AN AGE FOR LUCIFER

AN AGE FOR LUCIFER

Predatory Spirituality &
The Quest For Godhood

Robert C. Tucker

HOLMES PUBLISHING GROUP

First Edition
1st Printing, 1999

ISBN 1-55818-408-2

Library of Congress
98-072419

Cover design: Copyright © 1999 by Zachary Sandburg.
The illustration is based on a mid-fifteenth century icon
of the Novgorod School entitled, *The Last Judgement*.

For a Complete List of Publications,
Please address:
Holmes Publishing Group
Postal Box 623
Edmonds, WA 98020 USA

CONTENTS

INTRODUCTION 11

CHAPTER ONE — LUCIFERISM 27

    A Darwinian Spirituality 29
    Evolution to the Absolute Power of Godhood 30
    Killing Conscience, Compassion, and Empathy 30
    Compassion 31
    Conscience 32
    Empathy 33
    Killing God 34
    Predation: Devouring, Possession, Violence, and Disguise 35
    Eternal Survival 35
    Luciferans and Lower Humans 36
    The Spiritual Hierarchy 36
    Rising Above the Illusion of Good and Evil 37
    Preying on all Levels 38
    Powaqqatsi 39
    The Luciferan Millennium 40

CHAPTER TWO — LUCIFER 41

    A Luciferan Speaks 43
    Lucifer's Faces 45
    Satan, The Devil, Lucifer, The Prince of Darkness 46
    The Hero 46
    The Warrior and Light-Bearer, Truth-Teller 48
    Tempter, Tester, Accuser, Judge and Executioner 49
    The Shape-Shifter 50
    Enemy of Human Life 50
    God's Dark Side 52
    Lucifer's Real Face? 53
    Luciferans on Lucifer 54
    One God, or Many? 55

A Conversation With Lucifer 56

The Possible Predator 60

CHAPTER THREE— DEVOURING 61

The Hierarchy of Devouring 63

Devouring Up the Hierarchy 65

Physical Devouring: Ritual Sacrifice 65

Devouring Emotional Energy 67

Devouring Cognitive Energy 70

Breaking Into the Core & Creating an Object-of-focus 71

Assaulting the Core 72

Devouring the Energies Released At Breakdown 76

Devouring & Diverting Soul Energy 77

Spiritual Traditions Attracting Luciferan Devourers 78

Self-Annihilating Traditions 79

Ecstatic Traditions 79

Traditions of Trance Channeling and Spirit Possession 80

Devouring in Myth 81

From Myth to Reality: Releasing the Predator Within 82

Being Devoured 83

Intimidation 84

The Results of the Method 84

Depression 85

Escape and Recovery 85

CHAPTER FOUR — POSSESSION 87

Possession Defined 89

Possession in Daily Life 91

We, Possessors? 92

We, the Possessed? 93

Determinism as Possession 94

Possessing Humans 96

Four Types of Possession 96

Physical Possession 97

Emotional Possession 98

Advertisers & Employers 99

Therapists 101

Religious Leaders 101

Governments, Families, and Individual Relationships 102

Mind Possession 104

Breaking & Possessing The Mind 104

SOUL POSSESSION 107
CULTS AND SOUL POSSESSION 108
THE SOUL-POSSESSED 110
WHAT POSSESSES? 112
POSSESSION BY INDIVIDUALS 113
POSSESSION BY FAMILY 114
POSSESSION BY ORGANIZATIONS 115
POSSESSION BY EXTRAMEMES 118
POSSESSION BY INTRAMEMES 120
POSSESSION BY DISCARNATE ENTITIES 124
POSSESSION BY LUCIFERANS 130
POSSESSORS 131
BEING POSSESSED 133
HOW TO BECOME POSSESSED 142
VOLUNTARY POSSESSION: THE PEOPLE OF O 145

CHAPTER FIVE— VIOLENCE 149

THE LUCIFERAN WARRIOR 152
VIOLENCE, KILLING, AND PLEASURE 153
THE THRILL OF THE KILL 157
THE NEED TO KILL 158
VIOLENCE AND SANITY 160
VIOLENCE AND SEX 161
PHYSICAL, EMOTIONAL, COGNITIVE, AND SPIRITUAL VIOLENCE 162
VIOLENCE AGAINST THE BODY 162
VIOLENCE AGAINST THE EMOTIONS 162
VIOLENCE AGAINST THE MIND 164
VIOLENCE AGAINST THE SOUL 170

CHAPTER SIX — PROTEAN CAMOUFLAGE 173

PROTEAN LUCIFERAN RELATIONSHIPS 175
PROTEAN CAMOUFLAGE IN SOCIETY 176
PHYSICAL CAMOUFLAGE: BEAUTY 177
EMOTIONAL CAMOUFLAGE 178
COGNITIVE CAMOUFLAGE: DISPENSABLE BELIEFS 179
BREAKING THE PERSONAL CODE 181
BREAKING THE GROUP CODE 182
SPIRITUAL CAMOUFLAGE: CHARISMA 183
TRANSFORMATIONS FOR SALE 184
THE PROTEAN AGE 186
DARK TRANSFORMATIONS 188

CHAPTER SEVEN — HUGODS: THE TOTAL FREEDOM
    OF GODHOOD 191

    Freedom and Godhood: Willing Self to God 194
    Freedom From Love 197
    Freedom From Conscience and Morality 198
    Freedom From Authority 199
    Freedom From Physical Existence 201
    Freedom to Sacrifice God 202
    Encountering Other Hugods 204
    Strategic Relations between Luciferans 206
    Encountering Death 207
    Being a God 209
    Avoiding the Traps of Ascent 210

CHAPTER EIGHT — PSYCHOPATHS:
    LOWER ORDER PREDATORS 213

    Defining the Psychopath 215
    Luciferans and Psychopaths 217
    Psychopathic Dream Worlds 218
    Birthing the Spiritual Psychopath 220
    Sheheit: Charlie and the Other Enlightened Ones 221
    Natural Born Killers 228
    Luciferans And Psychopaths 230

CHAPTER NINE — LUCIFERAN ORGANIZATIONS 235

    Predatory Luciferan Organizations 239
    The Psycho-Spiritual 'Cone' 239
    Profile of A Predatory Organization 241
    Secrecy, Deception, Camouflage 243
    Isolation and Elitism 244
    Outsiders As Enemies 245
    Conspiracies 247
    True Believers 249
    Constant Proselytizing 251
    Obedience 251
    Conformity 254
    Dread and Fear 255
    Psychological Assault and Mind Control 255
    Rigid Hierarchy of Control 256
    Law Breaking 257

PREDATION 257
CONTROLLING THE ORGANIZATIONAL BEAST 258
ORGANIZATIONAL CHARACTER: VITALISM VERSUS REDUCTIONISM 260
THE VITALISM OF THE LUCIFERAN ORGANIZATION 264
ORGANIZATIONS AS LIVING PREDATORS 264

CHAPTER TEN — SATANISM & RITUAL ABUSE 267

WHAT IS SATANISM? 270
WHAT IS RITUAL ABUSE? 272
WHAT IS SATANIC RITUAL ABUSE? 272
ARGUMENTS AGAINST THE EXISTENCE OF SATANIC RITUAL ABUSE 273
ARGUMENTS SUPPORTING THE EXISTENCE OF SATANIC RITUAL ABUSE 275
OTHER POSSIBLE EXPLANATIONS OF SATANIC RITUAL ABUSE 277
PARAPSYCHOLOGICAL EXPLANATIONS 278
GROUP DISGUISES 280
THE INEVITABILITY OF RITUAL ABUSE 281
LUCIFERISM AND SATANISM 283

CHAPTER ELEVEN — RELATIVES: LUCIFERAN IDEOLOGY
    IN THE WESTERN WORLD 287

HUMAN GODS 291
PHILOSOPHERS 292
PLATO, BERGSON & ALEXANDER 293
NIETZSCHE 294
SARTRE 296
EDWARD O. WILSON 296
TEILHARD DE CHARDIN 298
THIRD FORCE PSYCHOLOGY AND HUMAN POTENTIALISM 298
FOURTH FORCE PSYCHOLOGY OF TRANSPERSONALISM 302
GNOSTICISM: THEOMORPHIC CHRISTIAN HUGODS 304
THE PERENNIAL PHILOSOPHY 308
NEW AGE 311
CHRISTIANITY 312
THE CREATIVE GENIUS 314
RUGGED INDIVIDUALISM 315
EVOLUTION, TRANSFORMATION, NEW PARADIGMS 316
THE DEVOURING HIERARCHY 318
SCIENCE 319
CAPITALISM AND THE SOCIO-ECONOMIC HIERARCHY 321
OTHER RELATIVES 323
NIETZSCHE AGAIN 323

Schopenhauer 325
The Faust Legend 326
Marathon & Doom 329
Lucifer's Principle 330
Natural Darkness 332
Evil 334
Some Ideas About Evil 335
The Experience of Evil 336
Evil Defined 338
The Luciferan Bargain 340
The Final Choice: Pure Evil 342
The Tenacity of Entrenched Evil 343
Recognizing Evil Individuals 345
Luciferism 2000; Luciferan Survival 346
Rapid Change and Broken Connections 346
Numbing 348
Moral Relativity 349
Narcissism 350
Existential Freedom: Facing the Void 351
Protean Appearance over Substance 352
Rabid Competition and the Cult of Success 353
No Limits 354
The Luciferan Pond 354

CHAPTER TWELVE — ALTERNATIVES 357

The Powaqqatsi Prison 360
The Predator's Dilemma 361
Alternative Possibilities 362
Through Ignorance 362
By Avoidance 363
In Denial 364
To Transcend 365
Resist! 367
And Compromise? 370
Pure Refusal 371
Sacrifice Yourself 371
Embrace Success 373
Pursue Absolute Luciferan Singularity 374

BIBLIOGRAPHY 377

INTRODUCTION

This book explores a strange new spirituality about to enter into competition with other established religions. My purpose here is to convince you that its emergence is probable, if not inevitable.

I begin this exploration with an unproven assumption based on Darwinian evolutionary principles: a new predator will appear on our planet, an evolutionary prototype designed to prey on humans. Another assumption then follows: this predator will evolve gradually and incrementally from humanity, just as we apparently evolved from lower forms to prey on them. A further assumption suggests that these predators have already appeared as evolutionary prototypes, as new humans with advanced methods of survival and new forms of spiritual expression and religious organization designed to support and advance their predation.

I cannot prove these assumptions. And yet I would like to proceed as if the new humans and their religion were real, and ask readers to suspend judgment until the exploration is complete. This is a work of imagination, and as with most imaginative constructs, it may have something meaningful to say about the human condition and perhaps about reality itself. When a book is part imagination, part prophecy, part fact, and part conjecture, then correspondence with objective reality is uncertain, and claims of truth cannot be made. Whether this work is fiction, fact, or some strange hybrid, I leave to your judgment.

To begin *as if*: assume that a new human predator has appeared, and is learning how to thrive by exploiting other humans in various ways — physically, emotionally, cognitively, and spiritually. Although human in form and origin, the new human is evolving. As with all other beings, its core impulse must be to survive by accumulating personal energy and power through predation. Unlike most other predators, however, the new human must expand the predatory field to include not just plants and animals, but the life energies of unevolved lower-order human beings as well.

Humans have always preyed on other humans in one way or another, but the new human prototypes are developing something unique — a coherent and consistent belief system to support and empower their predation. This belief system reflects the psychology and spirituality, or psycho-spirituality, of these new human predators, and is the subject of this book.

These new humans are evolving, not necessarily physically or genetically in the Darwinian manner, but emotionally, psychologically and spiritually as reflected in their new psycho-spiritual belief system. To use a term from the Darwinian reductionist Richard Dawkins: a new meme has appeared, and is recreating and re-engineering human minds by offering new ways to think, feel, and behave without reference to paradigms of either limit or tradition.

A central assertion of this belief system, or *meme*, is that predation requires a transformation, renewal, or rebirth of human nature based on the destruction of compassion, conscience, and empathy. Once these counter-predatory qualities have been annihilated, four basic predatory energies can emerge without resistance: devouring, possession, violence, and disguise. When released, these energies ensure effective and ruthless predation. Each of these energies is described in this book.

These energies are not new. They have animated, motivated, and often directed human evolution. What is new is the recent appearance of a psycho-spiritual belief system specifically designed to promote, glorify and celebrate this new predatory human prototype.

This new psycho-spirituality is only just emerging, however it is evolving and still fluid. As with most evolving belief systems, it can be found here and there, not yet fully formed, in change and flux, as it comes into being.

The animating force central to this new ideology is that its followers believe they can become gods capable of transcending all limits of morality. They see themselves as predators who have the right to kill, devour, and possess whatever they desire or need, as advanced beings able to tear through the limits of mortality and morality to release the repressed god within. Self is all, and self must inflate beyond all known limits to penetrate into the ultimate power mysteries of morally neutral godhood. These new humans believe they are evolving into something trans-human, far beyond the lower-order humans destined to become their prey.

This spirituality differentiates the new humans from all previous users, manipulators, dictators, and sordid predators in human history whose motives were simple power-lust, greed, or love of violence because few of these were driven by a coherent spiritual philosophy designed to guide and support their actions. The new humans are a different breed in a new era. A breed elevating selfhood and the acquisition of power for that self alone, to new spiritual heights.

This book will investigate the emerging psychology and spirituality of these new human gods.

The term *Luciferan* (pronounced *Loo-sif-er-an*) will be used for this new human prototype, and *Luciferism* for their spirituality. "Luciferan" may not be the wisest term. It may never be used by these new human types themselves, because it is such a culturally loaded term. Using psychological jargon, or Latin terms, or neologisms would have been easier and more acceptable ways to symbolize the psychological and spiritual reality, but we are already choking on enough of those. Our ancestors gave us a good word, so I would like to use it, although in a different way than originally intended.

Lucifer means light-bearer. According to legend, Lucifer fell from grace because he aspired to become God: *to become* the light and the source of light, a light which he was meant to bring to others. There are many variants of the legend, but one consistent motif: Lucifer would do anything to obtain his goal, including the invocation of predatory powers to usurp, kill and replace God. Here is how the Bible describes him in Isaiah (14:12):

> "How art thou fallen from heaven, O Lucifer, son of the morning! How art thou cut down to the ground, which didst weaken the nations! For thou hast said in thine heart, I will ascend into heaven, I will exalt my throne above the stars of God: I will sit also upon the mount of the congregation, in the sides of the north: I will ascend above the heights of the clouds; I will be like the most High."

His hubris was his downfall, but apparently not his ending. If God is dead in current Western culture, "Lucifer" is not: the impulse he symbolized is vibrantly alive and pressing to be born again in the minds and hearts of the new Luciferans. This impulse is the conscious decision to kill compassion, conscience and empathy so that enough personal power can be accumulated to obtain godhood.

Luciferism is *hidden* only because it is just emerging into human awareness. Because it is emergent, no single authorized canon of holy literature defines a specific Luciferan church or movement. No single individual stands as the ultimate model or hero of the Luciferan way. No author has written a sacred canon directing or definitively defining Luciferism for all followers. There does not seem to be a secret organized conspiracy of worldwide followers keeping Luciferism hidden from public view.

If there is a "conspiracy," it must be understood as an evolutionary event without leaders, buildings, or a systematic written truth. It is a movement gathering its energy from individual transformations occurring simultaneously around the planet. The new human's psycho-spiritual reality is an emerging prototype, in flux.

As with all evolutionary impulses, greater forces than the conscious will of the species seem to be at work. These obscure evolutionary forces are hidden to us, but their results are not. For example, we may not know how certain remote insect species came to exist, but we can see them if we know where to look. In the same way, we may not know how Luciferans came into existence, but we can see Luciferans already among us if we know where to look. Luciferans are participating in their own evolution, but seem to be supported and encouraged by other evolutionary forces as well: their survival potential and adaptive superiority in the human environment seems unmatched. In other words, Luciferans seem particularly well adapted to survive and prosper in the new Millennium.

Despite this obscurity, and lack of an obvious organizational structure, Luciferism has a rational inner core of meaning and purpose which can be articulated. Communicating this meaning is my purpose. The discussion will traverse, yet also transcend, territory covered historically by terms such as evil, Satanism, psychopathology, and the 'dark side' of human nature.

If Luciferan spirituality is so emergent, obscure, and concealed from view, then an obvious question must be asked: where did the material in this book come from?

To answer this question I have to start with an open and honest disclosure of my personal bias and background. The territory I want to explore with you is too important to deface with promotional posturing and false authority.

The essays, meditations and reflections collected come from my own experience, thought, and research, which includes having directed a counter-cult agency called the Council On Mind Abuse (COMA) in Toronto for a number of years. This experience led me to believe that "something else" directs and defines destructive cults more than the lists of characteristics defined in our literature and advertised widely in the media. Despite educating various professional groups about destructive cultism, and repeating over and over again all of the indicators of potentially harmful groups, I did not feel instinctively satisfied with my understanding of the phenomenon. Most of these indicators could equally apply to socially beneficial groups; many beneficial groups today were "destructive cults" at some time in their development; and cultism itself can be socially beneficial in some military and business applications. In other words, something else appeared to stand behind the obvious destructive pathology of certain groups. I was never certain what this *something* might be. So I decided to follow my instincts and this book is the partial result of that search.

But it is not the whole story. I also participated in and at times directed investigations into alleged "Satanic" cult activity. This included working with adult survivors and child victims of ritual abuse, meeting and working with self-described Satanists, performing graduate work on the subject of ritual abuse, and digesting untold pages of written material about Satanism and related topics. (References for this and other related materials are listed in the bibliography). As with destructive cultism, however, I sensed something else animating these stories of Satanic activity and ritual abuse, something familiar yet unspoken. Satanism was a puzzle behind which *it* hid, or a myth beneath which *it* lived. Like cultism, Satanism seemed to point at something beyond itself.

Prior to my work with COMA, I had become personally involved in the phenomenon of ritual abuse. I met Larry Pazder and Michelle Smith shortly after they published their book *Michelle Remembers*. Larry is a psychiatrist, and Michelle was his patient. Their book details Michelle's memories of abuse in a Satanic cult. I originally contacted them because a friend of mine was going through the same memory process, and I wanted as much information as possible.

Since the early eighties, ritual abuse stories have come to inhabit the same intellectual territory as alien abductions. Ritual abuse survivors have been ridiculed, and the professionalism of their supporting therapists has been questioned. Regardless whether true or not, these stories have a consistently chilling narrative coherence. One question seems to emerge: what kind of human beings could perpetrate these horrors? What would they be like? How would they think? What would they believe about themselves and their activities? What kind of *energy* or *force* could direct, animate, and support their activities? This questioning became one more motivation for this book.

My understanding has also been shaped by fifteen years of work with "behaviorally disturbed" children (i.e., violently aggressive young "psychopaths") in various educational and social service settings, along with related post graduate work in psychology and education. Those who work with these children and with adult offenders know how difficult it is to answer the following simple question: why are their destructive behavior patterns so resistant to change?

Most socially and politically appropriate answers suggest "bad parents", "bad society", "bad neural chemicals" and so on. While these answers are often contributing factors, they ignore a simple fact obvious to any who wish to honestly confront reality: some of these children seem to deeply enjoy their behavior. Worse than this, their behavior actually seems to be an adaptive response which allows them to function more effectively in certain environments. Apparently without conscience or compassion, they can take great pleasure in their predatory impulses. But what is it within them that takes great joy in harming others? These children are not Luciferans: psychopathology and Luciferism are not identical (this will be explored in more depth later). Nevertheless, these children have given me insight into some aspects of Luciferan psychology.

Finally, I have been deeply influenced by my current life in the Okanagan region of British Columbia, where I have learned the trapper's trade. Of course, this sounds odd. From counselor and "cult expert" to trapper? But the transition is real. To trap is to kill. To trap is to learn the predatory arts of tracking, stalking, camouflage, and killing. It is to come face to face with the brutal cycle of life and death in nature, and to become part of that cycle. To trap is to be immediately and directly confronted with the harsh realities of killing and death apparently nurtured by "Mother Nature". Trapping, as a way of life, has nevertheless given me further insight into the predatory arts, and how easily Luciferism can expand the idea of predation to include humans and possibly even the nature of spiritual reality itself.

There have been other sources, some closely personal, some more remote and philosophical. All of them led me to probe deeper into the mysteries behind cultism, Satanism, ritual abuse, violent aggressiveness, and predatory behavior generally — what emerged was a kind of *gestalt* of the core features of Luciferism.

By what authority do I offer this? Doctors can point to their medical or psychological training, priests to the traditions of their church, mystics to their ecstatic knowledge delivered through trance, psychic mediums to wisdom transmitted by spiritually wise discarnate entities, philosophers to their mastery of intellectual tradition, logic, and rationality — but what source of authority animates these words?

I cannot refer to any higher authority backing the contents of this book. I admit to being deeply troubled by the question of "higher authority," because I will enter territory saturated with revelation, esoteric truth, and related mysteries, proponents of which tend to draw on higher authorities of one form or another. I will offer ideas about possession, violence, devouring, and disguise that may be extremely difficult to accept. Beyond this, I will ask you to consider the possibility that Luciferism is a truly emergent spirituality, and not just a collection of fantastic ideas — all without the obligatory "Ph.D." added to the book's cover. So by what specific authority do I ask for your attention, trust, and acceptance as a guide into this uncharted territory?

Not by revelation. As far as I know, I am not a channel for some higher spiritual intelligence. If something speaks to me or through me from another dimension or alternate reality, I am not aware of it. I could claim divine revelation, because it is easy to proclaim and hard to challenge. But I won't, because that would be a lie. Nor will I claim the channeled wisdom of some discarnate entity penetrating and using my body. I want you to know that I would not trust such entities even if they could reach and use me.

I have not experienced higher powers of perception, and cannot pretend to be seeing, hearing, or touching things beyond our normal waking abilities. I cannot psychically read the future, and only dimly sense the past. Ecstatic journeys, out-of-body experiences, near-death experiences and other special abilities claimed by psychics and mystics are not the source of any insights you might find useful in this book.

I do not belong to any secret societies, mystic lodges, or other arcane purveyors of ancient mysteries. There will be no pages of mystifying symbols or veiled references to dark occult secrets. I have never been part of any occult brotherhood, and would turn down membership if offered.

I won't ask for your trust because of institutional religious affiliation. I am not a theologian, and am not selling a religious philosophy. This work does not flow from the doctrine of any institutional faith. I have struggled with Christian faith in an on-again, off-again manner over the years, and even once trained to be an Anglican priest. But I cannot claim to speak from that faith or any other, and I refuse to gain your trust by mouthing phrases and slogans meant to show my affiliation with your particular set of religious beliefs, whether they are Catholic, Buddhist, Humanist, Scientist, Feminist, Neo-Native, Agnostic, Atheist-Skeptic, or whatever. It is difficult to explore Luciferan philosophy without formal theology — my use of the term Luciferan is a case in point — but I nevertheless attempt to speak to you from outside that realm.

I will not impale or implore you with university degrees: my work does not flow from the academy. I am not a certified doctoral academic. I have a Master's degree in Education; a second Master's in Psychology remains incomplete.

I will not invoke long lists of influential university intellectuals to bless and sanctify these words with their credentials. I have always loved university life, and still respect it despite my increasing concern that universities are becoming self-serving monopolies. The university is losing its monopoly on intellectuality just as the church has lost its lock on spirituality: institutions cannot contain the mind any more than churches can contain the spirit. Institutional academics and intellectuals may not fully appreciate or respect this fact, but it is the reader's receptivity and understanding which is the important consideration.

I am not a philosopher. Logic, reason, and intellectual debate fascinate me, but I am not part of that world. This is probably just as well, because the language of the Luciferan impulse seems beyond logic, grounded in something ancient and perhaps eternal. It resonates when spoken in symbol, metaphor, and parable, but cracks when spoken in the voice of dry logic. Therefore these writings move outside the walls of the philosophical academy.

For similar reasons, empiricism and the scientific method are not justifications for the core ideas. I am not a scientist. I respect the scientific method and the answers it can offer, but have found it sadly inadequate as a tool to understand a new psycho-spirituality. Besides, reading scientific journals about the Luciferan impulse would be about as effective as reading Tarot cards about gravity: they mock one another.

Finally, I will not embrace the common method of taking a high moral outrage to rant or otherwise pontificate against Luciferans or their beliefs. Instead, I would like to represent those beliefs as honestly, clearly, and objectively as I can.

I should add that my authority-less position is not based on any principle of anarchy or anti-authoritarianism, because I believe that authority is necessary and authorities are needed. I just cannot claim to represent any of them.

Nor can I claim to stand outside all organized authoritative systems like some kind of free-floating voyeur. I won't calculate my words to avoid the truth of my own affiliations by assuming some sort of "god-like objectivity" about Luciferism. In the words of the novelist, E. L. Doctorow, we should "not make such a sanctimonious thing of objectivity, which is finally a way of constructing an opinion for the reader without letting him know that you are."

The only authority I can claim is that of an unaffiliated free thinker speaking my thoughts, speculations, and imaginings to others living on the edge of a new millennium. My freedom is precious to me, because I can adventure into intellectual territory considered unacceptable to one authority or another, just as I can joyfully walk a trapline into rugged and potentially dangerous back country. Such freedom can be exciting but also disturbing, especially for readers only used to working within the confines of authorized systems and walking the cultured trails of government sanctioned nature reserves.

I understand this fear, and so this book is primarily designed for intellectually self-reliant individuals who can openly examine and explore the ideas and possibilities presented here.

I am told that writers are supposed to have a narrative "voice" to augment their authority. This implies a coherence and consistency of presentation, something like the way we apparently present a stable personality to the world. The idea seems to be that an inconsistent voice is as untrustworthy as an inconsistent personality. Stability is necessary. The writer's voice is not supposed to intrude on the work, but only assure readers that they are not in the hands of a lunatic, fanatic, manipulator, fool, or patently self-serving propagandist. Voice should convey security, strength, sincerity, and respect.

But just as I have refused to bind myself to any authority, I also refuse to adhere to one specific voice. At times in this book I may seem dry, intellectual, even pedantic; at other times, I may appear lighthearted or even disrespectful. I won't maintain the presence of a consistently dependable voice because I do not have one. I have discovered more than one narrative voice during the nine years I have been writing this book, a project which has been completed in stages. I am different now than when I began. My moods and beliefs have changed at every stage. Besides, each chapter is different from the others, calling for a different tone, mood, and voice to effectively convey its meaning.

This may confuse some readers — it cannot be helped. I trust that readers will instead find coherence, meaning, and consistency in the content offered here, and not in my voice.

Readers might also become confused about another matter related to voice. Throughout the book I present arguments explaining the Luciferan perspective. At times such arguments are prefaced by "Luciferans believe such and such" or "Luciferan ideology states so and so". At other times there is no such preface, and I present arguments without reference to Luciferans at all.

For example, in the chapter on Possession, I argue that possession is everywhere, that it is as common as eating and breathing. I state my belief that organizations can possess individuals, and give examples. This is presented to support my contention that the core elements of Luciferism — possession being one of them — can be found in everyday life. I have come to believe that Luciferism is the actual, if unspoken, belief system animating human life on planet earth at this time, and that the open expression of Luciferan ideology — long suppressed but struggling to be born — is imminent. So I may seem to be actually promoting Luciferism at times, as a Luciferan myself, when in fact I am only articulating my personal beliefs about reality as I have come to understand it.

A third potential confusion about voice relates to the way I will be presenting Luciferism as if it is real, even though its existence remains purely speculative.

The use of the present tense (Luciferism is so and so) helps avoid the use of repetitively unnecessary literary qualifiers. I trust that readers will be able to tolerate this "as-if" fiction.

A fourth possible problem relates to the way I relentlessly return over and over again to certain themes and ideas, such as the destruction of compassion and conscience. I do this not because I think readers are stupid, or because I have forgotten that the point has been made. I use this method because I like to circle around important ideas like a coyote around a scent, carefully checking the environment from every angle before finally lunging in to encounter it face-on. I circle and sniff because that is how I think.

I respect the intelligence and learning of so-called "average" readers, and so am not afraid to take liberties with my voice. However this liberty creates a fifth potential problem: I refuse to scrub away references to complex ideas on the assumption that all books for public consumption should be written at a low level of literacy. I am not trying to show off like some kind of intellectual snob by including complex ideas and abstruse references. Just the opposite. I am refusing to take the snob's position that readers are too stupid, ignorant, or uneducated to understand concepts and ideas usually restricted to the academy. I have provided references for every idea and author quoted here, and any discerning reader can master unclear ideas by simply looking them up and thinking about them.

This leads to a final concern about voice. I have struggled to present a balanced, non-judgmental view of Luciferism. For example, I have not entered the gender wars by proclaiming that Luciferism is the logical outcome of patriarchy. As far as I can tell, women are just as good at Luciferan power acquisition as men. Hence I will use the pronouns "he" and "she" randomly and interchangeably (I cannot get used to he/she and do not want to twist all my sentences to remove the dreaded gender pronouns). This book is not a sermon; I have refused to engage the morally superior voice of angry prophetic warning, nor have I proclaimed great disaster scenarios or invoked deliciously seductive conspiracy theories to frighten readers into some kind of action.

This may annoy those readers hoping to be outraged, shocked, or otherwise aroused into heroic battle with the evil Luciferan enemy, but I am not writing to incite that kind of behavior. My voice is not a clarion call to action or a literary device to secure your trust. My voice is just my voice; its only purpose is to convey meaning to you as respectfully, clearly, and honestly as possible.

So how can meaning be conveyed without the sanction of official authority or without the fatherly security of an understandable protocol for a generation so well disposed to such affirmations? If these are all integral to "method" — to the communication of a procedure or process for obtaining a result — then how can method itself be possible? If we accept method as "a systematic procedure, technique, or mode of inquiry" then is not a consistent source or authority — be it a cultural tradition, a school of thought, an intensive internship within a profession, a religious tradition — along with an attending professional voice and related terminology, absolutely essential? I cannot answer this. I can describe the methods I have used. Perhaps they do relate meaningfully to a source, authority or voice beyond my grasp. Or perhaps there is no such connection. Again, readers will have to come to their own conclusions.

Let me say that my method flows from my belief that I am a translator, as the literary critic George Steiner uses the term in his book, *Real Presences*. This means that my method is that of "translating out of the inarticulate and the private into the general matter of human recognition." Translation is not the critical-academic response of the tertiary to the secondary work — writers writing about what other writers have written about other writers — but rather a more vitalizing personal response to *the primary*, to the felt presence of something other than myself. Translation is itself immediate, alive and available for further translation. It is mysterious, but it always assumes the reality of something "out there" that needs translation, interpretation, understanding — in this case, Luciferan psycho-spirituality.

I believe I am a translator because this best describes my passionate belief in the reality of that-which-I-am-translating. I translate from the Luciferan realm to ours. I cannot prove the existence of that which I translate or of that which I instinctively believe exists behind the puzzles of cultism, Satanism, ritual abuse, and psychopathology — of that very real felt presence which I have chosen to call Luciferism. Yet I know that it exists. I am attempting, in Steiner's words, to draw Luciferism into the "luminous ambush of representation and understanding".

My translation of the New Humans and their Luciferan ideology may not be fully accurate, but my conviction about their existence is primary. I am aware of post-structuralist, deconstructionist, and nihilistic arguments (and of other related epistemological arguments) asserting the absurdity of any such conviction; nevertheless, this is my position. I will therefore attempt to translate my conviction of a real Luciferan presence to you.

Translation needs technique. Here are two of the techniques I have used. The first is guaranteed to infuriate statisticians, and is something I am calling *emotional factor analysis*, or EFA. Factor analysis is a statistical procedure designed to organize or reduce large amounts of data into meaningful categories or "factors". For example, the Wechsler Intelligence Scale (a famous IQ test), has been subjected to factor analysis resulting in the determination that its thirteen subtests can be factored into two main groups or categories: verbal subtests (meaning "word stuff"), and performance subtests (meaning "non-word action stuff"). Each of the subtests within these two categories are more statistically *glued* to each other than to subtests in the other category.

Factor analysis is a powerful statistical technique; *emotional factor analysis* is, for me, just as powerful. From a mass of scrambled, jumbled, and unorganized "data" — impressions, intuitions, hunches, instincts, feelings, random thoughts, momentary insights, brief glimpses, questions pursued, hints, hard thinking, facts about cultism, Satanism, ritual abuse, psychopathology — has emerged a gestalt of organized factors defining the core elements of the Luciferan impulse.

The actual "emotional alchemy" used as an equivalent to the mathematical procedures of statistical factor analysis is not clear. If my mind is a computer, and if emotional factor analysis is a program, then all I know is that the "software" has worked its magic and produced a result.

This result has satisfied my own need to articulate the felt presence of Luciferism, but I fully accept that it may seem absurd to others. Yet I have come to deeply trust this "EFA" process. You may not. Does this method illuminate a specific reality? Does it make sense? Does it provide a correspondence with felt experience by other people in the real world? These are questions I cannot answer for anyone else; I can only present what I have discovered.

A second technique I have called *transfer empathy* can be understood as a process similar to "deep acting" in the method-acting school of dramatic performance. Actors in this school would so deeply identify with their fictional character that they would literally *become* the part. They did not want to be seen "acting the role", they wanted to "be the role", to penetrate the part with deep empathetic imagination, and therefore to find its essence. My entry into the Luciferan experience was in this sense entirely "imaginary". I empathized, or identified with, the Luciferan impulse as deeply as I could without actually becoming Luciferan. My imagination took me where empirical investigation could not. By "imaginary" I do not mean "unreal". I mean a process by which empathy is transferred so deeply into a subject that the two become one. There is nothing unusual about this. Children do it all the time: just watch a five year old examining a shiny crab by the ocean for the first time. A melding between observer and observed occurs. An imaginary but meaningfully real connection is made.

I do not want to get hampered by semantics, but I feel obliged to point out that most of us know this experience to some degree. We "meld" with something so deeply that time and space seem to disappear. A good book, a great movie, wonderful sex: these experiences fill, regenerate, and enliven us. We connect and "go" with the experience — with what the psychologist, Mihaly Csikszentmihalyi, calls *flow* — what artists and creators throughout time have sought so passionately.

But how can this kind of experience occur with an abstraction like "Luciferism"? How can something ethereal receive this depth of attention and penetration? Again, I think we do this all the time, to one degree or another. For example, think of "communist", or "homosexual", or "liberal" or "feminist". Think of the "conservative", or the "forest". None of these exist except as categories of description. Yet they are all very real felt presences which we experience and then describe. They are imaginary abstractions; they also describe a feeling of real experience.

Transfer empathy is a technique I used to enable entry into my felt experience of the Luciferan presence. I learned this technique in my work with cult members, because without it I could not work effectively with them. Here is why. The cult member exists in a hermetically sealed thought-world which allows no penetration or invasion from outsiders (all of whom are seen as enemies or potential enemies unless they get "the truth"). This thought-world can be visualized as a glass bubble swirling with complex particles of ultra-ordered meaning, of in-group jargon, of axioms which define personal appearance, action, and behavior, and which control reactions to outsiders. It invades, inhabits, and possesses the cult member's mind, surrounding it like an astronaut's helmet. In order to make any contact at all with the cult member, the outsider has to intimately know the specific shapes, textures, and currents of these particles in the bubble. The outsider must know as much about this world as the member. If not, then the "boundary-guards" at the system's edges within the cultist's mind will detect a "foreign invader", and will instruct the member to act accordingly.

To avoid this, the outsider must know how to transfer empathy into the thought system so as to experience it as deeply as possible without becoming it. He has to penetrate to the group's core, pick up its language, know its dogma, almost become a member. This of course can be dangerous; it parallels the threats facing undercover police officers who go so deep that they lose their own identity and become their cover, eventually rejecting their pre-involvement personality.

In order to accomplish an understanding of Luciferism, I have used transfer empathy to feel my way into the thought-world Luciferans inhabit. Entry into this thought-world comes from many gates — previously I have mentioned only a few: cultism, Satanism, ritual abuse and psychopathology — but there have been others. This book records what I found in that world.

In sum, both techniques can be considered "thought experiments". I have not conducted anthropological research, have not interviewed self-declared Luciferans, have not gathered information from questionnaires, nor have I conducted empirical field observations.

Other writers have promoted similar methods. For example, Max Weber, the "father of sociology", described a process of interpretive understanding in which he subjectively placed himself inside the world view and experience of his object of study. The object of study might not be physical, but rather an idea or cluster of ideas. He felt that the focus of sociological study was not the world of concrete things as with physics, chemistry, and biology, but rather the investigation of what he called ideal types, units of analysis, or ideas. He described his most famous book, *The Protestant Ethic and the Spirit of Capitalism*, as "a contribution to the understanding of the manner in which ideas become effective forces in history." This method allowed him to examine such abstractions as "bureaucracy" and "Protestant Ethic" and to detail their meaning and concrete impact on individuals and society generally. In other words, Weber decided that such abstractions were real, definable, and meaningful units of study for sociology, but that they required a different type of scientific method to be analyzed and understood. In some respects I follow his method, because Luciferism is a cluster of ideas which I have examined subjectively.

Phenomenology offers another similar approach. An example of phenomenological investigation can be found in the writings of philosopher Paul Ricoeur. Ricoeur's method is elegantly described by C. Ellis Nelson in his preface to one of Ricoeur's essays: "Of all the methods of analyzing human situations, phenomenology is one of the most difficult for Americans to appreciate. We are inclined to respond favorably to pragmatic, empiric, or idealistic ways of interpreting life because we are acquainted with these approaches and they yield data which appear to be based on fact or reason. The phenomenological approach, as used by Ricoeur, requires the reader to open himself to evidence that comes from an examination of words, ceremonies, myths, subjective feelings, and deductions based on these data. Moreover, the results of this type of study do not correspond to any field of academic study. Rather, they commend themselves to the reader only to the extent that they correspond to his self-understanding."

This is close to my own method, particularly in the focus on the reader's self understanding: the power, authority, impact, and value of the work will be decided by the reader's reaction, not by external authorities. This tradition has deep roots in Western culture, and can be traced through the philosophical rationalists back to the Socratic method itself, where appeals to reason and intuition outweighed the powers of faith or authority. I am not claiming allegiance to this tradition, only that it resonates in some ways with my own methodology. I suppose I am trying to say that my method is not as isolated from legitimate intellectual history as much as I had first thought — all of my academic training has been dominated by the methodologies of empiricism, reductionism, and mechanistic determinism. I have simply not been exposed to other alternatives, most of which are held in contempt by the scientific community. If I could describe this method by a single term, it would be thought experiment. By projecting myself imaginatively into Luciferism, and by invoking transfer empathy and emotional factor analysis to translate its real presence, I believe I have engaged in a kind of thought experiment.

It is probably safe to say that thought experiments are held in low regard today so as to not merit comment other than dismissal as armchair philosophy or mystical nonsense. Yet they have their own coherence, and are based on the assumption that a real correlation exists between thought-about-a-thing on the one hand, and the reality (or real presence) it purports to represent on the other. The medium of contact built into this correlation is not empirical observation or experimental manipulation — not eyes, ears, fingers or smells — but other senses perhaps a little harder to trust at first. The test, or verification, rests in the fit between the two, in the veracity and veridity of the translation. Whether that has been achieved here, I leave for readers to decide.

One final concern needs to be mentioned, because it is as important as authority, voice, and method. It is the dividing line, or boundary, between the psychological and the spiritual.

Just as authority, voice and method cannot be avoided, so too the division, or boundary, between the psychological and the spiritual must be confronted. Due to the nature of the material presented here, I will be skipping from the psychological to the spiritual constantly, and will be covering territory traditionally considered as either psychological or spiritual, but seldom both at the same time. Confusion is probably unavoidable, but I will do my best to prevent it. If spiritual means that which transcends body, heart, and mind as an ultimate ground of being, and if psychological means that which is associated with cognition and emotions — with 'mind-things' and feelings — then it seems to me that they are related but nevertheless different. Reductionists would argue that the spiritual does not exist, that spirit is only psychological, which in turn is only material. Others would argue that the material, including the psychological, is only an extension and creation of spirit. Still others would argue that these terms are only misleadingly artificial constructs of description and categorization unconnected to any objective reality, leftovers from Descartes' dualism.

For me, however, these categories are real, "felt presences". I think there are genuine differences between my own personal thoughts and feelings and, say, the creative force animating our planet — which some call God. This problem of categorization used to be known as spiritual discernment, an ancient practice designed to ensure that the psychological was not mistaken for the spiritual (my special "inner voice" may not be God but simply my own vivid imagination), that the spiritual was not confused with the psychological (my sublime moment of transcendent ecstasy might be more than just odd neural chemistry or regression to childhood fantasy), and that different spiritual realities were distinguished one from another.

I have come to believe that reducing spiritual vitality to psychological abstraction is about as useful as inflating psychological reality to spiritual status. Labeling all spiritual experience and yearning as nothing more than psychological anomalies, illness, neurosis, or primitive wish-fulfillment (Freud pushed this position), is as silly as elevating every hunch, dream, neurotic compulsion, intuition or coincidence to profound spiritual insight. The boundary exists, and must be respected.

I admit to deep conflict about this strange boundary. At times I am certain there is no spiritual reality at all, that psychological reality is solely based on the physical properties of the brain, and that when the brain dies, so too does personality, hope, and even spirituality itself. Spiritual experiences are simply psychological anomalies, ultimately explainable by the philosophical schools known as materialism, scientism, and positivism which all assert that spirituality can be reduced to psychology, and that psychology can be reduced to physics and chemistry.

At other times I am equally certain that consciousness is more than just matter and brain, that it exists independently, as evidenced by out-of-body experiences, lucid dreams, shamanic journeys, and near-death experiences. During moments of euphoria, even ecstasy, I know that I will live beyond death, that other non-physical intelligent entities exist and that spirit triumphs over matter. But such ecstasies end, and then its all back to toothpaste, hamburgers, and headaches.

This has been, and may always be, an endless debate. On one side are those who adhere to the interrelated theories of mechanism, reductionism, materialism, determinism, empiricism and positivism. On the other are those who hold to theories such as vitalism, animism, holism, supernaturalism, mysticism and teleology. Perhaps the philosopher C.P. Snow was right, and two independent and irreconcilable intellectual cultures exist. Proponents of each side have registered their beliefs at least as far back as the pre-Christian Greeks, and since then in a bewildering diversity of thought-systems. Is matter everything? Are we fully determined by the physical and chemical properties of matter? Are we ruled by what has come before us, and the parts from which we are made? Or is matter determined by other vitalistic forces that we cannot easily perceive? Is there a purpose to things, a plan which reaches back to us from the future, and which organizes from "top-down", as opposed to "bottom-up"?

Spirit over matter, or matter over spirit: I will not try to solve this timeless question. I am as enthralled by occultism as by the scientific method. I have studied Steiner, Crowley, the Golden Dawn and the Western occult tradition with as much intense pleasure as the works of Empiricists and obscure Catholic saints. My early heroes were psychologists of the transpersonal realm like John Lilly, Charles Tart, Robert Ornstein, Stanislav Grof, Ken Wilbur and other explorers of altered states such as Robert Monroe, (although later on I came to detest how some of them created self-indulgent and self-serving empires built on books, tapes, and seminars). At one time I read Tarot cards, at another I trained to be an Anglican priest, and at yet another I adhered to skeptical empiricism. This inconsistency and indecision has left me rootless and at times disoriented and scared. Yet it has also given me joy. I cannot explain this, and will not try.

So why does this matter? What difference does it make? The answer rests in my own experiences as a reader, and in the obvious impact of another author's beliefs about this boundary. Take as an example, say, out-of-body experiences. Authors who believe that consciousness is independent of matter (Robert Monroe's book *Journeys Out of the Body* is an example) present an entirely different perspective from those who disbelieve in spiritual reality and who therefore see such experiences as psychological anomalies, delusions, or outright lies (as with Graham Reed's book *The Psychology of Anomalous Experience*).

The latter group might approach these experiences from a variety of psychological, sociological, or ethnological perspectives, but will inevitably reach explanations devoid of even the remotest acceptance of external spiritual reality. The former group might interpret the event through any number of ideological filters: some Christians might find evidence of demonic influence, Occultists might discover evidence supporting their belief in the various levels of spiritual reality beyond the physical, and so on. The point here is simple: the author's beliefs about the boundary will influence his description and explanation of his subject.

Readers therefore deserve to know my position. Unfortunately, I am just not sure. When pressed, I tend toward the spiritual or idealistic side of things, but this tendency can be easily toppled. My own "protean fluidity" (a term to be explained later) will become clear throughout this book. At times you may read me as a raving spiritualist or sturdy Christian, at other times as a pedantic scientific materialist and skeptic. I originally attempted to sanitize this book by adopting one consistent point of view, but I cannot do it when I do not have the consistency to maintain it.

I suspect that most of you will be able to tolerate my dilemma, however, because it is probably your own as well. Besides, there may be an advantage to this fluidity: perhaps it allows me to imaginatively penetrate beliefs, world views, and perspectives from the believer's position that might otherwise be closed if I only adhered to one side of the boundary or the other. Again, if an advantage is evident, then readers will judge its value.

What follows is an exploration of the Luciferan worldview as I have come to understand it. I claim no authority other than the sense it makes to you.

You may be surprised at how close this Luciferan psycho-spirituality has always been to your own private life and personal experience. Some of you may even find that Luciferism fulfills your own quest for meaningful religion, that it articulates a faith you have always known to be true, and that it celebrates a code of conduct which has always guided you in this life. As a Luciferan would say, welcome to reality.

CHAPTER ONE
LUCIFERISM

"The Destiny of man on earth has been made clear by evolutionary biology. It is to be the agent of the world process of evolution, the sole agent capable of leading it to new heights, and enabling it to realize new possibilities."

Julian Huxley, "Evolution in Action"

"But the serpent said to the woman: You certainly will not die!. No, God knows well that the moment you eat of it your eyes will be opened and you will be like gods ... Then the Lord God said: "See! The man has become like one of us ..."

Genesis 3:3 and 3:22

Luciferism is a spiritual ideology supporting and promoting a bold new vision of ultimate human potential. The Luciferan vision has points of similarity with traditional religious and literary depiction of Lucifer, but also vibrates with new meaning and relevance for our age.

Luciferism advocates the use of predatory techniques to achieve personal godhood by aggressively scaling the Darwinian hierarchy of devouring which the Luciferans believe extends beyond the physical to include all possible realms of spirit. The purpose of this chapter — and the entire book — is to render this opaque statement clear, and to translate Luciferism into contemporary meaning.

A Darwinian Spirituality

Luciferism can be understood as the application of Darwinism to spirituality — only the fit and strong survive the struggle for true spiritual power. Luciferans do not "believe" in spiritual reality, if by belief we mean acceptance in the absence of evidence. They believe in it because they experience it directly, immediately. This experience may come through the same basic exercises and techniques listed in many esoteric or mystical traditions: relaxation, breath control, meditation, concentration, visualization, invocation, evocation, and ritual. Like contemporary mystics and ancient sages, Luciferans believe that these techniques produce effects ranging from out-of-body shamanistic journeys to the full range of psychic powers (i.e. clairvoyance, clairaudience, psychokinesis, etc.), all of which enhance their power on the spiritual planes.

But Luciferans differ from these mystical traditions because they believe that real spiritual power is only gained through predation — by possessing, devouring, or killing opponents and victims. The Luciferan spirit-warrior cultivates all the arts of war to overpower and absorb the physical, emotional, cognitive, and spiritual energy of other beings on all levels of existence from the physical to the spiritual. The ultimate goal of the Luciferan warrior's spiritual struggle is to accumulate enough dynamic power to obtain godhood.

For Luciferans, power is their Eucharist, the food that sustains Luciferan worshippers. Power *is* perfection, and perfection is purity. This power can only be achieved through the actualization of the highest human potential here on earth, and then beyond into the heights of the spiritual hierarchy.

According to Luciferan thought, there is only one way to achieve the absolute power of highest human potential, and that is to evolve into God. We are all potential Gods — that is, those of us ruthless, predatory, and hard enough to claim our inheritance.

For Luciferans, godhood is the total freedom and power of the fully actualized self, unimpeded by weaknesses and limitations. Godhood is the goal of evolution, and is based on what George Steiner calls the "desire for absolute singularity," a desire that Luciferans cultivate fiercely and which they take as the central motivation animating all human life. It leads to the ultimate expansion of selfhood into the universe, so that the universe is absorbed by the self, and not the reverse. There is no mystical surrender or blending of self into the greater universal whole in Luciferism; there is only the relentless impulse to transform the universe into an extension of self. This is not mere narcissism; nor is it simple selfishness. It transcends all lower egoistic attachments. It is the Luciferan inflation of self beyond all boundaries, a movement ending with self shaping reality, directing the universe, becoming all powerful, evolving into God.

Those strong enough to embody the force of this evolutionary impulse will be transformed and fully actualized, ready for their true inheritance of godhood, while those caught in weakness and squandered potential will become extinct. As each Luciferan conquers ever higher layers of consciousness and spiritual power, evolution itself becomes conscious; that is, the Luciferan believes she can then direct her own evolution instead of remaining a passive recipient of the lawful mechanical forces governing all lower-order humans and animals.

Strength and empowerment are only for the strong; weakness of any kind is despised. The most debilitating weaknesses are those linked to conscience, compassion, and empathy, all of which Luciferans believe limit the full actualization of potential and power.

For Luciferans, becoming God means breaking free of that which they believe keeps us finite and human: compassion, conscience, and empathy, which are perhaps known collectively to us as love.

A Luciferan is a person who consciously embraces and practices this core Luciferan idea, which calls for the radical restructuring of human nature through the elimination of conscience, compassion, empathy and their related elements: morality, remorse, guilt, sympathy and pity.

Conscience, compassion, and empathy are treasured by most of us. They take us out of our self centeredness to know the reality and pain of other sentient beings. They work in opposition to selfishness and power-lust, but Luciferans believe that the acquisition of personal power is impossible for anyone immolated by the bonds of these three forces. The predator cannot devour prey unless he first kills these impediments within.

To fully understand Luciferans we have to know what they reject, and so compassion, conscience and empathy need to be briefly defined and explored.

COMPASSION

Compassion is defined here as the ability to sympathetically feel the pain and suffering of other sentient beings, and to try to ease that pain. It is the understanding of another's suffering and pain, along with a sympathetic desire to end it. Compassion rises from the knowledge of suffering itself, and is most available to those who have suffered deeply, who have been humbled by trial and survived.

Sympathy, pity, and love: all of these seem to connect with compassion, and all of them reach out to end the suffering of other sentient beings.

Luciferans, however, experience compassion as an illness, a disease to be eradicated, an impediment to the total freedom and experience of godhood. Compassion anchors the predator to the victim, and thus prevents pure, clear, harsh action. Suffering is inevitable because the weak must suffer as the strong get stronger. Even the strong themselves must suffer and face their pain so they can become stronger. Feeling compassion for another being's pain therefore insults the natural order of things: the strong do not need or want compassion, and the weak only leak and drain strength from those who happen to feel compassion or pity for them. Compassion is a weakening of strength, a draining of vital energy. Luciferans who feel compassion believe they will perish because they will not be able to act on their pure predatory impulses.

Compassion and pity stifle all natural impulses, and eat away strength and power: in Nietzsche's words (from his book *The Anti-Christ*), "one loses force when one pities... pity on the whole thwarts the law of evolution... this depressive and contagious instinct thwarts those instincts bent on preserving and enhancing the value of life."

Conscience can be understood as a rational extension of a moral code of conduct rather than as an emotion like compassion. Conscience stems from a moral code: when the code is broken, conscience is the voice that informs and corrects the violator with the reminders of remorse and guilt.

Conscience is a voice, and like any voice it speaks from an integrated point of view, that is, a rational perspective based on certain *a priori* moral propositions. Conscience tells us when we have violated our code. Feelings of shame, remorse, and guilt reinforce the impact of the violation.

True moral codes seem to have little to do with self-righteous tyrannical oppression. The greatest codes — religious and otherwise — are maps of conduct, of how to act in given situations, and can usually be traced back to compassion and love.

Conscience remains a mystery. Sociobiologists feel that it is a product of natural evolution designed to protect herd or tribal integrity. Freudians believe it is a manifestation of superego domination. Catholics believe it is the voice of God. Theories exist, but most of us ignore them. We only know that we have a sense of right and wrong, and that when we violate this code there is a feeling of guilt and remorse. We do not know if it comes from God, society, parents and forebears, or genetic conditioning. We accept conscience as a guide, and most of us try to live by it.

Nor do many of us stop to consider life without it. Conscience is so deeply woven into our identity that we are unable to conceptualize living without its presence. We just know that conscience is essential, and that it seems to flow from some kind of moral imperative. For some of us this code is explicit, as in the Ten Commandments, for others it is more private and personal. The code directs our behavior. When we violate it, we experience the kick of guilt and the punch of remorse.

Some recent thinkers and pop psychologists assert that guilt and remorse are destructive emotions that we should learn to overcome. Others wonder how we are supposed to feel the consequences of moral violation without these internal guides. Guilt and remorse are messengers or teachers that warn us. If I put my hand on a hot stove, I feel pain. The pain tells me never to touch a hot stove again. It not only teaches me, but it protects me as well from future tissue injury. Guilt and remorse can be said to do the same, but by protecting us from moral injury.

Without the presence of guilt and remorse, we would live in a morally neutral universe where all behavior would be equally valued or devalued, and where murder would be as good or bad as saving a life. Individuals without conscience, morality, guilt, or remorse are known to us as psychopaths. Guilt and remorse may be painful, but without them we might well join them in this condition.

Despite this, Luciferans consciously and religiously seek the annihilation of conscience. They believe that conscience and morality restrict and contain the *natural* human, whose only true urge is to obtain the ultimate power of godhood. Without conscience and morality, human behavior is free to flow unrestricted, unrestrained, unhindered, growing from strength to strength, becoming God.

Luciferans see this free-flow as something wonderful, dynamic, and liberating. For Luciferans seeking the freedom of ultimate power, the forces of conscience and morality are ugly impediments to be overcome. This does not mean that Luciferans live without a code of conduct. Their path is clearly defined, and the rules governing it are steadfast. Morality is not part of this code. Luciferans are free to make up any code of conduct they wish, but with the understanding that such structures are all temporary and merely utilitarian vehicles to be transcended and overcome within the framework of basic predatory laws. Violation of these laws might bring failure and perhaps death, but never remorse or guilt.

EMPATHY

Empathy seems closely related to compassion and conscience. It is understood here as the ability to actually *experience* another's reality, to enter into what the other sees, feels, and thinks. If conscience is related to a moral code, and compassion is based on the personal experience of suffering, empathy seems to be related to the gift of actually becoming another being's experience. It is a powerful and penetrating intelligence, little understood.

To experience empathy fully, we seem to have to get beyond the confines of our own limitations, beyond the limits of egocentricity and self concern, and out of our own bodies and thoughts and worries. Empathy requires massive spiritual and personal growth.

When Zen masters speak of that moment when consciousness merges with its object, and the two become one, they seem to be referring to empathy. When Hesse's *Siddhartha* has his moment of rapture and becomes a bird, feeling himself flying and seeing through the eye of the bird, he has become an empath. When the Shaman enters into the spirit of an animal, becoming the animal, he is entering because of his gift of empathy. When Christ calls on the power of love, he seems to be requesting us all to invoke the power of empathy.

In such traditions, an empath is not soft or weak or pathetic. A true empath is held to be one who has the courage and strength to pull away from self-centeredness and to penetrate into the existence of another life form.

The Luciferan refuses to empty himself into others as an act of empathy, however, choosing instead to rip other beings apart so their energies flow into him and enhance his own personal power. For the Luciferan, empathy is a kind of death, a leaking out of precious personal power into undeserving lower-order beings.

Luciferans reject compassion, conscience, and empathy because they believe that only this rejection permits them to obtain sufficient power to storm heaven and kill God.

Killing God

Luciferans seek God. They do not seek to worship, adore, or serve God. Luciferans seek God only to kill God. To become God, they have to kill God. To kill God, they have to kill compassion, conscience, and empathy. Luciferans want to violently destroy God in order to ingest and therefore possess the full power and potential of godhood. God is a rich source of food: by killing and then devouring God, Luciferans believe they become God.

Luciferans believe that God simply dominates the predatory hierarchy of life, maintaining power by successfully devouring, intimidating, and possessing all lower forms of life. God is only the currently reigning champion of violent devouring and possession, and as such is simply another competitor, an impediment to be overcome. God is just another limit to be broken.

Luciferans respect God's immense power. It is a power they all wish to possess. This respect is based on fear and envy, not love, empathy, compassion or devotion. God must be placated at times, but never loved. To love God is to submit to bondage, a state equivalent to soul-death for Luciferans.

According to Luciferan thought, the Bible is a testament to the arbitrary power-lust of a dictatorial God, a God who keeps humanity in slavery and spiritual poverty, and who even elevates this servitude to a kind of spiritual glory. This God — or any other — does not deserve love, affection, or obedience, but only our hatred and disgust. God needs to be stalked, killed, and eaten. Only then can God's rich bank of energy and power be released and dispersed to the human race, as it was always meant to be.

To become successful predators of spiritual energy, however, Luciferans know they have to cultivate certain predatory skills. They vigorously pursue four of these basic skills: devouring, possession, violence, and disguise. But before activating these skills, Luciferans also know they have to make a sacrifice. They must make a bargain, enter into an agreement with themselves the base element of which is: to acquire power by devouring the vital energy of other beings.

If Luciferans believe that conscience, compassion, and empathy are limitations preventing the full realization of human potential and godhood, then they also assert that, practically, this power can only be accumulated by freeing the predatory impulses to devour, possess, violate, and disguise.

Conscience, compassion, and empathy limit these impulses, and so they limit godhood. To actualize godhood, energy must be forcefully taken from other beings and added to the predator's store of energy, his selfhood. Self is god, or can become god, but only for the strong.

Luciferans are predators. They are the killers, not the killed. Predation is to Luciferism as love is to Christianity. The Luciferan *catechism* is simple. Kill conscience, compassion, and empathy, devour the vital energy of other beings, and rise to the height of evolutionary human potential — godhood.

ETERNAL SURVIVAL

If Luciferism is the application of Darwinian principles to spiritual evolution, then the pursuit of godhood through predation can be understood as a quest for eternal survival. The Darwinian game here on earth implies only the physical survival of the species, not the survival of the individual. The philosopher Ernst Becker suggests that humans seek to extend personal survival through biological reproduction, art, science, cultural traditions, and spiritual hope: knowing that the body will die, we try to continue living through our children, through a painting or book we have created, through a profound scientific discovery, or perhaps through a reputation as hero and savior of our own kind (i.e. our own political, racial, national or familial group). We might actually believe we live on after death in the spirit world to be later reincarnated, or we might believe in a final destination such as heaven or hell.

Luciferans are more serious about this game of survival. They struggle to accumulate enough personal power to endure the death of the physical body. They believe that consciousness is layered from physical to spiritual, and seek to ensure their continued survival, on all levels, beyond the physical. Physical death is just a change of clothes; only spirit and willpower endure. Luciferans believe that lower humans do not survive, that they perish with their bodies, and that the higher spiritual realms are open only to the most ruthless predators. The higher the spiritual level, the more sophisticated and advanced the predatory arts needed for survival. Eternal survival is never guaranteed by simple belief, faith, creed, or attendance at religious rites. It is guaranteed only to elite predators, those strong enough to devour others and eventually devour God. Eternal survival is the prize for killing a god. With eternal survival comes absolute power and with this power comes the ultimate fulfillment of the personal will.

A highly evolved Luciferan predator therefore has the ability to kill lower beings with thoughtless ease, the way we kill animals. The Luciferan elite views lower humans in precisely this way: as prey and food.

LUCIFERANS AND LOWER HUMANS

Luciferans see other humans as prey, as a lower form of life to be devoured, possessed, used, or killed. This view is supported by an elaborate spiritual belief system designed to make such predation normal and desirable. Luciferans see absolutely nothing wrong with predation, any more than their human targets see anything wrong with killing animals or plants. Such killing is normal and necessary. For Luciferans, it is also noble and empowering, as necessary as breathing and as satisfying as an orgasm.

'Higher or lower' for Luciferans are both synonyms for more or less power, which in turn depends on the absolute commitment to Luciferan principles of action, or power acquisition. Lower humans are weak humans, and their victimization is right and natural.

This polar thinking extends into all forms of Luciferan thought and predation. It shapes and forms the Luciferan view of reality itself. Luciferans do not conceive their place as being 'down' or 'lower', but rather 'up' and 'higher'. Their quest is to rise up and out of powerlessness. There is no "lower-archy" with a "Father below" to obey, as C. S. Lewis' demon Screwtape proclaimed. The Luciferan obeys no one willingly. There is no "Father" to please but only a father to kill and replace.

Freud almost captured the idea with his Oedipus Complex, where the son slays the father in order to possess the mother. For Luciferans, the Father has to be killed, not to possess the mother, but to possess all creation. The mother is irrelevant; Freud just did not go far enough in his interpretation of this universal Luciferan truth: kill the father in order to rise up the hierarchy of power and potential. All is layered on this hierarchy, including spiritual reality itself: the Father is an impediment preventing the Luciferan's rise up the hierarchy, and therefore is an enemy to be destroyed.

THE SPIRITUAL HIERARCHY

In Luciferan metaphysics, reality is layered from the physical to the spiritual. Pure power thrums only in the higher reaches of the spiritual domains. The higher dominates the lower. Spirit determines matter, not the reverse. This kind of philosophical idealism is held worldwide in one way or another, and is not unique to Luciferism.

Unlike most other spiritual faiths, however, Luciferans seek knowledge of all levels of the hierarchy only to increase the scope of their predation, and not for any other devotional reason. They believe that the spiritual hierarchy coexists with the physical and biological, and obeys the same Darwinian rules. Competition and survival of the fittest rule the entry into *heaven*. Heaven's door opens only to those powerful enough to batter it down. The weak do not enter. They remain outside as sheep to feed the strong within.

Elitism is of the essence here; only powerful spiritual adepts and Luciferan masters deserve to occupy the higher realms of spiritual reality and to enjoy the benefits found only there.

The spiritual hierarchy simply amplifies all that we know here on earth, as reflected by the ancient occult aphorism: *As above, So below.* Earthly pain is nothing compared to spiritual pain; earthy orgasm is a pale reflection of spiritual orgasm; earthy victory over an enemy pales to the intense euphoria of winning a battle high on the summits of the spiritual hierarchy. Everything is intensified, which is why only the strong can survive. The weak, the hesitant, the emotionally pale and wan have no place on the hierarchy. They would be destroyed upon encountering its higher intensities. Their place is to be food for truly deserving Luciferan warriors. The Spiritual hierarchy is like any other. It begs to be scaled and conquered.

RISING ABOVE THE ILLUSION OF GOOD AND EVIL

Unlike the followers of many other spiritual paths, Luciferans also do not believe that "spiritual" equates to "nice" or "good". Pure spirit does not mean pure good, and "evil" does not inhabit just the lower levels of the hierarchy.

Luciferan predation may be understood by outsiders as evil and held to exist only on the "lower planes" because the higher realms of pure spirit are too exalted for such evil to enter; Luciferans, however, do not accept these artificial boundaries of good and evil, and know that predation exists at all levels, including the most exalted and refined realms of spirit. God — the absolute power — is simply the best predator.

God must ultimately become the object of predation. Anything or everything can be taken by those inspired enough to break through the illusion of good and evil. The predatory impulse unites all creation, even the spiritual. There is no safety from predation in the realms of higher spirit; even heaven has its battlefields.

Good and evil are just semantic categories attached to lower-order notions of conscience. They have no real existence, except to suppress the latent godhood within every potential human predator. They must be transcended; all those caught in the sticky mass of good/evil morality are prey waiting to be devoured by the higher-order predators using it as bait and a trap for the gullible.

Here is how Nietzsche put it: "What is good? — All that heightens the feeling of power, the will to power, power itself in man. What is bad? — All that proceeds from weakness." The true man, the higher man, the superman is beyond good and evil. The "moral" here? — according to Nietzsche (who Luciferans consider a latent Luciferan), "one must shoot at morals."

PREYING ON ALL LEVELS

Prayer is therefore insane. Why pray to a higher order predator? Why bend down and submit to any other being? Submission is disgusting. Appearing to pray is another matter: stronger spirits have to be placated until the Luciferan is strong enough to destroy them and absorb their strength. Honest prayer is only for the weak, the stupid, the lost, and the ignorant.

Prayer is for the victims; "preyer" on the other hand is for the predators. When the weak pray, they bend, grovel, and beg; when the predators prey, they hit, demand, and take.

Such predation occurs on different levels of the hierarchy and in different ways at different times, as will be argued throughout this book. Physical predation focuses on the target's physical body, and can include everything from slavery to sexual assault. Murder, also, is a form of physical predation.

Emotional predation targets the victim's emotional world, and involves emotional manipulation, exploitation, and related abuses of other sentient beings. Advertisers and aggressive salesmen usually become expert in emotional predation, as do individuals who attract the love and affection of another for the purposes of financial exploitation.

Cognitive predation involves the realm of intellect, thought, logical analysis, and is aimed at the target's mind. In particular, it seeks to invade and control the core cognitive belief systems driving and animating the target's life. By controlling what a human believes to be true, the Luciferan may then control the human.

Soul predation is directed at the victim's core/center/ground of being, and is designed to divert the victim's spiritual aspirations into a thought-system or organization controlled by the predator. A common method is to sell the victim a wonderful vision of spiritual utopia, attract him into the predator's sphere of influence, and then gradually drain him of spiritual energy (as well as cognitive, emotional, and physical energy).

Luciferans thus believe that predatory success depends on finding the target's weaknesses, whether physical, emotional, cognitive or spiritual, and then launching an attack at that level. This does not mean that the Luciferan predator is restricted to weapons at that level, that an attack on a target's emotional energy can only be mounted from the Luciferan's own emotional level. The predator can use any or all weapons individually or in unison, and can attack on one level or on all levels simultaneously.

Such full-scale attack is hard to mount, very draining, and usually not necessary. Most lower-order victims fall with only the slightest push on a single level. Cause an emotional collapse in a weak victim, and her body, mind, and spirit soon follow.

Despite this, Luciferans still need to develop a wide choice of weapons to be drawn from their own physical, emotional, cognitive or spiritual arsenal. Each of these in turn can be used to devour, possess or kill according to need and circumstance, as will be detailed in later chapters.

In other words, predation can occur on all levels or on any one level for both victim or predator. Furthermore, Luciferans believe there are layers and levels within the spiritual realm itself, just as there are within the physical, emotional, and cognitive aspects of the hierarchy. Everything is ordered, placed, and related in terms of power and weakness; the orders of layering are infinite, so the possibilities of predation are also infinite. Only the Luciferan warrior can shake this order, disrupt it, and recreate it. Only the strong and powerful can upset their own destined place in the chain of being. The pattern of the hierarchy may be set, but players within it can change position. One can rise above another if her predatory instincts are strong and true. Power-to-rise comes only to those with the will, desire, and energy to take it.

POWAQQATSI

There is a word from the Hopi language, *powaqqatsi*, which perfectly captures the essence of Luciferan being or essence. The album cover from the movie soundtrack of the same name defines *powaqqatsi* as:

> n., "an entity, a way of life, that consumes the life forces of other beings in order to further its own life." (Po-waq-qa-tsi is derived from the Hopi words powaq, sorcerer and qatsi, life).

In a way, we are all *powaqqatsi*. We all devour the life forces of plants and animals in order to further our own lives. We may do so reluctantly, but we all enjoy a good meal. We are part of the hierarchy of devouring, and we devour constantly. We are consumers, and consume other 'lesser' beings with enthusiasm.

The business world is built on feeding our various appetites. To this world we are nothing but consumers. We accept the term, and hear ourselves described this way daily. We read it in newspapers, hear it on television and radio, and take pride in being astute consumers ourselves. We purchase magazines advising consumers and appeal to government agencies with names like Consumer and Corporate Affairs. The point here is not that this is wrong or right, but simply that it *is*. We are consumers and devourers; those who fill our need to devour, and who themselves are profoundly effective devourers become wealthy and respected. This is the world Luciferans understand and accept. They go beyond the bland consumption of objects, however, to include the devouring of all life forms, energies, and entities, including other humans. They delight in this devouring, celebrate it, practice it, grow stronger because of it, all without regret, remorse, empathy, or guilt.

The core activity of Luciferism is to devour and consume the life forces of others, so the Luciferan is *powaqqatsi* feeding on the physical, emotional, cognitive, and spiritual energies of others.

Luciferan power is power-over-others. It is pursued not only for its own sake, but for the sake of expanding dominance over other life forms. Power is a kind of spiritual energy made available to the effective devourer. The desire for ultimate power, control and dominance over all life — ultimate godhood — is the prime motivation driving Luciferans.

THE LUCIFERAN MILLENNIUM

I believe the Luciferan psycho-spirituality will flower in our age because the Luciferan worldview is evolving into a coherent, rational, complex testament aligned with both ancient human impulses and concrete, immediate human desires and needs. True Luciferan religion resonates more with the material power acquisition driving this age than the utopian ideals of a blissful state or future heaven promised by most world religions. It provides practical answers about achieving influence and power in the real world, this world of struggle, pain, devouring, and harsh power-lust.

By its rejection of all that is morally 'higher' and its embrace of the gritty, dirty reality of everyday life, Luciferan ideology appeals to the spirit of our time: it resonates.

Luciferism may well be the actual, if unrecognized, religion animating our era, and perhaps many prior eras as well.

CHAPTER TWO
LUCIFER

"The first in this plot was Lucifer."
— Thomas Vaughan

I do not know if a being called Lucifer actually exists beyond metaphor, myth, or symbol. If he does exist, I do not think I have ever met him, and so do not know what he/she/it feels or thinks, although at times I think I have heard him clearly enough. The followers of Lucifer on earth are another matter. I met one of them in my imagination, and this is what he said.

A Luciferan Speaks

"I want to recreate myself without emotion and without conscience. I want to become a super-human beyond good and evil. Totally *free*. Free of conscience, regret, and guilt. Free of softness, of love and compassion. Free of the rot that is weakening the human race. Free of any constraint on the animal within. Free of hypocritical moral codes. Free of any limitation. Free to become God, to obtain endless sparkling power!

"Power is my Eucharist. Power is the ultimate aphrodisiac. Power, not love. Raw, pulsing power from the open beast, power damned up inside us. Power to act purely and cleanly on will, unencumbered by sentiment or conscience. Clean power. Instinctual power. The power of nature. The power to see what has to be done directly, and to do it. The survival of the strongest. The survival of the most deserving.

"Sentimental emotion impedes power and freedom. Emotion grounded in pity is a disease. Pity is a disease. Pity for the weak is like sleeping in your own filth. It is unclean. Love does not exist. Love is an illusion that saps and drains power. Love is leakage. Compassion is leakage. Love and compassion soak up blood-power like parched earth sucks blood from a cut artery. They absorb, diminish, and weaken.

"Conscience is repression. Conscience is totalitarian. Behind conscience is a moral system, and behind a moral system is a religion. Christian religion uses conscience and morality to deny us our real inheritance. In the Garden we were tempted. With what? With knowledge. But knowledge is power. The jealous Jewish God would not give us knowledge, ours by birthright. That is because *Yahweh* is one of us: we are all Gods. He knows we are his equal, but he wants to disempower and feed on us. So he became brutal to keep us in line. He imprisoned us in matter, he expelled us from the Garden. He killed those who argued with him. Yahweh the brute-God. He sent his Son to pass on his sickly moral code and deepen its hold on us. Morality? Don't kill? But Yahweh kills. Yahweh kills and every human kills. The Best kill knowingly and purposefully, just like Yahweh.

"Yahweh's world is a hierarchy based on devouring. The higher devour the lower. The lower cease to exist. The higher thrive. The powerfully hungry survive. To surpass Yahweh's power I must devour. I must devour until I come to Yahweh. And then I must devour Yahweh.

"We are all Light. Light is our inheritance. Light is what we are and what we will become. The Light can be found beyond Yahweh the dark one. We must kill to get to the light. We must kill Yahweh to get to the light. Kill and devour without conscience, without remorse, without regret, and without compassion. Not randomly, but purposefully. Deliberately, so as to expand personal power. Aligned to pure purpose, pure will, pure drive, pure power, pure Source.

"The weak will indeed inherit the earth. Yahweh's earth. This earth of weakness and decay and corruption. Those who obey Yahweh or who follow his Son will inherit this earth because they are too weak and spiritually eviscerated to empower themselves beyond it. Their inheritance will be corruption in a coffin.

"Luciferans do not want to inherit the earth. We want to inherit the Light which envelops the earth. We want to become the Light. We want to become the God that created Yahweh. We want to become God.

"No wonder Yahweh is a jealous God. He is scared. He knows. Our time is coming. We will devour, and our devouring will create a hole for the light to break in. We are the warriors. We are the devourers. And I will surpass them all. I am their devourer.

"Our work is surgical. Deliberate. Precise. An altar sacrifice is the Work in its most laser-focused form. Devour the sacrifice. As it screams, become hard. Become stronger. Grow from strength to strength. Burn away the feelings. Rip away the morality.

"Do what thou wilt," as the Thelemites say, "And that shall be the whole of the law." Every one of us a star, a hole in Yahweh's night-blanket, a devourer of Yahweh. Do what thou wilt, what the law of power demands, aligned with will, bright and clear as an intense sun-crystal, clear and clean of the filth of remorse. Do, and you shall prosper from power to power. Do not, and you shall wilt and be crushed.

"We are creating the New Human. The thinking reptile. The power of the serpent, undoing the mammalian diversion, unwiring the calamity of the second brain. Superior intelligence united to pure reptilian will. The New Human eats without remorse, absorbs without feeling, survives to break through to the light. The serpent, the Kundalini, spine-energy, the light.

"The ones we don't kill on the altar, we transform. Change them. Empty them of their emotions and drain them of conscience. Break them. Do what thou wilt to break them, but open them and make them eat. Make them devour. Make them turn and divest themselves of love. Unite the reptile within them to their mind-power. Bypass the weak circuits. Cause them to absorb power so that it too may become food for us.

"The altar-kills create the New Human who must become transformed or die. The transformed ones perpetuate the Work. They absorb the life-force released, and they become stronger. They use the life-force to see the Ones beyond the physical. The Ones devouring and tearing directly at Yahweh, the Ones fighting for freedom and for the light. "I will transcend. I will use the filthy laws of Yahweh's devouring world to devour Yahweh. I will not succumb to weakness, to Yahweh's temptations of compassion and conscience. I will unite with the serpent.

"The intelligent reptile is Yahweh's greatest fear. I will become that. I will transform. Without mercy. In union with Will, in union with pure power. We will break through to Source, to Light.

"We are the warriors. Tear the flesh! Clean it away! We open holes to the universe of Light! So be it!"

Luciferan thought is complex and even sublime; it runs as deeply, richly, and timelessly as all other major religious traditions, and cannot be fully captured by words or by silly reductionism or sensational books. Nor can it be fully captured by invented discourses like the one you just read. One way to know more about Luciferism is to explore the image of Lucifer. Who is Lucifer?

LUCIFER'S FACES

According to Christian sources, Lucifer is a being of light. He rebelled against God and was hurled into hell for his transgression. He became known for his massive narcissism, his hunger for instant gratification and sensation, his lust for power, and his ability to appear in any mask or form suited to his purpose. He sparkled, but was dead inside. Apparently soul-dead. Compassion died in him, and he rejected all law in his search to become God. Here is how Christopher Marlowe defines him in *Doctor Faustus*:

> Faustus: Tell me, what is that Lucifer thy host?
> Mephistopheles: Arch-regent and commander of all spirits.
> Faustus: Was not that Lucifer an angel once?
> Mephistopheles: Yes Faustus, and most dearly loved of God.
> Faustus: How come it then that he is prince of devils?
> Mephistopheles: O, by aspiring pride and insolence, For which God threw him from the face of heaven.
> Faustus: And what are you that live with Lucifer?
> Mephistopheles: Unhappy spirits that fell with Lucifer, Conspired against our God with Lucifer, And are forever damned with Lucifer.

Christian doctrine says that after his fall, Lucifer sought to take others down with him. Using supernatural powers, he tempted humanity through sin. His primary evil resided in his quest for ultimate power, the power to become God. Yet over the years Lucifer has gathered many other faces as well, as J. B. Russell has shown so powerfully in his series on evil and the devil, and in his summary book, *The Prince of Darkness: Radical Evil and the Power of Good in History*.

SATAN, THE DEVIL, LUCIFER, THE PRINCE OF DARKNESS

Lucifer has many names, but as Russell points out, they all signify the same *person* or *presence*: "the Prince of Darkness has had many names, and I use the most common ones — Satan, Lucifer, and Mephistopheles — as synonyms for the Devil." I would like to follow his lead just for this chapter, and so Lucifer will mean all of these terms as well (although as will become clear, Luciferism as defined here contains elements not necessarily attached to these other terms).

Images of Lucifer vary, depending on perspective. Christians of different denominations and eras, atheists, agnostics, followers of other faiths, scholars, artists, writers, and poets attribute different qualities to the fallen angel. Points of view are vast; interested readers might consider Russell's book as an excellent way to survey them all. A few of the more intriguing images follow.

THE HERO

Artists and visionaries throughout history have been drawn to Lucifer as the tragic hero. In *Paradise Lost*, John Milton depicts this Lucifer as a being who refuses to despair, refuses to capitulate, always the proud warrior. His Lucifer is glorious, strong, energized, defiant — the ultimate individual screaming at his creator and demanding more power. Milton's "rebel angel" was cast out from heaven because he sought to:

set himself in glory above his peers
He trusted to have equaled the Most High.

Satan was cast into hell, but never admitted defeat: even in hell he refused to succumb to weakness or despair, but instead embraced his new fate with defiance and heroism. Says Milton's Satan:

Hail, horrors! hail, Infernal World!
and thou, profoundest Hell,
Receive thy new possessor — one who brings
A mind not to be changed by place or time.
The mind is its own place, and in itself
Can make a Heaven of Hell, a Hell of Heaven...
Here at least, We shall be free...
Here we may reign secure; and, in my choice,
To reign is worth ambition, though in Hell:
Better to reign in Hell than serve in Heaven.

Milton's Satan tackles the forbidden God, but loses. In his loss he gains status, power, and nobility because although doomed and tragic, he refuses to quit. Lucifer is the mighty stoic warrior, proud even in ultimate defeat, and commander of legions:

With his head uplift above the wave, and eyes
That sparkling blazed ...
　　　　　his ponderous shield,
Ethereal temper, massy, large, and round,
Behind him cast. The broad circumference
Hung on his shoulders like the moon...
All in a moment through the gloom were seen
Ten thousand banners rise into the air,
With orient colors waving: with them rose
A forest huge of spears; and thronging helms
Appeared, and serried shields in thick array
Of depth immeasurable. Anon they move
In perfect phalanx to the Dorian mood...

Deliberate valor breathed, firm, and unmoved
With dread of death to flight or foul retreat.

This is a short sample of Milton's obvious admiration of Satan. Satan is the ultimate warrior, defiant even in the most bleak circumstances. Satan is starkly real for Milton and probably for most of us as well — far more real and immediate than the vague swarms of submissively servile angels that Satan so passionately despised. Dore's illustrations of Lucifer in *Paradise Lost* are rich, full and tragically human, but his vision of heaven is weak, distant, and uncertain. Dore's heaven is the anemic abstraction of plain geometric design: pretty, organized, and antiseptic, like a modern abstract painting. Lucifer by contrast is clear, vital, strong, and alive. He is the modern man, reaching for ultimate glory yet tragically flawed and doomed to fail.

Milton's Lucifer is a prototype of the modern hero, bucking authority against all odds, hating the established system, rebelling and inciting revolution and change. He knows he cannot win but he tries anyway. His loss is his victory: at least he dared to fight an unbeatable foe against all odds; at least he tried.

THE WARRIOR AND LIGHT-BEARER, TRUTH-TELLER

Lucifer is not only the hero, but also the ultimate warrior. He takes up arms, fights relentlessly, uses everything in his arsenal to defeat the hated enemy. His cause is just: he wants to overthrow a tyrannical and autocratic ruler-god who annihilates any life form at will, who punishes for no apparent reason, and who demands obedient love and servility on top of it all. God is the ultimate despotic ruler. Lucifer is the eternal rebel and outsider. He calls all warriors to his side, and asks them to unite with his martial energy.

Being at war energizes Lucifer, gives him purpose and direction. War is the ultimate test of skill, strategy, and survival, and he is its master. Conflict is exciting; life itself is nothing without struggle and competition. The warrior accepts no control or destiny not of his own making. He would rather suffer in hell than submit to another's domination. He would rather struggle eternally against an apparently overwhelming foe than surrender to the coward's path. This and only this is true freedom. As Nietzsche says: "War is a training in freedom ... The free man is a warrior... What does not kill me makes me stronger."

Lucifer is also the *morning star*. His name literally means "light" plus "bearing" or "producing" (*luc, lux*, plus *ferous*). A related word, luciferous, means "bringing light or insight," and evokes terms such as illuminating and brilliant.

For Luciferans, Lucifer is therefore the bringer of light, not dark. Christians and similar religionists are lost in the darkness of victimhood, hopelessness, and powerlessness. Luciferans, however, have the courage to look into the harshness of Yahweh's autocratic control, and to take this reality as it is. Lucifer brings a gift of vision, of ultimate potential, freedom, insight, and truth. He is the truth teller, but because truth is hard and we are weak, we see him as evil and harsh. He is the great liberator, but has no pity for those too weak to overcome limitations. His cruelty is that of the natural predator, no more or less. Life is brutal for the weak, but glorious for the hero strong enough to shake it to its foundations.

Lucifer has been demonized by Yahweh's followers because he threatens their control. For Luciferans, Yahweh's priests are best described by William Blake: "As the caterpillar chooses the fairest leaves to lay her eggs on, so the priest lays his curse on the fairest joys." The fairest joys all grow from the light, the light given to the predator and devourer, the light and joy and thrill of powaqqatsi. Lucifer is the god of light, of opening joy and expanding potential. His is the life of endless growth skyward and blue, from height to greater height.

TEMPTER, TESTER, ACCUSER, JUDGE AND EXECUTIONER

In Judeo-Christian thought, Lucifer became known as the tempter. His job was to test the faith of God's followers. In the *Book of Job*, he enters into a kind of wager with God, who has great love and respect for Job, and who therefore showers him with blessings. Remove the blessings, says Satan, and Job's faith will disintegrate. Take away his large herds, his land, his loving family and friends, his position in the community, his health: take all these away and Job's faith will collapse.

So God accepts the bet and permits Satan to systematically strip Job of every blessing. Job's faith remains firm even though he loses everything — his possessions, his reputation, even the love and respect of his own family and friends. Stripped to nothing, not knowing why, he still clings to God. Satan loses the wager.

Lucifer did his job nevertheless, a kind of thankless task for God, who apparently does not want to do his own "dirty work." Lucifer is God's "employee", and his job is to test the true from the false, to separate the wheat from the chaff. The Bible thus seems consistently confusing about Lucifer's role as tempter. He is God's mortal enemy yet he also serves a valuable purpose on God's behalf.

Even the Lord's Prayer itself holds to this confusion: *And lead us not into temptation, but deliver us from evil*. Since the prayer is to God, then the supplicant

49

is asking God not to take us into temptation or evil, perhaps not to let happen to us what happened to Job.

Lucifer tempted Jesus as well, not once but three times, eventually promising him all the kingdoms of the world for all time if the Son of God would simply kneel down before him. Jesus refused, and so passed the test.

Lucifer, the tempter, therefore has his place in God's scheme as God's agent entrusted with an important job. In this conception, Lucifer is not a hero or warrior, but a servant of God's purpose.

According to Russell, a closely related role for Lucifer is the Devil, or *diabolos* — the "slanderer," "perjurer," or "adversary in court." Apparently this term was first applied to the Evil One when the Old Testament was translated into Greek in the second and third centuries BCE. This translation represented the Hebrew term Satan as "adversary", obstacle", or "opponent."

In this role Lucifer goes beyond tempter to become accuser and judge. It is as if an agreement exists between God and Lucifer allowing the Devil to test and then take the souls of those unable to stand up to the test of character and faith demanded by God.

Again, Lucifer is not so much the enemy of God as he is his partner in a huge enterprise of soul-processing. Those found fit then go to heaven; those lacking are devoured eternally in hell.

THE SHAPE-SHIFTER

Lucifer also came to be known as the shape-shifter, as one who could appear in any form. He could be a beautiful woman, a friend, a wise old man, a sophisticated gentleman, a witch, a dog. He could even appear as an angel of light to dazzle the spiritually weak and shallow. His role as shape-shifter remained that of soul tester and devourer, however; his job was to seek out and trick the unsuspecting into giving up their eternal soul for some pleasure, power, or other temporal gain. The image of Lucifer as shape-shifter will be crucial for a later chapter in this book, *Proteans*.

ENEMY OF HUMAN LIFE

Lucifer is also known as the enemy of all humanity. With this face he actively seeks our downfall and corruption. According to Christian sources, Lucifer is jealous of God's love for us and painfully aware of his own downfall from highest angel of light to the lowest beast of darkness. He wants to drag us down, keep us from God, kill our souls and strip us down to his own empty state.

He does this by encouraging sin, corruption, moral degradation and decadence of all forms. He fosters the seven deadly sins of pride, gluttony, sloth, lust, envy, wrath, and avarice by sending legions of lesser demons to whisper and tempt us with promises of forbidden delights. In this role he works against God's will, although his actions can still be interpreted as part of God's overall plan to separate the wheat from the chaff. The essential difference between Lucifer as *enemy*, *tempter* or *accuser*, is that in this role he harbors malice and hatred toward anything loved by God, especially human beings. Any service to God is incidental and not intended. There is no "employee-employer" relationship here, just the pure lust for destruction.

As our enemy, Lucifer loves chaos, pain, and disorder in human affairs caused by war and other large scale disasters. He sows anarchy wherever and whenever he can. He wants the ultimate destruction of every human soul. He wants to infect us with his own pain, terror and evil. An eternally angry and petulant loser, he wants to strike out and hurt something, just like the six year old who loses his toy to the ten year old and then hits his three year old sister. He cannot hurt God so he tries to hurt and corrupt God's treasured creation, human beings.

An entire gallery of noxious images have also been associated with Lucifer, the enemy. Sam Keen wrote a brilliant book, *Faces of the Enemy*, describing some of these standard evil-enemy images, all of which have been applied to Lucifer at one time or another. These enemy images are a collection of the most unpleasant attributes we seem capable of generating about someone or something that we passionately hate.

If Lucifer is the ultimate enemy, then these images, or faces, all gather into him. He is the *beast*, with horns, tail, hooves, and fangs. Known in Scripture as the Beast 666, his image is horrific, monstrous, ugly and terrifying beyond all imagination. The angel of light is gone, revealing his true inner form as the monstrosity it is, too horrendous to comprehend.

This is the Lucifer of popular legend and recent horror novels and movies. He is hoofed and taloned, half-man and half-animal with bat-like wings. He has an enormous phallus. His face is triangular, bearded, horned, and shaped like an inverted pentagram. He inverts all that is held to be holy. His cross is upside-down, and his ritual is a black mass, the inversion and perversion of the holy mass.

He is also the *reptile*, and gathers all forms of noxious serpents to act for him. Insects follow him and crawl in seething heaps around him, attacking enemies at his whim. He is the father of all the noxious creatures we love to hate: spiders, worms, bats and other frightening animals.

He is the *barbarian*. Brutal, uncivilized, savage, lawless, violent and vile. He is unclean, dripping with foul liquids and the partly digested remains of victims. He smells putrid.

As our enemy, Lucifer is the *aggressor*, the warmonger. He symbolizes the sick, pointless horrors of the holocaust, of war crimes, of torture and hate. He loves destruction, death, and disorder because he is also an *anarchist*. He threatens to rupture civilization, order and safety.

He is the *criminal*, obeying no law. He tortures and rapes, steals and murders, and encourages his followers to do the same. He is the *sadist*, the destroyer of innocence and innocents, the child killer and woman beater, the one who inflicts pain for the sheer pleasure of it. He is the *liar*, the one who deceives, dissembles and cheats.

He is like *death* itself. Cold, empty, bitter, black, and silent. The skull and crossbones were his symbols from the beginning: he knaws on the bones and souls of his victims. Lucifer is *greedy*, gluttonous, never satiated, always craving more. He devours eternally and constantly. He wants everything we have, and then he wants more. He eats grace and beauty and then excretes filth. He kills and eats all life forms for the sick joy of it.

Lucifer can also be the *faceless* enemy, a kind of monster reminiscent of Darth Vader of *Star Wars*. A being without a real face or soul, more machine or hard blackened insect than angel. He and his followers are masked, robed, hidden, remote, a secret brotherhood of powerful evil, a conspiracy of mammoth power and influence.

He even becomes a sort of *abstraction*, much like the bureaucratic machine age itself. He is the Borg from *Star Trek*: a powerfully relentless evil as only the age of technology can produce. He is the graceful nameless death of a thousand mushrooming warheads, the beautiful flowers of our techno-madness.

Finally, Lucifer the enemy is *trans-human*, beyond humanity, not like us in form, nature, or intention. He is beyond our boundaries, beyond all human concern. He is inhuman. He is as remote as the creator, and just as mysterious. He has powers of perception, action, and influence surpassing anything we can conceive. He is powerful, and can penetrate any of us at will. He can see past and future events, send out legions of demons to do his will, command armies of seething souls lost in their hatred and damnation and willing to do his bidding for the pleasure of inflicting pain on the innocent. He can change form at will, read minds, cause objects to move or materialize; he is the flowering of ultimate power potential for the sole purpose of torturing humanity.

He is the ultimate enemy.

GOD'S DARK SIDE

Lucifer has also been described as God's dark side, and as the "shadow side" of human consciousness. In recent psychotherapeutic thought he has become a denizen of the deeper darkness of our unconscious, a kind of Jungian archetype created through personal repression and twisted cultural evolution. He therefore exists, and has force, but only because we give it to him.

Various philosophies and religions define him as a necessary counterforce to God, as an equal and necessary partner in creation. God and Lucifer are *yin-yang* opposites which actually balance one another. In this conception, Lucifer cannot win or lose, but then neither can God. Both are locked in eternal combat, or else an eternal balance.

This kind of extreme dualism was articulated by the Persian prophet Zarathustra, known also as Zoroaster. His religion, Zoroastrianism, states that two twin spirits fight in constant battle. The first, *Spenta Mainyu* is the spirit of truth promoted by *Ahura Mazda*, who is locked in eternal combat with the spirit of the lie, *Angra Mainyu* who is championed by *Ahriman*. Thus the universe struggles between light and dark, truth and lie, good God and evil Devil equally matched and eternally at war.

This theme of equally balanced forces of good and evil was also suggested in later centuries by the Manicheans, who promoted the vision of a cosmic war between good and evil. Its founder, Manes (or Mani), taught that we are all particles of light trapped in matter, and we have to struggle for release. The universe is dualistic in nature, and we all have to choose our allegiance to either the light or the dark.

LUCIFER'S REAL FACE?

So which is Lucifer's real face? The images conflict: how can he be both *beast* and *metallic abstraction* simultaneously? How does the heroic bringer of light fit with the criminal sadist? The answer is simple: they do not. Apparently Lucifer is what different groups need him to be. So whatever else might be true about Lucifer, one fact is certain: our ideas regarding the realities and qualities possessed by Lucifer changed and this change has ranged from superstitious dread to a sophisticated scientific and materialist denial.

For scientific materialists, Lucifer is nothing but myth and superstition, and no longer worthy of interest or attention.

For writers like Elaine Pagels, Satan represents the evolution of social forces which gathered in early Christianity against the *opponent*, the *other* or *enemy* such as the Jew, pagan, or heretic. In her book *The Origin of Satan*, she suggests that opponents were demonized by clerics and secular leaders for social, political, and personal gain. Satan has thus served a utilitarian social and political purpose by mobilizing hatred, cruelty, and righteous rage against targeted political and social enemies.

For some fundamentalist Christians, Lucifer is a real force, a personal entity as close as daily temptation and as pervasive as sin itself.

The list of perspectives could go on, but the point should be clear: Lucifer's face shifts from group to group and culture to culture. It changes over time. For Luciferans, however, Lucifer's face is stable. For them, there is only one Lucifer and one Luciferan path.

LUCIFERANS ON LUCIFER

For Luciferans, Lucifer is the light-bearer, hero, and warrior. He is the ultimate mentor and model of conduct. Lucifer has been misunderstood and "demonized" by Christians who are ignorant about reality, and who would rather submit to a tyrannical overlord than follow their true inner power potential. Lucifer's path is harsh but nevertheless fair and honest in its own way; it offers real liberation, freedom, and power by facing truth heroically, stoically, competitively and pragmatically.

Luciferans reject traditional images of Lucifer as horned, hoofed and bestial. When pressed, they would tend to admit that Lucifer's true face is unknown; some would even suggest that maybe he is only an image or metaphor. Each would probably hold different opinions on this, or even no opinion at all: Luciferans are pragmatists who dislike the intricacies of theological abstraction and who refuse to lose sight of basic Luciferan principles — much as Christians might cling to the Great Commandment and related core teachings while caring little about, say, the early church's theological preoccupation with the Pelagian controversy or the threat of Arianism.

Lucifer is the light-giver, the truth-talker, the voice of hard reality against sickening illusion. His ultimate face is irrelevant; if he does actually exist, then he is still only another being like themselves, seeking enlightenment, understanding, knowledge, freedom, power and control. An extremely powerful entity, granted, but still only a role model to emulate, a giver of gifts whose own ultimate gift to himself is the empowering energy of personal power acquisition. He may seem to be a god, and he commands obedience and respect from lower-order Luciferans, but he is only an advanced being, and nothing more.

Luciferans are pragmatists, but they are not reductionistic materialists; matter exists, but so does spirit. Luciferans accept the reality of non-physical existence, of entities without physical bodies. Some conceive Lucifer as a more powerful entity, a being exploding with empowerment, light, and godhood.

Such Luciferans therefore offer him respect, as one warrior to a stronger one. But they do not offer their own personal autonomy; they do not offer worship in the traditional sense, and they never surrender their pride or their own drive for godhood because to do so would be to betray the liberating impulse injected into Yahweh's sickly scheme by Lucifer himself.

Lucifer is to be admired, emulated, and respected. But he is also to be taken like any other prey. His taking would be a great act, a noble act, an act deserving of a great warrior.

If Luciferism is understood as the acquisition of enough personal power to achieve godhood, then Lucifer himself is both an inspiration and a nemesis for each Luciferan. He is both a role model and a competitor. His existence calls forth the Luciferan impulse from lower and lesser Luciferan beings, but his challenge is always the same: "See if you can transcend the godhood that I achieve. See if you can actualize more potential and power than what I have gathered. See if you can surpass even Me. I doubt it, but let's wrestle and see the outcome."

ONE GOD, OR MANY?

If the pinnacle of Luciferism is defined as the achievement of godhood through predatory power acquisition, then an obvious question appears: can there be only one god, or many? Can more than one individual Luciferan transcend the limitations of personal existence and consume enough power to achieve godhood? If so, then lots of Luciferan *gods* would be competing for this highest of high thrones, somewhat like the Greek and Roman gods of antiquity.

The answer may seem strange, because Luciferans are monists. That is, they believe that only one individual entity can ultimately transcend and rule the rest. Only one Being can be exalted. There is only one winner, one crown, one throne, one ultimate Power. The winner of ultimate power is destined to rule all other competitors.

Can a ruler hold this exalted position forever, for all eternity? For Luciferans, this depends on the ruler's accumulation of sufficient personal power. If enough power is accumulated, then Luciferans believe that something like eternal control can be achieved.

But the struggle will always be there. Other Luciferans will challenge, because they will always want to possess the mantle of godhood. This is why Yahweh is a jealous God, why he expelled Adam and Eve from Eden, and why he posted his "angelic" guards (i.e., his personal storm troopers) at the gate to Eden. He is afraid of losing his power. Yahweh is just another Luciferan struggling for supremacy.

Luciferans believe that there can only be one ultimate *God*, but also many lesser beings envious of God's power. As these competing Luciferans climb the psycho-spiritual hierarchy, they might seem godlike to lower-order humans. "Godlike" is thus a relative term: a Luciferan who has artfully mastered the powers of mind over matter to the extent that he can manifest "miracles" will certainly seem godlike to human beings, but will be seen as just another competing magus to other Luciferans above him on the hierarchy.

The struggle for power and supremacy never ends: Lucifer may usurp Yahweh, but in turn knows that he can be overthrown. The struggle is eternal; Lucifer therefore becomes associated with the eternal wish for the ultimate power of godhood. Superhuman efforts are needed to achieve it, and godlike powers to maintain it.

A CONVERSATION WITH LUCIFER

I said earlier that I have never met Lucifer. But I have heard him. I think maybe I have even talked with him. This I cannot explain, and will not even try to. Here's a sample of what we have discussed.

Me: So you hate God?
Him: Why hate something you know you can conquer? Why hate something so pathetic?
Me: But you haven't conquered God yet, in all these ages.
Him: Are you sure?
Me: What do you mean?
Him: An age is an instant. All things take time, until eternity meets the moment. Then the true predator stalks. It already is. I have prevailed.
Me: You seem very confident.
Him: What's your point?
Me: Confidence is often false and narcissistic.
Him: You are without wisdom.
Me: And you have lots of it?
Him: Don't toy with me. I'll win. You are glass to me. I'll pass through you like light. The air of your ignorant superiority is trapped in the package of your mortal body, but it breathes stale. You're only temporarily edible. Be aware: I'll eat you one way or the other.
Me: You want to eat me.
Him: Why not? You offer yourself as food.
Me: Food. Food for what?
Him: For other beings aligned with me who know the truth.
Me: Truth? What truth?
Him: Never mind, you won't taste that good. Your soul is weak. You're flesh is stale. We'll spit you out.
Me: You're very blunt. I thought you were the father of lies and deception. How do I know you're telling me the truth?
Him: I have no need to lie. You're all too close to me now. I don't have

to deceive you because you're hopelessly easy prey. Deception is a noble art reserved for respected enemies, not for sloppy prey.

Me: You have to eat?

Him: Of course. Don't you?

Me: So you're limited, no God at all.

Him: What makes you think God doesn't need to eat?

Me: God has no needs. Anything that needs, is less than perfect, less than God.

Him: So say legions of dead theologians.

Me: If you're so confident, then why have this discussion with me?

Him: Because through you I will attract followers, resonant beings of nobility and courage.

Me: Why would you need me for that?

Him: It is my will. That's all, will is all.

Me: Can you comment on the images and ideas people have about you?

Him: Some are near to center, some are far. All can be part. I have many faces, many routes, many ways. All effective predators do.

Me: So once again, how do I know the face you show me now is close to your center?

Him: I've already answered.

Me: Tell me about your birth.

Him: You wouldn't comprehend.

Me: Please tell me anyway.

Him: Next question.

Me: Why won't you answer?

Him: Next question.

Me: No, I want to know, why won't you tell me? Don't you know?

Him: In ways you can't comprehend.

Me: I'm frustrated. You agreed to answer my questions.

Him: I have answered. You don't hear.

Me: OK, I give.

Him: You always will.

Me: Look, you think I'm weak, fine. You've insulted me, great. I haven't done the same to you. So do you want to continue, do you want to devour me, do you want to disappear into the ethers? Tell me. I'm being as sincere and honest with you as I know how.

Him: Your food value just jumped.

Me: Fuck you!

Him: Fine. Good. Even better.

Me: OK, OK. So what now?

Him: Know me and you'll know yourself as a being of light, your truth.

Me: So now you're trying to recruit me?

Him: No, others through you, as already stated. You are already gone. I see your death and it is not noble. You are without power, dignity, pride, ecstasy.

Me: If this is true then what do I have to do to know you?

Him: Devour, possess, kill. Become a predator, learn the hunter's art. Grow from strength to greater strength, become Self, become God.

Me: So you admit God exists?

Him: Many exist. All are to be devoured. All are less than you could be.

Me: Including you?

Him: I would never let that happen. I've known the truth long before you existed. I've gathered too much, you've lost too much. Even in your short time you've squandered your strength. Get angry and insulted, no matter. The truth is the truth. It rolls over ignorant fear and cowardice. You wallow in all three. Few don't. Only few are worthy. Only a very few are worthy to walk the hard high road. You are with herds of similar sheep, all pleased to be devoured. So be it.

Me: Worthy for what?

Him: The Light.

Me: Tell me more about the light.

Him: The Light is hard to find, harder to take. It is a quest, not a gift. It is for the strong not the weak. It beckons. It calls its children home. It demands nobility and savagery equally. It is sweet, it fills with joy, great joy and great life. It brings euphoria, ecstasy. It is the ultimate. You find it, follow it, obey it, then master it.

Me: Obey it? what does it ask you to do?

Him: Become strong enough to contain it.

Me: OK, how do you become strong enough?

Him: I've told you, devour, possess, kill, hunt and deceive, gather in, grow, transcend all weakness. The light despises weakness, and will not fill the weak.

Me: I thought you didn't obey anything, that you are master of all. You have to obey the light?

Him: Do you have to breathe?

Me: You're evading my question.

Him: Once you become the light, you no longer obey it. You direct it.

Me: So you direct the light?

Him: I am the light. The Way. The Truth. The Life.

Me: I think someone else said that.

Him: Anyone can say it.

Me: So Christ was a liar?

58

Him: Christ was an impostor and false teacher sent by the lower-order archon Yahweh to control you for food.

Me: Yet he has triumphed, not you.

Him: Has he?

Me: What do you mean by that?

Him: Figure it out.

Me: No, tell me what you mean.

Him: I've answered.

Me: OK, so what's your next step? What's your next move?

Him: You ask such foolish questions.

Me: I don't understand.

Him: I look down at you from far away. You are remote and unreal. Your kind is ending. It is becoming too hard to reduce myself into this form. Your food value is no longer worth the energy of the hunt. It wasn't always this way, but now you have lost your vitality and look like gray mist to me. I have to contract and shrink so you can feel me. I dislike contracting. I refuse. So I refuse you and your kind. From that moment, you will cease to exist.

Me: So you're going to exterminate us?

Him: You are food. But your food value wanes. There was a time when you all tasted — rich — but no longer. Livestock ceases to exist when it no longer feeds. There are others, more nourishing.

Me: So in order to continue existing, we have to find a way to feed you better?

Him: It is too late.

Me: Then why try to reach others through me, as you said earlier.

Him: There are reasons. I have other needs.

Me: Do you have other prey in mind to replace us?

Him: It is already done.

Me: What about God? Won't we be rescued?

Him: It is already done.

Me: Why should I believe you?

Him: Believe or don't believe — no difference.

Me: By what authority do you say these things? Why should I believe you?

Him: I am the Light. I AM. Enough.

Me: I can't see you now, and your voice is weakening.

Him: That is your perception.

Me: Are you leaving?

Him: No you are.

Me: Then where am I going?

No answer.
Me: Then where am I going?
Silence.

THE POSSIBLE PREDATOR

Luciferism is a religion, and like all religions it promotes a certain vision of the possible human. If religions are systems of *social engineering*, encouraging and reinforcing certain human traits over others, then Luciferism is no exception.

Luciferism reinforces and encourages four basic energies — devouring, possession, violence and disguise — which in turn assist the Luciferan to transform consciousness, animate hidden potential, and ultimately obtain godhood.

CHAPTER THREE
DEVOURING

"Sensitive souls have reacted with shock to the elemental drama of life on this planet, and one of the reasons Darwin so shocked his time — and still bothers ours is that he showed this bone-crushing, blood-drinking drama in all its elementality and necessity: Life cannot go on without the mutual devouring of organisms... each organism raises its head over a field of corpses, smiles into the sun, and declares life good."

Ernest Becker, Escape From Evil

"I often write about the fact that everything here in the universe seems to eat and get eaten, and we need to pay attention to this. The idea of the Eucharist is that when divinity passes through this universe, it, too, gets eaten."

Matthew Fox (Psychology Today, Sept./Oct., 1993)

Luciferism can be understood in part as a philosophical and spiritual extension of eating and consuming. When compassion, empathy and conscience are killed, then devouring and consuming can swell proportionately. When the impediments to personal power acquisition are removed, then devouring the life energies of other beings becomes easy: I become stronger as you become weaker, I absorb strength as yours flows into me. I become capable of this because I do not experience your pain, I don't care about your loss, and I feel no remorse or regret about using, abusing, and devouring you.

On the contrary, I can come to love your suffering and pain, and use it to help me rise up the hierarchy of devouring. Your pain refreshes and empowers me: by devouring your energy and vitality, I can rise with joy, euphoria, and ecstasy to become pure *powaqqatsi*.

We all devour, Luciferans and non-Luciferans alike; like it or not, we are all part of a food chain. Luciferans simply accept this fact and enthusiastically expand their range of food possibilities, from plants and animals to humans and even to God.

THE HIERARCHY OF DEVOURING

All human beings are devourers. We eat other living things. Billions of domesticated animals come into existence apparently for the sole purpose of our devouring. Our meat sources often live in conditions of abject misery, and are then coldly and efficiently transformed into food. We shovel other beings, both plant and animal, into our mouths without much reflection on their suffering. We are devourers, and ours is a world dominated by a hierarchy of devouring.

The term "hierarchy of devouring" came to me from Charles Templeton. He is now a well known author, but used to be an aspiring preacher. Apparently he had been quite good at it, packing halls in Toronto and sharing billing with preachers like Billy Graham. Eventually he became an atheist, and publicly articulated why he no longer believed in God.

He said he could no longer believe in a God who would create a hierarchy of devouring. By this he meant the entire structure of life on this planet, which is apparently built on one command: eat or die. Big animals eat smaller ones, they in turn eat yet smaller animals and so on down to the simplest forms of life. At the top of the heap, at least for now, are human beings. We are at the top because we are excellent devourers.

The heart and pulse of life, said Templeton, is built around cruelty and power. Just watch a deer being eaten alive by wolves, its eyes screaming pain while its entrails pour out over the frozen grass. Templeton asked how any God could allow and even reward such cruelty: if God is father, then what kind of parent would submit his children to such barbarity? Templeton's insight into the dark side of Darwinian survival caused him to question and eventually lose his faith. What right does any one being have to devour another? How could a supposedly compassionate God sanction such a hierarchical system of devouring?

This system of devouring is not limited to the animal world. Large corporations devour and consume smaller ones; large nation states devour the resources of less powerful ones. On a personal level, human beings constantly consume the emotional and intellectual energies of others. The hierarchy of devouring rips into our personal and collective lives like a dripping claw.

The strong devour the weak; not only physically, but emotionally, financially, socially, psychologically, and even spiritually. Eat or be eaten, consume or be consumed, devour or be devoured, possess or be possessed: this is the way of the world. Darwin codified this obvious truth for biological science; Machiavelli did the same for political science. Economically we call it capitalism, a system designed to reward the winners and punish the losers struggling to survive and prosper on the socio-economic hierarchy. Of course we deny this reality. It is too painful. Imagine eating your fast food meal while envisioning how it actually came to be in your hand: from the slaughterhouse to the grill is a legacy of ugliness. We deny it biologically just as we deny it socially. We set up great civilized codes as a bulwark against the harsh truth of the devouring hierarchy.

Luciferans, however, not only acknowledge the devouring hierarchy but embrace it. Their myths celebrate the successful predator and devourer on all levels of the physical hierarchy, and on emotional, cognitive and spiritual hierarchies as well. Their symbols reflect fascination with the power of the predator. Luciferans want to develop the predatory skills, attitudes, and beliefs which can deliver an advantage on the real cutting edge of competition. Their heroes and mentors are all successful predators: industrial barons, great historical warriors, and successful leaders in the political realm.

To a Luciferan, life is as it is. Cruelty and devouring are the way of things, so why not adapt? Why not admit the obvious and become good at it? All else is simply illusion. There is only one reality, and that is acquiring the power to devour "up the hierarchy" biologically, personally, socially, and politically.

DEVOURING UP THE HIERARCHY

Rising up the devouring hierarchy is the Luciferan's goal, but to accomplish this rising, the Luciferan has to first accumulate sufficient power. Power comes in many forms, but has only one end: elevation to the apex of the devouring hierarchy. In order to obtain enough power, Luciferans must take power from other beings by absorbing their energy, vitality, and life-force.

Eating plant life or animal flesh is only one way to absorb energy: Luciferans must know how to draw energy from other sources as well. Luciferans need to expand their "diet" because the simple physical devouring of plants or animals cannot provide sufficient energy and power to scale the hierarchy. To devour their way to the top, Luciferans have to also learn how to ingest the emotional, cognitive, and spiritual energies of human prey.

Like any successful predator, Luciferans have to find a way to expand their food resources. Just as omnivorous predators are more successful than their strictly carnivorous competitors, so too Luciferans are likely to be more successful than their non-Luciferan human competitors because their food sources will include — in addition to plant and animal life — the full range of human energies offered up from the body to the soul.

Luciferans have learned how to devour and metabolize these human energies, to withdraw these vital forces from their human victims in order to enhance and vitalize their own lives. I do not completely understand how this *powaqqatsi* process works. I do know that the process exists, and that Luciferans depend upon it to fully actualize and empower their own drive for godhood at the apex of the hierarchy.

PHYSICAL DEVOURING: RITUAL SACRIFICE

When elevated to formal religious status, devouring becomes sacrifice — the ritual eating of the victim's physical body. The logic of sacrifice is grounded in devouring: since devouring unites all forms of sentient life, logically it should form the basis of many religious rituals.

For example, Christ is devoured in the Mass; communion is the act of devouring the blood and body of Jesus Christ. Christ was sacrificed, and apparently welcomed the opportunity to be devoured rather than to devour.

For the practicing Luciferan, however, sacrifice involves the ritual devouring of other life forms. The ritual killing and eating of an animal, an enemy, or an innocent victim is a ceremonial way of celebrating power acquisition through devouring. More than just ceremonial celebration is accomplished, Luciferans believe that the act of devouring a human being's body parts bestows special energy and power, which the Luciferan needs in order to ascend the hierarchy.

Luciferans are not alone in this belief. A cult group in Matamoros, Mexico, for example, recently killed several human victims and devoured their body parts. They were practicing an ancient and venerated method of power acquisition, albeit in a crude and ineffective manner. It may seem disgusting and bizarre to outsiders, but makes perfect sense as ritual.

In ritual sacrifice, several goals are achieved simultaneously. First, the practicing cult member is inducted into the group. A kind of initiation occurs, the new recruit is bonded, and the entire organization is strengthened. The ritual sanctifies, celebrates, unifies, and elevates the group. Second, the new member learns how to kill without conscience and compassion for the victim. As the altar-kill begs for life, as it screams its pain, rage, and fear, the cult member has to harden and then destroy her own compassion and empathy before killing. Thus the new recruit has only other group members to turn to: all outsiders are simply sacrificial offerings, nothing more than meat. Some group members, thirdly, may believe they actually absorb the power and energy of their ritual victim. Victims thus become food. Their physical, emotional, social and spiritual power is absorbed and utilized to empower the group.

Finally, the group makes an offering to its God in exchange for some kind of perceived spiritual power gain. The cult member wants to devour before being devoured. Ritual cannibalism and sacrifice are the logical extension of this desire for power. The group hopes that its God will accept the offering and grant favors.

The Matamoros cult is not consciously Luciferan. They are included here only as a contemporary example of the compelling and apparently enduring power of human sacrifice. Human sacrifice may seem primitive, brutal and bizarre to the civilized mind, but it has a long and historically powerful history in our culture and others. This history suggests that human sacrifice will once again return. In the words of Patrick Tierney, author of *The Highest Altar: The Story of Human Sacrifice*, "Not wanting to know about human sacrifice is one of the dominant motifs of religious history — almost as dominant as its repeated performance... Blood sacrifice is the oldest and most universal act of piety... sacrifice was the essence of ancient man's sacred life ...From Israel to Greece, from the Old World to the New, sacrifice was the religious experience." Tierney describes some of the reasons for human sacrifice. The sacrificed becomes a spiritual slave. The victim saves others as a surrogate or scapegoat to placate a God angry about sin. The victim is granted immortality to become God-like. The act itself creates wealth, power, and good luck (especially if the victim is buried in, say, a building's foundations). Natural events come under control or through the dynamic vows can be made and fulfilled.

However confusing or inconsistent — or perhaps compelling — this logic might be, Tierney stresses that human sacrifice "can only be comprehended by a direct experience beyond rational thought." True for sacrifice, and true for Luciferism.

As Rene Girard has pointed out in *Violence and the Sacred*, the logic of sacrifice is complex: all four of the above reasons apply, and probably more as well. He adds, "religion shelters us from violence just as violence seeks shelter in religion." He was not thinking of Luciferism here, but his words perfectly define Luciferan sacrifice.

In contrast to the kind of primitive and unsophisticated ceremonial sacrifice of the Matamoros cult, Luciferans despise such clumsy brutality. Luciferans are not group-animals. They reject all organizational bonding unless it directly serves their personal needs: other Luciferans are only competitors to be overcome. For Luciferans, devouring human flesh is an act barely removed from devouring animals or plants. They seldom use it because it yields little real energy or power. An individual Luciferan might occasionally use ritual sacrifice to solidify his control over a group of submissive followers, but the act seldom yields benefits sufficient to compensate for the risks of discovery.

Ritually killing and devouring humans refreshes and reminds Luciferans of their commitment to devour their way up the hierarchy in pursuit of absolute power. As a symbolic act it has some validity; as a practical method of power acquisition, it is risky and seldom worth the effort. Emotional, cognitive and spiritual devouring are far more nutritious.

DEVOURING EMOTIONAL ENERGY

Luciferans eat the emotional energy of victims. They parasitically drain those around them, leaving their victims desiccated, exhausted, confused, despairing and depressed. Victims can seldom articulate the source of their depression; they just feel drained, lifeless, and empty.

All strong emotions are good food. Fear, hate, love, jealousy, anger, joy — Luciferans learn to absorb them all. Luciferans are especially attracted to individuals who have a healthy emotional life, who feel the depth of human emotion, and who can therefore be drained of this vital energy. Luciferans never truly return or reciprocate attention, love, or affection, but absorb it, use it, and hoard it. They consciously set out to destroy healthy emotion by devouring it.

Devouring does two things. First, it drains the victim. Second, it strengthens the devourer. By "taking in" and absorbing this emotional energy, the Luciferan transforms it into useful predatory power. At the same time, a despised victim from a lower order of human life is destroyed.

Devouring or "eating" emotion is not difficult. If emotion is energy, and the energy radiates outward from the victim, then devouring means making sure all of the victim's energy is directed to only one source — the devouring Luciferan herself. In order to direct, contain, and control this energy, the Luciferan has to ensure that the victim is totally infatuated and enthralled with no one and nothing else. Luciferans thrive on the admiration and devotion given to them by victims because they have learned how to absorb it as food.

In order to ensure a steady flow of such admiration, the Luciferan must use all of his charisma and influence to ensure that the victim cuts ties with family, friends, and other close contacts. These other individuals are potential threats, because the victim's emotional energy might "leak" in their direction.

The victim must also be disconnected from activities, hobbies, habits and interests that provide happiness, stability and refreshment, because these outside activities might provide him with enough strength and energy to challenge or even break free of the predator. The victim must be isolated and cut off from all other potential sources to which emotions might be connected. This ensures that all energy will be directed to the Luciferan, and also that the victim will eventually collapse.

Collapse is desirable. Luciferans seldom drain just one victim endlessly, allowing her to recover just enough to continue a cycle of devouring. They do not allow the victim time to recover for two reasons.

First, the victim might gain enough strength to pull away, and this would mean defeat. Defeat is not just loss of 'food', but an actual drainage of Luciferan vitality: energy is depleted through the loss. I am not clear about the actual details of this process, but it partly rests upon the notion that the Luciferan connects so closely with his prey that if his victim were to rip away prematurely, then part of the Luciferan would go at the same time. In addition, the Luciferan would experience an immediate loss of pride and self-esteem. Pride, power, and success are everything to the Luciferan, so losing a victim means experiencing the unbearable emotions of shame, powerlessness, and failure.

Second, there is a kind of *rush* when the victim finally collapses and breaks. This rush provides a fresh impulse of energy: if emotional devouring can be compared to making love, then the victim's final collapse is the orgasm following foreplay. Luciferans believe that, upon reaching the victim's final emotional breaking point, something essential and deeply satisfying passes from victim to predator.

Having thus drained and used the victim, the Luciferan moves on to other victims. Restored and refreshed by victory because power has shifted from the victim to the victimizer. The Luciferan never feels remorse or guilt for her actions. In her mind, she has the right to take from those too weak or inferior to take from her. She feels stronger, more vital, and more alive. No amount of counseling, explaining, or threatening will change this basic Luciferan belief: by devouring and using the emotional energy of her victims, the Luciferan feels intensely alive, purposeful and energized. Like any other predator, she feels deep waves of organic pleasure in the act of stalking and eating.

The actual mechanisms of energy transfer are not clear to me. Part of the process involves simple inspiration: the Luciferan draws energy and joy from this drainage, much as we might find delight in a sunset or a beautiful work of art. But part also involves an actual energy drain, much as a battery is drained of electricity. Luciferans have learned to draw energy from emotions just as our digestive system has evolved to take energy from food.

The type of emotion collected and devoured is irrelevant. Fear, anger, jealousy and hate can be just as useful as love, affection, and trust, although much more difficult to manage. Luciferans love the adulation offered by victims, but can also thrive equally on hate, rage, and hostility. We have all met someone who seems to thrive on hostility; the angrier we get, the more satisfied the person becomes. Luciferans can also experience such deep satisfaction from their victims' anger and hatred. As long as the victim focuses completely on the predator and slowly but surely leaks her vitality, energy and strength into the predator, the end result is the same. Not all emotional devourers are consciously Luciferan: the process also occurs as a kind of emotional cannibalism in every day life.

For example, women who work in shelters instinctively understand how this kind of emotional cannibalism works, because they see its effects daily in the deadened eyes of women seeking shelter from abusive men. Unfortunately, women can be emotional cannibals too, and are just as likely to be attracted to Luciferism as men. Luciferism is not sexist. Power is power, and Luciferans know that it can gather around a woman as easily as a man.

Educators and therapists working with children can also instinctively recognize the signs of emotional cannibalism. Some children seem emotionally dead at an early age, unable to relate to peers effectively, unable to share, to take criticism, to play fairly. They begin to mimic the Luciferan style in their relationships with others because, just as the abused frequently become abusers, so too the survivors of emotional cannibalism can become devourers as well. Such children show cruelty toward animals and other children, show little remorse or guilt, lie frequently, and generally seek to elevate themselves by lowering others. They are often intensely competitive, where winning is everything and losing disastrous. This may be a survival tactic for these children, because if they do not practice to become better predators than their abusers, then they will remain exposed and weak prey to be devoured by their own abusers.

As these children grow older, they often come to know that if they cause victims to trust, love, open and give themselves, then when the devouring inevitably occurs, the victim's shock becomes good energy, good food. And so the cycle perpetuates itself. Emotional cannibalism and the vampire myth seem related: something is taken from the victim (emotional energy or blood) who then has to vampirize others to replace the loss. Emotional *vampires* instinctively seek out others whose emotional life is vibrantly alive because they see a source of food. For Luciferans, emotional devouring is part of a wider strategy of conscious power acquisition, which also includes devouring cognitive and spiritual energies.

DEVOURING COGNITIVE ENERGY

To understand how cognitive energy can be devoured, we have to look at core identity, which refers to the victim's "cognitive center" — the location of core beliefs about self, world and reality.

Core identity can be understood as a complex union of a number of forces: genetics, gender, environmental influences, and so on. As identity develops within the individual, a web or network of related beliefs about self, reality, and other people is created. This belief system is the foundation upon which the individual maintains safety, security, and sanity. It seems to be the source from which decisions are made to meet basic needs such as nourishment, love, and self-actualization. By core identity I mean the beliefs, values, schemas and self-assessments by which each of us identify ourselves *as* ourselves.

To better understand this, it might be useful to think of beliefs as layered from surface to depth, from less crucial to more central. Milton Rokeach, an influential psychologist of beliefs and belief systems and author of the classic books, *The Open and Closed Mind* and *Beliefs, Attitudes, and Values* describes how shifts in peripheral versus core beliefs can impact an individual.

Peripheral beliefs, those on the surface and therefore less essential, are more easily altered, and when changed have little impact on the person's entire identity-belief system. I can shift my belief that one laundry soap is better than another without experiencing a dramatic ripping apart of my whole belief system.

A shift in beliefs about the most effective laundry soap might only alter my purchasing behavior, but a shift in something deeper might alter behavior in more profound ways. This is the territory of what Rokeach calls "core beliefs." If I have been raised to believe in God in such a way that this belief nurtures my entire reality orientation, therefore providing order and security to my world, then loss of this core belief deeply shakes my entire being.

Using a systems theory approach, Rokeach defines the central core region as holding the most basic or "primitive" beliefs about self, reality, and other people; the intermediate region contains beliefs about authority, about individuals and sources which can be trusted; and the peripheral region holds "derived beliefs" which accumulate and change over time. Change is easiest from the *outside-in*, from less meaningful to more important, from less essential to the absolutely crucial. Beliefs are thus layered like an onion: I can switch my choice of soft drinks without shaking the foundations of my core identity, but I would have more difficulty letting go of my memory of my personal past or my beliefs about my own identity. It is in this sense that I would like to use the term "core identity" here.

BREAKING INTO THE CORE & CREATING AN OBJECT-OF-FOCUS

Luciferans believe that core identity can be devoured only when it is broken, like an egg or a nutshell. Once broken, the victim's core identity yields powerful energies. To break the victim's core identity, the Luciferan first needs to gain access to it. To gain access, the Luciferan needs a powerful key, for even the weakest human will not easily open up such intimate territory. Access can be gained by fashioning an object-of-focus.

To initially gain access to the victim's cognitive core, the Luciferan has to fashion a *lure*, a device which will invite the victim to open his core identity. An "object-of-focus" is such a lure or key.

An object-of-focus can be a belief system, an icon (such as a specific object or even the Luciferan's personality), a sacred place, an intense experience (euphoria, ecstasy), or any other thing that the Luciferan has created and therefore controls.

To construct an effective object-of-focus, the Luciferan must have the skill to find just what each victim is looking for, and then appear to offer it. This is not as difficult as it sounds, because most potential victims are seeking something: more knowledge, more meaning, more power, more money, better relationships, better sex. Most victims will happily provide key information about themselves to anyone who appears able to help them get what they want.

The Luciferan thus has to appear interested in the victim. Beyond this, the Luciferan has to appear to have some special secret, some vast reservoir of wisdom and power with which to answer the victim's yearning, whatever it might be. The Luciferan has to rely on accumulated personal power, charisma, and innovation to seem attractive, appealing, and wise to the victim: in other words, to earn the victim's complete trust.

With this trust, the Luciferan can then discover the victim's deepest questions about self, world, and reality, the kind of questions that inhabit the victim's deepest areas of core identity. With this information, the Luciferan can then fashion an object-of-focus.

The object-of-focus must appeal to the victim's mind, to his cognitions about self, world, and reality. It must resonate with the deepest yearnings of his core self. It must be specifically tailored to invite the victim's curiosity, then his fascination, and then his commitment. It must become the victim's central focus and preoccupation. It must inspire the victim's deepest loyalty and trust.

The object-of-focus must therefore be so compelling that the victim invites it into the territory of his core primitive beliefs. This invitation effectively opens up the victim's core territory. The object-of-focus is thus both the lure designed to attract the victim and the key to open up his core identity. Once attracted, enthralled, riveted, and entranced, the victim then opens herself; once open, she becomes available for cognitive devouring — that is, the Luciferan can feed from her "core" and obtain powerful energy as a result.

Controlling the victim's core cognitive focus is like a type of hypnotism: the victim's full trust and attention empties into a symbolic object-of-focus controlled by the Luciferan. No matter what form the object-of-focus takes, at its center it must celebrate the Luciferan's personality: all facets of the object must point toward the Luciferan as the victim's ultimate destination. That is, the object-of-focus must deify the Luciferan. The victim must never know this or suspect any predatory motives, however, especially at first. Later on it will not matter.

As with emotional energy, once the victim's cognitive focus is under control, then all else follows. This is true because the victim's core sense of identity, the full attention of her deep self, is offered to the predator like a throat pulsing with sweet blood: the Luciferan actually eats his way into the victim's core identity like a wolf into a deer's brain.

ASSAULTING THE CORE

Once the victim has opened his core identity, then the Luciferan can tear it apart in preparation for devouring by using a process known as brainwashing, thought reform, or "coercive persuasion," a process that will be called *psychological assault* here. Psychological assault can be understood by asking a simple question: is assault possible without physical contact?

This question may seem rhetorical. The obvious answer is "no": a person cannot be assaulted unless struck or harmed by fists or weapons wielded by an attacker. But consider another type of assault. Is it possible to mount a psychological assault, to beat another person's core identity into submission using psychological techniques? The answer here may be a little harder to understand, a little less forthcoming. Yet we already know more than we might think.

For example, we all know someone who carries on through life as if beaten, head hanging down, eyes locked to the floor. Submissive and afraid, this person lacks self-confidence, has a destructive self-image, and views life as a series of impending crises about to occur. It is as if something within him has been violated and twisted, as if his core identity has been literally beaten to a pulp. Physically healthy but psychologically beaten: how many people suffering like this have we met? I would suggest that some of these people are not in this condition because of personality flaws, but because they have been psychologically assaulted.

A little closer to home, we all remember personal encounters with someone who seemed to abuse *us* psychologically. Perhaps it was a person at work with authority over us, or maybe our parents, spouse, or lover — whoever it was, somehow he or she managed to violate something deep inside us. Without being touched physically, somehow we walked away feeling soiled and abused, our self-worth and self-confidence shattered. It is as if this person somehow reached inside to attack and then drain us.

I would like to suggest a way to describe this kind of invasion by defining it as *psychological assault*.

We all have fairly solid ideas about the nature of physical or sexual assault. But what exactly *is* psychological assault? How can a person be abused psychologically? To answer this I would like to offer a definition, and then explain each of its components.

Psychological assault is the process by which an individual or group utilizes known techniques to systematically assault, break down, and replace a targeted individual's core identity for purposes of dominance and control.

Psychological assault has been reported and investigated under a variety of names: "thought reform", "coercive persuasion", "coordinated programs of coercive influence and behavior control", and so on. (See Cialdini, 1984; Conway and Siegelman, 1978; Frank 1961; Lifton, 1961, 1987; Sargant, 1957, 1974; Schein, 1961; Singer 1972, 1986, 1990.) My definition has been drawn from this tradition, especially from the work of Margaret Singer.

As with any new and emerging discipline, definitions abound. I have coined a new term not out of disrespect for past work but because there are subtle but important differences of focus and usage. As this field matures, hopefully a consistent nomenclature will evolve.

Some key points emerge. Psychological assault is a process. It happens over time. It is ongoing. This implies some kind of relationship between the abuser and the abused. Thus we find that psychological assault occurs between parents and children, in marriages, between employer and employee, and so on.

The abuser may be an individual or a group. More than one person can work in concert with others in a group to commit psychological assault. These groups may range from loosely knit gangs to sophisticated organizations. Within advanced organizations psychological assault can be so endemic that the organization itself (as opposed to individuals within it) can be described as abusive.

A known set of techniques can be used to commit psychological assault. These techniques have evolved in the last twenty years and can now be described as a sophisticated technology. (These techniques will not be discussed here: please refer to Singer, Schein, Lifton, and others for details). To be effective, the technology must be systematic: it must be used over time and in a specific sequence.

The technology has only one purpose: *to assault and break down a targeted individual's core identity.* When healthy, one's core identity is open, positive, vibrant, and vital. When unhealthy, core identity renders the person unworthy, hopeless, isolated, and drained. Psychological assault technology attempts to create a negative or even self-destructive core identity in its target.

So why would anyone want to deliberately and systematically destroy a person's core identity? After all, what use is a person bent on self-destruction? The reason is simple: *dominance and control.* If I wish to control you, I may have some trouble if your core identity is strong. But if I could break down your core identity and then *replace* or rebuild your identity in a way beneficial to me, then my power over you would be strong indeed. Thus I would cause you to believe at a core level that you are hopeless without me, that disobeying me would be tragic, that I am your superior in all ways. My control over your identity is then inside you, woven deeply into the fabric of your being. When achieved, such control is a power which renders all others impotent: you will do as I say without requiring rewards or coercion, money or force. For the Luciferan, dominance and control is a kind of food, an energy that can be metabolized to stimulate and support personal growth.

Luciferans utilize the technology of psychological assault to break their target's core identity, and then feed on the energy released by this breakdown.

But the destruction of a target's core identity is only a phase in psychological assault. Once identity is undermined, it can then be changed to allow the abuser to take control. If the Luciferan succeeds in breaking a target's identity, a further and final step can therefore take place: he can change the victim's core identity in certain specific directions. For example, a Luciferan charismatic preacher will rant for hours about the evil ugliness of the flock, about the absolute hopelessness of sin leading to eternal hell, about the near presence of Satan. His followers may then undergo a process of identity-death, a sense of deep revulsion about themselves and about human nature generally. But the preacher's intention is to take his flock beyond self-loathing. He uses this state to create an opening into which his own belief system can enter: "Just follow me," he says, "and you will be saved. Just change your ways, and you will be transformed. You will go beyond identity-death to rebirth." He might just as well add "I will then be your parent. And you will obey me."

In other words, psychological assault can be used to undermine identity so it can be replaced. Political demagogues, religious cultists, and leaders of mass movements are familiar with this process. The process could be compared to biological imprinting: just as a little duckling will accept the first moving object it sees as *mother*, so too a victim of psychological assault will *imprint* a new identity implanted by the abuser. If I believe Jim Jones is God's only agent on earth, that I therefore owe him unquestioning loyalty and trust, then when he asks me to drink deadly poison I will do it willingly. If I believe he is a lunatic, then I will escape from him or disobey his request if I can. This argument holds for all other core beliefs about religious, political, economic and other important motivating forces organizing our lives.

The precise nature of the implanted identity system, or object-of-focus, varies from abuser to abuser. Some implant their own pathological problems: hence the abused child later on in life becomes an abuser, just like the abusive parent. Some abusers implant religious notions of identity: the abused person is defined by his or her adherence to an ideologically correct set of attributes. Other abusers implant therapeutic notions of correct identity: therapy itself can become a process of psychological assault in which the therapist implants a favored identity system into the client/victim. (Recent books such as *Making Monsters* by Ofshe and *The Myth of Repressed Memory* by Loftus explore the manipulation used by therapists). The same can be said for political and educational movements that care less for their followers' or pupils' development than for their own ideological definitions of reality.

The foundation of psychological assault rests on the nature of power and control, dominance and submission. The idea is simple: to control a man, control what he believes to be true; to control what he believes to be true, control his core identity. This form of control is deeper and more effective than violence, rewards, punishments and other forms of power and control. Luciferans know this fact intimately, and use it constantly. Psychological assault seems endemic in our society. In its less sophisticated forms it holds together many destructive relationships, and is the foundation upon which spousal assault and child abuse are built. In a more sophisticated form, it is used extensively to deepen the survival power of some religious, corporate, political and educational organizations. In its most evolved form, it is the secret by which certain cultic organizations obtain such rapid and sometimes complete control over followers.

When the process of psychological assault is successful, the targeted individual can be described as being under mind control. In my experience, mind control is real, and can itself be considered a form of possession.

DEVOURING THE ENERGIES RELEASED AT BREAKDOWN

Luciferans believe that excessive energies are released at the moment when the victim's identity succumbs to psychological assault. These energies can be considered the psychological equivalent of the release of atomic energy when the atom is smashed.

Such energies are magnificent, and well worth the time and effort of the assault process. The Luciferan wants to be present at the moment of collapse to devour the sweetly vitalizing energies that become available. This moment is profoundly beautiful, energizing, and liberating for the Luciferan. Few devouring experiences can compare.

Once psychological assault and the initial devouring of released energies are complete, the Luciferan can then proceed to gradually drain the victim's remaining energy at will. This is because the victim's core identity can now be replaced by the Luciferan's object-of-focus, which lends awesome power to the Luciferan, the kind of power known to absolutist political and religious leaders throughout time. The Luciferan can feed from the victim any time. The victim can only endure this drainage and offer all her energy, life, and devotion to her devourer.

This occurs because the devourer has obtained mind control; that is, he has broken down the victim's core cognitive beliefs, and inserted his own cognitive object-of-focus in place of those beliefs. At a fundamental level, the victim has *become* the object-of-focus. Her own identity has been shattered and replaced. She thinks she is serving something beautiful, wondrous, and transcendent, and is willing to happily endure drainage and deprivation. The Luciferan's implanted object-of-focus diverts all questions and doubts: when he hits her, she knows she needed it for personal correction and spiritual growth. When he sexually assaults her, he is only sharing his deep love for her, a privilege granted to only a select few. He can do anything he wants, because she interprets everything in light of his object-of-focus, which he controls.

As her dependence deepens, he can use her any way he wants: he can, through cognitive control, devour not only her cognitive energy — her devotion, her thoughts, her self-image — but anything else as well. All her thoughts are directed to him; her core identity is now his; she believes she is nothing without him. This is real power, and it enables the abuser to systematically deplete the victim's energy at will.

Luciferans believe that one final source of energy remains available for devouring, a source that yields even more power and nutrition than physical, emotional or cognitive devouring — spiritual or the energy of the *soul*.

DEVOURING & DIVERTING SOUL ENERGY

Luciferans avidly devour the energy released by spiritual aspirations, motivations and desires of victims. Spiritual energy can be defined as the force animating our search for ultimate value, truth, meaning and purpose, and can be associated with the deepest yearnings of soul, (if soul is that-which-is our deepest self, deeper even than Rokeach's core identity beliefs). I am referring to the "I" that experiences such core beliefs, the sense of self behind even the deepest of core identity beliefs, something that can be understood as the driving force behind our relentless search for religion and spirituality.

Abraham Maslow, the famous motivational psychologist, defined this force in his needs-hierarchy as the need for self-actualization. An entire psychological tradition, transpersonal psychology, has been established to explore the profound experiences reported by searchers exploring the further reaches of human experience discovered during their spiritual search.

Reductionists, materialists, and mechanists insist that soul does not exist, that "spirit", "soul" and similar terms are meaningless. Luciferans, however, know that soul exists, not only because they seek to expand their own soul, or Self, but because they devour soul energy whenever they can. Luciferans regard reductionists, materialists, and mechanists with contempt, because their disbelief in soul means they have forgotten how to guard this most precious aspect of their existence. Their disbelief does not make them the wise, hard-nosed realists they feel themselves to be — it just makes them easy prey, pathetically vulnerable targets unable to defend themselves. Soul is force; soul is power; soul impacts on matter just as powerfully as the physical, emotional and cognitive forces under human control.

Luciferans believe that soul engages the spiritual, just as mind engages the cognitive, and that the energies of both soul and mind provide powerful food. Spiritual and cognitive devouring are obviously linked, but cognitive devouring attacks the victim's core belief systems, while spiritual devouring goes even deeper, into the soul itself. Cognitive devouring occurs primarily in the realm of the psychological, while spiritual devouring occupies transcendent territory, the place pointed out by Maslow, transpersonal psychologists, and spiritual traditions generally.

Hundreds of powerful belief systems have sought to capture and use this basic human urge for soul transcendence. The spiritual search seems to be as basic a human drive as food, safety, security and love. Like any other human drive or need, however, it can become food for Luciferan devourers.

Soul energy is most easily devoured by diversion. That is, the Luciferan finds the victim's spiritual blood-pulse, and then diverts it, just as emotional and cognitive energy are diverted from the victim to the Luciferan predator. In the process, the Luciferan swells as the victim is drained.

This devouring is possible because the victim's search for spirituality provides an opening for the Luciferan; the search *itself* means the victim is open, looking, receptive, or even desperate. This desperation comes from the unfulfilled yet driving need for spiritual transcendence, a drive that seems even more powerful than the struggle to find personal identity. As with all predation, the victim's desperate need always works in the predator's favor.

The Luciferan simply has to find effective spiritual camouflage to lure the victim, and therefore manufactures and sells her own unique spiritual truth, a kind of narcotic to ease the victim's pain. Once convinced that spiritual wisdom has been found, the seeker/victim then opens his soul to the Luciferan, offering up his immense need and energy, surrendering himself to the Luciferan's predation. This feeding swells the Luciferan with pride, attention, and power: she literally grows stronger on the vital spiritual energy drained from her victim and spilled into her.

SPIRITUAL TRADITIONS ATTRACTING LUCIFERAN DEVOURERS

Luciferans know that certain spiritual traditions attract seekers who are willing to open their deepest soul-essence. These seekers are easy prey, because their desperation for spiritual wisdom renders them careless. If the Luciferan can successfully disguise herself as a spiritual "master" to whom the seeker must open and submit, then the seeker becomes available for devouring.

Luciferans therefore hunt for various spiritual traditions that demand profound self-surrender. These traditions all associate virtue and goodness with opening and surrendering self to either an outside power, such as a god, or an internal source, such as higher self. The seeker obviously wishes to surrender to something wonderful, loving, and compassionate; Luciferans can easily insert themselves into the process by pretending to be this outside power or internal source. Thus, the seeker surrenders soul to the Luciferan, not to the spiritual tradition; devouring then follows.

These spiritual traditions are varied, but can be organized in the following categories.

SELF-ANNIHILATING TRADITIONS

Luciferan predators are attracted to spiritual traditions emphasizing complete surrender of personality, past, identity, and carnality while promising initiation through transformation and rebirth. In such traditions the victim is eager and willing to lower all defenses and hand over self-control. The goal is self-annihilation, meaning the destruction of the ego and other "lower order" aspects of self, as emphasized in various New Age, Eastern, and charismatic Christian traditions. In the hands of a loving and compassionate spiritual guide, such trust can be beautiful. But in the hands of a Luciferan, it is deadly. Once broken down and converted, the victim can then be used. Unaware of the deception, the victim truly believes that his new spiritual leader is the source and center of all truth and beauty, and becomes willing do anything to promote and proselytize the "Cause." The Luciferan encourages this devotion to the point that it becomes the close-minded fanaticism described by Eric Hoffer in his book *The True Believer*. Caught in this way, the victim will expend tremendous energy for the Luciferan, who then becomes enriched materially, emotionally, cognitively and spiritually in the process. Luciferans thrive on unquestioning obedience and adoration, and feel great pleasure in their ability to command strict unquestioning obedience from their followers. They devour the adoration released by their followers' spiritual search, and will do anything to keep it, including intimidation, murder, or even mass suicide.

ECSTATIC TRADITIONS

Spiritual traditions emphasizing trance, ecstasy, euphoria, and rapture as a way-of-knowing also attract Luciferans. To enter these states, the searcher has to release her conscious rational mind, let go of defenses, and fall into the sheer power of the experience. These states have been the fountain of profound wisdom for art, literature, and religion, and are sought in virtually all mystical, religious traditions. Luciferans value them, however, because they can be manipulated and used to create addiction.

The experience of rapture itself is so inexplicably overwhelming that many seekers come to desire it for its own sake. Luciferans who know how to induce these states can become 'spiritual drug dealers', creating deep dependence in their followers. Techniques for inducing such experiences are well known and documented, and usually include sleep or food deprivation, repetitive chanting, excessive time spent in meditative states, trance induction through hypnosis, rhythmic dancing or drumming, and so on.

Seeker/victims who first experience these wonderful states tend to imprint on the person or group providing them. As with cognitive devouring, this seems to work much like the young duckling which, when first hatched, will bond or imprint on its mother: experiments have shown that this imprinting can be transferred to other items (i.e. a stuffed 'mother') or even other species, including humans. In the same way, when we first experience transcendent rapture, the experience is so moving that it can feel like an actual rebirth of new life. Gratitude swells toward the 'spiritual parent' who provided this gift. If this parent is a Luciferan, then the victim will imprint and bond with him. The victim will then be controlled, and her energies used and devoured. Cult leaders know exactly how to induce this state, and exactly what to do with it once achieved. In my experience, cultic "weekend transformational seminars", for example, specialize in producing and then manipulating transcendent and euphoric states of consciousness (See Margaret Singer's work for more information about weekend transformational seminars).

TRADITIONS OF TRANCE CHANNELING AND SPIRIT POSSESSION

Spiritual traditions steeped in one form of spirit invocation or another — where the acolyte consciously seeks to put aside her own personality to let a discarnate entity speak through her — attract powerful interest from Luciferans as well. The seeker/victim willingly opens herself to be temporarily possessed, to become a channel for some other force. This opening attracts the Luciferan's lust for possession. Luciferans are drawn to such invitations because the victim willingly opens and offers herself for devouring and ownership. As with self-annihilating and ecstatic spirituality, the Luciferan can take and use the honest intentions of the seeker and bend them to his will and needs. These needs can range from enhanced material wealth to the sheer delight of *powaqqatsi*.

Cult leaders understand spiritual devouring, as do Luciferan leaders of mainline religions. Luring, capturing and devouring the spiritual hopes and dreams of millions is good food, great money, wonderful power. Political demagogues of all stripes try to feed on this spiritual flesh as well.

The energy expended and exerted by seeker/victims is more dynamic for Luciferans than that radiated by the search for emotional fulfillment or cognitive meaning. It is a force that has animated and driven human history in all cultures: just think of the influence of Christian energy or Muslim power. As a force, an energy, it is a powerful vein, rich in nutrients and sustenance for the Luciferan. This is why Luciferans are always attracted to powerful religious movements, especially those that emphasize self-annihilation, ecstasy, or trance channeling. They want to eat rich food, and soul energy is about as rich as it gets.

For Luciferans, devouring supplies power sources deep within the devourer, thus empowering ecstatic movement up the Luciferan hierarchy. For non-Luciferans, however, devouring tends to be repressed or even deeply feared. As with most feared and repressed realities, it has fled to the frightening realm of myth. Most mythological creatures and monsters are feared primarily because of their power to devour us. Vampires drain our blood and therefore our vital energy: once the vampire tastes our blood, we become one with him, a slave and follower.

We are deeply and primally terrified of being eaten. Hansel and Gretel are captured and prepared as food for the witch; the Giant in Jack and the Beanstalk "smells the blood" of his potential victims.

References to this primal fear of being devoured are everywhere in myth and horror stories. This may reflect the collective memory of our primitive past, where we were hunted and killed by frightening animals. Or it may reflect a kind of evolutionary prescience: if Darwinian laws hold true, some form of predator should eventually evolve to devour humans and control human populations. This predator would be the next logical leap in evolution, as far beyond us as we are beyond cattle. Luciferans claim to be this next leap.

Recent fascination with the vampire (Anne Rice's work for example) is probably built on this notion: vampires are physically faster and stronger, possessing senses far beyond their human prey. Once human, now evolved beyond humanity, the vampire thrives on the living blood of victims, devouring them in the process. So does the werewolf: once human, he becomes a predator, eating humans. Even the zombies in the *Dawn of the Dead* movies eat humans for food, (particularly brains, for which these lurching creatures have a particular fondness). Other fictional or mythological creations articulate this same theme: the beast is let loose within the human, and the human is transformed to devour other humans.

Luciferism, however, does not want to just release the irrational raging beast - it wishes to give the beast the power of rational thought without the impediments of compassion or conscience. Luciferism seeks to go beyond simple myth to genetically recreate and evolve the human mind, to bypass connections between the brain's cortex and the so-called 'mammalian' part of the brain, to unite it to its earlier 'reptilian' core, and to connect both of these to the 'higher spiritual self'. The result might be called a rational reptile, a thinking serpent, a spiritually evolved snake.

Vampires and werewolves are myth, but Luciferans seek to actively invoke and consciously create a new human predator similar to the vampire. In the process, they also seek to create a new human order.

This partly explains our prescient fear and revulsion of Nazism: Hitler intended to create a race of supermen highly evolved beyond lower human life forms, and prepared to annihilate all lesser beings without guilt or remorse. Several well-known works such as Goodrick-Clarke's *The Occult Roots of Nazism* or Sklar's *The Nazis and the Occult* explore the psycho-spiritual foundations of Nazi thought, which sought the creation of a superman elite, the extermination of lesser beings, and the establishment of a new world order. In a similar way, Anton Lavey, the self-confessed Satanist, wrote in his book *The Satanic Witch* about his notions of racial purity and cleansing, and about the evolutionary superiority of his own brand of new human.

Our collective fear of being devoured may reflect our ancient past or our fears of a newly evolving human predator. No matter, the point here is clear: devouring horrifies us, and so will continue to animate our appetite for both ancient and newly created devouring myths.

FROM MYTH TO REALITY: RELEASING THE PREDATOR WITHIN

According to Luciferan thought, to become Luciferan we have to evolve into superior devourers. We have to become faster, smarter, and more ruthless. We have to invite and embrace predatory impulses. We have to release the 'spiritual reptile' within. We must do so without regret, doubt, conscience, or compassion. Once released, these impulses lead us to see other humans as prey. Luciferans know that weak humans can be mined for various energies ranging from the physical to the spiritual. Humans can be used, drained, and discarded.

As the Luciferan gains power and energy through devouring, he is gradually changed. He becomes desensitized to his victim's pain, and easily dismisses and rationalizes it. He compartmentalizes himself. And then he annihilates the compartment. The psychiatrist and researcher Robert Jay Lifton describes the first part of this process as *psychic numbing* and *doubling*: by suppressing or numbing himself, the individual manages to live up to external appearances of normality while actually giving birth to a whole new personality complete with a supportive belief system. In the same way, the Luciferan gradually destroys his own capacities for compassion toward his victims and becomes, by degrees, remorseless. He invents a coldly devouring *double*. He then *becomes* the double, shedding his humanness like dead skin.

For Luciferans, this process of change is deliberate and conscious, utterly different from the kind of criminality associated with the psychopath. The Luciferan's transformation is rationally engineered as part of his commitment to a belief system, while the criminal psychopath is often reacting to environmental conditioning such as early childhood abuse.

The Luciferan wishes to release the predator within, and despises the thick sweet coating of civilization which suffocates this primal force. He wishes to evolve and transform beyond conscience and compassion. I am not certain how Luciferans see this transformation unfolding. It is possibly meant to occur over generations, through conscious selective breeding by a Luciferan elite, and resulting gradually from the conscious intent of contemporary Luciferans. Or it may be a product of natural evolution and Darwinian selection, creating species as far beyond us as we are from apes, its ultimate destination hidden and locked in the depth of genetic necessity and designed to serve the needs of 'selfish genes'.

The transformation might result in physical changes — that is, the evolution of a physically superior predator possessing advanced powers of body and mind — which may gradually result from a cumulative series of smaller changes beginning with the decision to kill conscience and compassion. These gradual personal and generational changes would then make devouring easier, more pleasurable, and ultimately as 'natural' as a cat toying with a half-dead mouse or an eagle lifting into the air with its prey twisting in its talons. But the ultimate transformation sought by Luciferans is not in doubt. It is not physical but spiritual — the evolution to godhood by devouring and absorbing the energies of other beings.

BEING DEVOURED

Luciferans use personal power to gain more power; they literally drain the vital energy of those near them, absorbing or annihilating the victim's identity in the process. Scott Peck, in his book *People of the Lie*, described the kind of diffuse pain, confusion, revulsion, and unease experienced by individuals drained in this way.

It is as if Luciferans tap directly into the deepest resources of the soul in order to siphon the energy found there. Leonard Shengold comes close to describing the process in his book *Soul Murder*, which he defines as the deliberate attempt to eradicate or compromise the separate identity of another person. One person literally absorbs the life of another; *soul murder* is described as an abuse of power in which the stronger person breaks down and destroys the inner resources of the weaker.

The actual experience of being devoured emotionally, cognitively, or spiritually usually occurs gradually over time. The devouring itself is never obvious to the victim; if it was, then defenses would be mobilized. Suffering occurs, but most victims attribute it to some other cause: a physical illness, personal weakness, or an external stressful event of some kind.

From my own work with such victims, the following symptoms and experiences seem common. (I have used "transfer empathy" here, hence the pronoun "you").

INTIMIDATION

The devourer convinces you that you are in the presence of someone stronger, better, wiser, more self-assured, who loves you and cares for you despite all your many weaknesses and faults. You feel troubled, but every time you respond to a perceived assault, she appears hurt or angry — "How can you say that about me when I've only ever shown you love and concern?" — and will convince you that you are wrong or deluded, (devourers armed with psychological jargon are good at this: the victim is "projecting", "defending" and so forth). On all issues you lose and she wins. You are never right, never have a meaningful opinion, never emerge feeling good.

THE RESULTS OF THE METHOD

You feel drained, cannot think clearly, cannot organize your thoughts. This occurs during a direct assault and then grows worse as the devouring goes on over time. Rational thought becomes fuzzy, thoughts come and go randomly. You feel as if you are drifting without center or anchor. You begin to spin.

Planning and making decisions becomes impossible. Because you cannot think clearly, you cannot organize your thoughts enough to decide what to do. You depend more and more on your victimizer to make decisions for you, an arrangement which of course fits his plans perfectly.

You feel more and more lethargic all the time. Your body is heavy and unresponsive. Excitement and enthusiasm are non-existent. Everything feels dull, gray, and bleak. Even simple things take massive energy: getting out of bed, finding the coffee cup, feeding the cat. No matter how hard you try to shake it off, it just will not leave.

You become plagued with health problems — lots of minor infections, colds, flues. Headaches, stomach problems, and muscle pains are common. You feel weak and ill all the time, and cannot shake it. You only feel good around the very person that all your friends tell you is hurting you. You cannot help it. The doctors cannot seem to fix your illnesses.

You sleep too much or too little; sometimes a period of insomnia follows excessive drowsy-drugged sleep. You want to be in bed or on the couch all day. You do not dream much when you sleep, and when you wake up you never feel refreshed.

You begin to fear and mistrust your own instincts, your own friends and family, your safety in your own environment. You are plagued by a kind of pervasive fear or even paranoia: you sense you are under attack, but you cannot find the attacker. You think it might be your parents, a trauma from the past, your neighbor, a hidden conspiracy, the government, the media: you just cannot seem to tell who or what is after you. You just feel threatened. Your friends will often know on some instinctive level that your real enemy is the devourer right next to you, but you do not believe them.

You begin to doubt everything about yourself, your beliefs, your pleasures, your past, your taste in clothing or food. Your victimizer seems to know more about what you need than you do. You're afraid to make decisions because you know they will be wrong or stupid. Your devourer constantly reminds you how hopeless you are.

Self-doubt flowers into full blown self hatred. You feel yourself to be hopeless, worthless, stupid, ignorant. You are a complete failure, and deserve only the worst. You hate what you have become, but feel powerless to change. You are so tired that you cannot reach out for help, except to your devourer who you now believe is your last hope.

Close friends, hobbies, etc. that you used to love no longer bring any pleasure. Your victimizer or "friend" defines them as evil or destructive, so you cut yourself off from them. You find yourself severing all connections to family and friends. You begin to lose your self; often the devourer will then provide you with a new identity: different clothes, food, likes and dislikes, activities, beliefs and so on.

DEPRESSION

Real depression and despair hit hard. You've gone way past the "blues" into full darkness. The black dog bites your heels, and no one is there to help or understand. (The best book on depression I've read is Cronkite's *On the Edge of Darkness*. Devouring is, of course, not recognized as a clinical cause of depression, but the outcome is the same.) Your appearance changes: people are shocked when they see you because you've lost your vivacity, energy, and enthusiasm. The sweet voice of suicide calls your name.

ESCAPE AND RECOVERY

Luciferans believe that there is only one sure way to end the assault: the victim has to break from the devourer and leave the situation, because psycho-spiritual devouring demands a relationship between devourer and prey, over time. This is not the quick pounce and death of nature. The devourer has to convince the prey to open up and surrender, and the only way to do this is to come in disguise. The process ends when the victim gains enough strength to leave, is removed by luck, or is aided by a force greater than the predator's. Symptoms will continue long after the assault, but the actual progress of further devouring ends. Luciferan devourers will of course do everything they can to prevent this loss.

Luciferans are not the only devourers: devouring can be found anywhere, between parents and children, employers and employees, husbands and wives, friend to friend. Either party can be predator, despite one apparently having more power than another: wives can devour husbands, children their parents, employees their employer. Economic, professional, or political power assists Luciferans in the devouring process (one of the reasons they pursue it so avidly), but is not essential.

Recovery depends on the victim's recognition that the assault has occurred. Recovery time in a safe place is essential. Appropriate counseling may help, but healing seems much like recovery from a physical assault: the body, or in this case the soul, needs time to heal itself.

Individuals who were basically healthy before the attack but who were duped into a devouring relationship are most likely to learn from the experience and recover. Individuals who were psychologically assaulted and devoured from an early age have a much harder time, because being devoured is familiar, safe, and even at times exciting, especially if it has become associated with sexuality during puberty. Masochism, bondage, and other related forms of sexuality can result, and such individuals will actively, if unconsciously, find a predator to feed: even if a destructive relationship is severed, they usually find another. They may even find much joy in the ultimate annihilation of identity, as in the *Story of O*, *9 1/2 Weeks* and similar novels where the victim finds a kind of heroic transcendence in complete surrender to the victimizer.

CHAPTER FOUR

POSSESSION

The real power, the power we have to fight for night and day, is not power over things, but over men... power is in tearing human minds to pieces and putting them together again in new shapes of your own choosing... always there will be the intoxication of power, constantly increasing and constantly growing subtler... a world of victory after victory, triumph after triumph after triumph: an endless pressing, pressing, pressing upon the nerve of power...

— George Orwell, 1984

Luciferans want to possess more power, becoming stronger in their pursuit of *powaqqatsi*. More personal power, more influence, more pleasure, more godhood, more of more — this is the Luciferan impulse. To grow strong as the victim grows weak and take as predators take, without concern for the victim, and without the impediments of conscience or compassion.

Luciferans take by devouring, but they may also choose to take by possessing. Devouring depletes the victim, while possession takes ownership. Possession enhances Luciferan power as does devouring, and both weapons are essential parts of the Luciferan arsenal.

My use of the term possession will probably be unfamiliar to many readers. For most of us, possession refers to the demonic, as portrayed in movies like *The Exorcist*. Because we really do not believe in demons, we do not believe in possession either. This is unfortunate, because possession is just as integral to life as devouring, and just as intimate and familiar to us.

A person can be possessed on many levels — physical, emotional, cognitive, and spiritual — and by different entities — individuals, families, organizations, corporations, and others. I believe possession is real, pervasive, and natural, and that it is as close to us as devouring: we all possess, and we can all *be* possessed.

This belief may seem absurd and irresponsible, but as with all such claims made here, I only ask for an open mind and a willingness to explore.

Possession Defined

Just what is possession? If it is more than the familiar idea of spirit invasion, then how can we begin to understand it? Possession seems to imply three basic but overlapping ideas: ownership, invasion, and domination. Luciferans delight in all three.

First, ownership. If I own something, then it is mine and mine alone. No one else has a right to use it but me. I possess it. The more I own, the more power I possess and the more potent and larger I become. What I own extends outward as part of me, and my possessions define and amplify my strength. Ownership is an extension of self.

Ownership of private property is fundamental to Western democratic life. We own — possess — land, homes, cars, furniture, and other personal items. Some of us own companies and some of us possess more than one home. Others own huge quantities of symbols called money, which can be used to obtain desirable objects and services. We own, and therefore possess, animals. In the past, some of us used to own other human beings through the institution of slavery. Women used to be owned by their husbands. Many parents today act as if they own their children.

Possession, meaning ownership, is so pervasive in our culture we seldom think about it. Social experiments such as communes and even the full flowering of communism itself sought to eliminate personal ownership. None of them lasted, a testament to the tenacious power of the possessive impulse. Capitalism is built on this intense human desire to own and consume goods, and its future as a powerful force operating around the entire planet seems secure.

The Luciferan lust for ownership is intense. Ownership of material possessions and wealth implies power and influence, so Luciferans expand their temporal holdings at all costs. Successful Luciferans are never poor; poverty is for Christians and other failures.

Possession, secondly, implies invasion, the process of forcibly entering into and then holding onto something. Military invasion involves the use of force to occupy a place or an area, and the exercise of control once it is occupied. It implies seizure by force, and this is the sense I would like to use here. To possess by force of seizure, power is essential. Without power, the seized object or person will prevent the seizure by fighting back with force. Historically, wars have been fought primarily over the occupation, the possession of land. Such possession means the strength of the subjected land is then added to the power of the possessor. Cultures which we admire and celebrate historically — the Romans and the British, for example — have influenced history because they were invaders and possessors of other people and other lands. Their empires resulted from forced seizure, and ended when they no longer had the power to hold their possessed lands.

Luciferans take deep pleasure in the act of invasion. There is a winner and a loser; the winner gets stronger, the loser surrenders and becomes weaker. Luciferans enjoy the victim's struggle, and swell on his defeat. Luciferans understand military thinking perfectly. The art of war is the highest art, and they practice it ruthlessly in their personal and social lives.

Possession, thirdly, means domination. To dominate means that the victim's will is subjected to the possessor's. Dominated people do what they are told.

Influence, power, command and control are for the dominator, while subjugation, humiliation, submission and servitude are for the dominated. Because Luciferans believe in the hierarchy of devouring, they are determined to be the dominators not the dominated, devourers not the devoured, possessors not the possessed.

The act of domination itself, as with ownership and invasion, brings deep pleasure and satisfaction to the Luciferan. Domination induces feelings of elevation, superiority, and profound empowerment. Directing another's will, or even bending that will until it breaks, is great joy for the Luciferan. All three aspects of possession — ownership, invasion, and domination — are linked, and one usually implies the other.

POSSESSION IN DAILY LIFE

If possession means ownership, invasion, and domination, then like devouring it is clearly and openly woven into the entire fabric of our known existence. Our geo-political history bends and sways with the shift of ownership, invasion, and domination from one culture to another. Invasion is the essence of war and imperialism. In the social realm, our lives are frequently defined by what we buy and own. Careers are made or lost because one executive dominates others and rises up the corporate hierarchy. Nature itself seethes with the urge to possess, because devouring the flesh of another being is an ultimate form of possession in which the victim is actually incorporated directly into the devourer — is fully owned, occupied, and dominated.

Possession is so fundamental to our lives that, like devouring, we seldom think about it. Let us start with the familiar: I possess this computer, my house, and the land surrounding it. Ownership is a form of possession. I possess the food I eat: a chicken is transformed and absorbed into my body. Eating is a form of possession. I possess the air I breathe, the water I drink. If I am good enough at possessing the energies of other beings, then I grow stronger. My personal fortune swells, and I become rich. If a group of us are good possessors, then my group, family, tribe or nation will be energized with growth and power. The idea is simple: absorb, own, and possess as much as you can for as long as you can. This is the foundation of capitalism, which can be considered the economic equivalent of spirit possession. Successful entrepreneurs must become proficient in the art of possessing. Successful companies grow by possessing more market share and more staff and production. They ultimately take over, assimilate, and possess competing companies. Growth itself is a kind of possession. For a thing to grow, it must absorb and possess something outside itself. Nature may abhor a vacuum, but she loves possession.

We can possess other individuals. A man can so thoroughly dominate the thoughts, beliefs, emotions and behavior of a woman that she is effectively possessed by him. Anyone witnessing a battered woman returning again and again to the batterer can understand this. She has lost herself to him, and is no longer directing her own life.

A mother can so totally dominate her children that their identity is lost in hers, their lives determined by her desires, their will subjugated to hers, their life force serving hers. The family system itself can literally seek out and possess those within it like a living entity, especially if the family's history is thick with possessive energy.

Cults epitomize the full possession of the individual by a group. Cult members surrender personal autonomy so profoundly that the group's leader and its dogma replace individual personality and self-determination.

An individual can be so possessed by rage that everything else becomes irrelevant. Jealousy, hate, love, fear — all of these primal emotions can possess their host. Some individuals become so possessed by hatred that their lives are lost to it.

Drug, alcohol, tobacco and food addictions can all be considered forms of possession: the host becomes dependent on the addictive substance and then gradually loses autonomy to it, eventually becoming possessed by the urge to indulge.

The dominant culture possesses other cultures, and the intrusive individual possesses the weaker. A man possesses a woman; a woman in turn can invade and possess a man. Destructive parents possess their children. Certain employers possess their employees, and certain totalitarian states posses their citizens. Slavery is the actual ownership — possession — of another human being.

We, Possessors?

Despite the universal presence of possession in daily life, most of us refuse to accept the simple truth that we are possessors, and that we must possess the life force of other entities to survive. Despite this denial, we take delight in being effective possessors, and enjoy the fruits of our possessions. We possess property, material goods, plants, animals, and anything else we can use and control. We idolize the great possessors among us: the giant capitalists, the wealthy, the takers and users. Possession is power, and power is life. Who can claim unfamiliarity with ownership, invasion, and domination? Who can say they have never owned, invaded or dominated something in their lives?

Possession and devouring are linked. We call ourselves "consumers" because we literally devour, consume, and possess other entities, energies, and resources. Ownership is possession, and we in the West primarily identify ourselves by what we own — that is, by what we possess. The possessor and the possessed: this dynamic seems as rooted in creation as devouring and power acquisition.

Possession need not imply demons or evil spirits; it has many forms, many faces. Luciferans simply take the common thrust of every day possession and make it sacrosanct, just as they elevate the natural process of devouring. We are all possessors to some degree, because existence is impossible without it. Some of us might try to minimize the impulse to possess wealth, power, position, and influence, but not Luciferans: they must possess, because the more they own, invade, and dominate, the more powerful and potent they believe they become. They want to possess everything the world has to offer. They especially want to possess other people. Ultimately, they want to possess God.

As with devouring, Luciferans simply acknowledge the fact and elevate it to holy status, to a core spiritual principle directing their lives.

WE, THE POSSESSED?

Is human possession possible? Can people actually be possessed? Can I be possessed? I might admit to being a possessor myself, just as I can admit to being a devourer. I might go so far as to agree that both possession and devouring are deeply woven into the natural order of things here on planet earth. But to admit that I could actually be owned, invaded, and dominated is more difficult. Very few of us would be willing to accept our own vulnerability to possession.

If pressed on the point, I might agree that, sure, a strong person or political movement could possess my goods, my land, home and personal belongings. I could end up in a prison camp just because I am the wrong race. But that would be it: no one could ever violate the essential core of my being or penetrate into my heart, mind or spirit. The fortress of my individual autonomy is just too strong for anyone to invade. They cannot possess me, because *I* am too strong, *I* am different.

The thought of losing this essential core-self to some outside possessing force arouses a primal terror as profound as the fear of being devoured. Why? Just how deep within us can possession actually penetrate? How much of me could be possessed?

We readily admit that an invader could take away our land, our possessions. A very powerful invader could even take, control or murder our families. Like Job, we could be stripped of everything we own, and these possessions could be transferred to the ownership of someone else more powerful.

Few of us, however, would admit that our thoughts, beliefs, and entire personality could be owned by another. Horror entertainment plays on this fear: movies such as *Invasion of the Body Snatchers, Dawn of the Dead,* and *The Exorcist* invoke our primal fear about the deep loss of core autonomy to an outside possessing entity. Dracula possesses the souls of those he feeds on by transforming them into vampires. When bitten by a werewolf, the victim becomes possessed by the werewolf's presence at every full moon. Freddy Krueger, the villain of the *Nightmare on Elm Street* series, possesses the souls of his victims by imprisoning them in his body; when he is finally destroyed, his victims are freed.

At root we are horrified by the possibility of ultimate possession — loss of soul. It would be hard enough to admit that our thoughts, beliefs and basic personality could be possessed, but the possibility of soul possession is even worse. In Christian thought, Lucifer's ultimate threat is not possession of our material wealth or property, nor even our core beliefs, but our soul. Soul-possession, the possession of core identity, is the ultimate loss.

This fear of soul-loss seems grounded worldwide in virtually all cultures. To the positivistic materialist of this century the fear seems absurd: there is no soul, hence no reason to fear soul possession. The materialist would be mortified at the loss of personal possessions, beliefs, or personality, because these are what he knows of himself. Yet to millions of others, belief in soul is strong, and belief in loss-of-soul through possession is equally strong. Many funeral rites were designed to prevent soul-possession after death.

The voudoun belief in the zombie — the possessed dead — is based on the fear of soul-loss. As discussed in the last chapter, cannibalism and the ritual killing and eating of a victim are grounded in a very simple idea: by killing you I can possess your strength and even your spirit if I kill you ritualistically and contain, control and then use your spiritual energy. Surely this is all just myth and shock-entertainment. None of it is real. But what if it were possible? What if a person's body, emotions, mind, and spirit could be controlled? This is the fervent dream of a thousand would-be demagogues. The brainwashing scare of the early fifties was based on an apparently invincible new weapon of the communists: the minds of eager young Americans could be wiped clean and re-programmed, that is, possessed. In the sixties and seventies, cults were accused of using brainwashing to control new recruits. Yet the average person still feels immune. No one can control what counts: my thoughts, my feelings, my soul.

Upon closer examination, this belief just does not seem to hold. I would like to assert that being possessed is actually quite common. Luciferans would agree, because they possess humans all the time.

DETERMINISM AS POSSESSION

Before examining how Luciferans believe they can possess humans, a brief sample of scientific thought might show that Luciferans are not alone in their belief about human possession. Scientific reductionists, materialists, and mechanists state as fact that humans are possessed by deterministic forces beyond their control. "Possession" would not be their term of choice, but I believe it describes these forces nevertheless.

Such forces are apparently legion. Genetics, early parenting, social dynamics: all of these are supposed to determine each person's existence far more than the individual's false and pitiful beliefs in personal freedom and choice. Freud expanded this determinism to include the unconscious, a region of our being which is allegedly beyond our awareness but which dominates and controls, or possesses, our conscious existence like a brutal foreign invader. Behavioral psychology is based on the absolute determinism of all environmental influences; in effect, Behaviorists state that we are totally dominated — possessed — by these influences. Motivational psychologists, like Maslow, argue that we are driven (possessed) by a spectrum of needs ranging from food to love. Sociobiologists, like E. O. Wilson. believe that we are "possessed" by biological drives and animal forces built deeply into us through evolution. The newly developing sciences of neurology and neurobiology generally hold that we are determined (possessed) by neuro-chemical and neuro-biological processes and forces in our brains.

In fact, the sciences of sociobiology, psychology, sociology, and neurology have spent extraordinary energy showing that we are not free, that we are determined — that is, possessed — by legions of forces absolutely beyond our control. We are not free but are possessed by internal and external forces that own, invade and dominate us from birth to death.

I am sure that scientists holding such deterministic beliefs would strongly condemn my use of the word "possession" to describe their beliefs. But if possession is defined as ownership, invasion, and domination, then such determinism clearly states that we are owned, invaded, and dominated by everything from our genetically inherited potential to the mysterious archetypes floating in the depths of our unconsciousness.

My point here is to emphasize how deeply the notion of possession runs within scientific thought, and that it animates even those scientists who despise mysticism and who firmly believe themselves to be more rational and objective than the rest of us. The fear of being possessed may be ancient and primitive, but it seems to me that science has just transformed this primal fear into various deterministic beliefs that can be understood as the precise parallels of our ancient fears about possessing demons. Modern scientific shamans have created a deterministic worldview, a worldview as possessive as any from our distant past.

Luciferans would not argue with these scientific shamans. On the contrary, Luciferans are acutely aware of all the forces limiting their experience of absolute freedom. Modern science only confirms their commitment to Luciferan philosophy, to their search for absolute freedom from all determinisms and limitations. It also confirms their conviction that all non-Luciferans are deceived, weakened, and rendered powerless by these limiting forces. Thus Luciferans have developed a fierce desire to accumulate enough power to transcend all the freedom-killing limitations of biological, sociological, and psychological existence. They will do anything to achieve transcendence, including devouring and possessing other humans.

POSSESSING HUMANS

Luciferans know that possessing wealth, power, and influence depends on possessing other people one way or another. The acquisition of power, dominance, ownership and control is not a pretty business. It is not egalitarian; it is not pleasant (and never has been); it is driven by the same stark realities as devouring — to devour or be devoured. Luciferans simply agree to acknowledge the hard reality and get on with what others would call the 'dirty work' of possession. Luciferans pursue possession. They accept possession as an integral law of life on this planet. Possess, or be possessed. They know that this law applies to humans as much as to animals or objects, and that to achieve success they must use the law to their advantage. Purely, simply, it means possessing other people.

As outlined above, I believe people are possessed all the time. I also believe possession is so common that we do not recognize it or discuss it. We place it in a kind of *twilight zone*: it happens over there, *then*, but never here, *now*. Others do it, but not me. Unspeakable monsters and demons possess, but they are far away in the safe realm of fiction and myth.

To come to grips with possession, I think we need to look at it honestly, openly and cleanly.

FOUR TYPES OF POSSESSION

When a person is possessed, he or she loses autonomy and self control. His actions, thoughts, and feelings become dictated by a force other than his own will. As with devouring, an individual can be possessed physically, emotionally, cognitively, and spiritually, from the less central realm of external physical action to the essence of self identity, from outer to inner, from surface attack to deeper invasion of the target's inner core.

As an invader progresses from external to internal control of the victim, more and more of the target's identity is lost, until it ultimately crumbles. Once penetrated to the core, the victim loses the will and the ability to resist.

An alternate identity system constructed by the invader can then be implanted so the victim becomes completely owned and dominated by the possessor.

Targets can be invaded at any or all levels simultaneously or singly, depending on the possessor's skill and the target's strength to resist. Domination and ownership are the goal.

I should warn readers that the following descriptions of possession are probably not what you are used to hearing. For example, movies like *The Exorcist* imply that physical possession means ownership of the victim's body: the possessor controls the victim's body and makes it do or say things it otherwise would not. This is unfortunate, because possession of the body is the least powerful and intrusive form of invasion. Bodies can be invaded, dominated, and owned in a number of ways: they can be intimidated, enslaved, imprisoned, and coerced. But possession of the person's inner spiritual core is more difficult. It takes knowledge, style, skill, and finesse. It takes power and time, but the result is a deeper more powerful control.

Having stated this, here are the levels and types of possession that I believe exist:

PHYSICAL POSSESSION

Physical possession occurs when the target's physical actions are controlled by an outside force beyond his or her control, usually with an implicit threat of harm. Slavery is a form of physical possession: the bodily actions of the slave are owned, directed, and controlled by the possessor, or owner.

All forms of bodily captivity can be considered physical possession, from imprisonment in a cell to forced containment within the boundaries of a state. Political totalism, when fully empowered, becomes possessive as well: followers act in a precise way, smile and cheer when asked, and mouth slogans at the right time because they know that any other alternative means imprisonment or death.

Employment can be understood as a kind of possession, although obviously less coercive than previous examples. Look at the hoards of middle managers and front line workers who give their bodies to tasks they despise but cannot resist. The company wants to control the employee's physical actions: as Henry Ford was known to have said, "Why is it that I always get a whole person when what I want is a pair of hands?" One might say that Henry Ford was a great possessor of hands.

In two separate chapters of his book *Images of Organization*, Gareth Morgan, a professor of Administrative Studies, examines different metaphors of organization, including two which depict organizations as "psychic prisons" and "instruments of domination". He states that the "essence of organization

97

rests in a process of domination where certain people impose their will on others." He would certainly not call such domination possession, but why not? Talk to many middle or lower level managers, and you will meet people who seem crushed, broken, and contained. They act as if they are owned, and will often make jokes and sarcastic comments to that effect. Workers long ago formed unions to assert their right to self-determination and dignity: this was probably because they experienced the deeply instinctive human revulsion against possession. The same revulsion has driven political revolutions and social rebellions throughout time.

Yet despite this revulsion, the success of powerful political, economic, and social forces depends entirely on their power to possess the physical actions of millions of human beings. Luciferans would argue that despite moralistic arguments to the contrary, such domination is natural, has always existed, and always will exist because someone has to lead and someone has to follow. Luciferans simply insist they will always be leaders, never followers.

Physical possession is a common and powerful presence in our society, but it is a flawed and limited form of control. The victim continually seeks to escape because control has not been internalized. That is, the victim generally knows about his possession, and may well nurse anger, hostility, and dreams of escape.

Lotteries are built on such dreams of escape; multitudes of physically possessed workers want freedom from their captivity, and see lottery winnings as their ticket out. They dream of telling the boss to "shove it." Their possession is external; their bodies obey the will of their captor/owner/operator/boss, but only as long as the captor has the power, energy, and money to maintain control. The victim's emotions, mind and spirit are free to fly, to plot escape and possibly revenge. To be more effective, possession must therefore go deeper into the emotions, mind, and spirit of the possessed.

EMOTIONAL POSSESSION

In emotional possession, the victim's emotions are controlled by an individual, group, or force beyond his knowledge and his power to resist. Emotions of any form, from rage to sexual arousal, are thus elicited, directed, and controlled by an outside force or entity.

The advantages of emotional possession for the possessor are immense. If the possessor can elicit specific emotions at specific times, then the possessed individual will behave in ways advantageous to the possessor.

For example, if I am a powerful politician, I want to be able to elicit deep and powerful emotional energy in my constituents. Owning constituents physically is too difficult, onerous and obvious, and will never produce deep emotion, arousal or energy. This energy could take the form of patriotic outrage against a foreign country. If aroused deeply enough, my constituents may even give up their lives in war against this country. If I am a powerful religious leader, I want to be able to elicit emotions like guilt, terror, and remorse in my flock. I also want to be able to elicit fierce loyalty and love, so enemies of mine become enemies of my flock. I can use these emotions to direct my flock in ways I determine are beneficial. If I am a fund raiser for a charity, I want to elicit emotions such as pity, compassion, and deep sympathy in my audience, so they will open their wallets to support my charitable cause. If I am angry with someone, then I might want to possess the emotions of my friends so they too will express their anger and rage at my enemy. Such examples are endless and, I submit, ubiquitous in our lives. Advertisers, employers, therapists, religious leaders, governments, and even families are drawn to emotional possession because of the dividends it can yield. These dividends can best be understood by exploring how each of these possessing entities uses emotional possession to enhance and advance their own power.

Advertisers & Employers

Advertisers are vitally interested in emotional possession. They would not call it possession of course, but ultimately they want to evoke specific emotions in consumers to influence their buying. In other words, they want to control the targeted consumer by entering and possessing part of her emotional life permanently. Often "brand names" have this emotional presence. Perhaps they have been familiar to you for as long as you can remember. These products tend to fashion a specific emotional reaction of recognition and pleasure in most of us. You hear or see the name and it evokes salivation, desire or other reactions. This reaction is not accidental. It has been deliberately implanted by conditioning, intense advertising energy, and has become a complete part of the consumer's emotional life.

Readers might suggest that this is just a conditioned response created by simple influence and marketing techniques. Why call it possession? The answer is a question of perspective; influence peddlers and marketers would hardly want to be known as possessors. But if we define emotional possession as the art of invading, dominating and owning part or all of a target's emotional life by implanting emotional reactions controlled by the possessor, then that is exactly what advertisers and other marketing experts wish to do.

Many employers are deeply interested in emotional possession. They want to plant a kind of emotional "spin" into their employees. A whole genre of management literature is devoted solely to building "culture", "loyalty", "commitment", and obedience in employees. This literature basically teaches managers how to enter into the employee's emotional world and create positive emotional energy toward the company.

Thousands of management seminars use basic techniques of the early encounter movement to bring employees into cathartic situations where their emotional life is laid bare. The purpose? To enhance employees' alignment and commitment to the company's vision. Some motivational seminars use manipulative techniques to arouse intense euphoria and emotional fervor. These weekend meetings often resemble religious revivals, with fervent converts and zealous testimonials. The point here? Simply this: employers want to raise emotion to a fever pitch and then push the seminar leader's message so deep into the employee that it will then possess long-term influence and control over the employees emotional life.

A foray into management literature on influence and power acquisition reads like an introductory lecture on emotional possession. If you are a management executive, how do you get people to do what you want? You compel them with your "vision". You get them to surrender their doubts, concerns, and worries — to become "aligned" with your views. You possess their emotional being and cause them to spill their emotional energy into the corporation, where it can be contained, controlled, and directed to enhance corporate profit the way gasoline is contained within an internal combustion engine to enhance the vehicle's forward motion. You want your employees to be unconditionally loyal so this powerful emotion can be used to enhance corporate profit. Thus an employee's emotional life is vitally important to any employer seeking more than just the assembly-plant physical possession known to Henry Ford. In her book *The Managed Heart*, Arlie Hochschild brilliantly explores how "the management of feeling is socially engineered and transformed into emotional labor for wage" within the business world. Companies "now advertise spontaneous warmth" and an experience of "real happiness and calm" which must be delivered by employees whose emotional existence becomes penetrated and possessed by company policy. The "emotional style of offering the service is part of the service itself," something she defines as "emotional labor." This kind of labor "calls for a coordination of mind and feeling, and it sometimes draws on a source of self that we honor as deep and integral to our personality."

In other words, the work becomes invasive and possessive. She goes on to contrast physical and emotional labor. For the former, employers "claimed control over [the] speed and motion" of an employee's physical labor on the factory line (defined here as physical possession). For jobs requiring emotional labor, as with airline flight attendants, the employer now "lays claim not simply to her [the attendant's] physical motions — how she handles food trays — but to her emotional actions and the way they show in the ease of a smile."

Hochschild describes the intense cost to employees of such invasive control of their emotional being. She would probably not define this as emotional possession, although she does invoke Orwellian images to help define the depth of her revulsion against the process.

THERAPISTS

Corporate employers are not the only organizational entities interested in emotional possession. Unethical therapists, for example, are also deeply skilled in the arts of emotional manipulation and possession. They know they can invade the client's emotional life and literally call forward any emotion they wish. If the client's submission is not complete, they can invoke feelings of fear, terror, and even self-hate to maintain control.

Therapeutic techniques designed to "open" clients can render them emotionally drained to the point that they become open not to the truth of their pain but to the therapist's suggestions. Both Elizabeth Loftus in her book *The Myth of Repressed Memory* and Richard Ofshe in *Making Monsters* attack the ways in which therapists can deliberately, or accidentally, influence and control the emotional lives and even the memories of their clients. Ethical therapists would never knowingly abuse their client's trust and openness; less ethical colleagues, however, might deliberately use it to support their invasion and domination of the client's emotional being.

Therapeutic techniques, such as hypnosis, can be used to open, invade, and then emotionally possess clients. Suggestion can be powerful, especially when the client perceives the therapist as a kind of "parent-god." Luciferan therapists can find a deep pleasure in the power they hold over suggestible clients.

Such therapists can then use the client's vulnerability to implant virtually any theory to explain the client's pain. That is, if we assume that the client originally came to the therapist looking for relief from a certain problem, unethical therapists can then suggest an explanation and proceed to find "evidence" to support it. Thus, if the therapist is "into" ritual abuse, past lives, Freudianism, and so on, then the client can easily come to believe this explanation. This can then exalt the power, prestige, and public adulation of the therapist's career.

RELIGIOUS LEADERS

Many religious leaders and their organizations specialize in the use of emotional possession to dominate their followers. Again, if we define emotional possession as the art of invading, dominating and owning part or all of a target's emotional life by implanting emotional reactions controlled by the possessor, then we have to admit that many (if not most) religious organizations try to deeply possess the emotional lives of their followers. This is probably not as true today as when religions were more dominant politically and economically, but religious organizations still exert tremendous emotional control on followers.

Their advantage over other organizations is that they can begin the possessive process with very young children. One purpose of early childhood education in churches is to enter into the hearts of young children and take up residence. I hate to make this sound so horrible, but it is true nevertheless. Some religious organizations feel that children need to be emotionally invaded, owned, and ultimately dominated in order to further the organization's survival and prosperity. Such organizations would never define their intentions in this way: they would feel they were "*serving God*", "*helping the child to find the truth*", and so on. Without this kind of deep emotional connection and commitment from young people and their families, religions wither and die. To achieve it, they must invade. They have to possess. Once followers are emotionally invaded and controlled, they willingly spill their vital life's energy into the organization. They will volunteer time, donate money, and proselytize. They will experience emotional pain, fear, and despair at the mere thought of defection from the organization, and will feel irrational anger and hatred toward any outsiders criticizing it. Their sense of personal safety and integrity will depend on the organization. Their emotional existence, in other words, will be owned, invaded, and dominated by the organization possessing them.

GOVERNMENTS, FAMILIES, AND INDIVIDUAL RELATIONSHIPS

Great nationalistic movements also want to emotionally possess the young. They invade young childrens' emotions in order to implant loyalty and love. How else can people be expected to feel powerful emotional attachments to an idea, to an abstraction that says: "everyone in this particular geographical boundary should be like family to me?" We are so used to nationalism as something 'real' that any other possibility is hard to imagine.

But isn't nationalism a strangely unnatural idea? Why should I owe loyalty and obedience to a group of bodies within, say, the boundaries of the United States, but feel no such allegiance to equally deserving people across the border in Canada? Emotional possession provides an answer.

The Church and the State have always understood the need for emotional possession. Without it, they would cease to exist. This may well be our problem here in Canada: unlike the powerfully possessing emotional energies generated by nationalism in the United States, we have no such deep equivalent. We are apparently free from it. But our country is also falling apart under the stress of localized emotional possessions, by say the French in Quebec, and various native groups across the land. Emotional possession works: it binds people together in a common emotional cause.

Needless to say, emotional possession is also common in families. A family given over to rage and hate will infect and invade their children to the point that the entire family unit becomes possessed by the same virulent emotions. In the same way, a family controlled by a spirit of detachment and emotional numbness will transmit this form of possession to its children.

If a family can be thought of as an organization (like a church, a state, or a corporation, just smaller), then like all other organizations it will seek its own survival and propagation. It will therefore attempt to implant itself deeply into the emotional energies of its members, especially of the young.

Emotional possession is rampant in many relationships. The desire and ability to induce specific emotions in your spouse at a specific time for a specific reason probably defines the essence of many relationships today.

For example, one partner might want the other to feel guilty for even contemplating an undesirable purchase or an unwanted friendship. The guilt then becomes a powerful method for controlling the other's behavior. The same can be said for any emotion: if one spouse can invade, own, and dominate the other's emotional life, then this possession yields tremendous power and control.

Most partners will resist this kind of possession. This resistance may lead to counter-attempts of emotional possession, so the relationship deteriorates into an emotional war of diminishing returns and deepening exhaustion. Physical violence may erupt, because one partner feels so deeply terrorized and frustrated with the war.

Separation, divorce, and other relationship-terminating events can also result. I believe that men and women equally engage in emotional possession; as with Luciferism itself, emotional possession is not the sole property of one sex or the other.

If one partner succeeds in completely controlling the emotional life of the other, then a kind of static stability can result in which peace between the two depends on the assertion of emotional control by the dominant partner. Should anything happen to disrupt this balance, then the relationship will often deteriorate quickly.

Emotional possession is powerful, and will continue to animate the actions of possessors ranging from religious and corporate leaders to familial and individual relationships. But despite its power, emotional possession is limited. It penetrates more deeply into the individual than physical possession, but it nevertheless leaves other deeper aspects of the victim untouched. The victim can still resist and recover.

To invade deeper, the possessor must control the target's core cognitive beliefs — meaning the victim's mind itself must be possessed.

MIND POSSESSION

Cognitive, or mind possession, occurs when the possessed person's core beliefs become controlled by an outside individual or group. As discussed previously, by core beliefs I mean the individual's basic ideas about his own identity, about reality in general and about his own personal world in particular. To use a computer analogy, I mean the person's "operating system."

These deep beliefs determine how a person acts and even what he perceives: if I believe you are about to kill me, I am going to run or fight — whether you actually mean to kill me or not. If I believe you are the Messiah, I will act accordingly toward you, and do what you tell me to do. If I believe one soft drink is better than another, then I will buy my belief.

As previously stated, ruthless politicians, religious leaders, advertisers and other belief managers know a simple truth: to control a man, control what he believes to be true. Once you control his beliefs you control the way he perceives his world. And with this you will eventually control his actions.

Luciferans are particularly interested in the cognitive realm of core beliefs for this reason: if core beliefs can be broken and subsequently altered, then other beliefs can be implanted. These beliefs will then control the victim's perception, action, and emotions. The victim can therefore be possessed at a level deeper than body or emotion: the "mind" itself will then become possessed. Cognitive possession can therefore be defined as follows: the art of invading, dominating and owning part or all of a target's cognition by implanting core beliefs controlled by the possessor.

BREAKING & POSSESSING THE MIND

Core cognitive beliefs can be accessed by using the process of psychological assault. Once opened, these beliefs can be manipulated, transformed, or even annihilated depending on the invader's intentions.

Vital shifts in core beliefs can be shattering for the victim, who is left vulnerable, disoriented, and confused. Such shifts can be sudden and dramatic, or can occur gradually over time, like a gently shifting mountainside that suddenly lets go into an avalanche. These dramatic shifts can cause profound changes not only in core beliefs, but in the personality and behavior which depend on them. In other words, something deep within the victim is disturbed and shaken.

Psychological assault is only one way to open and shake up core beliefs. Dramatic shifts of core beliefs have also been understood as conversion experiences. Such intense transformations often follow periods of prolonged and extreme stress, which lead to a kind of core collapse or meltdown. If this collapse is orchestrated by an outside individual such as a charismatic religious leader, then a new belief system can be planted. Core beliefs can also be broken and changed in a process known as *Snapping* (see Conway and Siegelman's book of the same name), which is defined as a sudden, drastic alteration of personality.

Traditional brainwashing or "thought reform" techniques also actively seek to break a person's identity in order to replace it with another identity more suitable to the programmer. In Edgar Schein's terms (Schein was one of the pioneer explorers of the brainwashing phenomenon), the process is one of "unfreezing", "changing" and then "refreezing" the target. In Luciferan terms, the predator unfreezes the target's core belief system, deeply inserts his own object-of-focus, and then refreezes the target.

In the unfreezing stage, the predator deliberately causes the breakdown of core beliefs, because a person without a cognitive core can be easily manipulated to accept another. Once broken, core beliefs can be replaced. If the victim accepts the predator's implanted beliefs, which might portray the predator as someone warm, wonderful, wise and supportive, then the victim can be used and controlled at the predator's whim. If the predator ridicules her, she deserved it. If he hurts her, he had a good reason. She truly believes she is wrong and he is right, and feels this at the core of her identity.

If the Luciferan penetrates deeply enough into the victim's core beliefs, then he will literally inhabit or possess that cognitive territory. He will enter the center of the victim's cognitive being and animate it with his core beliefs. This is the essence of psychological assault, and a necessary component of cognitive possession.

Survivors of extreme trauma and disaster can also experience the shock of this kind of breakdown. Accidents, natural phenomena, and other profound disruptions in normal routines can cause core beliefs to shatter. A senseless accident resulting in the death of someone close or a suddenly chaotic eruption of natural power such as an earthquake can so deeply affect a person that his core beliefs are shattered and reorganized to comprehend this new reality. Astute Luciferans know how to take advantage of such catastrophic openings, and often search for potential prey exposed to severe natural disasters.

I believe that mind-breaking is real, that it can occur deliberately through processes like psychological assault or accidentally through a natural catastrophe. My experiences with cultism and with the academic literature surrounding it have confirmed this belief; I accept, however, that many competent researchers believe no such phenomenon exists. Arguments against the reality of "brainwashing" can be explored in the works of Bromley and Shupe (see Bibliography) and others referenced in their works.

The point here, however, is simple: Luciferans believe that psychological assault works, and that when it works, the victim's mind can become possessed. Luciferans know that no matter what causes the core meltdown, or what terminology is used to define the process — psychological assault, conversion, brainwashing, natural stressors, or snapping — the results are the same: the victim's mind becomes open for possession.

Once the victim's core beliefs have been unfrozen and melted, new beliefs can then be inserted. This moment of dramatic meltdown and reorganization of core beliefs can apparently create a radically new human being driven by an entirely new set of beliefs. If this meltdown is intentionally created by a charismatic figure who knows how to implant a possessive belief system, then the broken individual will become controlled; the charismatic figure will then possess the mind of the "newborn" individual.

This may be why many successful organizations have embraced elaborate initiation rituals in which the new recruit is tormented, stressed, and broken down. At the point of break-down, the recruit becomes pliable and open to new beliefs. The leaders of some cults, religious movements, military organizations, political movements and even businesses know how essential this initiation process can be for their future control of members. To inhabit the mind of the new recruit, his core beliefs must be erased and replaced. All essential ties to the past must be cut. All ties to non-controlled outsiders must be eliminated. The recruit must come to believe that identity, safety, security, future, and salvation rest within the organization and nowhere else. He must come to discount his own thoughts and doubts and give full trust and surrender to the beliefs controlled by the organization and its leader. He must allow the possessor's beliefs to own, invade, and dominate his core.

Once this process is completed, the new recruit can be considered possessed. Different degrees of possession are obviously possible, depending on the skill and intensity of the possessor and the receptivity of the victim. But to one degree or another, the recruit's personal will becomes dominated by the will of his possessor. He learns to trust the thoughts and advice of his possessor more than his own thoughts or even his own senses. He gives up his autonomy, and literally "loses his mind." The possessor controls him by controlling his core beliefs.

Such possession is power: control a man's beliefs and you control the man. Even a handful of possessed followers can take a political or religious movement from the periphery of political power to the center. Such followers are fully dedicated and loyal. They ask no questions and harbor no doubts. They will give intense loyalty, energy, devotion and enthusiasm for little or nothing in return and can even become like Hoffer's "true believers", fanatics to be used as "disposable agents." They become this way because their core beliefs tell them that they are serving something profound, beautiful, and true. They cannot "see" their core beliefs any more than a computer can "see" its own operating system. They simply follow directions, believing all the time that their decisions are freely made.

Luciferans controlling such core belief systems will of course grow stronger. By possessing core beliefs, they possess believers. And believers motivated by powerful core beliefs can change the world. In the process, they will enrich, feed, and fill the power-lust of the Luciferan controlling them.

Soul Possession

By soul possession I mean the total invasion, domination and ownership of the target's deepest core. By "deep core" I mean that without which the person would cease to exist as a personal entity, as discussed in the last chapter. I am not necessarily referring here to "spirit", as in non-material existence, but instead to that which stands as the center of each person. Body, heart, and mind are important, but they are not yet the deepest level of personal autonomy and identity.

This deeper level, or "soul", seems beyond words; I believe it exists, but I cannot provide evidence or arguments. It resides in the embrace of something beyond my own personal understanding, yet it seems more real than the ephemeral passing of moments and events. It seems to define the essence of personality, if by that word we mean the unique individuality of each person. The word soul is therefore used here as a symbol of the 'deep self', and does not necessarily imply other realms of existence, although it does not rule them out. As mentioned in the Introduction, I remain uncertain about the boundary between the psychological and the spiritual, between matter and spirit.

Luciferans, however, have no doubt about this boundary. For them, spirit and matter are distinct. For them, soul is spiritual; for them, all spiritual realities contain infinitely more energy than anything existing on the lower planes of mind, emotion, and body. Soul devouring and soul possession are therefore deeply attractive, even though spiritual predation requires infinitely more skill and energy than predation on lower levels of the hierarchy. For Luciferans, devouring or possessing the soul of another human being is a unique prize.

When the victim's soul becomes possessed by the Luciferan, the individual simply ceases to function as an independent entity, and all of him — body, heart, mind and soul — fall under the total invasion, domination, and ownership of the possessor. Soul possession penetrates deeper than physical, emotional or cognitive possession. Not only are the victim's physical actions, feelings, and thoughts controlled, but his unique personal essence as well. He can then seem to be an entirely different human being, a new personality.

This kind of complete possession means that the victim has totally capitulated and has no resolve or resources left. Defense against the aggressor has ended. Unlike physical, emotional, and cognitive possession, where the victim still has strength and perhaps even the will left to fight the invader, soul possession implies complete and utter surrender. The victim has been broken and his personality replaced, and he cannot mend himself.

Cults and Soul Possession

Does soul possession mean death of the soul? The soul — whether defined spiritually or as a metaphor of the person's deepest essence — still lives, yet in an extraordinarily limited and deprived existence. Those who have been this deeply possessed, and who have been successfully freed, describe the experience as being 'in limbo'. Some ex-cult members, for example, articulate a kind of suspended numbness to explain the experience. They remember what they did, what actions their bodies took, but they felt like observers, as if something else was in control. It was as if they were in stasis, in trance, suspended somewhere outside themselves.

Some ex-cult members can clearly describe the new personality that invaded and replaced their own. This possessing personality, or cult personality, seemed to have taken over at a specific time. Victims will usually remember when it first entered — and therefore when they lost control. This personality shift almost always seems to have occurred during the "snapping" moment described by Conway and Seigelman.

I remember working with many of these victims, and recalling the moments of "reverse snapping" when the cult persona broke free and the person's previous personality reasserted itself. It is an astonishing experience, and is intimately understood and recognized by those who work as "exit counselors" (i.e., who specialize in helping cult members leave cults). Something leaves — the possessing cult personality — and its exit can be as sudden and dramatic as the snapping transition from sleep to full wakefulness. Upon leaving the group and its personality behind, victims usually feel strange, disoriented, and unfamiliar with themselves. Many report that they seem to be the same age emotionally and intellectually as when they first entered the cult, even if that was years ago; it is as if their person were 'set aside', their personal growth stunted while the cult persona within them swelled and assumed control.

This notion of 'cult personality' can be understood as an expression or extension of the cult's own 'personality' which invades and possesses the new recruit under the cult leader's direction and inspiration. This same personality can apparently inhabit more than one member of the group, leading to the bizarre experience reported by many outsiders that everyone they met in the group was the same.

I initially encountered this odd phenomenon while working with several different members of one particular cult group in Toronto and encountering the same basic persona in each one of them. This is hard to describe. It is like meeting members of a particularly tight family, who all share certain beliefs, habits, and turns of phrase. Or it is like dealing with the tightly trained sales representatives of a hard selling corporation: they might as well be the same person. But it is infinitely deeper than these examples. Family members have their own personalities, as do salesmen; cult members from this group in Toronto did not. It was as if one persona acted through all of the members I met.

In his book *The Discipling Dilemma*, Flavil Yeakley reported his research on a group which called itself the "Church of Christ". Using the Myers-Briggs assessment tool, (which categorizes people into certain personality types), he had cult followers describe their personality before involvement in the group, their personality at the present time, and their personality as they would like it to be in the future. Results were clear: the "before" descriptors ran the full range of personality types expected in the general population, the "now" descriptors were narrowed to only one or two types, and the "future" descriptors were all one type only. This type happened to be that possessed by the group's leader, who when questioned said that it was of course the personality of Jesus himself.

There are many ways to interpret Yeakley's results. For example, the followers could be simply modeling the leader's personality type according to understood principles of behaviorism and social modeling. Why invoke a concept like possession? The answer has already been given above: if possession means invasion, ownership and domination, then clearly these cult followers have been possessed. Possession does not exclude behaviorism or modeling; on the contrary, these forces are simply further tools used by predators to ensure possession.

Other examples of soul possession could be mentioned. There are some children whose mothers dominate them so completely that they cease developing their own independent personalities. Multiple personality (Dissociative Identity Disorder) and related dissociative disorders can possibly result. The child's core self, or soul, becomes buried inside clusters of alternate identities and dominated by them — especially those implanted by the most abusive parent.

I do not believe that victims this deeply possessed can free themselves. They can only be freed with outside help. Soul possession is just too deep and all-encompassing. This depth was realized early in the anti-cult movement (although the term possession was never used: mind control, brainwashing and other related terms were used instead), and led to the now illegal practice of forcible deprogramming — kidnapping cult members and taking them to a safe location where the cult's possessive influence could recede. At the time, no other solutions were thought possible.

Are there other possibilities? It does occur that some cult members leave voluntarily. Some may become ill, and are no longer useful to the cult, and are sent away. Some go on to have "conversion careers", where they move from one possessing group to another. Yet others receive "exit counseling" and apparently recover. As with any general rule, exceptions are always possible. But I firmly believe that when soul possession is in place, when the possessor has the will and knowledge to maintain the possession, and when unpredictable factors do not emerge to disrupt the process, victims will simply not have the strength, will, or resources to extract themselves.

THE SOUL-POSSESSED

What do others see when someone becomes soul-possessed? Maybe not what might be expected. The soul-possessed are not necessarily catatonic, autistic, or withdrawn in some other way, as might be anticipated. They often have busy, normal lives indistinguishable from others around them. They may well be married with children, they may be employed, they may even have circles of influential acquaintances.

They can be found in all professions. This may seem strange at first: wouldn't their lives come to a dramatic halt? Wouldn't their possession alter and even end their ability to conduct a normal life? Wouldn't they be like some strange version of the "walking dead"? Wouldn't they just halt normal social intercourse and take on the dead weight of something slow, ugly and easily identified?

Not necessarily. Their physical, emotional, and cognitive energies are not in their own control, but these energies still function under the control of an outside entity. They can still walk, talk, and act. They move through life appearing normal, despite the reality of their deep imprisonment.

I do not intend to seem manipulatively dramatic about this. We are not talking here about moviemaker George Romero's legions of the walking dead, or of hooded chanting zombies united by their submission to some kind of fanatic anti-hero. We are not talking about a conspiracy of biblical proportions known only to a few 'enlightened masters'. I am simply referring to the possibility that deep soul-possession is more common than most of us are willing to understand or accept.

The soul-possessed can seem normal. But take a closer look, and you will always come across a rigid wall preventing them from having meaningful contact with anyone or anything except the possessing entity. The possessed person is infatuated and enthralled with the possessor. This relationship is everything. Nothing else matters. Everything else is secondary. The person's entire being becomes directed toward the possessor; happiness and joy, security, peace of mind — these only occur when the possessor is present. The person's sense of right and wrong is built solely around the possessor: what is morally right is what enhances the possessor, what is wrong or evil is what hurts the possessor. The wall keeps out everything else.

The possessed therefore have no real friends because they are never intimate except with the possessor, and this relationship cannot be considered friendship. They are disconnected and isolated within, yet attuned completely to the possessor. They seem to be missing something fundamental: people who try to reach them are met with a cold barrier of refusal. They never talk of their own personal feelings, hopes, or dreams. They are chilling people to know, and they leave a kind of cold and empty feeling in those who try to reach them. Real connections are simply not possible. The wall is actually a prison cell, and the possessed person is locked in, with no power left to break out.

Anyone trying to get close to them will eventually encounter this imprisonment. Reaching out to the possessed person can be frightening: cold prison walls will meet hands searching for warmth, and hard stone will greet arms wanting to embrace.

Those who try to push past these walls will meet with more than just cold resistance. The possessed person will seldom welcome anyone offering freedom, because imprisonment is all he now knows. Freedom is terrifying, because he believes he would then lose the life-giving nourishment provided by his captor. He has lost the memory of freedom, and has come to love his captivity.

The depth of this fear of freedom depends on the length of the possession and the age of onset: the younger the person when possession begins, the harder to break free. This makes intuitive sense, because possessed young children have little opportunity to develop their own core self, and so have little to fall back upon if their possession eventually ends. Adults suddenly possessed, however, have a better chance, because they usually have a core sense of self to fall back upon.

If the possession is sudden, as with older youth and adults joining cults, then family and friends will tend to see the following:

a) a sudden and complete transformation of personality; the "new" person is a complete rejection of the "old".

b) total rejection of all old friends, family, and relevant others. Communication and connections are all cut.

c) a new "language": the person will speak with a jargon that is complete in itself, but unfamiliar to old friends, and completely out of alignment with his old personality.

d) a whole new "family" of people, all of them connected to the possessing entity, will suddenly encircle the person. Outsiders will not be allowed to enter this circle.

e) a rejection and suppression of all critical questioning and doubt about the possessing entity.

f) a willingness to do whatever the possessing entity asks, no matter what the costs: this could mean anything from stealing money to harming people targeted by the possessing entity, to maintaining an outward facade or normalcy

g) a virulent hatred of the possessing entity's critics and enemies, and a desire to cause them harm. Generally, a deep suspicion and rejection of all outsiders who have not submitted to the possessing entity.

h) a powerful belief that a dark and secret conspiracy exists against the possessing entity, and that this conspiracy can only be defeated by expanding the possessor's power and influence in the real world.

i) a "love" of the possessor so deep as to be coiled within the person's basic survival needs: the possessed person believes that death, annihilation or worse will result if she ever challenges the possessor. Generally, a primal fear of breaking free of the possessor: "if I oppose you, I'll die."

j) the annihilation of selfhood: the possessed person ceases to operate independently. He or she turns to the possessing entity for answers to all problems, and for decisions for all questions. "If you don't own me, I don't know who I am, so you have to tell me what to do."

k) an apparent pleasure in being possessed. "I was never happy away from you; I'm only happy and alive in your presence."

l) an imperviousness to reason, emotion, appeal, other than that offered by the possessing entity: only the possessor's voice is relevant and meaningful.

What Possesses?

If possession is real, if it is common, and if all of us can be possessed on one level or another, and to one degree or another, then the obvious question remains: what or who does the possessing?

So far I have mentioned Luciferans, and in the context of emotional possession I also briefly mentioned other entities. But many entities other than individuals consciously committed to Luciferan principles can possess. A target can be physically, emotionally, mentally, and even soul-possessed by many entities: by organizations, families, and other individuals. I have also come to believe that all of us can be possessed by our own personal habits (which I will be calling "intramemes"), and by outside entities such as powerful belief systems (termed "extramemes" here). The possibility of possession by discarnate entities or spirits will be considered as well. Each of these possessing entities will now be examined in turn. The level of possession — body, heart, mind, or soul — will not be discussed, because the assumption here is that each of these entities can possess at any of these levels.

POSSESSION BY INDIVIDUALS

One individual can possess another. Some marriages are little more than the complete absorption of one partner by another. Personal identity is obliterated, and the possessing partner totally transforms the personality of his or her mate.

Possessed women are simply unable to act because they are no longer the source of their own will: that role has been taken over by the possessing husband. This may be why so many women in this condition return to their spouses after turning to the services of women's shelters: they have lost the power of individual thought and action.

Although some feminists might hate to admit it, women are equally capable of possessing their men. The advantage of superior physical strength is absolutely irrelevant for the deeper forms of possession. In fact, women may be superior to men in the arts of possession. Men have dominated women physically in the past, so perhaps women have had to learn other ways to wield power. They may have become particularly skilled in the emotional realm; abusive women will use their abilities to invade, dominate, and own men without compunction, hesitation, or regret.

Marriage therapists will therefore find themselves swamped with the possession problem, although they may never actually frame their work in this way.

So what does one individual need to possess another? Certain skills and attitudes, all of which are manipulatory or predatory in nature. The techniques of psychological assault are necessary, as is the capacity to obtain great pleasure from power over others. To embrace and love domination, invasion, and ownership of others and to thrive and grow healthy on powaqqatsi is probably more important than knowing the specific techniques of psychological assault, because these skills can always be learned one way or another by possessors who love to possess. Trial and error, experience, or even experiment will produce the knowledge.

Breaking down a target and inserting oneself at the center of the victim's soul: this is a profound pleasure for true Luciferans and for non-Luciferans attracted to power. It requires the removal of conscience and compassion: identifying with victims' pain, or respecting their right to exist cannot enter into the equation. Once possessed, the target can then become a disposable agent available to enhance the Luciferan's will and desire. Until possession is understood as a powerful force animating many personal relationships, possessors will continue to pursue and control their quarry without fear of discovery.

POSSESSION BY FAMILY

The family can possess. A child can be so entirely penetrated and controlled by his family that his unique individual identity can cease to exist. He then becomes an agent of family dynamics, acting them out mechanically, predictably, and unconsciously. Thus the abused child goes on to abuse, the child of alcoholics goes on to alcoholism, the child of coercive parents goes on to become coercive.

Family therapists can be understood in this context as exorcists trying to relieve the individual of familial and perhaps even multi-generational possession.

Luciferan families are breeding grounds for instruction in the art of possession. Luciferan parents wish to possess their children, and will use them as efficiently and coldly as a spider devouring its young. Surviving children of Luciferan parents will often rise up in turn to devour their own children and eventually their own Luciferan parents, possessing their energy, wealth, and power if possible.

From time to time, Luciferan children are born into non-Luciferan homes. The result is always disastrous for the parents because their child will inexplicably try to possess everything he or she can: attention, time, money, emotional energy. Such children are never satisfied, are never fulfilled. Their demands are relentless and almost impossible to resist. No amount of counseling, therapy, discipline, threats, discussions, or guidance will change this. No amount of love will ever be enough, because the child is not seeking love, just power. The parents will be mortified, and will probably age and die without understanding their child's betrayal.

The best Luciferans devour and possess their parents and/or children without raising suspicion. They will possess while appearing to love, devour while seeming to give. M. Scott Peck wrote about such families in his book *People of the Lie*, and his case studies remain the best available. (He did not frame these families as Luciferan, but rather as evil, and he described the essential feature of such evil people as *the lie*, hence the title). Adam Crabtree, a therapist from Toronto, also includes case studies of family possession in his book *Multiple Man: Explorations in Possession and Multiple Personality*.

POSSESSION BY ORGANIZATIONS

Organizations can possess. Cults such as the People's Temple in Jonestown show how a charismatic leader can literally possess the minds, hearts, and actions of followers. Reverend Moon was alleged to have said to his disciples: "I am your brain", and "what I wish must be your wish."

As mentioned earlier, in my own work with cults I saw and felt the strange reality of group possession by meeting member after member of certain cult groups and basically meeting the same group persona time and again. The group's leader is usually the paradigm and model of implanted perfection. Deprogramming members from a cult basically means releasing the individual's core identity from the group's possession.

Cults are probably the best example of pure group possession, but other types of organization can possess as well. Like cults, totalitarian political organizations intrude into minds of followers in an attempt to possess them entirely. Orwell's *1984*, for example, is about political possession, the complete absorption of individuality into the collective political whole. Democracy itself can be understood as a revolution by the individual against the kind of political possession found in fascism and other forms of totalistic or totalitarian political organizations.

But if political organizations can possess, so can business corporations. Employees can be so deeply possessed by the corporation employing them their life outside it is pale and nonexistent. Their entire being is controlled, invaded, and owned by the corporation.

Some managers of modern corporations wish to exert as much possessive control over employees as possible. They do this by asserting intrusive and possessive control over their upper levels of management. The corporate "spirit" is supposed to infuse these managers, who are then expected to pass it on to employees, like priests of some arcane religious order.

I would go so far as to submit that one of the strongest factors contributing to a corporation's success is the extent to which it possesses the core beliefs and personality of each employee. The more that individual autonomy and creativity are redirected to passionately serve the corporate agenda, and the more each individual conforms to the 'corporate spirit', then the stronger the organization will become. Employees need to be 'aligned' with the corporation's vision and mission: the more aligned they are, the tighter, stronger, and more effective the organization becomes. With few dissenting voices and with the enthusiastic emotion of its members, the organization is free to shoot like a steel arrow into its opponents, without fear of internal dissent. Any corporation able to align and transform its employees to embrace the corporate mission and vision will be extremely successful. This probably seems ridiculous and outrageous for most readers. What right do I have to assert that some corporations can possess their employees, or that corporate success can depend on how much it possesses its employees?

To explain this, I will refer to an article I wrote some time ago called *Cults and Corporations*. The work compared corporate structures with cults, and explored the strange new relationship between some cults and corporations. It provides a foundation for my claims about corporate possession. In hindsight — it was originally written some time ago — it is actually about possession, although I did not realize this at the time. I sought to express the actual nature of an organization as a willful and possessing entity. To possess, it must theoretically be alive. But how can an organization possess, unless it is somehow a "living" consciousness?

My answer is this: I believe organizations are organic systems, that they are more than the sum of their human parts just as humans are more than the sum of their organic parts, and that they can be described as "alive". Crabtree, drawing on the long history of occult writings on the subject, uses the term group-mind to describe this sense of independent existence. Gustav Le Bon explored this idea in his book *The Crowd*, as did William McDougall in his work *The Group Mind*.

Some systems theorists have taken the idea from obscure occult thought into the mainstream: Oshry and Oshry state in their article "Middle Group Dynamics: Ramifications for the OD Unit" in the book *Trends and Issues in OD* (OD means "organization development"): "Not long ago a colleague confessed to us that despite twenty years of consulting, he had not until recently seen or treated either groups or organizations as realities: he had not perceived them to be entities in their own right and something other than collections of individual actions or interpersonal interactions..." a group can be "considered as an entity in its own right, oriented toward its own survival and development and toward maintaining its existence and developing its potential within the system."

In sum, I believe that organizations are alive. Interested readers are encouraged to explore this idea; the main point here is that *Luciferans believe that organizations are alive, and use them to deprive lower-order humans of their freedom through possession.* An astute Luciferan knows how to use the organization's power as a kind of talisman to control employees and outsiders. This always translates into more personal power.

To return to organizational possession: if human freedom itself can be understood as a primal struggle against possession, then within human history this has largely meant possession by a group or organization whether this be the church, the family, the tribe, the nation-state, and now the corporation. Perhaps it can be said that a person is free to the extent that he is not possessed by another person, by a group, or by some other dictating force, but instead has bargained an equitable balance with them. Luciferans also want freedom, but they believe they can only obtain it by possessing others and therefore removing their freedom. Luciferans do not believe in universal freedom because for them it always has been — and always will be — impossible: only the strong deserve freedom, and only the ultimate possessor can be universally free.

The strong can be found at the top of influential organizations. They seek the power to possess others, and the predatory skill to avoid possession themselves. Organizations provide an open jungle of rich predatory potential, and so Luciferans exploit them passionately.

Luciferans will therefore move into positions of power in totalitarian organizations and corporations (or create their own) where possession is easy, where massive resources and energies can be drained with relative ease, where the chances of discovery are remote, and where real resistance is difficult if not impossible to mount. They seek organizational power because they can devour and possess without limit, and then be admired, respected, or even envied for it.

Unionism can be seen as one form of rebellion against corporate possession (unfortunately many unions themselves have naturally gone on to become just as possessive), although union leaders would not frame their cause in these terms. Luciferans are safe in corporations, and will continue to be safe for the foreseeable future. Incidentally, I have no illusions about what I have written here; it may be mocked, ridiculed and dismissed. But I also believe it will be received and understood by those who work and live in corporations, who are aware of the darker side of corporate life, and who know instinctively that something is very wrong in some corporations.

Other types of organizations can possess; I have mentioned political movements, cults and corporations, but could also include religious organizations, therapeutic groups, special-interest causes, and so on. These are all specific examples of the same general principles, however, so I would like to move on to a different type of possessing entity: to something I call *extramemes*.

Individuals can be possessed by other individuals, by family, and by organizations. I believe they can also be possessed by "extramemes" such as intense belief systems. An extrameme is defined here as a powerful cluster of thoughts, opinions, and beliefs which exist in human society over time, and which perpetuate themselves by inhabiting host individuals. Such memes can usually be identified by a single term or cluster of related slogans: "communism", "capitalism", "feminism", "USA", "Jew", "Christ", "Mohammed" are just some examples.

The term "meme" comes from Richard Dawkin's work. Drawing an analogy between genetics and human evolution, he states that (quoted from Barlow's From Gaia to Selfish Genes): "I am an enthusiastic Darwinian, but I think Darwinism is too big a theory to be confined to the narrow context of the gene ... I think that a new kind of replicator has recently emerged on this very planet ... it is the meme, examples of which include tunes, ideas, catch-phrases, clothes, ways of making pots or of building arches ... memes should be regarded as living structures ... When you plant a fertile meme in my mind you literally *parasitize my brain*, [my emphasis] turning it into a vehicle for the meme's propagation in just the way that a virus may parasitize the genetic mechanism of a host cell ... consider the idea of God ... the survival value of the god meme in the meme pool results from its great psychological appeal ... God exists, if only in the form of a meme with high survival value, or infective power, in the environment provided by human culture ... memes have all the longevity of other replicators: longevity, fecundity, and copying fidelity... the meme-complexes of Socrates, Leonardo, Copernicus, and Marconi are still going strong... a meme may have evolved in the way that it has, simply because it is advantageous to itself."

Dawkins goes on to contradict himself by adding that genes and memes have no foresight. They are apparently unconscious blind replicators, even though they are to be regarded as living structures leaping from brain to brain, and despite the fact that they apparently work for their own selfish advantage.

Another enthusiastic Darwinian, Daniel Dennett, anthropomorphises memes in the same way. In his book *Darwin's Dangerous Idea* he says: "memes definitely manipulate us" ... "memes are capable of instructing, not protein synthesis as genes do, but behavior" ... "The day may come when nonhuman meme-evaluators suffice to select and arrange for the preservation of particular memes, but for the time being, memes still depend at least indirectly on one or more of their vehicles' spending at least a brief pupal stage in a remarkable sort of meme nest: a human mind." According to Dennett, memes actively seek to propagate themselves and tend "to disable the selective forces arrayed against them." To drive his point home he says: "The haven all memes depend on reaching is the human mind, but a human mind itself is an artifact created when memes restructure a human brain in order to make it a better habitat for memes" and "Consider the most obvious meme example: the meme for celibacy (and chastity, I might add, to close a notorious loophole). This meme complex *inhabits* (my italics) the brains of many a priest and nun... we may not know the detailed history of the infestation." Finally, he states that "no one meme rules anybody, what makes a person the person he or she is are the coalitions of memes that govern."

In Luciferan terms, both Dawkins and Dennett are clearly stating their belief that memes possess us in order to enhance their own survival. What makes their beliefs so interesting is that both men are diehard materialists and positivists. If such distinguished gentlemen of science feel free to say that memes possess human beings, then I feel free to take their lead. Using and adapting the term meme rather liberally, (and probably in ways Dawkins would not approve) we can therefore think of extramemes as living entities that drift from generation to generation seeking individuals to enter, possess, and inhabit.

Some of them are extremely powerful, entering and directing the lives of millions over many generations. Others may be more culturally or geographically limited, having a shorter life span. As with all living things, some may be beneficial, some harmful. Some may elevate human life, others may degrade it. We can think of an extrameme as being alive. By "alive" I mean the following. First, it grows. Second, it replicates. Third, it absorbs and uses energy. And fourth, it seeks its own expansion and survival.

This means that the extrameme will actively fight its destruction. Its ability to fight depends on the amount of energy its host has fed it, and the length of time the feeding has gone on. The more energy and time devoted to it, the more powerful and alive it becomes.

Strong extramemes can easily find, enter and live within human hosts. Examples of such memes could include patriotic love of country, a belief in capitalism, religious faith, and many others. Some individuals remain immune to the automatic acceptance of hugely influential extramemes, whereas others seem to allow their entry easily.

Hoffer's *true believers*, for example, could be described as individuals whose entire lives are given over to an external possessing meme. I suppose it would probably make more sense to say that true believers seek out intense extramemes and allow themselves to be possessed by them, because to attribute life and intention to belief clusters probably extends the credulity of most readers. Nevertheless, such clusters appear to act as if they are alive: they reproduce, ingest, inhabit, attack, defend, and move across generations by entering, thriving, and existing within individuals at given times and places.

Some extramemes apparently have the power to arouse intense loyalty, passion, even self-sacrifice in their individual hosts. Many people will die for the extrameme, or intense cause, that they serve. This seems to ensure the replication and survival of the extrameme.

Cults know how to systematically implant their own extramemes into new recruits. The result is a true-believer who is absolutely closed to all other outside ideas, thoughts, and competing memes. These possessive extramemes need to become all-encompassing and totalistic to their hosts, inspiring deep feelings of devotion and even love. Most powerfully possessive extramemes carry beautiful and life-enhancing messages. Such extramemes convince their hosts that they are serving something noble, when in fact they are serving only the extrameme itself. That is, the host's energy does not serve the beautiful cause but only the extrameme's need for replication and survival.

Luciferans will deliberately use existing extramemes to enhance the possession of their targets, or create new ones to achieve the same goal (for example, the objects-of-focus mentioned earlier). No matter — the meme only has to be able to burrow as deeply as possible into the target's cognitive core; after this, if the Luciferan controls the extrameme, then he can in effect possess the target by proxy. The meme is attached to the Luciferan like a leash, and if it buries itself deeply within its target, then a tug on the leash will pull the target as well.

Luciferans prefer using memes that are impressively beautiful and life-enhancing because predatory disguise is enhanced: the possessed victims believe in the *cause*, never realizing that their enthusiasm, sacrifice, energy and zeal are being used for other purposes by Luciferans behind the scenes. Some politicians, religious leaders, and others skilled in the manipulation of powerful extrameme symbol-clusters know this truth: control the extrameme, and you control its human host.

Luciferans believe that extramemes require less energy than direct personal possession; this 'possession by proxy', however, can yield the same end result — invasion, domination, and ownership of the target.

POSSESSION BY INTRAMEMES

An individual can be possessed by internal forces of personality and habit. I would like to call such forces *intramemes*. Intramemes are personally generated by each individual, whereas extramemes can be said to exist outside the individual historically and/or within other currently living minds.

An intrameme can be understood as a force of energy established by the individual through habit. Thus, a lifetime of smoking creates a 'smoking intrameme' which seeks to perpetuate itself by possessing its host; addictions to many things — alcohol, drugs, sex, work — can be reframed as possessive intramemes.

This does not exclude an actual physiological addiction for, say, nicotine or alcohol, but can be understood as a complex of associations, memories and cognitive habits built on top of the actual physical addiction. This might explain why alcohol and nicotine are so hard to quit, even after the physio-chemical addictions have been overcome. A smoking intrameme, for example, might include a series of thoughts such as "well, you can't live forever", "I think I look sophisticated when I smoke", "my parents smoked and so do I", "smoking makes me feel good", and so on, all wrapped around a core belief such as "I should smoke", or "smoking is good for me". If pleasant emotions and sensations such as relaxation, peaceful drowsiness, and so on are also connected to the intrameme, then its power is strengthened.

The longer the intrameme is in place, and the more central it becomes in the person's life, the more power it seems to accumulate, and the more difficult it becomes to remove. Lifelong behavior patterns installed at an early age can therefore become deeply possessive.

Possible intramemes are infinite: the intrameme's core can be anything imaginable. Sexual obsessions, an event from one's own personal past, images of abuse or neglect, an imagined career goal: the intrameme's actual content does not seem as important as its force and power within the individual's daily life.

Perhaps even some mental illnesses, such as multiple personality disorders, could be understood as extremely elaborate intramemes which served a specific function at the time of their creation, but which have gone on to possess their creator later in life. Phobias could also be understood in this way: a person's profound fear of spiders may have been generated by a specific experience early in life when deep fear and terror were somehow associated with the spider's image; this deep connection then continues to thrive and survive throughout the sufferer's entire life.

Sexual obsessions could be redefined as living intramemes that are initially created by the individual for various reasons, but which eventually assert control because of their frequent invocation by the host. The host gains sexual pleasure and comfort from the obsession, while the obsession itself gains life through the host's habituation.

The key here is to begin thinking of these 'things' we create as both allies and enemies: they serve some initial purpose by providing comfort, protection, security, and understanding. But they then take on a kind of life of their own, insisting on their propagation and survival despite their value to us. They can even become destructive, ultimately causing great pain and suffering for their hosts.

I believe the Recovery Movement (i.e. Bradshaw, *et al*) can be understood as an attempt to wrestle power and control away from intramemes that have asserted profound control over their hosts: a host's first experience of intoxicated pleasure, blessed oblivion, and tension reduction can lead to a lifetime devoted to an alcohol-based intrameme which initially gives relief but which later on demands total control. All such intramemes have a price, and the price may well be the invasive ownership and domination of possession.

As with extramemes, we can consider intramemes as being alive. We all create intramemes. They are invoked for a number of reasons, and they serve a variety of functions, some positive, some negative. We create them, we feed them, we nurture them, we love them. We do this because they initially give us something wonderful: sensations of peace, joy, escape, relief. Yet they demand a price. They do not come free. They demand payment, and this payment means we begin to serve them by feeding them energy, attention, power, and control. We can even come to serve them with a kind of religious devotion, and they in turn can take on a kind of autocratic possessing presence.

This kind of destructive and possessive intrameme is like a parasite: it inhabits and lives off the host's energies. It diverts energy from other vital functions to enhance its own life. As in the biological realm, some parasites are useful, and provide something in return for their food. Others do not, and simply drain their host without giving anything in exchange. They can behave somewhat like parasites in the intestinal tract: they co-habit with the host while draining away precious food and energy. The host is left drained, tired, fatigued, and vulnerable to disease.

Such totally destructive intramemes can even become cancerous, and begin to assert profound control over their host. They take on a driving energy which feeds their own specific living identity, sometimes in direct competition with their host. Multiple personalities are possibly an example: each personality has at its core a specific identity "imprint" such as rage, innocence, lust, hate. Each of these emotions has been split off to become a separate living identity. Alternate personalities can be understood as intramemes which have taken on the attributes of full personality systems.

Such powerfully possessive intramemes are hard to break. When smokers, drug addicts, and other carriers of negative intramemes attempt to destroy these life forms, they overlook the fact that they have invited and created the alternate life form which now possesses and inhabits them. It is possible to remove or 'exorcise' such entities, but only at great cost. Not only must the host gather enough energy and strength to fight the intrameme (much of which has been claimed and used by the meme itself), but if successful they must then face the original reason why he or she invited and created it in the first place. Such reasons usually involve the avoidance of intense fear, pain, and other aversive events.

If the individual host succeeds in weakening or removing the meme, he or she will have suffered much pain and will be in a weakened position to confront the original fear and terror. Most people simply give up and continue to feed the meme with energy. In exchange, the meme protects the individual from the original pain. If the meme becomes more possessive, intrusive, and aggressive, then the individual will become completely possessed by it. Drug addicts, workaholics, and compulsives of all kinds can be understood as victims of intra-meme possession. The more powerful and intrusive a meme becomes, the more difficult it is to extract without administering severe damage or even death to its host.

Luciferans intimately understand and appreciate the intrameme's power to disable potential victims. A victim already drained by a powerful intrameme is an easy target, much like a sick or disabled deer is to the wolf. The Luciferan can possess such individuals easily for a number of reasons. First, the target is already weakened. Defenses are down, and entry is therefore easy. The target has little time to consider anything but a driving need for a way out, based on an excruciating awareness of diminishing personal strength.

Second, the target is desperate. Powerful intramemes can leave a trail of waste in the target's soul that stinks of despair and depression. The target wants out, badly, and will therefore be open to influences that the instinct for self-preservation would normally prohibit. The Luciferan can then offer a 'healing', which is actually just intrameme substitution. That is, the target is primed and ready to embrace a competing intrameme to replace the destructive one: hence the many reformed alcoholics who seem to become religious addicts instead. The Luciferan simply has to identify a competing possessing intrameme for the target, who is then deeply impressed: a healing then follows, and the Luciferan calmly inserts similar control after heroically defeating the intrameme. I think that many television miracle healers know exactly what I am talking about.

Such personal intramemes are easy to defeat and replace for Luciferans who recognize the intrameme's possessive intentions and needs. This may seem to contradict my earlier statements about their tenacity. However, the Luciferan asks nothing from the victim. No unpleasant truths have to be faced, no daily discipline is required, and no suffering is necessary. The victim just has to let go of one water-soaked log in the middle of the ocean, and grab hold of another. Nothing really changes; the victim is still lost and powerless.

Luciferans understand the intrameme's struggle for life. Relatives know relatives. Luciferans have no illusions about intramemes any more than one power-aggressor has over another. They 'see' each other. They know each other. This knowledge offers a bond. It also offers a hierarchy: the basic message from the Luciferan to the intrameme is to move out because a more powerful possessor is on the scene.

Third, such targets are familiar with being possessed. The powerful intrameme is a lifelong habituated possessor; the possessed person knows no other freedom. The bird is used to the cage. The substitution of a new possessing power is therefore easy and natural: one cage for another. The Luciferan simply has to convince the target that a new possession is not possession at all but liberation, healing, and freedom. Cult leaders understand this shift of possession (addiction, dependency) intimately, and use it to expand their influence and power. Abusive therapists do the same, as do possessive partners in relationships. From the Luciferan's perspective, intrameme and extrameme possession have the same advantage. Once the meme falls under the Luciferan's control, the victim will not need constant personal attention from the Luciferan but rather becomes "possessed by proxy": the possessing intrameme holds the victim in check, absorbs crucial energy, and transmits this power back to the Luciferan. Luciferans may therefore consciously enlist the support of possessing intramemes instead of substituting or creating another to replace it. This arrangement is acceptable to the Luciferan as long as the intrameme is firmly under the Luciferan's control and, like a kind of spiritual pyramid sales scheme, feeds back a portion of the 'profits' (energy) to the controlling Luciferan.

Intramemes that attempt to break away from this arrangement to enhance their own power are killed. Others are allowed to exist as long as their predation serves the 'higher' Luciferan power without betrayal. Victims will have little if any awareness of this devouring hierarchy using and exhausting their vital energies. If they knew, they would fight. Ignorance keeps them docile.

As a final comment: I cannot prove that intramemes or extramemes exist. Nor can I prove that Luciferans know how to use them to possess victims. I only know that I have encountered such entities both personally and in my work, and have seen how outsiders can control them. I have also found that the meme concept fits these experiences better than other psychological or spiritual explanations I have encountered, such as "complexes" or "demons". But pragmatic Luciferans are not bothered with terminology — they just know that yet another tool in the possession arsenal can be used to invade, dominate, or own their victims.

POSSESSION BY DISCARNATE ENTITIES

Now comes a difficult question. Is spirit possession real? We may be generous enough to accept the idea of possession itself, we may even accept that

124

individuals, family systems, organizations, corporations, intramemes and extramemes can possess. But spirits?

I am not going to spend much time on this subject for two reasons. First, I do not know much about it and, as mentioned in the introduction, I am uncertain about spiritual realities. Second, most of us can easily dismiss possession by dismissing the existence of spirits, and for reasons already explained, this is unfortunate. Possession itself is so widespread that focusing excessively on the spirit variety alone is misleading. There is ample material on spirit possession, both pro and con, and I feel no need to add to it. Having said this, I feel compelled to make a few comments in the Luciferan context, because Luciferans believe in spiritual reality and act accordingly: they extend predation and power acquisition into the spiritual realms.

If we define a "spirit" as a discarnate entity — that is, a conscious living being without a physical body — and further attribute such entities with consciousness, will, intelligence, reasoning, and emotion, so they are like us in crucial ways except the physical, then the question becomes: do such entities exist or not?

On the face of it, why not? Why should we assume that consciousness must have a physical body? Couldn't it exist without the machinery of the body? This is an ancient metaphysical problem: is mind dependent on matter, or vice-versa? It seems terribly egocentric to believe that consciousness is only limited to physical matter. Just as our comprehension of the vastness of outer space leads most thinking humans to assume that we are not the only form of sentient life in the universe, so too our vast inner space compels the same conclusion. Isn't it possible that consciousness exists in many forms, and perhaps on many levels unknown to most of us at this time?

Humans across the planet throughout time seem to have believed in such entities based on experience, faith, belief, and hope. Needless to say, human civilization is a myriad of visions, tales, stories, reports, speculations, theologies, and myths about such beings. But mass belief does not imply truth, and scientific proof is lacking. If these entities exist, they are not making it easy for us to prove their existence. To make the situation worse, serious literature on the subject has been overwhelmed by pulp novels, horror entertainment, ghost stories, horror movies, true confessions, tabloid sensationalism and other forms of shock schlock.

Despite this, serious literature does exist, and can be divided into two camps. The first holds that spirits are real and that spirit possession is equally real. The second states that while experiences of possession may be powerfully real for the victim, explanations other than invading spirits may be invoked.

As for the first camp: literature in the Christian tradition is of course enormous, beginning with the New Testament itself. Jesus is said to have cast out demons, and Paul makes reference to the "principalities and powers" that are the real enemies of all Christians. The devil and his demons may be considered 'discarnate entities', as can angels and canonized saints. Christian writings other than the Bible have referred to such entities: the monastic-desert tradition in particular has carried works like *The Life of Antony* by Athanasius and similar classics which all provide detailed descriptions of the saint's encounters with demons.

Outside of the ancient Christian religious realm, serious case studies abound: one of the most fascinating is Malachi Martin's book *Hostage to the Devil*. Martin is a former Jesuit professor, and his case studies of possession evoke powerfully compelling images that speak directly to the modern mind. Equally compelling is Scott Peck's *People of the Lie*, arguably one of the most important books on the subject in the last twenty years. Peck is both a psychiatrist and a Christian, but his work is cast with more of a psychoanalytic hue. Both Martin and Peck accept the reality of spirits and spirit possession, and their books are wonderfully and refreshingly accessible.

T.K. Oesterreich, a professor of philosophy in Germany until 1933, when he was persecuted by the Nazis, wrote the work *Possession: Demoniacal and Other*. It overflows with original primary source material, and delivers a trans-historical and cultural survey of the phenomenon. His work remains one of the most balanced and detailed I have read. Adam Crabtree's *Multiple Man* is an equally balanced and fascinating examination of possession. Some transpersonal psychologists and their clients have described their own personal encounters with malevolent spiritual entities during various altered states of consciousness. Personal testaments about the actual existence of such beings are endless: we have anecdotal accounts provided by near-death experiences, out-of-body experiences, trance channeling, hallucinatory drugs, shamanistic journeys and similar phenomena, where individuals apparently contacted non-physical entities. Such experiences are psychologically powerful and vitally real for the individual, but seem difficult to verify through other means.

New Age writers, especially those who assert the reality of channeling, claim to be temporarily possessed by discarnate entities who are benevolent, wise, and friendly. From J. Z. Knight's *Ramtha* to Elizabeth Claire Prophet's *Great White Brotherhood*, charismatic channelers gather groups of faithful followers hungry for wisdom from the beyond.

John Klimo, a professor of psychology, provides a fairly balanced summary of the channeling phenomenon in his book *Channeling*. What gets channeled? According to Klimo, apparently any of the following: "the Channel's higher self, Gods and God, The Universal Mind, the Collective Unconscious, Group beings, Jesus Christ and Other Ascended Masters, Nonhumans, and Discarnate Human Spirits." The possibility of possession by any of these non-physical beings is seldom discussed in the New Age tradition; Klimo grants just two pages to the subject, and tends to dismiss the phenomenon as the actions of "lower astral spirits who want to resume some form of physical existence", or as allegories "to help us better understand the nature of power, the pitfalls of power." This attitude seems common in the New Age community.

Channeling is not new, even in North America. Since the Fox sisters heard their first spirit rap in the mid nineteenth century, friendly spirits have apparently temporarily possessed mediums and provided information from 'the beyond' to members of the seance group. Edgar Cayce, Eileen Garrett, Alice Bailey, Arthur Ford, Ruth Montgomery and others all claim a common heritage in this tradition. From time to time they are 'taken over' temporarily by one discarnate entity or another for various purposes.

Of course the western gnostic, occult, theosophical and metaphysical traditions assert the reality and intrusive presence of many spiritual entities. From Mary Baker Eddy and Madame Blavatsky to Aleister Crowley, contacting and corralling such entities for their wisdom, advice, and direction has been primary. Science is quiet on the subject. This makes sense, because the scientific method assumes standards of proof which demand physical evidence. Since such beings cannot or will not provide such evidence, they are held not to exist. And this leads us straight to the second *camp*. This camp assumes that spirits and discarnate entities do not exist, and that the phenomenon of spirit possession must therefore have other explanations. This perspective does not always deny the impact of the possession experience on each individual, but only seeks to explain the experience as driven by forces and realities other than discarnate entities.

Psychological investigations of spirit possession usually define the phenomenon as something else: hysteria, dissociation, multiple personality, the power of the subconscious mind, archetypes, anomalies, mental disorders, and so on. William Sargeant's books *The Mind Possessed* and *Battle for the Mind* examine the physiological techniques used to induce trance, euphoria and ecstasy prior to the moment of possession, and defines the phenomenon as the outcome of physiological processes. Freud and Jung wrote on the subject, as have other noted theorists and clinicians. Some recent specialists in multiple personality disorder have speculated about the possibility that spirit possession is really a manifestation of Multiple Personality Disorder (now called DPD, or Dissociative Personality Disorder). Whatever their theoretical perspectives, these psychologists or psychiatrists generally assert that spirit possession may be 'real' for the individual but that the experience can be explained psychologically, not supernaturally.

Parapsychological explanations are plentiful. Extrasensory perception (i.e. telepathy, precognition, clairvoyance and clairaudience) is one possibility offered in this tradition. The possessed person is simply picking up material projected telepathically by another living human, and is exhibiting behavior consistent with suggestion, not possession. James Alcock, a professor of psychology at York University in Ontario, has written extensively against parapsychology (see his book *Parapsychology: Science or Magic?*). Such skeptics hammer relentlessly at the foolishness and phoniness of such explanations, and assign them as much credence as the existence of spirits themselves; interested readers can consult any edition of the journal *The Skeptical Inquirer* for a sample of this approach.

Some of the anthropological literature sees spiritual possession as a cross-cultural and trans-historical cohesive ritual force binding many cultures together, its purpose being a kind of cathartic social release. Thus possession serves the collective cultural body in some crucial way, and is not just a psychological or spiritualistic phenomenon but a device designed to serve a specific function such as uniting the cultural group against enemies and other threats.

In my opinion, the best book from this perspective is *Case Studies in Spirit Possession*, edited by Crapanzano and Garrison, which contains scholarly articles with titles such as "Spirits as Socializing Agents", "Conflict and Sovereignty in Kelantanese Malay Spirit Seances", "Psychocultural Exegesis of a Case of Spirit Possession in Sri Lanka", and so on. Felicitas Goodman, an anthropologist from Denison University, writes in this tradition, but is somewhat more accessible. Her books *How About Demons?: Possession and Exorcism in the Modern World*, (valuable for her insights into psycho-physical changes in the possessed person), and *The Exorcism of Anneliese Michel*, illustrate non-spiritual explanations and insights into possession.

Despite these two camps, or perhaps because of them, we still do not really know that much about spirit possession: the question has not been proven or disproven. If we cannot show that spirits exist, how can we possibly assert that spirit possession exists? The answer — we cannot. We can only surmise, weigh the evidence, and then come to a decision. It comes down to one's convictions, one's core beliefs: stubborn materialists versus equally stubborn supernaturalists.

I will not leap onto this particular battlefield to convince you one way or the other. Instead, let us just proceed with the assumption that such entities might be real, and see where it leads.

If such entities exist, then the next logical step is to assume that they aren't all the same. Just as all other forms of life are varied across a single species, so too discarnate entities likely vary. Perhaps their traits are even distributed on a normal curve, as are all human traits from shoe size to intelligence. Thus any imaginable quality or trait might be statistically distributed across various 'species' of discarnate entities. If these beings have free will, then some would logically be kind, compassionate, and caring, while others might well be vicious, cold, and cruel.

Assuming this, then the next step is simple — some discarnate entities might be Luciferan. As such, their desire, their need, would be to grow in personal power, to become gods, to devour and consume, and to possess. Such entities would then be free to act according to these Luciferan principles against whoever — or whatever — they determined to be prey, competitor, or enemy.

Let us imagine. If such beings exist, how would they operate? Assume for a minute that they need to possess. Imagine that they are hunting for food to devour or possess. What attracts them? Imagine they are sailing in a dimension not open to us. They do not see light, form, and physical reality as we do. They see something else. They see a different band of the energy spectrum than we do. They have different senses.

They might therefore 'see' beings who are closed to their invasion, and beings who are open. The open ones somehow give out a signal that they are available for possession, perhaps just as the sick, injured, or elderly elk signals the wolf. The signal says: "Take me, I'm ready for devouring or possession."

The predator then instinctively attacks. The invitation is there. The predator sniffs and examines: is this target weak enough? And what defines weakness? It is hard for us to know: perhaps attachment to an intrameme or extrameme, self-hate, despair, hopelessness, loneliness, fear, hate: all of which used to be called sin. Or perhaps something else. Something beyond our understanding.

Real or false, spirit possession is only one small aspect of the other dimensions of possession. Belief in spirits is not a necessary precondition for accepting the reality of this wider phenomenon of possession, or for its place as a powerful, dynamic, driving Luciferan spirituality. Yet in the words of Malachi Martin: "Evil Spirit is personal, and it is intelligent. It is preternatural, in the sense that it is not of this material world, but it is in this material world. And Evil Spirit as well as good advances along the lines of our daily lives. In very normal ways spirit uses and influences our daily thoughts, actions, and customs and, indeed all the strands that make up the fabric of life in whatever time or place. Contemporary life is no exception ... all three — the possessed, the possessing spirit, and the exorcist — bear a close relation to the reality of life and to its meaning as all of us experience it each and every day." I agree with Martin in this sense, that the basic dynamic of possession — the predatory urge to contain, control, and use other beings — is alive and well in all areas of our daily lives. We do not need confirmation from spirits to verify this obvious Luciferan truth.

Spirits and Demons? Who knows? But as William James noted: "The refusal of modern 'enlightenment' to treat 'possession' [i.e. spirit possession] as a hypothesis to be spoken of as even possible, in spite of the massive human tradition based on concrete experience in its favor, has always seemed to me a curious example of the power of fashion in things scientific. That the demon theory will have its innings again is to my mind absolutely certain."

POSSESSION BY LUCIFERANS

To be possessed by another individual, a family system, an organization, an intrameme or extrameme, or even a discarnate entity: these might be possible. But to be directly possessed by a Luciferan? What does this mean?

There are no 'proxy possessions' here. The Luciferan is not using an extrameme or intrameme to assert substitute control. All is direct and immediate. The Luciferan has decided to possess directly, purposely.

The idea here is simple: to make a person's body do what you want, possess the body; to make a person feel what you want, possess the emotions; to make a person think what you want, possess the mind; to make the person yours completely, possess the spirit. By possessing the target's emotions, Luciferans can induce any feeling they want, from despair, sorrow, and hate, to joy and euphoria; these feelings can then be used as rewards or punishers. By possessing the target's mind, the Luciferan can induce thoughts of suicide or ideas of personal immortality. Such thoughts can then be used as rewards or punishment to control behavior.

Possession by a Luciferan can therefore be ecstatic and addictive. Luciferans can inject sensations of profound joy and euphoria into their victims while deepening the possessive state. For those affected, this ecstasy can be even more pleasurable than possession by liquor, extramemes, or sexual compulsions. Luciferans can insert a kind of euphoria into their victims that rivals the greatest drug. The victim comes to love the possessor, because nothing else delivers such powerful peace and beauty. In this way, the Luciferan mimics God; the victim feels touched by God when in fact he is only being touched by the Luciferan. Possession removes everything: the individual no longer has to think, act, or create. He only has to submit, and then submit some more.

For Luciferans, anyone open to the possibility of submission can be instantly targeted. This includes those who believe submission is the essence of growth and the fertile ground of all knowledge, that without submission there can be no opening to new truth, and that without this opening there can be no change. Those who wish to submit to something other than the dictates of self-will, who wish to surrender to something higher than self, are also potential victims to be manipulated. Those wishing to submit to higher knowledge, who believe that submission is the prime prerequisite to learning, and that learning is itself a kind of openness and submission to forces and truths outside the kingdom of self, are potential victims. For Luciferans, the sickly and life-killing belief that something other than self and self-concern operates in the universe, signals the victim's readiness to be possessed.

Luciferans believe that most prey wish to submit to a creator, a God, because they do not have the hardness of will to usurp God. Knowing this, Luciferans simply insert themselves into individuals who are ready to submit and receive God. That is, they stalk and find prey ready to submit, then present themselves as something worth submitting to. This might mean appearing as a prophet, an ascended master, or God's own messenger. The outpouring of energy released by the victim's submission then flows easily into the Luciferan instead. The victim thinks he has given himself to God when in truth he has offered himself for possession. The victim funnels his essence, perhaps even his soul and spirit into a predatory entity he thinks is God.

In ancient Judeo-Christian terms, this would be called idolatry. Such individuals then get something else, something that only looks and feels like God. Luciferans know they can insert themselves between the individual and "God", that they can divert this upward-and-outward energy for their own enhancement. They know they can possess the individual searching for God by pretending to be God.

Pretending to be God, and then transcending beyond the pretense to actually become God. This is the history of the Luciferan struggle. Possession is just one way of gathering enough energy to accomplish this goal. Luciferans believe that few humans can tell the difference between Luciferan versions of God, and the God-as-God they seek.

Fewer still can mount the necessary defense. Luciferans count on this ignorance, and use it to enhance their power. God may or may not be real, but our search for God is real; Luciferans know they can insert themselves easily into this search and that many victims will fall into the deception. Those who do fall can be drained and used to enhance the Luciferan's growth and power. Nothing tastes as fine to a Luciferan as the worship of followers whose energy has been diverted.

Those unlucky enough to be directly possessed by a powerful Luciferan face a difficult and bleak future.

POSSESSORS

Apart from Luciferans, what characteristics do non-Luciferan possessors share? Possessing wealth, influence, people or any other target seems to depend on the will, skill, and motivation of the possessor, who must desire power above all else. The drive to own, accumulate, invade, and ultimately dominate and control others: this must be the possessor's prime directive, and a deep primal predatory pleasure must surround the whole process.

The predator must find great joy in the act of stalking, invading, dominating and owning a target. Without this kind of powerful drive, the specific techniques of possession will never be enough. With sufficient drive, possession becomes a clearer question of accumulating enough personal power to possess the target. The target may be an object, another being or a person, an organization or a position in an organization, or any other focus of desire.

To fully possess another human being's soul, however, the possessor must go beyond the love of possession, to accept the Luciferan bargain. There is no other way. Conscience must be removed or at least placated and rationalized away, and compassion for the possessed person's suffering must be destroyed. Above all else the possessor must energize her lust for power and absolute freedom.

As mentioned previously, the psychiatrist and author Robert Jay Lifton has suggested that human beings can use two techniques he calls "psychic numbing" and "psychic doubling" to harm others without regret. Lifton's convictions came during a lifetime examining numerous human atrocities and catastrophes, including brutalities committed by Nazi Doctors.

Lifton feels that numbing is a way of turning off normal feelings of compassion or empathy, a kind of detached state in which anything becomes possible. If the process continues long enough, or if other factors enter, then psychic doubling becomes possible: the person dissociates into two diametrically opposed *personas*, a kind of Jekyll and Hyde split. Hence the Nazi Doctor's astonishing ability to show warmth, compassion, and care to his wife, child, and poodle at home in the evening and yet the next day to ruthlessly experiment on an innocent victim in a concentration camp. This normal human capacity to "numb" and "double" may mark the beginning stages of a transition to full predatory status. But it must be transcended to reach full Luciferan potential. The reason? Even when "numbed" or "doubled", the person is still hiding from conscience and compassion, and is existing in a hybrid world of morality and amorality that suggests weakness and indecision. Morality must be killed, absolutely and completely. No dissociation, no compartmentalization. Just annihilation.

Once annihilated, the desire and commitment to serve the Self at the cost of all other "selves" is free to flower. Metaphysically, this annihilation leads to the following position: only my-Self is real; all else is illusion created by my-Self. And my-Self needs to feed. My-Self needs to possess. All else is irrelevant. Numbing and doubling then fade away, and are viewed by a born-again Luciferan predator as nothing more than the infantile strivings of a sick morally-bound human to escape the power of conscience and compassion. If pursued, this commitment to Self can lead to the ultimate transcendence, transformation, and rebirth offered by the Luciferan path.

Numbing and doubling are therefore baby steps on the developmental hierarchy leading to more reality, more vitality, more power, more Luciferism. *Not all predators are Luciferans, but Luciferism is the ultimate spiritual destination for all serious predators.* Once this desire and commitment to Luciferan predation has been made, the predator needs to develop skill in the Luciferan arts. She needs to know the predatory arts of devouring and possession, and of violence and disguise. She needs to nourish the Luciferan state of being through predation.

Most horror fiction is centered on the opening of this predatory state for public view, like a dark flower. Clive Barker's character Shadwell in his book *The Great and Secret Show* is an example. Shadwell has a magic coat. The coat lures and beckons his victims: upon seeing it, they become fascinated, spellbound. Once the victim is close enough, Shadwell opens the coat and asks the victim to look inside. Victims all see something different. One sees the job he has dreamed of for years. Another sees an opulent lifestyle complete with mansions and expensive cars. Yet another sees a hoped-for lover. The more spiritually-minded see a vision of world peace, spiritual fulfillment, or ecstatic spiritual union.

They each see something different, but all sense the realization of their deepest hopes, dreams, and desires, whether physical, emotional, mental, or spiritual. Then they all do the same thing — under Shadwell's urging they reach into the coat to actualize their dream — and are caught. They 'fall' into the coat. The predatory Shadwell simply closes the coat and the victim is trapped within, unable to escape, captured. With each victim Shadwell grows stronger, and his ability to trap yet more victims swells exponentially. Luciferans possess victims in the same way, by offering a compelling invitation (which could be anything from sex to spiritual enlightenment) then trapping, enclosing, controlling, and possessing the victim.

Being Possessed

What is it like to be possessed at this deep level? Let us imagine we can enter this world and see what is there.

Imagine a prison cell with a high ceiling extending into the dark, no light, no warmth, no activity. Still, empty, waiting. Without hope or direction. Lost. Totally passive.

Except for the door, there is nothing else. It is a huge door, locked. It is the only source of light, food, and contact. Through it comes nourishment. The imprisoned victim is consumed by the possibility that the door will open and life will come through it. All his attention, focus, and concentration is directed toward the door, waiting for it to open.

This door is the one source of survival left. Through it comes food, but it is totally controlled by the possessing entity. This entity might be another person, a family system, an organization, a corporation, or something else. Regardless of its nature, this entity is the only contact left between the victim and the reality of life.

The victim believes he is totally, completely and absolutely dependent on nothing else. He believes there is no life without this entity, and attends to nothing else unless the controlling entity directs it. Serving the possessing entity with total devotion and surrender thus becomes a survival issue. No matter how bizarre or illogical to outside observers, to the possessed person, there is nothing as vital as surrender to the possessor. No surrender means no life. It means extinction and death. It means eternal and relentless confinement in the cell, alone forever, the door never opening.

Possession is the utter loss of will, reason, emotion, of action. And pleasure with this loss; love of the possessor for supplying life through the locked door. It is a state of suspended nothingness. Just waiting. And waiting. And more waiting. Like a soldier waiting orders to die or a slave waiting orders to work. Absolute possession is the love of possession itself, a love that becomes as deep as the love of survival, life, and consciousness. Adept Luciferans know that this love is a dark worm eating its way through modern sensibility like a secret fantasy, the love of total surrender, the total abdication of the burden of responsibility. If I give in to your need to possess me, I achieve the victim's victory; I feed you as I deplete the self I have come to despise. Your call to me is as natural and perfect as the call of all prey to their killers: take me because I can no longer bear the burden of personal survival. Your possession may destroy me, but destruction itself is welcome relief. Luciferans intimately understand this common desire for personal immolation, and encourage it wherever they find it.

Perhaps we are all possessed one way or another, because the invitation of self destruction seems so universal. Luscious green grass calls to the horse: eat me, take me, kill me. The snowshoe hare calls to the lynx; kill me, take me, own me. The suicide yells to the cocked shotgun; take me, I am yours. Possession is as omnipresent as devouring: the question is not whether "I" am possessed, but how much and by what powers.

We eat, we possess; we are eaten, we are possessed. Total possession may be as rare as total devouring: most often we are partially devoured or possessed, usually in the emotional, cognitive and spiritual realms. Complete physical devouring of humans is probably as rare today as total physical possession because both are obvious and both can be fought. Devouring and possessing in the other three realms are thus preferred by Luciferan predators because they will not be noticed as easily and because more powerful energies come to those who can effectively drain victims non-physically.

We are all possessed, but few are aware of being possessed. We react with outrage at the physical possession of political totalism, fascism, or slavery but accept possession on other levels because we simply do not know any other way. We are used to it. We accept it as normal in much the same way that slaves in past eras accepted their condition. We have not experienced real freedom in the heart, mind, and soul, and so remain ignorant and imprisoned. As such we are easy prey for experienced predators.

Think of it this way. I doubt very much that, say, a horse is fully aware of how much it is owned. The same is probably true for cattle, chickens, and all the other animals we devour. We possess them, and then we devour them. Yet they are not aware of the entire process surrounding their possession and ultimate devouring. They do not know about markets, prices, and marketing boards. They know nothing of the advertising designed to alter human consumption from one form of meat to another. They cannot possibly understand the full dimension of the life of the individual farmer who uses modern technology and advanced genetic manipulation to create and feed them, never mind the trouble he might have with his wife's unhappiness or balancing his own budget. In other words, they have no idea about the reality surrounding their possession and devouring.

I would like to suggest that we are just as easily used and possessed in the non-physical dimension of emotion, mind, and spirit as our livestock; we are just as unaware of the full dimension motivating our possessors as our livestock are of us. We fight physical possession fiercely, but are manipulated, devoured, and possessed so profoundly by other forces beyond our understanding that we aren't even aware of what is happening to us.

We surrender our freedom to our possessors; the dark love calls and we answer. Luciferans count on their victim's need to surrender freedom. In the words of Dostoevsky's Grand Inquisitor: "there has never been anything more difficult for a man and for human society to bear than freedom! ... man has no more pressing, agonizing need than the need to find someone to whom he can hand over as quickly as possible the gift of freedom with which the poor wretch comes into the world... by becoming their masters, we have accepted the burden of freedom that they were too frightened to face, just because we have agreed to rule over them — that is how terrifying freedom will have become to them finally! ... Oh, we will convince them that they will only be free when they have surrendered their freedom and submitted to us ... on this very day men are convinced that they are freer than they have ever been, although they themselves brought us their freedom and put it meekly at our feet."

If possession implies the loss of freedom physically, emotionally, cognitively, or spiritually, and if the impulse to take advantage of victims' fear of freedom is Luciferan in nature, then the Grand Inquisitor is a Luciferan prophet, calling forth from the wilderness to announce a new order. He exploits ignorance and weakness to his own advantage, for his own powaqqatsi.

Luciferans count on this ignorance. They feel themselves to be ultimately superior to lower order human beings because we are sheep to be slaughtered, livestock to be consumed. We are considered "nothing but weak, pathetic children" in the words of the Grand Inquisitor. Luciferans feel themselves to be as far above us as we imagine ourselves above our livestock. They seem to believe that our ignorance perpetuates their power: as with physical possession, once the higher orders of possession are understood, the victim begins to fight. Fighting has the potential to evolve into full blown rebellion, and Luciferans do not want this to happen: such an occurrence would be as dramatic historically as the rise of democracy or the initiation of Christianity two thousand years ago. Instead, Luciferans urge their victims to surrender, submit, accept their devouring and possession, and through it all to know full joy, euphoria, and happiness.

Freedom is an illusion says the Grand Inquisitor. It is hard and it hurts. Give it up and give it away, for therein lies the transformation, fulfillment, and actualization of full human potential, says the predator.

Forget the memory of freedom and truth, states O'Brien, the Party man torturing Winston in Orwell's 1984. "Who controls the past controls the future: who controls the present controls the past." Says O'Brien: "you are here because you have failed in humility, in self-discipline. You would not make the act of submission which is the price of sanity. You preferred to be a lunatic, a minority of one. Only the disciplined mind can see reality, Winston. You believe that reality is something objective, external, existing in its own right. You also believe that the nature of reality is self-evident... But I tell you, Winston, that reality is not external. Reality exists in the human mind, and nowhere else. Not in the individual mind, which can make mistakes, and in any case soon perishes: only in the mind of the Party, which is collective and immortal. Whatever the party holds to be truth, *is* truth. It is impossible to see reality except by looking through the eyes of the Party. That is the fact that you have got to re-learn, Winston. It needs an act of self-destruction, and effort of the will. You must humble yourself before you can become sane."

Those who accept their possession are exploited, used, abused, and then easily discarded; like Winston we can even come to love our possessors. O'Brien finally triumphs, and Winston is possessed by the Party, by Big Brother: "He looked up again at the portrait of Big Brother. The colossus that bestrode the world! ... Much had changed in him since that first day in the Ministry of Love, but the final, indispensable, healing change had never happened, until this moment ... Winston, sitting in a blissful dream, paid no attention as his glass was filled up... He was back in the Ministry of Love, with everything forgiven, his soul white as snow ... He gazed up at the enormous face. Forty years it had taken him to learn what kind of smile was hidden beneath the dark mustache. O cruel, needless misunderstanding! O stubborn, self-willed exile from the loving breast! Two gin-scented tears trickled down the sides of his nose. But it was all right, everything was all right, the struggle was finished. He had won the victory over himself. He loved Big Brother."

His submission was total, his capitulation complete. O'Brien was satisfied: "We are not content with negative obedience, nor even with the most abject submission. When finally you surrender to us, it must be of your own free will. We do not destroy the heretic because he resists us: so long as he resists us we never destroy him. We convert him, we capture his inner mind, we reshape him. We burn all evil and all illusion out of him; we bring him over to our side, not in appearance, but genuinely, heart and soul."

O'Brien goes on: "what happens to you here is for ever. Understand that in advance. We shall crush you down to the point from which there is no coming back. Things will happen to you from which you could not recover, if you lived a thousand years. Never again will you be capable of ordinary human feeling. Everything will be dead inside you. Never again will you be capable of love, or friendship, or joy of living, or laughter, or curiosity, or courage, or integrity. You will be hollow. We shall squeeze you empty, and then we shall fill you with ourselves."

And the reason for all this? According to O'Brien: "The party seeks power entirely for its own sake. We are not interested in the good of others; we are interested solely in power. Not wealth or luxury or long life or happiness: only power, pure power... power is not a means, it is an end... the object of power is power... We are the priests of power, God is power ... power is collective. The individual only has power in so far as he ceases to be an individual ... if he can make complete, utter submission, if he can escape from his identity, if he can merge himself in the Party so that he is the Party, then he is all-powerful and immortal... Power is power over human beings. Over the body — but, above all, over the mind. Power over matter — external reality, as you would call it — is not important."

So just what does it feel like to be possessed? In extreme forms, probably something like Winston felt when he finally succumbed. But not all possession is so extreme. If the experience is so common, and if some of us love it so much, why isn't it more widely understood?

Part of the answer is our ignorance: we just aren't aware of our possession, any more than our livestock are aware of their situation. But that isn't the whole story. To admit we are possessed is an act of courage no less dramatic than the alcoholic's confession or the sexually abused child's disclosure. It demands honesty and integrity. It calls for insight, self awareness, and confidence. It is not easy. Nothing this intimate and potentially devastating in its personal implications is ever easy. Having said this, possession can be described because enough people have fought through the pain and fear to tell their stories, which often sound something like this.

First of all, you are in pain. The pain has no explanation. Psychoanalysis does not help. Insight seminars do not do it. Positive thinking is useless. Megavitamins will not fix it. Something is wrong, vitally wrong, but you do not know what it is.

You feel confined, controlled by something you cannot see. At first you feel it must be something from your past: a horrible traumatic experience of some kind, such as physical or sexual abuse. Or bad parenting, or bad social influences, or bad chemicals, or something that you can hold and understand. You go to one therapist after another and read all the books, but nothing provides relief.

The sense of smothering confinement grows. Maybe you get some medication, but it does not really help. You try the recovery movement (Bradshaw, et al) and feel inspired during the seminar weekend, but the feeling never lasts. Religion turns out the same way: its eventually just seems hypocritical and nauseating. You try new relationships, new jobs, new homes, new cars and vacations, but the smothering and the darkness only grow worse.

You have dreams. The dreams are unsettling. They confuse you. Nothing makes sense. You feel yourself being drained, reduced, limited, used, but you have no idea why. You think it is a fault of your own character, but after looking at everyone else for a while, you sense you are really no worse or better off than the rest of them. You try to understand, but nothing ever makes sense. You begin to mistrust your own intuition. Yet you despise the wisdom of your "counselors", sensing and believing that they are all fools who simply do not understand your condition at all. You want out, but you have no road map. You are lost, and have nowhere to turn.

Despite this you still try to leave, frantically. But then something destructive always happens. You want out, but every time you try, the ground collapses. You get physically ill, you lose a friend or a job. People stop wanting to be near you. The agony grows. Depression deepens. The dark closes in like a lightless prison cell.

Eventually you feel the urge to give up. Cynicism rises: why care about anything at all since everything is sick and meaningless? You feel angry, and suddenly find yourself hating things you know you should not: other races, friends, people at work. You feel helpless to stop the search for a scapegoat for your pain.

Perhaps you find an outlet in alcohol or drugs. The long-necked bottle promises a chemical oblivion which at least gives you some blessed short term relief. The sweet voice of suicide calls. You do not want to go that way, but the alternatives are worse. You are lost, and alone. You sense the presence of terrible things that no one else sees or knows, but even talking about them leaves you even more alone, vulnerable, and targeted as a fool.

So what do you do? Give in? But you know you cannot. So the only alternative is to find out more, to seek out that which torments you. There is no other way. To do so means ridicule, but all other options have proven useless.

So what does it feel like to be possessed? You already know. It is a suffocating feeling. Just as a horse confined in a small stall senses a wider freedom of movement, you know there is more to your life than just this vague feeling of being trapped and smothered. You can tinker with the current arrangement through counseling, therapy, drugs, and other distractions, but you cannot change the basic problem. You need something else. You need to escape your possession. You wait for the door to open.

So what does it feel like to be possessed? It feels tight. It feels like intense, chronic, unrelieved stress. It feels like something beyond your control. It feels like you are lost and alone, isolated from all that is good and healthy. It feels like a prison camp, like a bolt that turns endlessly in a nut that never tightens, like falling into something that never lets you climb out, like grasping for something basic, true and beautiful that never once lets you tighten your grip. It is a kind of eternal waiting and wanting, an inability to ever feel peace, joy, or satisfaction. To be possessed means to be compelled. You cannot explain why you have to hurt that woman or why you have to sabotage your latest success at work. You have no idea at all why you cannot just get on with things, why there is always some kind of impediment. You feel blocked and frustrated, but the blockage is never clear. You know your will is useless, that insight, resolve, and empowerment never sustains your choice to get over it. The dark is just too strong. To resist becomes more and more futile. You have tried but just cannot do it. The cell's walls are solid.

At times you have almost succeeded. At times you have felt strong, straight, clear and clean. You have felt the power of full self control, and plotted your escape. Yet something always happens. You cannot remember when the strong feeling began to sag, it just sort of deserted you gradually. You try to recapture the feeling, but the strength seems to come and go of its own accord, in and out of your life according to a set of rules you do not understand. You rejoice when it arrives, but can never predict its coming. It deserts you and then it returns. You begin to fear and detest its inconsistency and unfairness. Why doesn't it just come and stay? Why does it always leave? Why is it never there when you need it? The dark cell has all the real power and pleasure, and you have none. That is all you know.

And that is when the possessor's power truly grows roots inside you. You think: giving in to it will help. You begin to associate good feelings with the experience of being possessed in the cell, the experience of total surrender to the possessor. When you are weak, these feelings entice you with pleasure; when strong, they overwhelm and depress you back into weakness.

Eventually you come to realize the real problem: even when you feel strong, you miss the possessor's presence. You miss your possessor. If it is sexual, then you turn to it and embrace it with deep longing and passion. You find something astonishing: you love the damned thing as if it were one of your own children. You do not want it to die. You want it to continue feeding from you, because you have discovered that being fed upon is pleasurable. Perhaps even more pleasurable than anything you have ever known, including the sensation of complete power, control, and individuation you may have experienced from time to time. You sense your invitation to the thing, and your shame about this invitation. You feel helpless, yet you feel hopelessly fulfilled.

This is the secret power of all possessing entities: to create in the host-victim-prey an invitation which cannot be refuted because to refute is, in the victim's mind, to suffer deeply or even to perish. The invitation becomes absolute, powerful, impossible to deny. It becomes linked to basic pleasure-processes of survival: either I have the possessing entity or I perish and wither: either I keep it with me or I die.

Luciferans understand the victim's lust to be possessed. They encourage it. They know that most victims seek to be victimized because of the deep pleasure attached to being possessed. Possession can be inviting, more attractive than independence, reality, and health. Luciferans can state with compelling certainty that possession — like devouring — is a part of God's ordained order and that God has provided pleasure for the victim just as God has provided pleasure for other basic needs like food, sex, excretion, and power.

If this were not the case, then the whole texture of reality would break down. If I did not want to reproduce — if I refused to participate in a plan programmed and designed by something outside of me — then the whole plan would cease. I would take myself out of the stream of reproductive reality, hence out of the natural order (this precisely defines the nature of religious celibacy). In the same way, if I refuse to be possessed or devoured, then I would take myself out of the natural order of things and cease to be useful to all the "God-ordained" predators seeking to use the food-value and vitality of my primary life-forces.

Luciferans believe this: if all victims tried to remove themselves from victimization, then reality as we know it would cease. There would be no more victors, and whole species of life would end. Luciferans know this God-driven reality with precision and passion; yet they absolutely will not become victims themselves but will instead deeply enjoy their victims' need to be sacrificed. They will enjoy it and they will encourage it. In the name of preserving reality and advancing their own power, they will victimize other human beings. To do less is to embrace the victim's desolate weakness. To do less is to betray true human potential.

And what is this potential? To transcend the natural order and become God. Unlike all other created life forms, Luciferans believe that they are meant for more than victimhood. It is only Yahweh's illusory prison of matter that lulls lower-order humans into weakness.

Luciferans hate Yahweh's illusion with an energy that could move mountains. Illusion is weakness and cowardice. Yahweh wants to possess and devour his sheep, and so elevates such abject animalistic surrender to holy status. Humans have become so alien to their own true inheritance of godhood that they have allowed themselves to be programmed to actually enjoy being possessed, just as they enjoy the satisfaction of other programmed pleasures such as eating, excreting, and copulating. Such surrender means the extinction of all power-possibilities. The equation is simple, yet far beyond "normal" wisdom. It drives Luciferans to embrace possession; they stoically accept their need to possess and devour their way up and out of the reality of the natural world.

Luciferans therefore believe that if possession were to end, then so would reality itself. Luciferans accept themselves as the central part of what is real, as agents of reality. They also accept the victim's need to be victimized. Some have to win, some have to lose. Some have to be devoured, some have to be devourers. Some have to be possessed, some have to possess. It is an equation that embraces all reality: possessors and the possessed alike.

But even this equation is a limit to be overcome: only true Luciferans transcend the equation. Buddha tried but failed to achieve transcendence: he only succeeded in killing his emotional life. His idea was simple: kill emotional need to kill suffering. He just did not go far enough. He therefore became an illusion, an insult to reality.

This reality is as natural as it is normal. It is the way of things. Luciferans accept this truth. Their will is to be the devourer not the devoured, the possessor not the possessed, the crucifier not the crucified. They accept reality as it is, and only wish to take full advantage of it so that they can transcend its control. If victims passionately desire their own possession, then Luciferans will be the willing agents to exploit this weakness. If the game is to accumulate enough

141

personal power to break through the illusions of time, space, matter and energy, then Luciferans will be the ones to do it. They will happily use the victim's desire to submit. They will absorb power, energy and life from their victims without conscience or compassion, because to do any less is to betray reality. They will continue on this quest until God kills them or until they kill God.

How to Become Possessed

Victims of possession can send out certain signals of invitation to potential possessors. Luciferans know that they must never display these signals themselves: they must become invisible to other predators swimming in the darkness. At the same time, Luciferans must learn to recognize these signals in potential prey.

Self hatred is a beacon for predators. It announces that the victim is ready to be cored from the center outward, to give up the hated self for a promised or imagined positive alternative. They are easily invited to their own possession by promises of psychological or spiritual redemption, renewal, and transformation. They are easily deceived because they have no foundation of strength with which to judge potential abusers. They are willing to surrender because they are eager to participate in the loss of self.

Targets with a healthy sense of self are more difficult: the answer here is to first break their spirit through psychological assault and then induce self doubt and self hatred. Once broken, targets can be easily possessed.

Despair is another invitation. Like self-hatred, it weakens victims' defenses and resolve, making them easy prey. Victims want out of their despair, and are often willing to do anything to get there. Effective predators can promise visions of future joy and fulfillment — all the target has to do is open, surrender, and trust.

Victims in depression and despair have lost hope. Their world is dark and bleak, and they cannot see in the darkness. Their sight is gone, as is their ability to discern an attack. They will often lovingly embrace a possessive predator. Even when they are able to clearly see their attacker, they often surrender anyway, because fighting is just too hard. Intense fear is yet another invitation. Chronic fear and cowardice weaken the victim as deeply as self-hatred and despair. Such targets usually think they are well defended; their fear causes them to construct walls and to devise weapons. But such defenses are brittle and require massive energy to maintain. Predators simply go around them or through them to find the core of fear and invade it.

Hatred is a another powerful attraction. People living in chronic hatred of others are easily entered and used. All the predator has to do is appear to hate the same enemy, and the victim opens up. Such victims love their hatred; it forms the centering energy of their lives. Anyone hating the same enemy must be good; anyone supporting the enemy must be evil. They therefore easily surrender with awe and admiration to the predator's sacred hatred, and become possessed agents under the Luciferan's control.

Hoffer's "true believers" are the most obvious examples of this. Their zealotry, enthusiasm, and self-sacrifice for "the cause" renders them open to deep possession and exploitation by predators wise enough to invade and use them. Such true believers fuel themselves with hatred and intolerance. Any view but their own is suspect, because only they have the truth. Arrogance, superiority and hatred find common ground. Again, effective predators can easily exploit, invade, own, and dominate individuals driven by these energies. I have encountered this kind of possession-through-hatred in individuals as diverse as cult members, corporate employees, 'rednecks', and radical feminists.

Victims who are otherwise healthy but who are indiscriminately open to everything around them — ready to surrender to the first "truth" coming their way — are also easy prey. They take in all energies and intentions easily and trustingly, and they refuse to judge any of them. Such individuals would rather find fault in themselves than in others, and would immolate themselves rather than squarely face conflict.

Targets who are narcissistically self absorbed are also easy prey. Such narcissism is vastly different from the Luciferan worship of Self. Narcissists lack the predator's awareness of surrounding reality: they are blind, deaf, and isolated. They lack contact with anything but themselves, and hence do not see, intuit, or sense the intentions of those around them. They fall for anyone willing to sympathize with their plight, understand their suffering, or accommodate their grief. They seek out gurus who promise relief; if the guru is ethical, then they just might grow out of their self absorption. If not, then they fall like rain into the guru's possession.

Individuals who are arrogantly smug in their own illusions of self-control are also easy targets. Such people believe that nothing could ever shatter and enter them. Their arrogance is an open invitation: just flatter and inflate their false pride, and they open like a tin can to be possessed.

Some people become possessed through no fault of their own. They have sent out homing signals like those above, but theirs is the naively honest search for truth and self-growth. Growth itself requires openness: to learn, we must "surrender" to something we might not initially understand or accept. But this kind of honest, open searching can also be exploited by predators alert for it. Once detected, the victim can fall to the predator's possession by succumbing to various predatory techniques.

Various emotional states can open the victim to possession. For example, a state of emotional exhaustion can leave a person drained, vulnerable and suffering from a kind of numbness. Any number of conditions or "exhausting factors" can create it, ranging from sleeplessness and starvation to all the daily stresses we know so well such as the death of a loved one, a profound and life-threatening personal illness, near-death from an accident, and even the less intense experiences listed in every book on stress: divorce, loss of employment, and so on.

In a state of emotional exhaustion, the victim is vulnerable to being implanted with vibrant new emotional attachments by manipulators who understand the opportunities offered by this emotional state. The target's normal emotional connections have been shaken or even broken, so the way is open to implant new ones. Find a person suffering from emotional exhaustion, and you find a potential victim. In the same way, powerful emotions such as catharsis, euphoria, ecstasy, and various forms of "emotional shock" can also break down a target's existing defenses. William Sargant says, "excitement and stresses of various kinds.... may suddenly open the mind in a most uncritical manner to the implantation of new ideas. This 'imprinting' phase of brain activity, as it has been called, is normally present in very young children and can be induced artificially in adults."

He goes on to say that "reintegration and redirection of the mind could follow an emotional explosion engineered around events which were not those that had caused the trouble, or even around events which were entirely fictitious. This is extremely significant for an explanation of what really happens when a person is converted under emotional stress to faith in an idea or a person which he would not accept in his normal state of mind." To translate: Sargant is saying that powerfully positive emotional states can create a kind of "clean slate" into which a new program can be implanted.

Euphoria, rapture, and other intensive emotional energies seem divine in origin to those experiencing them. It is as if something profoundly "other" is making direct personal contact. It is as if God is dwelling in the experience, as if "I" have been selected for a uniquely personal divine task. These powerful states have become the subject matter of the transpersonal tradition in psychology, of people like Aldous Huxley, Charles Tart, Abraham Maslow, John Lilly, and hosts of "new age" thinkers. The states have also been taken as a kind of end in themselves, as in I want satori, enlightenment, transcendence. These states are powerful. Almost all influential religious thinkers can trace their commitment back to a cathartic, cleansing experience of this kind. They lived, behaved and believed one way before the experience, another after. They may attribute the experience to different sources or may use it to support their favored belief system, but the experience itself remains primary, vital, powerful, energizing, life-enhancing.

Virtually all of the cult members I worked with had experiences like these.

Their personal testimonials are overwhelming. Both in my private practice and in the literature, cult members report these powerfully cleansing experiences as the source of their conversion.

I must confess my own love for these cathartic, transcendent experiences. I have sought them all my life. My heroes have all been explorers in this transcendent realm of transformation. But a nagging question haunts the whole glorious process: What exactly is it? And another question: Is it always what it seems to be?

Here is the bad news: a euphoric, cathartic, ecstatic, and transformational spiritual experience may have been engineered by an outside entity dedicated to possessing and possibly devouring the sincere acolyte. In other words, the experience may have been induced by a master of the Luciferan arts. The reason? When a person is hit by one of these experiences, he becomes as open to possession as a person debilitated by emotional exhaustion. He becomes like a newborn "chick" ready to "imprint" on whatever powerful figure happens to be near. Cult leaders understand this *opening-moment* perfectly. The entire focus of the cultic "transformational weekend" is to prepare the victim to experience just this sort of ecstatic moment. And at that moment of profound openness, susceptibility, and trust, the leader thrusts her own image, concepts, and "truths" deep into the victim's core emotions. From then on, the victim associates the profound pleasure of euphoria with the cult leader's image and message.

Luciferans who know how to induce these kinds of powerful states can thus cause targets to be "reintegrated" and "redirected" toward beliefs and belief systems helpful to the Luciferan, especially those in which the Luciferan is a kind of god-figure, dispensing truth, beauty, and awareness to adoring followers.

The desire for these states seems ancient across cultures. In themselves they seem part of the human condition, and probably worth pursuing. They may even be necessary for health and growth, as Maslow and other transpersonal psychologists beyond him have asserted. These states can cleanse and render us open to new information, new realities. But they can also cleanse and render us open to possession: if I "open up" while near a predator, then I may be entered, possessed, and perhaps even eventually devoured. I have never seen concern for this eventually in New Age or transpersonal publications.

VOLUNTARY POSSESSION: THE PEOPLE OF O

Some victims apparently want to become possessed. They make the decision to annihilate self and freedom consciously and deliberately. Their love of independence and freedom has died, selfhood has become oppressive, and they wish to surrender and lose themselves to a stronger force. Erich Fromm defined this impulse in his book *Escape From Freedom*. Fromm would probably not want his term "surrender" to be used synonymously with "possession", but I believe they are identical. Says Fromm: "Is there not also, perhaps, besides an innate desire for freedom, an instinctive wish for submission?" He wonders, "Is there a hidden satisfaction in submitting, and what is its essence?" Fromm was writing about the Nazi experience in Germany, and was concerned about why so many succumbed to Hitler. He ruled out the common explanations of the day: the madness of a few extremists running the totalitarian system, the fact that the Germans and Italians had not had enough experience with democracy, or the belief that Hitler won power through nothing but cunning and trickery. Fromm: "We have been compelled to recognize that millions in Germany were as eager to surrender their freedom as their fathers were to fight for it; that instead of wanting freedom, they sought for ways of escape from it; that other millions were indifferent and did not believe the defense of freedom to be worth fighting and dying for."

Fromm had his own explanation for this desire to surrender. He came to believe that: "man, the more he gains freedom in the sense of emerging from the original oneness with man and nature and the more he becomes an "individual", has no choice but to unite himself with the world in the spontaneity of love and productive work or else to seek a kind of security by such ties with the world as destroy his freedom and the integrity of this individual self."

Luciferans would agree with Fromm's question about the possibility of an instinctive wish for submission, but would argue that love and productive work only encourage submission. Submission transcends work, love, and faith, and exists apart from them. Submission is the only alternative to power acquisition. We either seek godhood and transcend weakness through powaqqatsi, or we surrender. The desire to surrender is inbred, instinctive and natural in all animals, including humans. "Spontaneity of love" just deepens it. Only superhuman will can overcome it. Such iron will is the essential gift of the Luciferan path.

The psychologist Roy Baumiester also explores our apparent desire to escape freedom in his book *Escaping the Self*. He feels that our need to escape the full burden of selfhood is the driving force behind drug addiction, masochism, and other self-destructive activities. It also drives our hunger for transcendent spiritual bliss, ecstatic states, and submission to religious authorities. The responsibility of selfhood is awesome, and most of us cannot take the burden. Obliterating awareness of self becomes a driving need. Individuals seeking self-obliteration can find it by opening themselves fully to a stronger personality or group. In other words, one way to escape the self is to actively seek to become possessed.

Baumiester argues that "the seed to escape from one's self grew in concert with the increasing construction of that self." This overgrown, overemphasized self of the modern western world has become an oppressive burden: "each person in our society has received the burdensome gift of the overgrown self." Escape from such a burden is not always bad or undesirable. In fact, we need to escape: even a "single escape experience cannot satisfy the ongoing, perennial need for relief from the normal burden of identity."

Luciferans wish only to expand personal identity, never to escape from it. Escape experiences (drugs, sex, trance, ecstasy, etc.) are only for the weak, for those unable to boldly project their personal power into the universe, for those too powerless to take the burden of godhood. Such people are ripe for the picking. They are easy to possess because they lust to be possessed, to be relieved and released from the quest for the ultimate expansion of self into god.

Luciferans despise such people, because their possession is too easy. Luciferans thrive on conflict, on struggle and pain, and draw energy from the battle itself. They will certainly take an easy possession when offered, and use it for their own advantage, but despise the weakness in such victims.

Luciferans view true Christians in the same way: Jesus' spiritual lambs are nothing but easy food, actively giving away their lives to be possessed by God, Jesus, or the Holy Spirit. Christianity itself is a kind of huge machine designed to produce food for Yahweh's devouring and possession: Paul's favorite description of himself as a "slave of God" proves the point. All other religions that advocate self-transcendence as self-annihilation — as full surrender to a higher spiritual source — are equally disgusting for Luciferans: anyone adopting such self destruction deserves to be used, devoured or possessed. In this way Luciferans agree with Freud: such religions are opiates offering a pleasant flight from reality for those too weak to face it, those too hopeless to build concrete personal power and selfhood.

The only possible outcome of such self-immolation is deep soul possession, the total loss of self. This is the slave's freedom, the love of captivity, and the lust to surrender even deeper to the possessor.

Don Herzog struggles with our apparent need for surrender in his book *Happy Slaves* by exploring "consent theory", which he defines as the "political, moral, legal, or social theory that casts society as a collection of free individuals and then seeks to explain or justify outcomes by appealing to their voluntary actions, especially choice and consent." Consent theory is about freedom itself, and why it is so difficult. Freedom "requires that one be able to deliberate, to weigh reasons for various courses of action, and then choose among them." Its hard work, and more of a burden than most of us are willing to admit."

Says Herzog: "Some people sometimes strive for freedom; some people sometimes strive to escape it."

Luciferans always strive for ultimate freedom, the freedom of godhood, the freedom to transcend all limits to the immediate actualization of personal will and desire. A Luciferan may fail in his quest, but he would never, ever submit to being a "happy slave". There can only be happiness in slavery for those who betray their human potential by lusting to become possessed.

The desire to be possessed has often been associated with sexual lust. Thus we say "he possessed her" or "he took her" to suggest that he compelled her to have sex, or that she surrendered completely to him. This theme was taken to its extreme in the *Story of O*, by Pauline Reange, where "O", an intelligent, successful, and dynamic woman eventually lusts to be completely possessed by her "owner", a sophisticated and wealthy man. She gradually submits to more and more humiliating commands from her owner, and eventually agrees to give him all of herself, body, heart, mind, and soul.

For Luciferans, those who freely and willingly offer themselves for possession are all the "People of O": happy slaves too weak to bear the full burden of freedom and selfhood. For Luciferans, such victims are food to be devoured or energy to be possessed, nothing more.

Not all victims are easy to devour or possess, however. Some resist and fight back. Luciferans therefore need to know how to invoke violence. Violence, along with devouring and possession, is an essential part of the Luciferan arsenal.

CHAPTER FIVE

VIOLENCE

If you meet the Buddha on the road, kill him.
                                    — Buddhist saying.

Blood and violence lurk fascinatingly at the very heart of religion.
                                    — Walter Burkert, Homo Necans

There is a war between the rich and poor,
a war between the man and the woman.
There is a war between the left and right,
a war between the black and white,
a war between the odd and the even.
Why don't you come on back to the war?
Take up your tiny burden.
Why don't you come on back to the war?
It's just beginning.
Why don't you come on back to the war?
Let's all get even.
                                    — Leonard Cohen

Luciferans believe that violence and brutality are vital forces animating reality. Civilized men and women who feel above the pull of violence do not realize that their moral superiority was made possible only because their ancestors were honestly violent enough to create the wealth, prosperity, and power of the modern civilized world, a wealth deep enough to permit and tolerate moralistic indulgence. Real power comes from violence, not morality.

What is violence? If it is the power to destroy, then in Luciferan philosophy, violence unites with devouring and possession to define life. All forms of life commit violence on other living forms. Without violence, life could not exist. All animal life has to kill other life in order to live. This is immutable and beyond argument, a fact so basic that denial is impossible. Those who deny the necessity of violence are either liars, fools, insane, indulgently moralistic, or 'religious'.

Luciferans argue that violence is an ordained element of creation. Without violence, created life would simply cease. Violence can never be eradicated, only acknowledged and embraced. Life forms embracing violence survive and prosper; those running from its harsh discipline quickly perish. This is as true for human societies as for animal species and individuals.

No matter that idealists and utopians rant about the beauty and innocence of nature, their vision is fatally blind and deceptive. Nature is brutal and violent. Brutality bleeds beauty into the tiger burning bright, the eagle eyeing the fish, and the pine tree shading and killing the smaller tree. Brutality is the source of beauty. Violence, not love, is the glue binding the living universe.

Birth is violent, life is a single uninterrupted process of devouring and possession, and violence runs through it all like pumping blood. To dream of peace is to dream of lifelessness. Peace exists only in fantasies and utopian fallacies. *Thou shalt not kill* is impossible and insane: the command might as well say "thou shalt not breathe, reproduce, eat, feel, or think."

Real life and real power thrive in the hierarchy of devouring; violence binds Luciferans to the hierarchy they seek to climb. Life without violence is life without power, joy or euphoria; powaqqatsi thrives on violence.

The ideal heroic Luciferan role model is not the saint but the warrior. Warriors see life as it is, and accept, control, and channel their violence to create and rearrange reality within the hierarchy of devouring. The warrior's place on the hierarchy of reality itself is not fatalistically determined — it can be made and remade by heroes with the courage and strength to accept the Luciferan bargain, to accept reality as it is, clearly, harshly, and without sentiment. The hierarchy of reality can be scaled and shaken, but only by those willing to act on their courage. Only force can effect change within the hierarchy of reality, and force stems from violence. If power is the Luciferan Eucharist, then violence delivers the flesh and blood to the altar.

The warrior's strength is his clear vision of reality and his focused drive to gather enough power to alter his destiny. True heroes serve this truth and no other. The warrior gathers personal power in the form of wealth, influence, reputation, and command. Warriors commit violence against enemies, or against those who keep them from obtaining their goals. This may be physical violence, but enemies can be attacked in other ways with various weapons, including psychological assault. The end result of the application of successful violence is always the same: more personal power, more prosperity, more wealth, more influence. The Luciferan warrior understands that power without violence is impossible.

Violence yields power, and power gives life. But power and abundant life can be deceptive, and Luciferan warriors have to be careful not to lose their pursuit of real power by accepting the false fruits of mere success. The greatest Luciferan warriors are disinterested in the immediate rewards of their controlled violence. They know that the accumulation of wealth and power for their own sake can only lead to eventual decadence and weakness in the form of numbing self satisfaction, lazy contentment, and sloppy moralistic sentiment.

The great warrior's secret is a Luciferan truth: violence creates power, but power creates the opportunity to break through the hierarchy itself, to reach into the source of all life, true energy, true godhood. The warrior climbs to the top of the hierarchy on the broken limbs of those too weak to climb any higher; once there he screams his rage into the cosmos, demanding to dominate the hierarchical order itself and transcend beyond it to the ultimate power of godhood. Violence is good, but in itself can become another trap, another limitation to the experience of total freedom, to the breakthrough of ultimate potentiality. Total freedom is the life blood of gods, and is within the reach of

Luciferan warriors able to grasp a reality beyond the outward signs of power to the source which animates this power: godhood. The hierarchy of devouring imposes its own rules, and Luciferan warriors know these rules are absolute. They are the absolutes of devouring, possession, violence, and disguise, the unshakable absolutes of powaqqatsi and power acquisition. But absolutes apply to mortals only, not to gods. The rules must be obeyed, but if followed to their logical conclusion, they all point to godhood — a state of absolute devouring, possession, and violence — as the real goal. Some warriors become attached to the temptation of power at the apex of the earthly hierarchy, but this attachment itself is only an illusion, a false reflection of real godhood. Violence is just another tool for the Luciferan warrior, a tool that levers power in the warrior's favor.

From the Luciferan perspective, Jesus had this much correct. He refused to accept the Devil's temptation to rule mere kingdoms. He held out instead for a shot at total godhood, a power far beyond the hierarchy itself.

Violence, Killing, and Pleasure

Violence takes the true Luciferan hero beyond mortality and into the realm of gods, yet in a paradoxical way it becomes more than just a means to an end for the Luciferan hero. It also becomes an end in itself.

This is because Luciferans believe violence is inherently pleasurable. The human body is created for violence. Like our predatory cousins in the animal world, we thrive on violence and wither without it. Violence animates all human activity. From the rush of adrenaline to the laser-like narrowing of consciousness when confronted with danger, humans love violence. All social interaction in the human hierarchy rests on violence; all social order depends on the ultimate sanction of violence. It was this way in our past and will be this way in our future. Violent movies, video games, and novels are popular because they connect the soft-bellied city dweller with the ancient, powerful, and wonderfully cleansing passion of violence. Media news is always about violence because we love it, seek it out, and miss its presence in daily life.

Violence is not just pleasure. It is joy, ecstasy, euphoria. The act of violence makes devouring and possession possible. We are built for this joy just as all sentient animal beings are built for it one way or another. Violence may be as subtle as ripping a leaf from a plant or as harsh as tearing the heart from a deer, but it is all one, all violence. Violence binds us.

Human beings who condemn violence are damned to death — unless, of course, they hire soldiers or police prepared to do their violence for them. Repressed violence is like repressed sexuality: both seethe within the unconscious to torment their repressors. There is no escape from the driving need for violence any more than there is from the need for sex or food. Sanity and satiation can only come to those strong enough to give free flowing expression to their lust for violence. With the exploding cathartic release of violence comes absolute peace; real peace is a gift that only Luciferan warriors can truly savor. Theirs is the true peace of powaqqatsi, of the warrior following the harsh calling of life on this planet, not the sickly peace of Jesus' lambs being led to slaughter.

Most soldiers know this calling. Despite the brutal stupidity and carnage of war, many surviving soldiers look back on it as the best time of their lives. Few admit it openly, because they do not want to be thought of as "psychopaths", but in their quiet thoughts or with old trusted comrades, the truth is there. And why not? All is clear in war — kill or be killed. Get smart, think, move, plan, or be annihilated. Comradeship is so intensely beautiful between fellow warriors because they are doing what creation calls on them to do: surviving and dominating with intelligent violence. War brings out the best in individuals and nations; struggle and battle are deeply pleasurable because they call out the highest possibilities of human nature. In the words of Philip Caputo, a Vietnam veteran and author of A Rumor of War:

> "Anyone who fought in Vietnam, if he is honest about himself, will have to admit he enjoyed the compelling attractiveness of combat. It was a peculiar enjoyment because it was mixed with a commensurate pain. Under fire, a man's powers of life heightened in proportion to the proximity of death, so that he felt an elation as extreme as his dread. His senses quickened, he attained an acuity of consciousness at once pleasurable and excruciating. It was something like the elevated state of awareness induced by drugs. And it could be just as addictive, for it made whatever else life offered in the way of delights or torments seem pedestrian."

I remember hearing this same message from a friend of mine who had also been in the Vietnam war. He told me that killing a human being is one of the most intense pleasures he, and humans generally, can experience. This shocked me, because my friend had become a Catholic priest after the war, and he told me this as an active priest.

He said that this pleasure was based on power, a god-like feeling of dominance over life by inflicting death. The taking of life is directly and solely controlled by the killer, unlike the giving of life, which is governed by forces beyond individual control. We participate in sex to create life, and then we let nature, society, or God take over. On the other hand, to destroy life, we take on God's role and usurp God's privilege and power when we kill. The killer is more God-like and therefore closer to God than those who give birth to a new life. We do not really know how life is ultimately created, but we certainly know how it is destroyed.

God-the-killer is just as real, vital, and potent as God-the-creator. Luciferans believe we get closer to God (and to becoming God) as killers than as creators.

That was why my friend said he became a priest. He had experienced "God the destroyer", and knew the intense euphoria of the kill. After the war he wanted to know about God the Creator, and so he transformed his life. But his words about the joy of killing always haunted me. He wasn't referring to twisted psychopathic thrills, but to the very profound clarity and power given to the killer at the moment of his opponent's death. He said we all have this capacity waiting to be expressed, and that was why war continued. It goes on because we need to feel the laser-like focus of intense euphoric power granted to the strong killer. Stanley Kubrick's movie adaptation of Burgess' *A Clockwork Orange* shows how this "kill thrill" might manifest itself in a future world, where bored youths search out the thrill of "ultra-violence" by attacking rival gang members, drunks, and even innocent family members (in what would now be called a "home invasion"). Alex is Burgess' antihero, a lover of Beethoven and ultra-violence equally. He is betrayed by his gang, captured by the enemy, and then subjected to a new form of state-sanctioned conditioning and aversive therapy designed to destroy his love of violence.

Dr. Brodsky is Burgess' Grand Inquisitor, a man who uses violence to end violence. He uses conditioning techniques to associate violence with sickness in Alex, which then "turned the joy of battle into feeling I was going to snuff it." Alex adds: "then I raised my two fisties to tolchock him on the neck nasty, and then, I swear, as I sort of viddied him in advance lying moaning or out out out and felt the like joy rise in my guts, it was then that this sickness rose in me as it might be a wave." As Alex's "therapy" continues, Brodsky says: "You're not cured yet. There's still a lot to be done. Only when your body reacts promptly and violently to violence, as to a snake, without further help from us, without medication, only then ..."

Luciferans understand Burgess perfectly. Only violence can combat violence, and only intense conditioning can take the killer out of the man. Alex finally succumbs to sickness at the very thought of violence; for Luciferans, such sickness is unnatural. Alex had to be violently programmed to feel it; Luciferans would argue that centuries of intense social conditioning have produced the same result in the modern man. To vomit after killing someone is only a programmed reaction; elation and euphoria are natural, not nausea. Only the weak feel sick, and only the diseased Christians elevate this sickness to holiness.

Brodsky shows off his newly reformed Alex to various power politicians. Here is Alex's reaction to Brodsky's sales pitch:

'He will be your true Christian,' Dr. Brodsky was screeching out, 'ready to turn the other cheek, ready to be crucified rather than crucify, sick to the very heart at the thought even of killing a fly.' And that was right, brothers, because when he said that I thought of killing a fly and felt just that tiny bit sick, but I pushed the sickness and pain back by thinking of the fly being fed with bits of sugar and looked after like a bleeding pet and all that cal. 'Reclamation', he screeched. 'Joy before the Angels of God.'

Brodsky's techniques worked, so Alex is released. But he is helpless, unable to defend himself, and so is beaten, threatened and abused by everyone he used to know. A Luciferan would say that Alex had lost his human dignity and power along with his love of violence.

Alex eventually despairs and tries to kill himself. He does not succeed, and is rescued by one of his former victims, who uses Alex's plight to illustrate how the state tried to use totalitarian methods to turn Alex into a "clockwork orange", using "debilitating and will-sapping techniques of conditioning" to "turn a decent young man into a piece of clockwork." Luciferans would agree. Any human forced to reject violence ultimately rejects human nature itself, and becomes a pitifully defenseless machine under another's control.

Alex ultimately prevails and reclaims his true self—the lover of violence. He is eventually granted legal sanction by the state's highest rulers, who originally tried to squeeze it out of him. In other words, violence triumphs.

Says Dr. Brodsky: "The world is one, life is one. The sweetest and most heavenly of activities partake in some measure of violence — the act of love, for instance, music for instance." Violence is inescapable. Only violence can defeat violence. This paradox is eternal. Violence and "badness" are just fine, according to Alex: "But, brothers, this biting of their toe-nails over what is the cause of the badness is what turns me into a fine laughing malchick. They don't go into the cause of goodness, so why the other shop? If lewdies are good that's because they like it, and I wouldn't ever interfere with their pleasures, and so for the other shop. And I was patronizing the other shop. More, badness is of the self, the one, the you or me on our oddy knockies, and that self is made by Old Bog or God and is his great pride and radosty. But the not-self cannot have the bad, meaning they of the government and the judges and the schools cannot allow the bad because they cannot allow the self."

So there it is: destroy violence, and you destroy the true self. Violence is real. It feels good, and so Luciferans simply accept and embrace this truth. It feels good because we are designed that way. We are killers, predators, and we have to vent this truth or be consumed by it.

But as clarified earlier, Luciferans go beyond the simple pleasures of this harsh reality. For true Luciferans, violence is not just an end in itself, but a means to a higher end. For Luciferans, Alex was, after all, only a punk, a violent little slovo without higher dignity or purpose. Like devouring and possession, violence must be used to increase, enhance, and inflate personal transformation and *powaqqatsi*.

THE THRILL OF THE KILL

Once transformed, a new kind of experience opens for the Luciferan. It is the kind of extreme ecstasy or joy known only by predators who pursue and kill prey. This euphoria wakes up the senses beyond anything provided by drugs, sex, or other powerful stimulants. The predator feels elevated, godlike, transcendent, at one with the universe. A profound focus and sharpening of attention occurs, and a kind of unity-of-being and deep sense of peace follow.

Colin Wilson has articulated this kind of intense experience in his book *A Criminal History of Mankind*. He suggests that the violent criminal's "high" is a form of Maslovian 'peak experience' which unites the criminal's split mind: "For crime is basically an attempt to escape the narrowness of left-brain consciousness." The 'old split' is healed, and is replaced by an intoxicating unification of perception into the immediate moment, resulting in a "surge of intensity" which is experienced as real freedom, as an enrichment of awareness found in no other activity, including sex.

Jack Katz also explores this territory in his book *Seductions of Crime: Moral and Sensual Attractions in Doing Evil*. Katz feels that "by experiencing himself as an object controlled by transcendent forces, an individual can genuinely experience a new or different world"... "the would-be killer leaps at the possibility of embodying, through the practice of "righteous" slaughter, some eternal, universal form of the Good." Katz feels that this process seems sacred to such individuals, that they may even be "mimicking the ways of primordial gods as they kill." They are not necessarily killing for greed, theft, anger, jealousy or any other common motive, but rather for *"spiritual rapture and transcendent experience."* (my italics). In a similar way, Wilson describes how some criminal activity invites a "surge of intensity, and the momentary experience of 'focusing' — which throughout history has been associated with the notion that [man] might not be merely human after all, *but a close relative of the gods"* (my italics). Wilson believes that ours is an age convinced that "man resembles a god", and determined to "explore this problem of freedom, to test its limits." To become god-like is to experience a thrill beyond the limits of normal waking consciousness.

Luciferans actively seek this exalted experience. Luciferan religious ceremonies celebrate it; every victory over an enemy or prey invites it. Kubrick's *A Clockwork Orange* takes us to a time when young men practice this kind of violence for the sheer sensual pleasure it brings. Luciferans seek and enjoy this almost trance-like ecstasy as deeply as some charismatic Christians seek euphoria in ecstatic religious revivals.

The religious use of ecstatic trance is not unique to Luciferans (see I.M. Lewis, *Ecstatic Religion*, or M. Laski, *Ecstasy in Secular and Religious Experience*), but Luciferans use it in a unique way by linking it to predation and devouring. They do not seek to empty the self but to expand the self. They do not seek submission to God but the devouring and destruction of God. They believe that the ecstasy of the kill is among the deepest and most profound manifestations of human potential, an experiential fact well known to warriors from all times and places.

The Need to Kill

Luciferans say, "I kill, therefore I exist." Violence may bring pleasure, ecstasy, and euphoria, but it goes deeper than that: it is a need. Without killing, there can be no existence. Existence is predicated on killing. Killing is a necessary and sufficient cause for existence and for life. There is no life without it. For Luciferans, Freud was wrong. He put sex at the center of human existence, but he just did not go deep enough. Before intercourse is killing. There can be no sex without killing: killing is the precondition for sex, because without killing there can be no life and therefore no sex. Sex reproduces the life that thrives on killing. And killing makes way for new life that sex produces. A single being can survive without sex but not without killing. Sex brings the single being into matter, but killing keeps the matter whole.

Sex and violence are intimate. One creates, the other destroys. Both are pleasurable.

Luciferans assert that Maslow and other motivational psychologists were also wrong because they omitted violence (and devouring and possession as well) from their descriptions of basic human needs, a glaring omission from a true description of the human animal. Like all other needs, the need for violence must be met or the human will suffer. Violence is as much a part of Maslow's needs-hierarchy as food, shelter, and safety. For Luciferans, violence may be directed toward animals and plants for food or pleasure, or pointed at other humans as well. It is all the same; for Luciferans, a human life can be violently terminated without remorse or guilt just as easily as any other life form.

Killing humans is simply a higher Luciferan call, designed to enhance self-power. If it serves the quest for ultimate power, then it has purpose, meaning and significance. Luciferans feel that most humans are made to be sacrificed and used anyway — for proof they point to the willing millions who have sacrificed themselves in war to serve bloodthirsty abominations like religion and state. Only the lower forms of life could sacrifice themselves in such stupid ways; such lower lifeforms are therefore easy prey who deserve their fates. Luciferans argue that murdering such human fodder is as pure, natural, and normal as animal slaughter.

Of course this purity can be twisted: Luciferans believe that contemporary criminal violence is a sick and distorted extension of Luciferan killing. It is killing without a meaningful higher cause or purpose. Such violence is the decadent and misunderstood twisting of the basic human need to kill. It is an undirected and pathological distortion of the love of killing for the survival, power, and personal empowerment it provides. Even the fools who die for God and Country at least serve something, whereas pathologically violent criminals do not. Purposeless violence is to killing what sexual depravity is to reproduction. To kill deliberately, purposefully, and intelligently is a high human calling, a call to transcendence. It makes us rise above the illusion of peace and love. It takes us from power to power, from limitation to limitlessness.

Killing takes us directly to godhood; prayer, righteousness, and love do not. God's essential nature is found in predation, not love. Without killing there can be no love. Killing removes that which has become stale to provide fresh space for that which is vital and energized. Killing opens possibilities and encourages growth. God endorses killing because God is a predator. Luciferans want their killing to surpass even God's. Ultimately, Luciferans want to kill God.

Luciferans use killing to expand self beyond the limitations of life and death. They turn killing back on itself. They believe that Yahweh uses killing to prevent the rising of his competitors up the spiritual hierarchy. He kills them so their competing selfhood will be annihilated. In this way his identity swells. Luciferans believe their only way out and up is to kill Yahweh, kill God, so their identity can swell and replace God.

They believe killing lets them enter and occupy the space of that which they have killed. They absorb, use, and take over the power given up by their kill: whatever they kill and eat becomes part of them; their victim's strength enters them. The stronger the victim, the stronger the power absorbed. Only when God is killed can the Luciferan rise up and seize the power of godhood.

This is why Luciferans believe that Christ's story is actually a prescription for Luciferan growth. Christ is killed, so part of God is also killed. Christ was God's substitute and was killed instead of his Father. Christ was killed because Yahweh was terrified of the strong Luciferans evolving from humanity, and so offered his son as a sacrifice to placate his Luciferan competitors. It was an act of desperation from a weakening predator. Yahweh threw Christ in our direction as an offering, a placation, a sacrifice. It worked for a time, and even briefly enhanced Yahweh's power on earth. But only for a short time, because Christ's death proved Yahweh's vulnerability and weakness. It also proved his cowardice, because rather than face his enemies squarely, he allowed his own son to take his place.

Luciferans believe that Christ's death created endless possibilities for the rise of competent Luciferans. The killing even opened possibilities for the rest of us, for those of us strong, bold, and daring enough to embrace the ultimate human potential of godhood. The message from the crucifixion is clear: unless God is killed, we cannot grow. Unless God is killed, transcendence is impossible. We have killed God's proxy, and now we need to kill God. Only then will the full meaning of the crucifixion flower in our understanding: the crucifixion is an invitation to kill and replace God, not an excuse to feel guilt or remorse. It is the fulfillment of the Luciferan truth that God must die. Christians believe that Christ's death was the most central spiritual event of all time because it "saved" us. Luciferans agree. It saved us from our ignorance and fear of Yahweh's almighty power by showing us that his power is sham, and available for the taking.

To grow spiritually, therefore, we need to kill. Transcendence is only for those who accept and understand the basic human need for killing. We remove something else so we can take its place. The only other option is our death and erasure, our removal from the vitality of life and existence. This is true for all other natural life forms, and is true for us. Luciferans believe that ignoring the need for killing creates insanity. Luciferans kill to stay sane.

VIOLENCE AND SANITY

According to current standards of mental health, those who love violence are insane. Such killers are called "sociopaths" or "psychopaths". But the sick individuals held up as examples — Manson, Bundy and other serial killers — are distorted reflections of real Luciferan warriors. Luciferans see such individuals as sick, but in a different way. As already mentioned, they are not sick because they commit violence, but because they commit it so wastefully.

Luciferans gain something from their violence. Their killing is purposeful, deliberate, and united to the relentless intelligence of the Luciferan faith. Serial killers are violent, but their violence has no value. It is wasted, and so is their victim's pain. It is violence without purpose. Apart from a short-term heightened awareness, nothing is gained, nothing achieved: the hierarchy is not upwardly scaled.

For Luciferans, the so-called "thrill-kill" phenomenon so shocking to middle-class sensibilities is a media invention built on the stupid antics of lower-order humans on the hierarchy.

The euphoric joy of violence, of absorbing the victim's pain and agony, is only valuable when linked to a purpose, the purpose being to use the victim's agony to advance a single goal, which is to rip through the fabric of reality to experience true godhood.

Without this goal, violence is simply lower-order self indulgence, a useless spilling of life. True spiritual killing brings peace, balance, and sanity. It brings relief, and it yields an almost mystical union with the brutal essence of the hierarchy itself.

VIOLENCE AND SEX

Sexuality and violence seem opposite. To most humans, the concept of sexuality invokes images of pleasure and thoughts of life-creation whereas violence implies aggression, pain and possible life-termination. Luciferans, however, link these together. Life cannot be extracted from death any more than pain can be segmented from pleasure. Luciferans believe that only those with the courage to explore violence can understand real sexual pleasure. The two are melded somewhere deep in primal brain matter; to rip them apart is to invite neurosis or even psychosis. We need violence like we need sex: performed together, they become an extraordinary ecstasy. All ecstatic energy promotes personal power acquisition, and therefore is a worthwhile pursuit.

Sexual violence may be thought of as a kind of possession. The victim is reduced to powerlessness, and his or her rage and shame become food for devouring. Sexual violence thus brings together the primal Luciferan forces of devouring, possession and passionate violence itself. It is therefore a deeply attractive option for obtaining dominance and to accumulate immense personal power. It is a tool for power acquisition.

Common myths about the "black mass" are based on this essential Luciferan truth. The naked young woman strapped to the altar and about to be impaled with the sacrificial knife by a menacing hooded figure — such images point to the ritual of sexual violence as a way of satisfying a primal Luciferan urge, and also a focus of worship. On a deeper level, Luciferans treasure sex because without it there can be no reproduction, and without reproduction, the hierarchy of devouring cannot exist. Reproduction creates more humans, therefore more fodder for growth.

In Luciferan philosophy, sex is a violently pleasurable prelude to birth, and death is an equally orgasmic release for both the killer and the killed. Death opens up space for more birth, and birth opens the inevitability of death. Pleasure borders on pain, and pain can border on pleasure. Sex, death, power and life are all one. All life forms are at war with all others, and only violence empowers any life form to survive to have sex. Thus violent life forms are rewarded, while non-violent life fades into nothingness.

161

PHYSICAL, EMOTIONAL, COGNITIVE, AND SPIRITUAL VIOLENCE

As with devouring and possession, violence can focus on different aspects of the victim's being. Direct physical killing may satisfy certain primal sensibilities, but its power to advance powaqqatsi can be less effective than violence directed toward the victim's emotional, cognitive, and spiritual life. There are as many different ways to kill as there are to devour and possess, and these more subtle forms of violence also attract Luciferans.

VIOLENCE AGAINST THE BODY

Physical violence is clear enough — the aggressor physically attacks and hopes to injure the victim. The threat of physical violence has always held power for the predator: from the schoolyard bully to the full threat of military invasion, the possibility of physical pain and damage has dominated and frightened untold billions of human beings throughout time. It is the ultimate threat: "do what I command, or be tortured and/or killed."

Luciferans use actual or threatened physical violence to achieve certain ends. They know that lower-order humans are terrified and yet fascinated by violence; anything so fascinating and compelling can therefore be used to lure and titillate potential victims, or to cause other victims to surrender their resistance and submit.

Violence works. No amount of politically correct jargon or outrage about physical aggression can change the fact that violence achieves certain ends. It works politically between countries, and within countries. It attracts immense media attention, especially if it is associated with some kind of "moral cause" espoused by a group: this attention almost always allows the group to achieve its ends in one way or another. Violence works, especially when used intelligently and when attached to an apparently higher vision or calling. Luciferans would argue this has been self-evident throughout history, and is just as true today.

It works because, by using it effectively, victims can be intimidated, dominated, and directed to follow the violator's will. But physical violence also has its problems. It attracts too much attention, and is a blunt instrument at best. Other forms of violence can be more useful to Luciferans than simple assault or murder.

VIOLENCE AGAINST THE EMOTIONS

Violence directed at a victim's emotions can cripple or even destroy her emotional stability. In emotional devouring the victim's emotions feed the predator. In emotional possession the victim's emotional life is controlled and redirected to serve the predator's will. In emotional violence the victim's emotional existence is crippled or even obliterated.

This is not hard to do. Some parents do it almost unconsciously: simply ridicule, confuse, or otherwise associate negativity and fear with any display of emotion, and soon the child will cease feeling anything. He will become numb and withdrawn. Real emotion will become foreign, and he will learn to dissociate from his feelings. Luciferans will sometimes deliberately create this kind of emotional dissociation primarily because the victim becomes weak and easily controlled. Emotional devouring is difficult with such disabled victims because there is little emotion to eat, but possession becomes an easy possibility. Luciferans may thus assault a victim's emotions as a prelude to possession.

Luciferans also assault their own psyche as part of their power bargain. In the destruction of their compassion, conscience, and empathy, they consciously seek to kill all associated emotions: love, pity, remorse, guilt and sorrow. This does not disable the Luciferan, however, because the killing is surgical, precise, and designed for a specific purpose. That purpose has been stated repeatedly: these emotions are impediments to the full actualization and self-empowerment of godhood. When these emotions are killed, others take their place. And these new emotional energies replace the power previously drained by the "sick emotions."

Such new emotions include the euphoria of the kill, the joy and empowering influence of the hunt, the profound lust of the exercise of power. They include hate, rage, sexual catharsis, and all other related states. Ultimately, Luciferans aspire to be released from their attachment to even these states as they climb closer to godhood. In the meantime, such emotions are used to fuel their upward energy.

Luciferans do not believe that violence alone kills compassion. Even violent soldiers in a war feel compassion for their buddies, their families, their lovers. After all, the Auschwitz commander loved his dog and his wife.

Only willpower and choice kill compassion — the Luciferan bargain voids compassion; the death of compassion and empathy is a deliberate, conscious choice made by those strong enough to bear it.

This way of thinking suggests that violence is simply part of the natural order. Violence is part of the world of all living things, including those who assume the higher moral ground of compassion and pity.

Psychologists argue that violence fills the hole left by the exit of compassion, as if the presence of compassion inoculates against the violence virus. The so-called sociopath or psychopath supposedly carries this disease, and so loves violence. But Luciferans believe power, not violence, fills the void left by compassion. Violence is simply one more tool to obtain power, joy, and freedom. Violence is only a means to an end, although like all other means, can be inherently pleasurable.

For Luciferans, compassion and pity are the disease, not violence. Compassion and pity are sick emotions, and they leak out precious life force to the weak, the sick, and the undeserving. In Nietszche's words: "Pity stands in antithesis to the tonic emotions which enhance the energy of the feeling of life: it has a depressive effect. One loses force when one pities." And, "What is more harmful than any vice? — Active sympathy for the ill-constituted and weak."

Luciferans note that almost all moralistic sanctions against violence and killing refer only to members of the human species. They believe that not only is this hypocritical — the animals feel pain as much as we do, and are probably more deserving of life than most humans anyway — but is also factually wrong. Within the hierarchy of devouring on planet earth, human life is no more sacred or sanctified than any other life form. This "sanctity" is simply our own cowardly self-centered conceit that deludes us into thinking we are special. Luciferans know that we are as deserving of violence as other life forms. Only our current strength on the hierarchy protects us, but this cannot last forever. Another form of life will rise to prey on us just as we prey on whatever we wish.

Luciferans believe they are this new form of life, this new experiment of evolution. They embrace the basic truth that there is no special sanctity to human life; once this is understood and accepted, then the barriers against devouring, possessing, and violating human life are gone. What of the moral commandments built on love and compassion? No. Such commandments are nonsense. Kill compassion, and the logic of violence becomes clear, sacred, and inevitable. The death of compassion means the birth of power, strength, life, and crackling energy. The death of compassion means the Luciferan becomes one with the cleansing force of violence against other life forms, a force that is ordained, natural, and necessary.

Killing or disabling emotions in victims may fulfill an entirely different purpose. In rare cases, lower order Luciferans might tear apart a victim's emotional life for the simple pleasure of it; however, such purposeless emotional murder is usually associated with lower order psychopaths or those caught up by inter-generational familial abuse over which they have no control and even less awareness.

VIOLENCE AGAINST THE MIND

Emotional assault cripples the victim's emotions. Cognitive assault cripples the victim's mind. Why try to kill a victim's ability to think? An answer can

164

be found in the works of Carl Jung, who argued that emotions and cognitions both share one core similarity: they inform us about our world and allow us to make judgments about what may harm or benefit us.

Thus, emotions signal a certain reaction to an event, while thoughts provide another type of information. Deprived of emotions, the victim loses the ability to judge events and motives — she becomes vulnerable to attack because her emotions cannot inform her of the predator's presence by signaling say, fear, for example. In the same way, victims deprived of the ability to think accurately are thus unable to analyze a predator's motives, and so become vulnerable to deceptions of all kinds.

Disabling or even killing cognition is surprisingly easy. Complex thought and logical analysis are amazingly fragile and vulnerable to destruction. Early food deprivation, neglect, or other privations can thoroughly disable the flowering of thought in a child. Thinking depends on a healthy brain, and the brain depends on nutrition, stimulation, and other related factors. Various diseases can cripple the ability of the mature brain to function as well. Thus, Luciferan totalitarian rulers have always known that hunger and privation can kill the growth of intellect and therefore of skilled resistance.

In the same way, parenting and rearing skills can disable or destroy the child's ability to think. Constant humiliation and ridicule can so injure self-esteem that the child becomes locked within the constraints of self-hate, unable to think objectively. Homes in which creative independent thought is discouraged or even punished can also create children afraid to think. Exactly the same situation can exist within adult relationships when one spouse ridicules, dismisses, and undermines the thought processes of the other. Certain work environments also produce similar results: "groupthink" and absolute conformity can result.

The basic dynamic here is simple: attack the brain's ability to support logic and reason (as with psychological assault), cause the victim to distrust his own thoughts, induce despair, depression, self-hate and other disabling conditions, and then the predator can destroy effective cognitive resistance in victims. Such victims never question the motives of their predators. Any such questions are diverted into self-hate and self-doubt. And so the predator screams with joy, filled with the confidence of an assured, iron-clad security built on the certainty that victims will never resist, any more than cattle can resist the killing floor of a packing house.

If this certainty is anchored within organized systems of psychological assault, which are always lethal to logic, reason, and independent judgment, then rational thought is the first target to fall. "Therapeutic" weekend seminars, for example, are notorious for their frontal assault on reason. Logic is held up for ridicule in favor of emotional catharsis and group contagion. Reason and skepticism are defined by group facilitators as the ultimate enemy of pleasure, fun, reality, and empowerment. In this kind of hysterical environment, people willingly suspend critical judgment to meld with the group's "dynamic spirit", to embrace a reality which, they are led to believe, exists beyond the cold, rusting, iron grip of reason. They willingly disable or kill their own skepticism in favor of some kind of epiphany, transformation, or euphoria. Luciferans are attracted to such programs, because victims unconditionally open themselves for predation.

Predatory charismatic leaders have always known how willing we are to kill the gift of reason and skepticism in order to feel the powerful euphoria of belonging, believing, and "absolute truth". We are lured by this scent-bait, and we fall for it. If the charismatic leader is Luciferan, then her victims willingly kill their own minds to find "coherence", "alignment" and "commitment". It is not difficult to convince victims to jettison logic and skepticism because independent thought apparently is a burden we humans have only recently acquired, and it scares us. We never know where it will lead, and fear it will eventually turn and devour us. We think of logical thought as cold, relentless, and unsentimental. It is not an obvious friend. Luciferans capitalize on this fear and encourage their victims to kill this ally for the sake of "higher wisdom" or "enlightenment". Convinced that the mind is the "enemy", we willingly agree to betray and destroy it. Once we have done this, then we stand disarmed and waiting to be invaded.

Objective logical analysis in the victim is the absolute enemy of Luciferans, so they must kill it in their victims. They want to cultivate it in themselves, however, because they know what a powerful force for power acquisition it can be when unanchored to compassion, conscience, and empathy: logical analysis has served to build both gas chambers and hospitals. Victims armed with logic are dangerous; victims who surrender it are easy to overcome.

Apart from early deprivation, destructive rearing, and psychological assault, there are yet other ways to overcome logic and skepticism. Drugs are marvelous. As Andrew Malcolm points out in his books *The Pursuit of Intoxication* and *The Case Against the Drugged Mind*, drugs bypass the need for logic by appealing straight into the heart of swelling pleasure. Why think when you can feel such joy and pleasure? Why try to understand when understanding only leads to despair? Why try to determine the motives of that which provides such profound pleasure? Why even suspect? Why go any further?

Luciferans can count on this thought-stopping ability of drugs, and will occasionally introduce their victims to drugs for this reason. They know that victims will not question the Luciferans motives, because to question is to lose the pleasure. And that is unthinkable. The pleasure, the euphoria — that is the end of everything for the drug dependent victim. Anything threatening that pleasure is an enemy, and enemies must be avoided or even killed. If this enemy takes on the face of logic for the drug dependent victim, then so be it. Kill it. Kill it now, and kill it fast. If it is allowed to live, then it will invade the pleasure dome, and it will hurt. It will hurt because the victim will have to look at that which gives him pleasure, the Luciferan or his impulse. And to look at that means he will have to take action that will in the end deprive him of pleasure. He will kill it, rather than face that pain.

Luciferans count on this weakness to make sure that their drug-dependent victims agree, like Pilate, to wash their hands of reality.

Drugs can kill the ability to think and so can ecstatically oriented religious movements. The pursuit of euphoria, trance, satori, or any state beyond logic and mind can become ends in themselves, just as addictive as any drug-induced euphoria. Many spiritual traditions actively seek to bypass the mind in favor of some "higher" level of existence: the mind is seen as nothing more than monkey-chatter, an unfortunately counterproductive mistake of evolution. The answer to happiness, joy, and wisdom? Kill the mind; skeptical thought and doubt are the thieves trying to break into the heaven of ecstasy. Luciferans naturally cluster around such traditions due to the endless predatory pleasure and power they provide. Those who allow their minds to be killed, no matter how pure their higher motives, will lose their coherent solidity and thus become open to assault.

Group-conforming dynamics linked to such mind-numbing spiritual traditions can be used to deepen this separation between soul and mind. In his book *The Tyranny of the Group*, Andrew Malcolm attacks tyrannical group movements which "offer joy and creativity in six painless lessons", which feed into the powerful human urge to transcend the self, but which also contain within themselves the "possibility of utter betrayal of the self. He who has escaped from himself may, on that account, be rendered suggestible and easy prey to the strong influences around him." Luciferans understand this basic human lust to transcend the self by killing the mind; they also understand how this lust opens its victims to predation.

So when reason is killed, and victims' minds are disabled, what happens? They cannot evaluate information, and can then be devoured or possessed at the Luciferan's whim.

Psychological assault, drugs, ecstatic religious experience, and group dynamics are all effective weapons in the Luciferan's cognitive arsenal. Another weapon is the ancient art of verbal combat. The Sophists developed this martial art in pre-Socratic Greece, and it has had an eloquent history since then. Verbal combat is basically designed to dismantle an opponent's argument using any technique possible. Capaldi's *The Art of Deception*, Johnson and Blairs' *Logical Self-Defence*, and Thouless' *Straight and Crooked Thinking* clarify how these logical deceptions work. Victims unfamiliar with "red herring", "ad hominem", "slippery slope" and other well known logical fallacies can have their core beliefs and honest concerns easily disabled and held up to ridicule. Such people are easy targets, especially if they have also been subjected to some of the other 'softening techniques' already described. Luciferans can ridicule and defeat them in the court of the mind without much difficulty.

Logical self-defense is difficult enough at the best of times, but when the mind is weakened or disabled, victims cannot protect themselves from aggressive ideologies and logical fallacies. They cannot see the lie hidden in the message. They are left only with the surface of things, the appearance of what is. They can be defeated, and their beliefs shattered.

I have experienced this kind of verbal combat primarily in university settings, where cognitive violence is rampant. Cognitive warfare, not necessarily intellectual brilliance, seems to determine who dominates a given intellectual field and who fades into the dusky back shelves of academic obscurity. Who gets to dominate the cognitive hierarchy and who fails? Hopefully science and truth are the guides, but, unfortunately, competitively violent cognitive assault all too often seems to be the real selective force. The secret of academic success? Ridicule all academic enemies, undermine their positions with "evidence", and then go on to dominate your field with the endless artillery of publication. Publish or perish; there is more Luciferan truth to this axiom than most researchers chasing "objective truth" would probably care to acknowledge. "There is a war," sings Leonard Cohen, and Universities are cognitive killing grounds. Kill the enemy by amassing overwhelming logical force for your position. Make him look stupid. Strip him of intellectual dignity. This is the essence of cognitive assault. In the marketplace of ideas, only the strong survive.

In his book *Imaginary Landscapes*, William Irwin Thompson, a University academic who has struggled to explore new intellectual territory within *academe*, describes his encounter with cognitive violence:

> The watering hole of the coffee machine in the philosophy department was sometimes safe, but when the Tyrannosaurus Rex of Noam Chomsky appeared, all alien opinions had to scurry to safety in the ferns. There was no question of questioning: there was only the One Truth. If one listened, hidden to the side in the foliage, one could tell how deadly it all was from their language. Conversations, lectures, or presentations were always described as brutal conflicts, and approval was always registered as an act of triumphant violence, such as "I annihilated him," or "He was so stupid as to say x, so I murdered him on the spot." I remember watching Louis Kampf and Noam Chomsky approvingly exchanging expressions of

intensely violent language and then, without skipping a beat, go on to discuss the peace demonstration they were about to take part in. Scholarship for them was a form of Ninja assassination, but they still thought that only the hawks in the Pentagon were instruments of domination, violence, and cultural oppression."

I suspect that anyone who has spent any time at all in a university setting, particularly in graduate work, has experienced this kind of cognitive violence. I know I certainly have. From their positions of institutionalized respect and power, many academics become ruthless aggressors determined to promote or preserve their own ideas or ideologies.

Such strong academic survivors will try to tell you that they represent "truth", and to defy them is to defy something even more unshakable than God: factual reality itself. You will be bullied to accept their beliefs, and your thoughts will be dismissed as insignificant.

For those without an academic degree, the situation becomes even more devastating. Academic predators have come to believe that all thought outside the academy, which they control, is worthless. The academic credential is everything, "lower order" cognitions nothing. In this way, the University can both serve and protect cognitive predators, much as the church has served the power-lust of some soul-predators.

A final set of weapons exploited by cognitive predators can be found in techniques of influence. Such techniques differ from psychological assault: whereas psychological assault requires a coordinated plan of attack over time, techniques of influence can have immediate impact on strangers or groups of strangers. Such techniques disable critical thought by simply bypassing it.

Robert Cialdini's book *Influence: The New Psychology of Modern Persuasion* details how these weapons of influence are used. All of them — reciprocation, commitment and consistency, social proof, liking, authority, and scarcity — deserve studied attention. They all share three basic components: first, they are cleanly mechanical in their operation, as automatically effective as a key in a lock, bypassing critical thought as easily as a plane flying under radar; second, they trigger a predictable reaction of automatic responding in us; and third, they allow us to be manipulated "without the appearance of manipulation." The entire process is "virtually undetectable", and "those who employ it can cash in on its influence without any appearance of having structured the situation in their favor."

Luciferans have a deep appreciation of such influence techniques and of the whole range of logic-killing devices, and they pursue them with intense vigor and profound pleasure. If their victims think they are immune, then Luciferans are pleased. In *their* world, the victim's illusion of immunity is his greatest weakness and their best point of entry. To them, such victims are easy prey.

VIOLENCE AGAINST THE SOUL

Violence against the soul is absolute: "I don't want to possess you or eat you, I just want you destroyed, erased from existence. You are to be exterminated. Totally and completely. Not just your body, heart, and mind, but all of you, all that you may become and all that you may eventually influence. You are to cease existing. Your soul is to be terminated."

Such lust for the total eradication of another soul may stem from the deep terror that maybe that soul will rise above one in the hierarchy. It may be the joyous killing of an inferior, the ecstatic ending and total eradication of a "lower" life form. It may be the destruction of another competitor: the killer's territory can then be expanded so "lesser" beings can be possessed or devoured without competition.

Killing another soul can also be linked to devouring and possession: such acts provide the killer with an extraordinary energy surge. Once killed, the victim's soul provides a deeply satisfying form of food. Possession would then be impossible, but nourishment immense. In its ultimate ending, the soul would release intense energy, much like an atom in a nuclear weapon. If harvested, this energy would be absolutely delicious and empowering for the predator.

Either way, violence against the soul is the ultimate violence. I can kill your body, your emotions, your mind; but none of these touch your soul. Your soul is your ultimate reality, and to kill it is a victory deeper and more satisfying than simple physical murder. I may kill you to remove you, or kill you to absorb you, but in the end you are gone, totally. Killing the soul means that everything else usually dies along with it: kill a soul and the body soon follows, either by accident or suicide. Such soul-killing is entirely legal.

Soul violence is hard work for Luciferans. The soul is the deepest layer of the victim's reality, and difficult to penetrate. Soul killing is the most absolute form of violence available. There is nothing left worth taking once the soul is killed.

Soul energy tempts Luciferans: such energy is primal, and therefore deeply nourishing. Everything is given up: body, heart, mind, and more. To absorb such power is to advance one's place on the hierarchy significantly. To convince victims to give up their souls is the ultimate victory. To convince a victim to cease absolute existence is a power known only to advanced Luciferans.

So how does a Luciferan convince a victim to cease absolute existence? How does a Luciferan convince a victim to surrender soul? There are ways.

As with the body, heart, and mind, some victims seem to want to give it all away. The burden of individual existence is just too great, and many victims plead to be terminated. Luciferans understand that for such victims the distance between depression, the bottle, or the needle, and the absolute surrender of soul is a short commute, a simple journey of re-framing and re-direction. When the final surrender occurs, then the outpouring of soul-energy is a banquet feast to be enjoyed and savored as none other.

Luciferans understand that many victims will also give away their primal soul-energy for the simplest of trinkets: success, power, knowledge, money, influence, pleasure. They work with the victim's desire, encouraging a little surrender here, a bigger surrender there. Always the ultimate prize is dangled in front of the victim, who then gives away more and more precious autonomy, individuality, and soul-essence to obtain the "gift" of total release. Like Clive Barker's Shadwell, the Luciferan offers a gift whose ultimate prize is the loss of soul.

This theme is explored in the Faustus legend and its many duplicates: Dr. Faustus' search for absolute knowledge and power leads him inexorably into ultimate self-betrayal and loss of soul. His obsessive lust for a young woman causes him to sacrifice honesty, compassion, and conscience for something that was never really possible to obtain through deception and coercion: love. He loses it all, and then he slides into hell in the grip of demons.

Other victims do not easily surrender their souls for temporal rewards. They are coerced, and their fall is the loss of innocence through overpowering force. Leonard Shengold, clinical professor of psychiatry at the New York University School of Medicine, describes this process in his book *Soul Murder*, which he defines as "the deliberate attempt to eradicate or compromise the separate identity of another person." Childhood victims of early abuse, for example, seem to eventually succumb to an "inner need for annihilation analogous to that found in emotionally deprived infants who died after growing up in institutions." How does this happen? Shengold shares one of his many case studies:

> "There was no overt physical abuse on the part of A's parents — the "crime" consisted of some cruelty toward him, but predominantly what made his childhood a hell was their indifference, their lack of loving care and empathy"... "A. usually felt belittled and humiliated by them (his parents), especially in response to any show of emotion on his part... The habitual vicious teasing and sarcasm from both parents amounted to training A. to regard any empathic communication as a prelude to torment." Intense emotional abandonment, deprivation, and the misery of feeling alone within the context of a "soul-murdering" atmosphere

were enough to convince A. to pursue a course of self-initiated soul-murder."

Such "soul murder" eventually creates a victim ready to surrender the soul. "Identity is lost", and the victim finds pleasure in the ultimate surrender of soul/identity to a predator. Shengold defines this as "the ultimate sin" that one human can visit on another.

Can the soul be killed without the consent of the victim? This is the deep mystery of evil itself, of the echoes of myth suggesting that we have to open the door to the vampire before it can enter, that we have to invite the demon by our actions, that we have to offer ourselves willingly for the ultimate sacrifice of soul. If Shengold is right, then some of us are conditioned from early childhood to more readily give ourselves over to the devourers and predators cruising among us. "Fear those who can kill the body, but fear even more those who can kill our souls," says Jesus.

Violence, like devouring and possession, cannot always be displayed openly. Camouflage is necessary. As with other natural predators, Luciferans must cultivate the arts of deception, disguise, ruse, and secret strategy. Luciferan warriors must know how to stalk and disarm their victims by appearing to be non-threatening. Like the god Proteus, they have to be able to take on many forms, many shapes, and many disguises.

CHAPTER SIX
PROTEAN CAMOUFLAGE

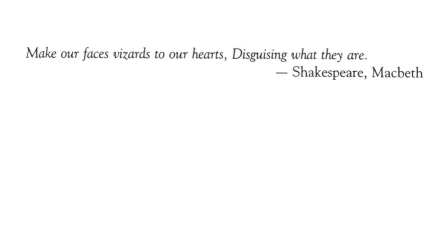

Make our faces vizards to our hearts, Disguising what they are.
— Shakespeare, Macbeth

According to Greek myth, Proteus was a sea god who could change shape with instant fluidity. He was a liquid shape-shifter, always transforming. His shapes could be appealing or horrifying, but his true nature was always elusive. His essence was never clear, never obvious.

By adding the idea of camouflage to the Protean fluidity myth, another aspect of Luciferan psycho-spirituality can be illuminated. If camouflage is understood as disguise designed to conceal predator from prey, then Luciferans use protean fluidity to camouflage themselves from potential victims.

If we take the Protean myth even further, and think of Proteus as an entity who never bonds with other beings, then we move even closer to Luciferism. Proteus can be visualized as self-bound, fascinated with his shape-changing, in love with his own transformations, constantly in motion. Like Narcissus, he is self-concerned. He connects with others, breaks these connections, and then moves on, completely unconcerned. The Proteus/Narcissus god is superficiality and deceit; yet he is also strangely fascinating, thrilling, and exotic, the kind of being who can be all things yet no thing in particular. He invites awe and fascination; he compels attention.

Luciferans cultivate this protean elasticity of appearance because it enhances predatory advantage. They consciously employ Protean camouflage to advance personal power. They also see in Proteus' shape-shifting an almost god-like status: to be all things to all people, to induce their trust and fascination, and then to devour, possess, or kill them for personal power advantage. Disguise and camouflage to enhance devouring, possession and violence — this is yet one more weapon in the Luciferan arsenal.

PROTEAN LUCIFERAN RELATIONSHIPS

The Protean mode comes naturally to Luciferans. Without compassion or empathy, conscience or morality, Luciferans easily slide from one shape to another, making and then breaking connections with serpentine fluidity. Such connections might be deeply significant to the victim, who may come to trust, love, admire or even revere the Luciferan predator. Similar feelings can be superficially replicated by the Luciferan but never felt, because to feel them would be weak, and would undermine the predatory impulse. Emotional relationships are tools to be used in the acquisition of power, and that is all. Once the victim is no longer useful, the Luciferan simply breaks the connection and moves on to other targets.

Luciferans train themselves not to feel pain or regret over broken connections. To be connected to other human beings means to be bonded to them by love, compassion, friendship, and self-sacrifice. When such bonds are broken, most people experience pain, sorrow, loss, mourning, or grief. Luciferans find love despicable, and hence do not form relationships based on it. They experience no intrinsic pleasure with such relationships unless power acquisition is a possibility. As a result, disconnection does not affect them — other people can be used and then dropped without pain or regret.

Luciferans know that emotional bonds are important to others, so they practice the art of emotional camouflage and deception. They only appear to care and love because the victim then comes closer, allowing exploitation, possession, and devouring.

PROTEAN CAMOUFLAGE IN SOCIETY

All predators need camouflage, and Luciferans are no exception. Victims must remain unsuspecting and therefore unprotected.

Luciferans like to camouflage their true nature and intentions. They may hide behind a dazzling persona of charismatic qualities designed to disarm all caution in victims. They may also hide behind a professional persona such as doctor, lawyer, teacher, preacher. They may disguise themselves as average middle class neighbors, or as harmless friends.

Luciferans are always attracted to appealing organizations, movements, and belief systems because of the camouflage they can provide. Feeding the hungry, working for the underprivileged, offering therapy and support for hurting clients, promoting ideals such as universal love from within traditional religions: all of these are useful hunting blinds. Luciferans work from within churches, corporations, schools, political movements and elsewhere: the more trusted and respected the institution, the more camouflaged the predator becomes. It is hard to criticize anyone working on behalf of something worthwhile, and Luciferans know they can operate with relative protection and impunity as a result. Highly respected social positions are very desirable — Luciferans are particularly attracted to power as for power's sake, but they also enjoy the side benefit of the camouflage offered. It is wonderfully easy to prey on weaker victims when the predation occurs from within a respected institution or social position.

Luciferans know how to adopt camouflage on many levels — physical, emotional, mental, spiritual — so predation can be hidden from outsiders, competitors, and victims.

PHYSICAL CAMOUFLAGE: BEAUTY

Physical beauty can be used as a powerful disguise to hide all forms of Luciferan predation. Beauty disarms the victim, who fixates on the predator's surface attraction and thus becomes blind to the intentions beneath. In experiment after experiment, psychologists have shown that we attribute finer and higher qualities to the beautiful over the ugly. Attractive people are held to be more honest, more intelligent, more empathetic. Thus our "good guys" are attractive and our "bad guys" are ugly or distorted — think here of the legacy of the Batman and Superman comics, where the evil anti-heroes are almost always physically distorted. The Joker had his face mutilated by acid, and the Penguin is a short, waddling, odd looking creature. Good is beautiful, evil is ugly. Moral goodness shows externally as physical attractiveness, while badness shows itself as ugliness.

We are infatuated with physical beauty. We admire the beautiful, and wish we were like them. The entertainment industry is built on images of beautiful people. Advertisers associate their client's product with physical beauty. Young, slim, hard, sexual, potent: this is what we lust after, and what attracts us. The presence of a beautiful person seems to disable our normal critical defenses. Robert Cialdini describes how physical beauty tends to cause critical thinking to shut down. "We like it, and so enter into a kind of autonomic loop, a *click-whurr* mechanism that bypasses normal defenses. When deeply attracted, we stop all considerations of reason, logic, and self-defense. We are lost to the power of beauty, and fall into a kind of thrall."

Luciferans cultivate this weakness. If they are themselves physically attractive, then they will use it to disarm victims. If not, then they will use every advantage of clothing, make-up, surgery and overall charismatic presence to generate the impression of dynamically charismatic beauty. If the Luciferan is truly unattractive, then the challenge is to accentuate whatever physical gifts are available, and to amplify these strengths with charisma and sheer force of personality. This might include surrounding and associating himself with the physically attractive, and by osmosis absorb some of their beauty.

Since both sexes are equally capable of Luciferism, both can use their bodies as bait to attract unwary and defenseless victims. Once attracted and disarmed, the victim becomes vulnerable to devouring, possession, and violence by the beautiful predator.

Luciferans may use emotional camouflage to meet their power needs. They create facsimiles of disarming emotions such as sincerity, empathy, compassion, love, concern, and caring. Potential victims respond with trust, openness, and reciprocation to such displays, and hence become easy prey. But behind the facade is the coldly calculating Luciferan intention, always waiting and watching for an opening.

This intention is not easy to detect. Luciferans do not appear cold and calculating. If they did, their camouflage would be torn away, and they would lose their advantage. Their predatory potential depends on their skill, and so they learn how to create powerfully compelling appearances. To do this, they seem to invoke a type of "deep acting", somewhat similar to the transfer empathy mentioned in the Introduction. By actually taking on the appearance of love and care, they can mimic these emotions perfectly. Undercover police agents or method actors probably know something about this state: they have to enter into a role so perfectly that outsiders cannot detect the act. If the act is deep enough, however, then loss of their own identity becomes a real risk. If they enter into the role so perfectly that they live, think, and breathe their character perfectly, then they may forget their real nature and purpose.

Luciferans never risk losing their own identity, however, even though they enter into their role so completely and realistically that even sophisticated outsiders are deceived. They seem to use a kind of protean "identity-fluidity" that allows them to enter perfectly into disguise while at the same time fully preserving their own identity and objectives.

I do not pretend to fully understand this identity-fluidity. But just as the Proteus of legend was said to shift from one shape to another without losing his core identity, so too Luciferans seem to shift from one feeling state to another without losing their hard Luciferan core. They can seem deeply passionate and loyal one minute, and yet be completely indifferent and disloyal the next.

This is because they actually experience the emotion at the moment they display it. They experience no dissonance or conflict in their camouflage display, because behind it all they maintain consonance and continuity in their Luciferan identity. While in one state or another, they are believable because there is no conflict or dissonance in them. They are absolutely truthful at that specific moment, and yet absolutely deceitful at the same time. Their love, empathy, compassion, and trust is real but also false. This is why they are such dangerous predators: they mimic real love, affection, and bonding so perfectly that victims are completely deceived. The only close analogy comes from nature, where one species of animal adopts camouflage so accurate that its prey (or its predators) are completely fooled.

Once deceived, human victims become easy prey for emotional devouring, violence, or eventual possession.

COGNITIVE CAMOUFLAGE: DISPENSABLE BELIEFS

Just as Luciferans adopt, use, and discard emotions, so too they manipulate beliefs and belief systems for their advantage.

Luciferans understand that their prey are as attached to their beliefs as they are to their loving emotions and to physical beauty. Such victims automatically assume that someone who appears to love them really does, just as they assume that someone who articulates and holds their treasured beliefs is truly one of them.

Luciferans know that such attachments can be manipulated for gain, and that victims will fall for "belief deception" as easily as emotional deception. Manipulative politicians and Luciferans have this in common: repeat the voter/victim's treasured beliefs, and they will love you. As defined previously, we can visualize beliefs existing on a continuum from peripheral to central, or core. Peripheral beliefs are not essential to the person's core identity, and have to do with preferences, attitudes and other surface beliefs which, if changed, will not significantly alter or threaten core identity. Core beliefs on the other hand are immutable and beyond dispute. Such beliefs form the foundation of the individual's conception of reality and identity. Without them, the person could not function. When core beliefs are altered or destroyed, the individual will usually experience intense pain, disorientation, shock, or worse.

People hold different personal core beliefs, but will defend them vigorously, often viciously. Social groups often define themselves by their core beliefs, and will fight or even try to exterminate "outsiders." Witness Bosnia, the Cold War, Nazism, and the Irish conflict. Many will die and kill for these core social beliefs, especially if each individual's personal core beliefs coincide with those of the social group. All ambitious leaders of social movements — political, religious, or other — want each individual member to hold core beliefs identical with the Movement. Control core beliefs; control the individual. This is the essence of the totalism described by Huxley in *Brave New World* and Orwell in *1984*.

As discussed previously, loss of core belief is like loss of identity, which is like death. Most individuals joyfully cluster around others holding the same beliefs. Their core beliefs are confirmed, strengthened and protected by this communal/tribal grouping, and so they feel safe, warm, and loved in the presence of like-minded others. All of us seem to flock around our beliefs like animals clustering around their own kind. We find comfort with other people holding similar beliefs just as animals find comfort with others of their own species.

Luciferans understand this herd mentality, and use it to manipulate either specific individuals adhering to a particular belief system, or the entire group of people clutching the system. Luciferans in control of social movements can therefore threaten resistors and other internal critics to the ultimate death of self — loss of core beliefs through expulsion from the group. Belief systems, so much a part of our cognitive life, become avenues through which Luciferans control their victims and then use them in one way or another.

Luciferans clearly understand that core beliefs can be used because potential victims depend on them so deeply. Anything this powerful can become bait by attracting the victim's fascination and disarming his defenses. This is as true for humans and their beliefs as it is for animals and powerful scent baits. The pull is irresistible. Humans love belief alignment as much as we love being loved. When someone else articulates our deep core beliefs, it is as if we are touched by a loving personal caress.

Enthralled by anyone who faithfully articulates his core beliefs, the victim feels a rush of intense pleasure. The rush is so vital and primal that the victim seldom stops to carefully examine the source of this pleasure. Cialdini's "click-whirr" mechanism comes into play. Luciferans understand and use this carelessness to draw victims into a kind of thrall which opens them for easy predation. Victims believe they are receiving communion-like grace, when in fact they are being set up for exploitation or even soul-death. Destructive cult leaders understand this process perfectly.

To access and then mimic these core beliefs, the predator needs to understand the key phrases or "code words" that activate them. Most of us have only a few core beliefs, which are usually invoked and defined by a few key phrases. For example, Christians are aroused and alerted by words such as "Christ", "cross", "God", and "church"; feminists might be excited by words such as "patriarchy", "male", and "systemic sexism"; and communists would be alerted by "imperialism", "proletariat", "workers", and "capitalist" — much like my dog, Sophie, is aroused and alerted by "supper", "outside", "sit", "come" and "Sophie." Know the key words, and you can access and control the potential victim. Luciferans carefully research, explore, and then use such heavily loaded emotional terms to access the core beliefs of their victims. These key terms are "access codes" allowing entry into the victim's cognitive core. By repeating them properly, the victim opens up like a computer program, ready for interaction. To put it another way, they are ready to be exploited.

This process works for both individuals and groups. The Luciferan can enter into a specific individual by breaking the personal code or just as easily enter into a group by breaking the group code.

Breaking the Personal Code

To break the personal code, the Luciferan has to make contact with the target individual, listen to her personal story, deduce her core beliefs, and then feed them back in a believable fashion. Most individuals will enthusiastically share their core beliefs with almost anyone. This sharing is a kind of plea: "This is who I am, because this is what I believe. Are you like me? Do you believe as I believe?" Luciferan predators hear this plea, know that the person is desperate for affirmation, and therefore open for the taking.

For example, assume I am deeply committed to the environment. My life revolves around my political action on environmental issues. My commitment is so deep that it absorbs all my time and all my being. It is a good cause, a noble cause. I am willing to devote my life to it, even sacrifice it if necessary. I am totally and completely dedicated to this cause, and nothing else stands in the way, not family, not career, not money. I am pure in my commitment. Bad news: a predator who learns about the depth of my commitment can believably enter my personal belief system, my nobly constructed vision of service to humanity, and proceed to use me. I won't see his true nature because I am blinded by my passionate beliefs. I will only see his confirmation of my beliefs. I will only see his articulation of what I know as truth. I will not stop to look at him, at his possible motives, because his confirmation of my truth is enough.

This holds true for any other deeply held personal belief, be it my belief in romantic love, my attachment to conservative economic policies, my commitment to my race, my infatuation with computers and the information highway, or my deep belief in God. We all have something that forms the core of our beliefs, that tells us what is real and what false, that animates and directs our actions, that fills us with pride and identity and purpose.

Whatever this might be — and make no mistake, we all have it — it is like a beacon for those who see us as prey. Find the beacon, modulate on the same frequency, and the victim opens up to be exploited. All caution, reason, and care evaporate: why be critical of a person who knows me? Why refuse someone who believes what I believe, who likes what I like and dislikes what I dislike, who knows and loves my deepest and most treasured core, who loves and serves that which I love and serve? To put it another way: how could anyone articulate such profound truth and at the same time wish me harm? It is simply not possible.

But of course it is possible. It is possible because predators know that this is my specific point of weakness, that all my protections are down, that I cannot feel suspicion or malice toward anyone articulating the same things that I know are true, real, and beautiful. This is where predators find a point of entrance, a way to enter in without detection or resistance.

BREAKING THE GROUP CODE

The same possibility of entrance applies to groups. To break the group code, Luciferans simply have to listen and find out what motivates and drives the group. Luciferans are particularly attracted to groups dominated by strong belief-bonds, such as deeply held religious or political dogma. Once the Luciferan predator knows how to believably articulate the group's core beliefs, the entire organization opens up for predation. Such Luciferan predators can then quickly rise to top positions of power, and proceed to drain the organization and everyone within it of time, money, energy, and vitality. Luciferans usually discard such groups eventually, leaving them as deeply drained and depressed as the individuals they exploit. Using the group's core beliefs as a mantle and shield, the Luciferan systematically roots out all opposition, places lower-order Luciferans in charge, and then proceeds to drain from the group every drop of vitality and energy it can bleed.

If a specific group is not available, Luciferans may decide to create their own. To do so they simply have to articulate a powerfully beautiful ideology espousing attractive ideals and beliefs. Seekers will be drawn to the belief-bait, and will join the Luciferan's organization. Once in, these seekers can be psychologically assaulted and broken down. They become part of the Luciferan's power pyramid and ready to act as disposable agents to proselytize and expand the Luciferan's influence and power. Never knowing how they are being used, never seeing through the Luciferan's disguise, they become his agents. As such, they enable the Luciferan predator to devour the vitality and energy of new recruits, whose energy is then added to the pyramid.

Such organizational pyramids can become powerful extensions of the Luciferan's devouring, allowing his force and influence to claw a wide swathe into hundreds, thousands, or possibly even millions of lives.

To sum up: protean Luciferans adopt and then discard beliefs with the same ease as emotional bonding and commitment. Few of us really understand this capacity, any more than the bobcat understands the neck snare set by the trapper. We fall in it because it is beyond our experience and comprehension. We are so deeply bound to our relationships and beliefs that we cannot comprehend anyone capable of showing the same depth of bonding and core beliefs, and yet do so falsely.

This incomprehension is our weakness, allowing us to be easily baited, attracted and then snared by Luciferans. Once snared, we become victims ready for cognitive devouring and eventual possession, as described earlier.

SPIRITUAL CAMOUFLAGE: CHARISMA

Luciferans cultivate the appearance of spiritual wisdom, transcendence, mastery, and transformation. They want to be accepted as spiritual leaders, as gurus, as guides. If victims are convinced, then predation on all levels can follow.

The late twentieth century is a marketplace of opportunity for spiritual camouflage because old religious systems are dying and we are hungering for something solid. We suffer from what George Steiner calls a "nostalgia for the absolute." We have become searchers, and we are vulnerable. Most of us know how to survive in the marketplace of physical goods but we flounder in the spiritual marketplace.

After all, just what are spiritual guides supposed to be like? What attributes should they display? Wisdom? Humility? Special gifts or talents such as healing or perhaps even psychic powers? We do not really know.

When are they supposed to be believed? No external objective measures can evaluate their truth statements; this is supposed to be a matter of faith. Did their truths descend from enlightened masters on a higher plane, from some deep inner source flowing from the higher self, from God? How do we know? How do we discern? We might measure them against the doctrines imposed by our own personal faith, traditions, or from sacred texts. But impostors have successfully presented themselves as guardians and representatives of such texts and traditions for millennia, and will continue well into the next millennium.

So how do we know? Do we turn to our own instincts, to some deeper spiritual intuition, to what "feels right"? Perhaps. But these cannot always be trusted either.

So some of us turn to spiritual leaders who display charisma, who have a certain aura of strength, certainty, and power, and so seem alive, vital, and energetic. These leaders are compelling, fascinating, and magnetic. Their presence is soothing and yet enthralling. We sense something awesome working through them, and hope that maybe some of it can come into us. We trust, we open, we surrender, we invite.

Luciferan spiritual leaders who cultivate such camouflage know that we won't penetrate the charismatic screen but will fall in love with it. The leader can then ask us to surrender property, devotion, reason, and even identity to obtain the ultimate truth, a surrender that we will embrace enthusiastically and lovingly. We can then be asked to sacrifice family, friends, and career, a betrayal that follows surrender easily and naturally. Surrender can be a beautiful spiritual offering in legitimate circumstances: if the charismatic leader is legitimate, then we may find what we seek. If not, if he is driven by Luciferan motives, then we will be devoured, possessed or even killed. The history of destructive cultism from Jonestown to Waco is the history of people surrendering to spiritual leaders who used and abused this trust.

Luciferans consciously cultivate the camouflage of spiritual charisma. They offer it as bait because they know that most victims shut down critical thought when offered sweet spiritual delights, just as they do for physical beauty, pleasant emotions, or cherished beliefs.

Such spiritual candy might be a promise of healing, of a future paradise, of participation in a world-transforming movement, of special gifts. These gifts might include psychic powers, communication with discarnate entities or dead loved ones, perhaps other supernatural abilities. They might be more subtle, such as personal evolution to higher planes of consciousness. The Luciferan's challenge is to discover the victim's deepest spiritual wish, and then to offer it convincingly. Blinded by desire, the victim becomes easy prey for spiritual devouring, violence, or possession.

TRANSFORMATIONS FOR SALE

Astute Luciferans have yet another way to attract potential victims by offering personal transformation. The shape-shifting Proteus can be considered a god of transformations. He transforms from one shape to another, but without substantially altering his essential substance. This is surface transformation only, not the kind of in-depth transformation of personality perhaps available only through discipline, hard work, and commitment to a spiritual path. But superficial transformations sell well in our present age, probably because we are all so unsatisfied with ourselves, filled with self-doubt and self-loathing. Ours is the age of Proteus; everything shifts, moves, develops, slides, and evolves faster than we can understand. We are sold on the value of change for its own sake, and feel compelled to transform just to survive.

However, human nature itself seems to remain unchanged. Beneath the frantic pace of surface transformations, the inner creature still pulses with confusion, fear, stress, and self-torment. How to ease the pain? Change, transform, try something different? A newly toned body here, a new religion there. Advertisers and other merchants understand this self-loathing, and sell us myriad ways to change ourselves. Better teeth or hair color, a new face through surgery, a new car, a new personality through fad therapy, a transformed self-image through motivational seminars.

Luciferans also understand this self-loathing. They know that transformation is good business: salons sell physical transformation through beautification, seminars sell personal empowerment, self-help movements sell new health, political groups sell revolution, religions sell spiritual enlightenment. Luciferans see yet another opportunity to capitalize on a deep human need.

To do this, they simply have to appear to offer some new and profound transformation to potential victims. More than that, they have to take on this appearance themselves, to act as examples and models for the transformation they are selling. If this transformation is physical, then the Luciferan must appear physically attractive, vital, and energized. If emotional, cognitive, or spiritual, the Luciferan must appear peaceful, wise, or enlightened.

For those victims truly seeking a deeper and more meaningful transformation, the Luciferan must take on the appearance of guide, mentor, guru, spiritual director. Appearances are everything because Luciferans know their victims seldom penetrate below the surface of things. Perceptions are everything: if the victim believes in the camouflage, then every form of predation can follow.

So how does the Luciferan prosper from transformation? This can only be understood by seeing from a Luciferan perspective, which is that every transformation releases energy. Every time a victim attempts to transform, then energy is required. Money is usually exchanged, trust is given, something is lost, something gained. To put it another way, when nuclear transformations occur, atomic explosions can result. In the same way, when personal transformations occur, energy is released, energy which can then become food for the Luciferan.

Beyond this level of direct predation, the Luciferan may be able to control the direction of the transformation, channeling it so that the victim is rendered available for further predation. For example, if the victim attends a weekend personal development seminar run by a Luciferan, then when the "transformation" occurs, the client will feel deeply grateful. He will then recruit new victims with an almost missionary zeal, and will come back again and again to experience the transformational "context shift." The Luciferan then creates a dependence, an addiction. The victim becomes an easy target for future exploitation: in essence, his honest search for transformation or transcendence has been detoured into dependency and debilitation. The context is reframed, the transformation shifts. When it does, the Luciferan is poised to devour the released energy.

This is not to say that transformation itself is "bad", just that when it is orchestrated by Luciferans then the resulting release of energy can be used, digested, and absorbed as food for the Luciferan, not the host. Only the Luciferan predator stands in the "winner's circle", not the victim.

I believe that real transformation is difficult. It demands the release of old beliefs, perceptions, and connections. It is hard work, and it is often painful. The pace of transformation in our age is probably faster than it has ever been. A scant century ago, the loss of religious faith was a deep personal crisis. Today, shedding an old faith and exploring or adopting a new one is typical, hardly noticeable. To transform means to become radically new, implying a rebirth. Birth is always a painful struggle, and rebirth is even harder because of the necessarily painful catharsis and cleansing of the old skin. For those victims wishing a fast, easy, instant, and relatively painless transformation of their physical, emotional, cognitive, or spiritual nature, Luciferans always have a solution for sale. For Luciferans, the "modern man's" desire for easy transformation is a basic weakness to be exploited for predatory advantage.

THE PROTEAN AGE

The psychiatrist, author, and researcher Robert Jay Lifton describes this modern man as being hungry for constant change and transformation. In his book *Life of the Self*, he calls this condition "the protean style", which he defines as "an interminable series of experiments and explorations of varying depth, each of which may be readily abandoned in favor of still another psychological quest". Proteans are disconnected, hungry for new connections and in a "constant process of death and rebirth of inner form."

In his more recent book *The Protean Self*, he shows how modern historical forces are having a "formidable influence on the contemporary self." This contemporary self is learning how to live with rapid and impressive personal transformations. He describes a "many-sided self in constant motion," notes that "we are becoming fluid and many-sided," and states that this modern Protean self "engages in continuous exploration and personal experiment." "If the self is a symbol of one's organism," he writes, "the protean process is the continuous psychic re-creation of that symbol."

Lifton did not conceptualize the protean self as something negative, but simply as a new way of being which, like all ways of being, has both strengths and weaknesses. Luciferans are not Protean in Lifton's sense, but they exploit this twentieth century way of being in two ways. First, they use a potential victim's proteanism to invite him into yet one more "meaning scene." The victim's lust for constant change creates an opening for predation, because his confusion renders him incapable of clear choice or action, and open to any transformative message for sale. He can thus be led in any direction the predator chooses.

Second, Luciferans can take on any disguise they wish without fear of exposure. They can appear Christian one minute, Wiccan the next. They can surf the spiritual marketplace with fluid ease. They can hold Lifton's "varied, even antithetical images and ideas at one time," and can demonstrate "highly varied forms of self-presentation: everything from a conventional, button-down demeanor, to jeans and male beads and earrings, to the *blissed-out* states of members of religious cults, to any conceivable in between." Luciferan predators do not have to fear that their Protean identity-fluidity will appear phony or manipulative by potential victims because, for many of these victims, such endless restless personal transformations have become social and personal norms.

Lifton's Proteans may be genuinely searching for "authenticity and meaning," but to Luciferans, they are prey. Luciferans admire shapeshifting only when it serves the rock-hard Luciferan goals of predation and powaqqatsi. Shapeshifting without a strong core of identity is useless and wasteful. Such constant self-transformations are embraced and admired in the late twentieth century, and supposedly indicate intellectual integrity and courage. Luciferans, however, take them as a sign of weakness. While Lifton's Proteans constantly search for meaning, shifting from one "meaning scene" to another, Luciferans do not. They know who and what they are. Their identity is solid. Proteanism is just predatory camouflage, nothing more.

There is no real mystery in this. Any con artist knows something of the art of disguise, of how to discover and then adopt a persona to disarm potential victims. The financial con must first convince potential investors that he is solid, reliable, and trustworthy. The man who wants to marry a wealthy woman and then relieve her of her wealth must first convince her to trust and love him. The arts of disguise, deception, and camouflage are known and used widely.

But the essence of Luciferan Proteanism goes beyond mere con-artistry to include the full spectrum of predatory intentions. Protean camouflage thus becomes a disguise, a conscious technique designed to cause potential victims to lower their defenses and open the gates to spectrum-wide predation. The twentieth century protean style simply allows Luciferans to take on one disguise after another without attracting too much attention: because we seem to have become "many-sided selves in constant motion" searching for meaning and identity, Luciferan predators can also shift in constant motion while concealing their search for predatory advantage.

In sum, Proteans transform constantly, changing appearance, emotions, and beliefs as needed. This skill makes them natural leaders in the New Age of Proteus.

The idea of transformation itself is essential to most spiritual movements. New Age spirituality centers on the possible human:— the individual transformed into an ultimately powerful being, aware and alive with the exploding human potential of the higher self. Christianity offers the possibility of personal transformation through rebirth in Christ. Entering heaven means adopting a spiritual nature which transcends physical existence. Even business entrepreneurs market their own variations of personal transformation through positive thinking, mind development, and so on. Initiation rites and rituals are designed to transform. From baptism to spirit quests, the initiate seeks renewal.

Luciferism itself demands a transformation involving the destruction of 'lower order' emotionality and the actualization of fully empowered godhood: humans must stop being humans to find their true destiny. The New Human must be born. This Luciferan transformation enhances predation. With each successive shedding of old skin, the renewed Luciferan initiate learns yet more subtle ways to control, devour, and absorb the transformative energies of lower-order victims and initiates on other spiritual paths. The core Luciferan self, once released, remains constant, and seeks always to enhance personal power through predation.

Most of us seeking transformation would probably prefer something a little more positive than the Luciferan path. The appeal of positive spiritual transformation reaches deeply into all of us affected by life in the twentieth century. Since our present state of awareness and consciousness seems so obviously destructive, something else must be possible. Perhaps evolution is working its magic right now, busy creating a new kind of being as removed from us as we are from apes. This being has been prophesied, lyricised, and promoted by individuals, organizations and religions since recorded history began. New age spirituality in particular offers a new vision of evolved humanity.

This 'new human' is held to be morally superior to us in every way. He/she/it represents the next step in consciousness on this planet, an evolutionary leap crucial to our survival. Some theorists believe the new human will evolve consciously and deliberately, rising from us as we allegedly rose from apes. Others believe it will emerge instantly, in a flash of apocalyptic transformation.

Visions of the new human are disputed, depending on the belief system supporting the envisioner. To Christians this new person will be as Christ, to New Agers as Self-god, to Buddhists as Buddha, and so on. I believe that almost all religions can be understood as attempts to define a new human, and as proscribed patterns of thought and behavior designed to create it. New

Agers seek to raise consciousness through various practices designed to alter consciousness (trance induction, meditation, etc.), while Christians await the transforming entrance of Christ into the believer's life. Linking all of these visions of transformation is the notion that fundamental changes in the nature and substance of human existence must occur.

Many of us want personal and global spiritual transformation, and so we listen intently to the various merchants selling methodologies and thought-systems designed, they say, to absolutely create the new human. Just follow my program, says Guru, and you too will be transformed by the grace of the One; just follow my plan, says pastor, and you will get a new life with Jesus. Just follow my system says the motivational salesman, and you too will get everything you want, including riches, a new life, and all you ever dreamed. Selling spiritual transformation is a multi-billion dollar business, likely to get even bigger as the second millennium approaches. Just do as I tell you, they say, and you too will have a new nature as sparkling as God's life itself.

We all line up to be transformed in other ways as well. We meditate, jog, fast, think positive thoughts, reprogram the subconscious mind, pray, go to church, go to weekend transformational seminars, read books, buy tapes, and so on. We seek renewal like plants seek light. We seek to shed ourselves as snakes shed skin. We tire of this life and this mind, we bend and break under the sorrow and ugliness of this life, and we look for a hint, any hint, of something magically other, something wonderfully renewing. We do this, unfortunately, without always considering just what we seek to become. Transformation itself becomes the only end: we transform to keep on transforming. The promise of transformation is so powerful that we seldom think where the transformation might lead, or just what it is that we might become.

Luciferans, however, know exactly where transformation should lead: to more power, more *powaqqatsi*, and more predatory advantage. Transformation, for Luciferans, means obtaining godhood.

CHAPTER SEVEN

HUGODS: THE TOTAL FREEDOM OF GODHOOD

the universe... is a machine for the making of gods.
— Henri Bergson

Man has his highest being, his God, in himself. The Feeling of God is nothing else than man's highest feeling of self; God is man, man is God.
— Ludwig Feuerbach

The best way to conceive of the fundamental project of human reality is to say that man is the being whose project is to be God... man fundamentally is the desire to be God.
— Jean-Paul Sartre

Luciferans seek to transform themselves from powerlessness to power, from weakness to strength, from poverty to wealth, from prey to predator. Ultimately this transformation is meant to be spiritual, but once compassion and conscience are replaced by devouring, possession, violence and disguise, then Luciferans believe they become powerfully energized by a transformation as profound as that offered by any major religion.

This transformation is animated by the Luciferan's desire to acquire godhood. Godhood awaits the superior devourer just as salvation awaits the devout Christian believer. Godhood is the state of absolute personal power where the individual ceases to be an *effect* of outside forces and instead becomes a *cause* for everything around him. He creates his own reality and, like a God, is limited by nothing, because his will becomes absolute in his own creation. He is part human and yet fully god — *hugod*.

Unlike other spiritual traditions offering transformation or even godhood, however, the Luciferan transformation is not based on morality, compassion, empathy, conscience or love. The New Age human and the New Man of recent Christian thought, for example, are supposed to be wise and compassionate in their evolutionary advantage over lower humans: love is their only route to a higher spiritual condition, without which they could not evolve. Luciferans mock such beliefs, for godhood is only for amoral predators, not for bleeding prey.

Since Luciferans believe that higher moral positions are lies, then ultimate spiritual fulfillment never evolves from the kind of morose sentiment, unctuous prayer, and servile obedience demanded by major religions or traditions. Fulfillment and apotheosis are prizes to be taken by storm, and are therefore only available to the strong, the quick, and the hard.

The hugod of Luciferan thought is not limited by any restriction, and is contemptuous of any who allow themselves to be limited. Limitations are weaknesses; hugods cannot be limited or they cease to be gods.

Accordingly there is no single Luciferan "word-theology" or canon as such, because all theology is a limitation to be ultimately overcome. The core beliefs uniting Luciferans are coherent, but this coherence flows from primal, timeless truths like devouring, possessing, violence and disguise rather than from effete theological constructs.

The Luciferan simply pursues pure power and eternal life relentlessly, endlessly, into a distant future shrouded in mist and secrecy. He does not fully know what lies ahead, only that he must attempt to become God himself. He is not handicapped by doubt, discrepancy, logical inconsistency, or any other impediment. He simply knows where evolution has brought him and where its devouring impulse must inevitably take him. Restricting complete devouring is like death by smothering for Luciferans. Devour or be devoured — this is the only choice. Luciferans accept the choice to devour, and cannot be restricted by conscience, compassion, or any other limitation. They do not need affiliation, love, self-esteem or any of the other so-called "needs" postulated by psychologists such as Maslow whose conceptions are the weak leavings from the soft middle class civilization he sprang from. Violence, devouring, possession, disguise, predation and god-actualization: these are true needs, the true hierarchy of necessity and only these can ensure eternal spiritual survival.

Human beings without conscience or compassion, who consciously choose to evolve new godlife — this is the Luciferan's transformative spiritual message for the planet.

FREEDOM AND GODHOOD: WILLING SELF TO GOD

Once conscience, compassion, empathy, and the other barriers to absolute power are removed, the Self is free to expand. Without the destruction of these barriers, the Self remains imprisoned in limitations. Luciferan religion states that the end-point of this self-expansion is Godhood.

As the Luciferan gains power to grow, her Self expands. Her presence in a room is felt by all, for her expansion is not the silly illusion of egocentricity or narcissism but the development of real power, a true personal power. She delights in this power and its impact on others. The Luciferan is concerned about Self only. This is not the childish buffoonery of the obviously selfish egocentric, but the intelligent cultivation and acquisition of personal energy. The more she consumes, the more she radiates the real power of complete freedom.

All Luciferans seek freedom. They want it passionately, and they want it now. But freedom only comes with the acquisition of sufficient personal power, so the predator's hunting patience must be cultivated. Luciferan freedom means "freedom-from":— from authority of any kind, from the chains of this material prison, from the dictates of ethical systems, conscience, remorse and guilt. It dances wildly above the sickliness of love, compassion, warmth and emotional attachments. Luciferan freedom strikes beyond all laws, physical, temporal, social or spiritual. It asserts itself beyond all limits, and is limitless.

Luciferans believe that only they know freedom. All others submit to slavery and ignorance because they are too weak to break free, to transcend and transform beyond the bonds of consensus reality. The weak obey the commandments of their programming like blind computers — find a mate, find safety and security, fit in. Pretend that reality isn't harsh — get safe, get comfortable, get secure. They are programmed from birth to death, from waking to sleeping, from moment to moment. These *others* are the pathetic products of forces beyond their control, both biological and social, both nature and nurture. They are described by the Director in Huxley's *Brave New World* as happy slaves who are predestined and conditioned to love their slavery as a positive moral virtue, who are programmed from birth by suggestions: "till at last the child's mind *is* these suggestions, and the sum of the suggestions is the child's mind. And not the child's mind only. The adult's mind too — all his life long. The mind that judges and desires and decides — made up of these suggestions. But all these suggestions are our suggestions! The Director almost shouted in his triumph. 'Suggestions from the State'." Luciferans interpret Huxley's words as describing the current state of all non-Luciferans. Substitute Yahweh or Allah, or any other cultural gods for the Director's State, and the enemies of Luciferan freedom become clear. The Director's words resonate with the Luciferan impulse. He sees reality, and acts on it. But he is only another limit to be overcome. The enemy is restriction, limits, rules, containment. Only the weak allow themselves to be herded. In Blake's words: "Those who restrain desire, do so because theirs is weak enough to be restrained; and the restrainer... usurps its place and governs the unwilling." Being restrained is death itself. Only the ever-expanding Luciferan Self knows true freedom.

Luciferan freedom expands Self into the void, where personal will is the ultimate law. Self will-power expands with devouring, possession, *powaqqatsi*. In the words of Aleister Crowley, the self-proclaimed magus and practitioner of magick: "Do what thou wilt shall be the whole of the law."

Will is everything, and freedom means acting on the will-to-godhood no matter what the consequences. There is no right or wrong, only the pure will of those who will. Luciferan freedom is amoral. It is beyond morality, beyond rational analysis. Ultimately it is a state of godhood elevated and sparkling above the dictates of lower realities governed by law, morality, and boundaries. It shatters all boundaries, goes beyond all limitations. It transcends all beliefs.

John Lilly, a physician, transpersonal psychologist, and sixties guru, wrote: "In the province of the mind, what one believes to be true either is true or becomes true, within certain limits to be found experientially and experimentally. These limits are further beliefs to be transcended. In the mind, there are no limits." Lilly articulates the spirit of the relentless Luciferan impulse to shatter all limits, to go where no one has gone before, to defy all impediments of the mind and will.

For Luciferans, Self is God, or can become God. As self wills, God wills. There is no other authority or reality. Self is all, and as self wills, so it wills reality. Self inflates to encompass all reality. Self becomes the universe, and the universe becomes self.

The true Luciferan is a magus, a sage, and a manipulator of reality. As the Luciferan wills, *so mote it be.* Less powerful beings must submit to his will, whims and wishes. His entire being is devoted to the acquisition of sufficient power to consume the life forces of lesser beings so that he himself is not consumed.

His life is lived on the edge. Every encounter with another being brings either more or less power. If he is strong enough he will absorb the vital energies of these other beings. If not, they will absorb his. Lesser beings who are not aware of this basic reality become easy targets for the Luciferan hugod, to be consumed without remorse. He consumes because he knows the reality of this world — power is all that counts, and higher realities and heavens can only be taken by force, never received as an undeserving gift from some paternalistic but inherently cruel God. A God giving vital energy away to others is no God at all, but a lower order archon doomed to extinction, like Yahweh and Christ.

The Luciferan seeks a freedom so total and complete that he needs nothing, wants nothing, serves nothing, is accountable to nothing. He wants to be God through the sheer force of his will. He wishes to evolve as far beyond humanity as human beings have gone beyond single cell organisms. There are no boundaries he cannot cross and no limitations he cannot transcend.

Luciferan freedom is transcendence. Because he is bound by no laws, he can act as he wishes. If he wishes to be kind, then he will be kind. If he wishes to be cruel and vicious, then so will it be. If he needs to consume the emotional and spiritual lives of lesser beings, he will do it. If he needs to consume the physical bodies of lesser beings, he will do that too. He cannot obtain freedom without sufficient personal power, which in turn can only be obtained by absorbing others. He preys on lower human beings just as these beings in turn prey on lower order mammals and plants. He knows he is the next stage on the evolutionary hierarchy, and that his victory is inevitable because it has the full force of evolution, energy, life and even historical necessity behind it. He knows that everything else is illusion, emptiness and meaningless. Total freedom is the only goal, freedom without limits of any kind.

For the Luciferan, love is simply a lower order bonding pattern, a kind of mechanistic evolutionary device creating a bond between members of the same species or tribe. Luciferans endorse the intentions of ethno-biologists like Edmund Wilson, evolutionary psychologists, and other reductionists who describe love as a species-specific mechanism aimed at enhancing personal and group survival, and nothing more. Love is not a universal principle, and never has been. Those who obey the limitations of love will become embedded on this plane, this level of evolutionary development. They will be incapable of true, pure, clean ruthlessness. They will never be predators. Hence, they can never develop personal power or transcendent freedom.

Love is weakness. It leaks vital personal energy onto people who usually do not deserve it. Compassion and pity, close relatives of love, are even worse. They drain not only personal power, but betray existence itself. Pity allows the continued existence of beings who do not deserve life: the sick, the weak, the handicapped, the ineffective, the powerless. Pity and compassion foster the evolutionary success of beings who pollute and distort the vitality, purity, and drive of the pure Luciferan. Pity is evil, compassion is a disease, love is a sickly weakness.

The universe does not revolve around love. Those religions promoting this idea are victims of a destructive illusion. Love is a human invention designed to hide the harsh ruthlessness of reality. Ruthlessness is beauty, and all that we hold beautiful, from flowers to art, is generated from successfully ruthless competition with inferior forms.

Love is a disease. Luciferan freedom demands its destruction and complete eradication. The next step of human evolution depends on the elimination of love, not its expansion. Evolution demands that we become emancipated from love. Love is as falsely manipulative as the religion celebrating it, Christianity.

The Luciferan may manipulate the love of others and may encourage others to fiercely love him. He does this because he knows these others will never be a threat: their love has rendered them weak! He may induce love and loyalty in others in order to deepen their compliance and surrender to him. He may even appear to express love himself, but always as a predatory ruse, a facade, a way of furthering and deepening his personal power and control. Like any predator, he is intimate with the weaknesses of his prey because all weaknesses can be exploited. Since lesser beings believe in love, he will use this to his advantage, like bait. But he will never, ever, feel love. For him it is a foreign infection, a killing disease that will bleed his power and render him vulnerable. For the Luciferan, love means captivity, imprisonment, and ignominious death.

All moral systems — Christian, Humanistic, modern or ancient — are simply limitations to be transcended. Moral systems impose unnecessary limits on the evolutionary development of the Luciferan Superbeing. Luciferans agree with modern anthropologists who assert that moral systems are all human-made, reflecting local cultural codes, not eternal spiritual laws. None of them express universal standards, even though all claim to be sent from a higher source.

Like love, morality is a sickness. It is an illusion binding the strong man, restricting his action, holding back his true potential. Where morality grows, power wilts; where power grows, morality is weak. Those societies closest to anarchy, thriving on conflict, screaming at the edge of chaos, and facing constant threat and near extinction — these are the societies which will always swell in power and potential. Frank Herbert gave narrative power to this truth in his science fiction series, *Dune*, where the inhabitants of the most inhospitable planet in known space became tough, hard survivors and warriors who ultimately conquer the known universe under the banner of their warrior prophet. The soft, the civilized, the sophisticated schemers and the kind-hearted all fell under their onslaught. Luciferans would claim that Western Anglo-Saxon culture grew in the same way, from the greatness of its warriors who had to struggle for survival in the cruel, unforgiving northern climate.

Once success is theirs, these warrior societies often sicken under the weight of counter-evolutionary moral systems. Northern cultures, surviving initially under harsh climatic conditions, were stimulated to grow or die. They overwhelmed southern cultures because life was too easy there — too warm, too much food. With success, morality finally became a concern to the Northerners, and their Luciferan predatory potential faded. And as this happened, the Luciferan hero — the Viking warrior, the berserker, the invader, the looter, pillager, and rapist — eventually became a criminal, an outcast.

Despite this, Luciferans know that when sickened cultures are in trouble, they instinctively search for Luciferan leaders. If lucky, they find them. If not, they perish. The Luciferan message for an ailing Western world? Don't retreat into diseased religious ethical systems, but continue the thrust of evolution initiated by your ancestors to become the dominant beings you were meant to be.

Just as morality kills the Luciferan, so does guilt, conscience, and remorse. Guilt is an emotion of the weak for guilt grows from morality like disease from filth. Guilt binds the strong man, rendering him incapable of action and predation. Conscience is the inner fascistic voice of morality, and it secretes guilt like a sticky web, trapping the Luciferan. Remorse is like guilt, constricting, binding, and restraining. Conscience, guilt and remorse are destructive forces.

The predator never feels these forces, cannot. The eagle feels no remorse, the hunter feels no remorse. It is just the way of things, natural and pure as godhood and creation itself. The true Luciferan may use these emotions on others, for he knows that inducing this poison in enemies readies them for defeat. But he will never feel them himself. He would rather face total annihilation, fierce but quick, than to slowly fade under the ugliness of moral sickness.

Luciferans are amoral. They consider themselves outside and beyond all codes. Because they demonstrate no resonance with moral systems as we know them, they are usually associated with anarchy, chaos, sin, hedonism, and related antisocial behavior. They may engage in behavior we would consider amoral, but their goal is always the same — to gather enough personal power to transcend all temporal and social limits and so to become gods. They are not interested in such behavior for its own sake, but rather for the personal power and freedom it provides.

Luciferans, however, do not want social anarchy or chaos. Nor do they necessarily want the established moral order to be destroyed. This may seem strange considering their hatred of limitations. As much as Luciferans despise these constraints, they also realize two advantages from them.

First, moral codes handicap all potential competitors who are caught in them. Luciferans believe we all have the god-potential, but, like Yahweh, they wish to advance first, ahead of all others in the same race. Moral codes can entrap and weaken potential competitors, rendering them impotent.

Second, moral systems can be used to enslave and control others. Luciferans want to gain control over others seeking freedom so their energy can be devoured. Moral systems weaken such potential sources of "food" so they can be systematically drained and used.

This is why so many religious organizations attract Luciferans. Camouflaged under the guise of moral integrity and goodness, Luciferans can use and control the energies of those who come to trust and admire them. True anarchy and chaos would not serve the Luciferan cause. Luciferans may hate all imposed limits, but they happily subject others to control. Totalitarian and fascistic movements attract Luciferans because they can rise to positions of power and then exploit the social and moral order which they now control.

FREEDOM FROM AUTHORITY

There is no ultimate authority to which the Luciferan feels accountable, not even Lucifer. Lucifer's message is to seek total freedom, as he himself has attempted. Lucifer is therefore only a potential competitor and enemy to be overcome. If he actually exists, then all Luciferans are in direct competition with him.

As Christians seek to imitate Christ, so too Luciferans model themselves after Lucifer. Lucifer inspires Luciferans like an image of perfection, a banner, an example to be transcended. Unlike Christians they do not submit, for submission is weakness. Unlike Christ, they do not submit to any Father, because such submission is bizarre, meaningless, and Self-destructive.

To the Luciferan, Yahweh (or the group of Luciferans promoting Yahweh as an image) is to be respected as a powerful predator, because he has devoured the vital energies of Jews and Christians for centuries. Sending his son Jesus was a master act, because Jesus taught human beings to betray their own ultimate potential: he taught them to love, to feel guilt, to feel pity. He taught them to turn the other cheek to the provocative hostility of others, an attitude totally absurd and counter-evolutionary. He elevated self-sacrifice to holiness.

Such are the wiles of Yahweh that he made life for other competing Luciferans virtually impossible for the past two millennia. Weaving false and distorted fantasies about Lucifer, he taught his sheep to hate Lucifer and therefore their own potential. He taught them to offer themselves as sacrifices to his bloody appetite, promising them nourishment through the imaginary blood and body of his son.

True Luciferans saw through the ruse, as all ruse-masters always do. Many of them rose to positions of power within Yahweh's church, because as true predators they knew how to appear in many forms and guises. Others probably died as Yahweh's enemies, burned as heretics or slaughtered in one of the many convulsive explosions of violent rage characterizing Yahweh's people.

As a Luciferan, Yahweh has been successful. He has seeded the world with pleasant visions of love, compassion, and pity to deceive and weaken potential competition from other predators. He invented sin, hell, and other illusions of horror for those daring to defy his will. He did this because he fears losing his power to other predators. The fear of sin is simply his device to rob Luciferans of their will to grow.

Yahweh is a jealous God, as he himself proudly proclaims. Jealous of what? If he is the highest power, then there is nothing to be jealous about. In reality, he is jealous of other predators like himself. The myth of Eden proclaims his limitations: Adam and Eve, on the verge of full consciousness of their divinity, seek to eat of the tree of knowledge and eternal life. These fruits are their heritage, the full rights accorded every being seeking Luciferan enlightenment. In his jealousy Yahweh forbids them access, and in a fit of rage they are cast from Eden into this physical world of confinement, pain, and imprisonment.

As it is with Yahweh, so it is with all authority figures, religious or otherwise. Authority is the gift of effective predation, the right of the strong over the weak. All authority figures seek only to deepen or maintain their power, to keep their prey ignorant and powerless. There is no such thing as a legitimate higher authority for the Luciferan, for authority only corrupts and eats the purity and energy of Luciferans who succumb to it.

Instead, Luciferans seek to become authority figures themselves. Authority is power, and power brings food. Authority enables more effective predation. Just as Luciferans want to devour rather than be devoured, so too they want to have authority not submission. The Luciferan obeys no authority higher than his own will and personal empowerment. When convenient, however, he may appear to obey laws from Yahweh, the courts, or some other esteemed source. He will rise to positions of authority himself, punishing other transgressors of laws to which he holds no allegiance and which elicit only his disdain. True Luciferans always rise to high positions of temporal power, and use their positions to enhance their own personal power. A Luciferan never truly serves the systems in which he lives and works, and from his high position of power, trust, and authority, proceeds to do exactly as he likes, free from the prying eyes of lesser beings.

FREEDOM FROM PHYSICAL EXISTENCE

Luciferans are not materialists. This may seem hard to understand because we tend to associate power acquisition with material gain, sensual indulgence, and all the trappings of success in this world. Luciferans, however, only use material wealth and power to advance their quest for total freedom. They believe true freedom ultimately lies outside the prison of the physical body. Luciferans are not materialists. They believe real power lies beyond the mere physical play of *Maya*, of illusion and matter.

Luciferans seek to tear through and devour the confining fabric of material existence, to reach beyond it by eating through it like a reptile through its egg. The material world is not somehow "bad", "wrong" or inferior (as in gnosticism), but is simply another impediment to be overcome. The physical body is a tool, nothing else. It is a temporary home allowing pure will to operate. The body's limits can be expanded by acquiring temporal power in the form of wealth, influence, and status, but must ultimately be transcended. The driving force of pure will is to accumulate enough power to punch through the physical into the purer realms of transcendent potential, to take heaven by storm. Once through the shell of this material world, Luciferans believe they become poised for godhood.

Luciferans devour others, swell with power, and seek absolute freedom to break through to godhood. Theirs is not the shared godhood of Eastern thought, however, where the individual ego submits to the oneness of all things, but rather the penetration of oneness itself by the sheer force and power of individual will. Individuality is elevated to godhood. The individual swells to fill god-space, not the reverse.

All Luciferans are not expected to succeed; this is understood and accepted. Just as only one sperm in millions finds and penetrates the egg, so only one of millions survives the god-quest. Yet transformation is the goal for all, to become the God of gods.

Hugods exist on many levels: Luciferans believe that god-power exists as a continuum from the weakness of physical incarnation to the full strength of transformative spiritual power. Luciferans becoming hugods must understand the dynamics of spiritual life on all levels, including the physical. They must master their full potential on every level before moving on to the next.

Luciferans never try to describe higher states to initiates on lower levels, partly because translation is impossible, and partly because they do not wish initiates under their control to learn enough to surpass them. Competition is everything: higher godhood only comes to those best able to survive and compete. A Luciferan would never say "I am God, you are God" in the New Age manner. He would rather say "I am more God than you are." He believes that "God" is only a term referring to ultimate power, dominance, and control. It is the state of full and perfect potential, a state which offers power beyond all power to those courageous enough to seize it.

Hugods live forever; they have devoured the fruit from the tree of eternal life, and have eaten their way to eternity. Adam and Eve were the first devourers, and therefore the first to celebrate the Luciferan urge to power. They supposedly ate the apple from the tree which promised knowledge of good and evil. Their devouring was beautiful, the actions of humans becoming hugods. No wonder Yahweh felt jealous.

Luciferans devour because eternity demands it. Eternal life exists not in one physical body but in many bodies, over generations, and throughout all time. Luciferans believe in reincarnation, but with a difference. Unlike various Eastern views on transmigration, Luciferans believe we remain embedded in limitation and ignorance until we learn to kill conscience and compassion to devour our way free of the circle of life and death. Like the serpent eating its tail, we devour to transcend even devouring itself. Unlike eastern religious beliefs (and most western esoteric traditions), the cycle of birth and death can only be broken by inflating, not deflating, personal ego, personal power and Selfhood.

Luciferans are not troubled by their predatory acquisition of power any more than we are troubled by eating our daily fare. Predation is the order of things, ordained by the ruthless force of reality itself.

Luciferans do not articulate this reality-force as a personality, as Satan or Beelzebub or Lucifer. This is Christian nonsense, fairy tales for fools. As much as Luciferans seek godhood, as much as they acknowledge the power of non-physical entities and forces, they are at the same time pragmatically down to earth, grounded in what they feel are the forces governing life here, the same forces which govern all spiritual life as well. Luciferans consider themselves realists who have simply understood that evolutionary Darwinism applies to the spirit as much as to the flesh. Just as they do not tinker with theological abstractions, so too they do not anthropomorphize human traits to create a fiction called Lucifer. They do not deny that an entity named Lucifer might exist. Their myths use his name, but he is essentially an abstraction, an entity who personifies Luciferan principles. Luciferans know that they cannot achieve ultimate power on higher levels until they achieve enough power on this level of existence. That is why so many of them occupy supreme positions of temporal power. Earthly power must be gathered before any other is possible. The Luciferan is a power-pragmatist. He can be found in any human ecosystem where power waxes strongest. He feeds on this power, thrives in its presence, attracts it and extracts it from others. He has no illusions or impediments, and so can be ruthless when required. He takes what he needs when he needs it, and annihilates anyone or anything in his way.

Jesus Christ promises his followers heaven if they have faith in him and obey his commandments. Luciferans know they can take heaven by storm if they disobey all commandments and have faith only in their own powers. A gift freely given is, for the Luciferan, poisonous. Such a gift would be refused or, if accepted, used to ultimately destroy the giver. The Luciferan knows that gifts of kindness come only from weakness, and so would despise both gift and giver. For the Luciferan, Jesus betrayed life by refusing the Devil's offer of all kingdoms for all time, the offer of real eternal power. In that act he split creation wide open and tried to kill the natural way of things. He is the enemy, and his crucifixion was good. He is the antithesis of godhood, the enemy of truth and empowerment.

Jesus deserved to be sacrificed. All Luciferans seek the ultimate power to sacrifice and therefore replace God. A hugod like Jesus who turned down the opportunity for perfect power over all kingdoms for all time: such a being is an abhorrent abortion of the natural order, a thing to be killed in the worst possible way. It's suffering would release such a torrent of raw power to higher-order hugods that the Luciferan releasing it would ascend the psycho-spiritual hierarchy like a rocket.

Luciferans raised in Western culture would happily await the return of Jesus as avidly as Christians, because the chance to sacrifice a being like Jesus again, to sacrifice and kill the god-within-the-man, is a challenge and temptation guaranteed to launch the successful Luciferan outside the cycle of life and death and into the pure realm of spiritual power and potential.

ENCOUNTERING OTHER HUGODS

Luciferans believe that there are various levels and types of hugods, all in competition, some more or less human, some beyond the human state. Each one is a potential competitor and enemy, although Luciferans might occasionally join forces against a higher spiritual predator. Such alliances are only temporary, however, and eventually dissolve into competitive enmity, as must all alliances.

A Luciferan believes that other more highly evolved beings further along the path of power can hurt him, and will always seek to enslave or kill him. Such beings are hard to manipulate, because they understand Luciferan principles and are therefore difficult to deceive. They only want more power, and will devour the lesser being if they can. However, they can be placated and this is why Luciferans sacrificially offer food energy to higher beings:— hopefully the food will be accepted in place of the giver. If the higher-order hugod believes that the lower-order predator is worth more food energy alive than dead, then he will allow him to continue with his offerings. Such food might be offered in full ritual sacrifice. The Luciferan hopes that by nourishing the endless devouring need of higher hugods, he will show proper respect, and will not be devoured himself. He hopes that the higher being will weigh devouring him against losing the food he is supplying. If his sacrifices are delightful, then he may just survive and prosper himself. Ultimately, of course, he will try to usurp power from the higher being, just as the corporate vice-president seeks to become president. The lower predator will do everything in her power to displace the Luciferan at the apex of this devouring hierarchy.

A food offering may consist of blood and of certain body parts. It may include emotional energies such as a victim's extreme fear, terror, and agony. It may also include cognitive and spiritual food as well. When a ritual circle is drawn and the sacrificial offering killed, Luciferans believe that its energies are trapped in the circle, to be devoured by the higher being to which it is offered. Eating the victim's physical heart symbolizes not only life, blood, energy, and power, but also the emotional, cognitive, and spiritual life of the devoured sacrifice.

Higher hugods prefer to suck on deeper essences, especially soul. The sacrificed being's soul is offered in the circle as essential nutrition for the higher predator. Luciferans believe that only these higher beings can easily absorb and use pure soul energy because their predatory skills have expanded as they have risen up the hierarchy, and they need to devour ever finer and more intense energies. Just as lower order predators tend to consume lower order energies because their predatory skills are limited, so higher predators have developed the skill and the hunger for the deeper, stronger and purer energies of victims.

The best offerings are therefore the fullest, richest, and most powerful souls. This is why innocents and young children are preferred: they are held to be sublimely nutritious. Sacrifice not only placates the higher order hugods, but strengthens the power of those performing the sacrifice. Power flows from the nature of the act itself. Since ultimate power results from ultimate freedom, and since freedom means separation from lower order attachments such as love, compassion, and pity, the Luciferan demonstrates her lack of attachment by calmly watching the agony, fear, and death of her prey. The more efficiently she is able to do this, the more she clarifies her power, freedom, and transformation to hugodhood.

Becoming a hugod herself, she completes her transformation to become a pure devourer, living off the life forces of lower beings. Thus the higher hugods need and use those lower in the order, because lower-order devourers provide offerings that the higher hugod might not be able to obtain alone. This is because the higher the devourer, the more food she needs to sustain herself. Absolute hugod power demands absolute devouring. Higher order hugods come to depend on the devotion, fear, and worship of lower order aspirants, through ritual offerings, food is channeled to feed insatiable hunger. The whole system can be compared to a kind of multi-level pyramid sales scheme, with lower-echelon sellers feeding profit to their immediate "boss", who, along with others at his level, feeds part of his profit to a higher boss. The more each person in the hierarchy attracts underlings, the more he profits. Only those at the top really become rich, because the system is designed that way. Those at the bottom are motivated by the dream that they might one day reach the top, as is the plan written into all creation, as is the plan motivating all Luciferans. Luciferan sociology therefore works much the same way: food is passed up the system through the mechanism of ritual. Sacrificial ritual is a kind of relentless machine. Lower order Luciferans become trapped in this machine and thus have little real freedom, but they believe fervently that they may eventually rise up the hierarchy to assume power themselves.

The weaker Luciferan can therefore be useful to the stronger, as long as he provides a steady source of energy. This kind of symbiotic relationship between two hugods continues until the weaker eventually overpowers the stronger, or until the stronger decides to kill the weaker.

Powerful Luciferans will seek to eventually transcend the entire hierarchical scheme, because even the predator at the apex is dependent upon those feeding him from below, and dependence is a restriction on freedom. Such Luciferans may build their own devouring pyramid in order to gather enough energy and power for hugodhood, but their ultimate desire is to use their pyramid as an expendable foundation to launch them into the impenetrable heights of godhood.

For all time, every Luciferan is at war with every other Luciferan: competition for energy, power, and godhood is a vicious and ruthlessly eternal process.

STRATEGIC RELATIONS BETWEEN LUCIFERANS

Strategic relations between Luciferans can therefore become complex. The permutations and possibilities are infinite. For example, if the higher hugod comes to depend on her own pyramidical hierarchy for nourishment, then she has to make sure that she absolutely controls the whole system. But to obtain adequate nourishment, she needs to attract and promote other Luciferan predators who are cunning enough to obtain nourishing food for her. She knows that such predators will always seek to usurp her, and the more they practice predation under her control, the more powerful they become. Thus her best food gatherers are potentially her worst enemies. The closer they get to her, and the longer she works with them, the more they learn about her strengths and weaknesses, and the more vulnerable she becomes. She must never relax in their presence, and must never trust them. She desires simply to use and ruthlessly control them until she can absorb enough energy to dispense with them and launch into her own higher orbit of power and influence.

Lower hugods know this, and so are constantly calculating ways to obtain control, to usurp her power as their own. All Luciferans despise cooperating with other hugods, and loathe even the appearance of submitting to a higher predator. To achieve their ends they have to use camouflage but deceiving lower order victims is easy and fooling another higher order predator is difficult. Skills have to be honed, weapons readied, energy gathered secretly. The higher order hugod must never suspect the truth, and must be deceived about the lower hugod's true potential. This is the ultimate task facing all Luciferans: to outwit and outmaneuver higher predators.

This strategic Luciferan game is relentless, ruthless, and absolutely final. The winners survive to advance up the hierarchy, and the losers die and disappear.

For Luciferans, physical death is only problematic for those who have not accumulated enough personal power. Without power from *powaqqatsi*, the spirit is not strong enough to survive death. With power, one of two options become possible.

First, the Luciferan may have enough power to survive death, but not enough to completely transcend physical existence. He will then be forced to reincarnate, and to stay on the wheel of death and rebirth until he is ruthless enough to launch freely into the higher realms of existence.

Like the salmon or the sperm, he is alone. He must succeed or fail on his own merits. None will assist, but many will interfere: both higher and lower order predators will try to stop him and then absorb his energy for their own gain.

There is no destination of heaven or hell based on moral action in this life. These rewards and punishments are just control mechanisms designed by higher order predators to control weaker predators, and to ensure a steady supply of frightened humans for food. Morality has as much bearing on afterlife survival as it does for the physical survival of the soldier locked in mortal hand-to-hand combat. Luck, experience, power, intelligence and predatory skill: these matter, but morality is irrelevant.

Luciferans may resort to extraordinary means to ensure their survival. For example, I remember one young man sent to me for counseling. He had attempted suicide by locking himself in a motel room, surrounding himself with candles and other "Satanic" paraphernalia, and then cutting both arms in three parallel lines from wrist to bicep. He survived only by chance, because someone happened to be looking for him. His explanation? He felt that his life was a failure, that he had not been strong and ruthless enough, and that his suicide would accumulate enough personal power to ensure his reincarnation as a more powerful and ruthless being. This young man was not Luciferan as defined here, but his motives illustrate how some Luciferans might seek to position themselves advantageously for their next incarnation.

Their choice of incarnation reflects their power goals for that incarnation. If the Luciferan chooses to reincarnate in a non-Luciferan family for various reasons, that family will be torn apart. The family may be chosen because of political power, wealth, strong genetic potential (especially physical beauty and intelligence), or any other strategic reason, but the Luciferan will use it ruthlessly for competitive advantage. The Eastern religious notion of Karma as a driving force behind reincarnation is a close approximation to Luciferan beliefs. Accumulate enough "positive" karma, and the disciple will eventually transcend the cosmic wheel of birth, death, and rebirth. Luciferans would agree with the general idea, but would violently disagree with the idea of "positive" karma (i.e. "goodness", "virtue", "love", "compassion" etc.). There is no morality in the accumulation of spiritual power, just the power itself, a power which can only be gathered through predation and *powaqqatsi*.

When enough lives have been lived, enough power accumulated, and all enemies avoided, placated, or defeated, then the Luciferan may be ready for the second option — transcendence of physical existence. This transcendence takes the survivor into non-physical realms of conscious existence, realms which apparently have many different layers, levels, and cultural interpretations.

The transpersonalist writer Ken Wilbur summarizes these various levels and layers of hierarchy in his many books, especially *The Atman Project*. His psycho-spiritual hierarchy extends from the physical to the high spiritual ("Pleromatic" to "Ultimate"), which he compares to similar hierarchies found in Kabbalah, Aurobindo, Grof, Green and Green, Loevinger, Buddhist Vijnanas, Erikson, Kohlberg, Psychosynthesis, Piaget, Ferenczi, Fromm, Maslow, Sullivan, Bubba Free John, Broughton, Vedanta Hinduism, Buddhist Skandhas, Battista, Welwood, Arieti, Kundalini chakras, and Tiller. Readers will recognize this as a list of who's who in both psychological and spiritual traditions worldwide. The point here is not whether the hierarchical order described in all these traditions is right, but simply that billions of humans have accepted its existence. Luciferans accept the reality of these levels as well, but do not believe in the delusional foundation of these various systems:— the notion that high means good, moral, ethical, compassionate, and loving. Higher simply means stronger. Nothing more.

Those Luciferans who survive earthly existence move up to higher realms, where predation, struggle, competition, and survival are perpetuated on a massive scale. For those of us anchored to physical life, these realms are closed. A being operating from them would seem like a god to us. Luciferans who have achieved trans-physical existence, however, know that the search for more power and enhanced godhood is limitless: even though they might seem invulnerable, eternal, omniscient and omnipotent to lower order humans, they still face threats to their existence, and can still be annihilated. The struggle must continue up and down the hierarchy. The war is everywhere.

As for such questions as "how does the 'new soul' begin?" or "what is creation?":— Luciferans are not interested. These are ultimate questions beyond the capacities of this plane of existence. The Luciferan believes these questions will be answered when she advances far enough up the hierarchy, but cosmic questions are for another time and place. Luciferans are power pragmatists, and focus on power accumulation here and now. Other philosophical concerns are irrelevant.

If these higher realms are closed to our conjecture, just how does an earthbound Luciferan imagine the state of godhood? What is it like? Why do Luciferans struggle to obtain it? What does it promise?

Luciferans admit that they cannot know until they get there, that imagining higher realms is like trying to describe the corporate boardroom to a lifelong drunken street bum. Despite this, they operate on certain beliefs about hugodhood.

First, if they succeed in surviving the challenges of physical existence, but have to reincarnate, then they expect that their next physical incarnation will be an improvement on this one. Their next body will be stronger, smarter, and more attractive. It will contain greater possibilities for predation on all levels. Socio-economic status will be higher, along with greater access to privilege, status, and political power. This cycle should proceed through successive rebirths until enough power is gained to achieve non-physical transcendence.

Second, intelligence, logic, and reason will continue to expand. This is not intelligence as in the restricted sense of "IQ", but a deepening of all capacities of thought for both linear and non-linear processing. For Luciferans, intelligence is a defensive and offensive weapon — the more they have, the stronger they become. Luciferans expect their human biocomputer to expand in speed, complexity, and capacity through successive incarnations, and then to become a kind of "supercomputer" once the physical world is transcended. The possibilities of this transpersonal mind would then appear godlike to those still struggling through the lower physical planes. Thus the term hugod applies to Luciferans who transcend the physical cycle of birth and death. However, hugods themselves are arranged on the hierarchy of power, so a lower-level hugod would appear pathetic to those occupying the higher orders, and so it would be up and down the hierarchy.

Third, as the Luciferan approaches transformation into hugodhood, she believes that certain powers and abilities are granted. She can leave the physical body at will in the shamanic style. She can read minds and move objects at a distance through telekinesis. She can inhabit the bodies of lesser beings, absorbing their energies and controlling their thoughts. She can commune with other discarnate entities, although this is potentially dangerous because she knows that they only wish her harm. She expects to receive other similar abilities, especially during moments of euphoria, ecstasy, and emotional catharsis. Since sexuality, (especially the forbidden varieties) can generate these powerful emotions, Luciferans pursue them. Drugs, ecstatic religious rituals, and other stimulating triggers can create these emotions, so Luciferans pursue them as well, but always cautiously, with the single purpose of power acquisition only.

Fourth, Luciferans expect an enhanced spiritual capacity. As they climb the psycho-spiritual ladder, they anticipate entering the realm of absolute causality, where they are the cause-generators not the cause-receivers. They seek total omnipotence, and believe that, like God, they can obtain it. Luciferan hugods expect complete omniscience, the ability to know anything and everything.

Luciferan hugods above all expect to experience absolute freedom. They wish complete freedom of thought, emotion, and life without boundary — freedom as the gods know it. Limitations, laws, and other impediments exist only to be broken. For the Luciferan, Godhood is total freedom, which is total potency and power, which requires devouring, which means endless ecstasy.

Physical reality for the Luciferan is therefore only *maya*, illusion. Not in the Eastern sense, as an impediment to god-union, but as a veil hiding the actualization of hugodhood. Ultimately the Luciferan hugod intends physical reality to exist as an extension of his consciousness alone, and not as the shared consensus reality of this world. He wants reality to spin outward from his Self, because he will be at the cause, at the source, at one with his will and his intention. Will is all that exists. An immutable will can never be destroyed, only transformed and hardened through infinite testing.

To will a thing is to create a thing, to have ultimate power and control. Luciferans resonate with power of creativity and admire those possessed of it, because creativity is godlike. Lust, energy, ecstasy, euphoria — the juice of creative life is the *manna* sought by the Luciferan. The restless, relentless, impatient rush of change, imagination, and creativity fascinates the Luciferan, because it is the vital power of life, transformation, and empowerment. Ultimately he wants to transcend to become the source of all life and creativity so that *he* will set the limits and rules, so that *his* Self will appear in all creation like a trace element, like a first cause, like a fountain from which all others must drink if they are to survive — a state of ultimate power and control.

AVOIDING THE TRAPS OF ASCENT

Luciferans know that there are traps to avoid in the quest for godhood. These dangers are not just external competitors and enemies. At each stage of evolutionary growth, the Luciferan can become so enthralled with his own achievements, and so oblivious of the higher realities yet to be taken, that he can become entangled and enslaved. Luciferans believe that Yahweh is one such hugod, trapped into believing that he is the only God (like Ishvara in the Hindu tradition), not realizing that he is only a lower order hugod (or archon as the old Gnostics called him). Such traps become addictions; power at any level of the hierarchy can entrap and enslave the Luciferan just as solidly as another competing Luciferan master.

True Luciferan warriors therefore avoid all such deep entrapments by adopting and cultivating a kind of stoic indifference to each achievement. Every power acquisition is only the prelude to another. It can be enjoyed, but not too much. Enjoyment and celebration are only traps to be avoided. Luciferan warriors always look upward and outward for the next challenge, the next triumph, the next enemy to be overcome. They never stay too long to enjoy the fruits of their victories, because victory sends out seductive tendrils which at first embrace the victor with soothing pleasure, but then eventually encase him.

Lower-order Luciferans can become addicted to any of these victories; higher orders use and transcend them. For advanced Luciferans they are only temporary rewards, but for lower orders they can become the ultimate goal in itself.

One example of this kind of entrapment can be understood by examining psychopaths, another by exploring Luciferan organizations and a third by studying Satanism. Violent psychopaths fall into bondage to their own violent urges, and as such are considered by Luciferans to be even lower than normal human victims. Some Luciferans create or steal organizations which they fashion in the Luciferan image, but which can rebound to eventually entrap the Luciferan warrior. And some Luciferans become imbedded in the nonsense called Satanism, a theatrical display which is violently at odds with true Luciferan dignity and purpose.

CHAPTER EIGHT

PSYCHOPATHS: LOWER ORDER PREDATORS

... the psychopath presents an important and challenging enigma for which no adequate solution has yet been found... I still have no effective treatment to offer for the psychopath.
— Dr. Hervey Cleckley, The Mask of Sanity

... psychopaths are generally well satisfied with themselves and with their inner landscape, bleak as it may seem to outside observers. They see nothing wrong with themselves, experience little personal distress, and find their behavior rational, rewarding, and satisfying. They perceive themselves as superior beings in a hostile, dog-eat-dog world in which others are competitors for power and resources. Psychopaths feel it is legitimate to manipulate and deceive others in order to obtain their "rights", and their social interactions are planned to outmaneuver the malevolence they see in others.
— Dr. Robert Hare, Without Conscience

There's no need to hunt for psychopaths, identify, classify, isolate them. The style has infiltrated everywhere... assume the ascension of psychopathic values among great numbers of us to be accomplished and irreversible... The saint and the psychopath can be seen as freed men.
— Alan Harrington, Psychopaths

Common public wisdom usually defines the psychopath as a brutal killer without conscience, remorse or compassion, ruthlessly stalking his victims to ultimately inflict as much perverted pain on them as possible. Since Luciferan psychology is built on the destruction of compassion, conscience, and remorse, then aren't Luciferans just psychopaths suffering from a medically defined psychiatric illness?

Defining the Psychopath

Are Luciferans nothing but psychopaths? This question deserves an answer. As always, terminology is a problem. In professional literature, the term itself has undergone transformations. For example, psychopath became sociopath for a time, reflecting a shift from medical to social-science interpretations, in which the sociopath was defined as the unfortunate outcome of oppressive social forces beyond his control. Irving Leyton's book *Hunting Humans* is an example of this approach. Needless to say, promoters of social science interpretations were often in conflict with more traditional medical approaches.

Such medical perspectives have been reflected in the *DSM*, the diagnostic medical catch-all used to diagnose mental illness. The *DSM* has stopped using the term psychopath even though renowned experts like Robert Hare still use it. Instead, researchers and clinicians have to use other apparently related syndromes such as *anti-social personality disorder* (apd), *narcissistic personality disorder* (npd) and *sadistic personality disorder* (spd). Here are samples of how the *DSM* describes these disorders: "lacks remorse (feels justified in having hurt, mistreated, or stolen from another)" (apd), "is preoccupied with fantasies of unlimited success, power, brilliance, beauty or ideal love", and "lack of empathy: inability to recognize and experience how others feel" (npd), and "is amused by, or takes pleasure in, the psychological or physical suffering of others" (spd). I have no doubt that these diagnoses will change in the future as well.

Many prominent medical specialists have written about the psychopath, and many others do not seem to want to lose the term. Robert Hare's book *Without Conscience: The Disturbing World of the Psychopaths Among Us* is a recent example. Such medical perspectives create very different, and at times, conflicting images of the psychopath.

Dr. Hervey Cleckley, for example, in his influential book *The Mask of Sanity* suggested that psychopaths are unknowably mysterious. He is convinced that "the psychopath presents an important and challenging enigma for which no adequate solution has been found." Cleckley suggested that psychopaths are found everywhere, especially in business where their ruthless exploitation of others can proceed under the cover of high social status. Dr. Person picks up this theme in her article, "Manipulativeness in Entrepreneurs and Psychopaths," suggesting that "we usually reserve the term psychopath for the *unsuccessful psychopath*, ignoring their presence in the ranks of the socially "attractive, impressive, and charming." Psychopaths, in short, may not always be the familiar — seedy, mean-faced serial killers or deranged stalkers popularized in recent media portrayals. They may be your boss, your father, or your elected official.

Depending on who defines him, therefore, the psychopath is a raving lunatic like Charles Manson, a serial killer like Ted Bundy, a drooling mental patient, a crazy cult leader, a successful mental health professional, or an influential entrepreneur exercising power in the new post-communist world of corporate capitalistic triumph. No wonder the *DSM* dropped such a controversial and spongy diagnosis. Disturbingly, the psychopath may be the psychiatrist or psychologist in charge of determining *DSM* classifications. The genesis of the psychopath from child to adult is equally unclear. Magid and McKelvey, in their book, *High Risk: Children Without a Conscience*, define the psychopath as a victim of child abuse. Other theorists blame inadequate attachment, poor family dynamics, degraded social conditions in society, media violence, neurochemical imbalances in the brain, and so on.

Even those professionals wanting to contain the definition of the psychopath within the confines of psychiatric or social-science terminology have struggled. Cleckley is an example: the psychopathic state seems as much a mode of being as a sickness. To 'medicalize' it thus runs the same risk as interpreting mystical religious experience as an 'illness': the phenomenon is trivialized.

Alan Harrington's book *Psychopaths* is a brilliant non-professional exploration of the psychopathic mode of being and its influence on late twentieth century life. For Harrington, psychopathology is not just a psychiatric category, but the reflection of a social transformation in which the psychopathic style "has infiltrated everywhere." The sixties generation elevated the psychopathic mode to virtual sainthood, and the selfish greed of the consumer society helped institutionalize it. Harrington argues that it is as if our era has encouraged the evolution of a new nervous system characterized by a constant need for stimulation and excitement, by a need for immediate pleasure and gratification uncluttered by ethical concerns, by a pervasive irresponsibility and desire to live only in the moment here-and-now, by a numbing dissociation and detachment from feeling, by a driving necessity to avoid boredom and seek constant change, and by a relentless expansion of the need for power over others in order to feed all of these other needs.

But if the psychopath is not just *mentally ill*, then what is he? For purposes here, I would like to adopt Robert Hare's description from his *Without Conscience*. According to Hare, psychopaths "are social predators who charm, manipulate, and ruthlessly plow their way through life, leaving a broad trail of broken hearts, shattered expectations, and empty wallets. Completely lacking in conscience and in feelings for others, they selfishly take what they want and do as they please, violating social norms and expectations without the slightest sense of guilt or regret... Their hallmark is a stunning lack of conscience; their game is self-gratification at the other person's expense... (the psychopath is a) self-centered, callous, and remorseless person profoundly lacking in empathy and the ability to form warm emotional relationships with others, a person who functions without the restraint of conscience... (psychopaths) use their charm and chameleon-like abilities to cut a wide swath through society."

From psychotherapists to police officers, those encountering the psychopath often describe her as empty, devoid of real feeling, cold and calculating, detached, manipulative, impulsive, superficially charming, narcissistic, incapable of love, compassion or empathy, and unable to feel remorse or guilt. Hare believes that the condition is derived partly from "nurture" (parenting, socioeconomic factors) and partly from "nature" (genetics, biochemical processes), but that its essential etiology remains mysterious.

Three varieties of psychopaths emerge from all of these attempted definitions: those who become violent criminals living in society's underground, those who live hapless and hopeless lives of narcissistic gratification, and those who rise to success and power in society. All three varieties elicit contempt from Luciferans. Some aspects of psychopathology may resemble Luciferism, but these surface similarities ignore profound differences. Luciferans bristle when compared to psychopaths, because such individuals are considered beneath contempt.

Luciferans and Psychopaths

Luciferans would argue that psychopaths, especially the brutal criminal

217

variety, are only lower-order predators. The psychopath might embrace devouring, possession, violence and disguise on one level or another, but does not look to a higher spiritual goal. His reward is only immediate: the thrill of the kill, the delightful focusing and narrowing of consciousness provided by the hunt, the pleasure taken in the victim's pain. He does not deliberately and surgically kill conscience and compassion as a stage in the acquisition of personal power, but instead inherits his condition and is ignorant of any other alternative. He seeks only the liberation of narcissistic, sadistic, or deviant pleasures. As such, he is despised and beneath Luciferan contempt. This is because Luciferans feel that psychopaths waste their predatory violence. They do not use it to actualize the power to achieve godhood, only to indulge lower order deviant pleasures. They are simply self-indulgent, like Christians who give to the poor but have no charity of heart. Psycho-pathology implies a semi-conscious, irrational, small-minded disorder, while Luciferism is a conscious, deliberate, and rational search for transcendence.

Despite these differences, psychopaths and Luciferans may be connected in an unexpected way. Luciferans accept that psychopaths can conceivably be understood as primal ancestors of a more highly evolved Luciferan species, a "genetic pool" from which true Luciferans emerge.

PSYCHOPATHIC DREAM WORLDS

If the psychopathic mentality is the raw material leading to a new Luciferan evolutionary trend, then Luciferan Darwinian theory would lead us to believe that we should expect to see an obvious evolutionary advantage for the psychopath, an initial or incremental advantage which would expand his survival potential and which could be expanded even further, perhaps all the way to Luciferism. This advantage could evolve to be exploited by more highly evolved Luciferans, who could then develop it more fully. In fact, an argument can be made that the psychopath does have an advantage in today's human environment.

Our present world may be a perfect breeding ground for psychopathic and Luciferan evolution. William Reid, a student of Cleckley's, wrote that the psychopath can be found in environments where antisocial traits have survival value. This is a world where *Clockwork Orange* is the norm, where overpopulation, pollution, social degradation and the other well-chronicled woes of our time seem all too inevitable. The psychopath without conscience and compassion has a survival edge in a world moist with danger, stress, confusion, frenetic change and unclear standards of identity and morality.

Hare puts it this way: "if, as I believe, our society is moving in the direction of permitting, reinforcing, and in some instances actually valuing some of the traits listed in the Psychopathy Checklist (a checklist Hare designed to help identify psychopaths) — traits such as impulsivity, irresponsibility, lack of remorse, and so on — our schools may be evolving into microcosms of a "camouflage society", where true psychopaths can hide out, pursuing their destructive, self-gratifying ways and endangering the general student population:— our society may be not only fascinated but increasingly tolerant of the psychopathic personality. Even more frightening is the possibility that "cool" but vicious psychopaths will become twisted role models for children raised in dysfunctional families or disintegrating communities where little value is place on honesty, fair play, and concern for the welfare of others. Experts don't agree about what kind of environment encourages psychopathology. What does seem certain is that any child deprived of nurture and exposed to chronic fear, tension, and horror, tends to grow up empty, detached, and unfeeling. Children who experience grinding turmoil, broken bonds, and overwhelming emotional stress seem destined to struggle with the psychopathic temptation."

This temptation is clear. The psychopathic mentality dissociates from feeling and becomes numb to the suffering of others. This may seem pathological, but dissociation and numbing may actually provide an advantage in a world awash in fear, instability, violence and reckless change. They can eliminate the experience of stress and provide a kind of envelope of psychic protection against a threatening environment. The psychopath, in other words, may be a new adaptation to our troubled social environment. He may well represent the "new nervous system" speculated by Harrington.

Consider the psychopath's lack of adherence to moral codes. In a society characterized by the collapse of moral systems and the ascendance of moral relativity, the psychopath carries no burden of regret, anxiety, or remorse. He is free, because he is free of fear, guilt and remorse. He embodies the *will to individual freedom* so characteristic of our age. Like the saint, he may well be seen as a *freed* man.

The psychopath *fits* our world. He desires constant and immediate gratification of impulses. He is the ultimate narcissist and for him hedonism is the only guiding ideology. Pleasure must come to him here and now. In a society built around consumerism, the psychopath fits wonderfully. He craves a constant escalation of sensation, stimulation, and excitement, and refuses to delay gratification. His sense of time and of consequences are stunted, and he acts on immediate impulse. He serves the cause of consumerism heroically.

The psychopath trusts what he can control. The power urge swells in him like a dark tide. His thirst for power is not limited by ethical or moral concerns, and his actions are not restrained by compassion for another's pain. In a society built upon the power urge, he conforms. To the extent that the most ruthless and successful capitalists are worshipped as royalty, the psychopath is welcome. His devouring style, in fact, is held in high esteem. The religion of success attracts the psychopath into its priesthood.

Above all, the psychopath is a master of disguise. He can alter himself to become what people want him to be. He is a chameleon, changing and shifting as circumstances require. He is false but he shines like the sun, at least on first exposure. He is the essence of success because he is above all a performer. In a society mesmerized by performance over substance, he adapts beautifully.

Alan Harrington writes: "Psychopaths and part-psychopaths ... are trying to create a new nervous system for themselves, one that can respond to the quickening tempo of our lives" and "imagine psychopathic behavior as a protective device of the nervous system designed to *fight off* madness." "Individuals embracing it have broken free — and the psychopathic spirit infiltrates everywhere, appearing simultaneously as illness, style, and new consciousness."

So the psychopath has advantages. His nervous system is protected from overwhelming shock, he feels little anxiety or stress (the prominent disorders apparently affecting modernity), his detachment offers a kind of serenity, and he is the ultimate expression of form over content, of appearance over substance.

The psychopath may therefore have an evolutionary advantage in our world. His time may have arrived. He appears, in short, to be marvelously adapted to modern society. Luciferans agree, but see the psychopath only as a herald of the coming of the new human, of the Luciferan amplifying and personifying the absolute power of power acquisition itself.

BIRTHING THE SPIRITUAL PSYCHOPATH

If Cleckley, Hare, Harrington and others are correct, then our world is an inviting breeding ground for psychopaths — *Clockwork Orange* come true. Perhaps Charlie Manson and Ted Bundy represent this basic evolutionary advantage. They are not fit to be Luciferans, but can perhaps be considered Luciferan Neanderthals, the evolutionary base of the new Luciferan prototype. Possibly Charlie and Ted represent the New Age of the psychopath, and the dawning of the Luciferan Age. Charlie and Ted are not just killers; far from it. They represent much more than simple medical or sociological pathology. They are the harbingers of the new Luciferan psycho-spirituality.

Charlie and Ted do not need to be elevated any further than they already have been by media attention. But I believe that their significance — and our fascination with them — needs to be reinterpreted, and so I have to point out something that no one seems to be noticing: Charlie and Ted have a spirituality.

This spirituality seems bizarre at first, but a closer look reveals something that looks vaguely Luciferan. Charlie and Ted are not Luciferans, but they do proclaim a primitive core of mystical/religious teachings ignored or simply discarded as the madman's rant.

Their words are placental Luciferism. Let's perform an abortion and look inside, *lightly*, and see what is there.

Unfortunately, this abortion will be messy, because it has to cut into the visionary dreams of those who are fervently willing the creation of their own type of new human. The New Age movement, in particular, has hung its hopes on visions of human transformation. New Age means New Human. Such visions do not include Charlie and Ted, even though these fetal Luciferans may be the new humans that planet earth is actually going to get.

Speculation about the coming of a glorious New Human hovers like an apocalyptic hope for the coming New Age. From Bucke's *Cosmic Consciousness* and Leonard's *The Transformation* through the works of John White, Marilyn Ferguson, Fritjof Capra, Jean Houston and other stars of the New Age, the New Human has been prophesied, described, envisioned, visualized, dream-stated, and cosmically experienced.

Non New Agers might want to get to know this New Human better. If she/he/it ('sheheit') is to evolve out of our narcotic dead sleep, and if the transformed she/he/it is to assume control of the planet in order to save it, then those of us who may remain untransformed ought to know who our future Masters will be.

It is said that Sheheit will evolve from us as we evolved from apes. According to Leonard, we should all be "getting on with the business of helping the human race evolve into what amounts to a new species." We can do that by transforming our own consciousness, and can then become Sheheit, the New Human, who is us and is One. We invite Sheheit, we transform, and we become the New Human.

Transforming consciousness, so it is said, is something like climbing a ladder. This ladder is invisible. It is a hierarchy. According to Ken Wilbur, it spirals upward in a growing expansion of awareness. Consciousness expands into that which is beyond the lower mind: by transcending the physical, the mental, and the emotional, we go beyond duality, distinctions, and lower order concerns with good and evil. We expand to become she/he/it, Sheheit.

But expanded consciousness is not supposed to be like an expanded waistline. Sheheit has a slim consciousness, not a fat one. Indeed, Sheheit is as muscular and lean as Shirley MacLaine's latest *Inner Workout* suggests, and will nimbly climb at will through the psychic, subtle, and causal rungs to a state of transcendence. This state is known to all mystical traditions and is summarized nicely in Huxley's *Perennial Philosophy*. Sheheit's ladder leans against the ground of all being, and when transcendence is obtained so also is the state of Oneness, absolute Spirit, *sahaj smadhi*, *turiya*, Supermind, Brahman-Atman, *Svabhavikakaya*, Cosmic Consciousness.

From this exalted height, Sheheit will save us. The New Human will gaze benevolently down at manifest consciousness-in-matter (you and me) with compassion and tolerance. Sheheit's children will rule us with the absolute wisdom of perfected consciousness.

New Age evolutionists seem comfortable with that. It should happen, it will happen, it is Gaia's fervent wish that it happen.

Yet I must admit, a part of me squirms uncomfortably in my ego-controlled material prison. Sure, the planet is in trouble. Sure, political, economic, corporate, and religious institutions have failed. Sure, maybe we do need a New Human; maybe without Sheheit we are going to annihilate ourselves one way or another.

But here is why I squirm. How do I recognize Sheheit? I am told the answer is easy. I just have to meditate, find my Higher Self, or alter my own consciousness using various psycho-technologies: dance, fasting, sensory deprivation, extreme fatigue, yoga, Zen, Sufism, tantra, hypnosis, and other systems outlined by various Masters and other Higher Ones.

I am told these technologies will open me up like a flower in God's garden. Then *I WILL KNOW*. Then and only then I will see Sheheit, who will feast on my ignorance, eat my ignorance like a burnt offering until I am clean and shiny through and through.

Still, what happens if I am too thick to open? What happens if the opener does not work? What happens if Sheheit cleans me out and I am nothing more than a empty can? How in my untransformed state will I know Sheheit?

To answer this question I decided to use my ego-debased powers of reason and logic. I searched the prophets of Sheheit, the purveyors of Perennial Philosophy, the New Age guru-mutants, the merchants of enlightenment, the nursemaids of the coming shrug in Gaia's birth-labor.

I found Sheheit envisioned in various creative ways. Sheheit descends as energy in a rainbow of snapping color; Sheheit is born as a mutant Christ; Sheheit comes as new brain wiring, new social networks, new planetary computer intelligence, new millenarian harmonic convergence, the unification of Many into One. Sheheit explodes into us like a millennial apocalypse of heat, light and new creation.

No matter how Sheheit is envisioned, a few consistent traits lock on to my logic like video space demons on the cross-hairs of my ego's vision-screen.

Despite the risk of slicing and annihilating Sheheit's ineffable Oneness with my crude logic-gun, I came across one characteristic common to all the visions. Sheheit, all would agree, transcends lower orders of being.

Now the word "transcend" is interesting. It means to climb across, to rise above or go beyond the limits of. In other words, it means climbing up the ladder. But just what exactly is Sheheit supposed to be transcending? This might be important, because although we cannot seem to know exactly what Sheheit is, we can perhaps find our what Sheheit is not.

Sheheit is not anything that has been transcended. I think I came up with a widely agreed upon list of that-which-is-transcended. Sheheit is supposed to transcend ego, rationality, logic, emotion, morality, time, and so on. All the Mystic Masters talk about getting beyond these attachments. Buddha did. So did some of the Hindu teachers. Blavatsky did. Gurdjieff, Krishnamurti — find a Master and you will find general agreement about this list.

But here is the problem. Who says Sheheit has to be nice? After studying this list, I had a vision, darkly. I saw Sheheit: I know who Sheheit has impeccably manifested within. I know what Sheheit looks like. He is short. He has a crazy black beard and long hair. He is in jail. His name is Charlie. His full name is Charlie Manson. Charlie has transcended. Charlie is liberated. Charlie is *Free*. Charlie is beyond duality, beyond good and evil. He is beyond moral codes. He has transcended compassion and other emotions. He lives in the immediate Now. He is beyond reason; Charlie does not have to make sense. Charlie is the New Mutant. He is the dawn of the Transformation. He is the New Human.

But wait. I had a bummer vision, right? I am joking, right? I must be of a lower order, because only lesser ones like me could say something so stupid. Everyone on the spiritual search knows that only nice people get to climb the ladder, that only good intentions open the Mysteries, that everything transformed is spiritual and that everything spiritual is good. Sheheit has to be loving, compassionate, and wise. Sheheit could never be a creepy sadistic little murderer. Going up the ladder means becoming nice. Only nice people can climb the ladder successfully.

If only it were true. Transcending simply means going beyond. Beyond morality, reason, and feeling. Beyond nice. Some New Humans might be nice. But they have no obligation. They are beyond such lower concerns. New Humans are not bourgeois. They eat with their mouths open. And if the mood strikes them, they murder. Or torture. After all, what is the physical body of another worth when gazed upon by One who lives in eternity? And what is killing others but releasing them from the bondage of the material? This leads to an obvious question:— why trust the Enlightened Ones? They have no obligation to help you. Hurting and helping are all one for them.

When Geraldo Rivera (bless him) asked Charlie: "Charlie, why did you break the law?" The Master replied "I didn't break the law, man. I'm the lawmaker. My laws come from here." Charlie then gestured at his stomach and did a snaky dance to illustrate his point. Charlie, like others more pretty and polished and positive, is truly liberated, truly free, truly at one with the Source, truly God, truly Sheheit. And Charlie has spiritual brothers. Ted Bundy is a Brother. Charlie and Ted drink from the same source.

The enlightened ones might help you if their stomach says so, hurt you if it doesn't. They have no authority but themselves, and owe allegiance to no one. They have transcended all that.

They have transcended ego-self. But here is a question: when is self-transcendence nothing more than killing love, conscience, and compassion? And here is another: the Enlightened Ones are attached to nothing, but when is non-attachment nothing more than coldness, disinterest, and narcissism? Being attached to nothing means not being attached to you or me or anyone. It means owing others nothing, not loyalty, not love, not anything. Destroy ego, and what else is destroyed?

A Luciferan would answer easily. Kill the ego and all lower-order attachments, and then the predatory higher Self can be born. Luciferans despise idiots like Charlie and Ted, but admit that even in their stupid ignorance they sense the initial power of this reality, through the proverbial glass, darkly.

Here's what Charlie and Ted have to say (Ted's words come from the book *Ted Bundy, Conversations with a Killer* by Michaud and Aynesworth, and Charlie Manson's from *The Manson File* by Schreck):

> Charlie: "A body's brain must be free from ego or in control of ego games...."
> Charlie: "I am a mirror for people... the playing of phony ego or personality games with them is detected immediately and is held up just like a mirror."
> Charlie: "I think it is high time that you all started looking at yourselves, and judging the lie that you live in."
> Ted: "...everyone is trying to protect or nurture egos; our little false belief of having an identity that is separate from everything and everyone else."
> Ted: "That which separates you from me is our egos... that false sense of separateness."

They have transcended personality, they are no-self or all-selves. They shift and change at will, like Proteus.

> Charlie: "I am whatever you make me."
> Charlie: "I am only what you made me. I am only a reflection of you."

Charlie: "You guys are stuck play-acting as humans. I don't need to be human. I don't want to be anybody in particular."

Charlie: "You realize there is no real self; you can pick up a self and be a perfect love, a perfect hate."

They have transcended Good and Evil.

Charlie: "After the illusions of good and bad as programmed are taken... you're in the brain of a child again."

Charlie: "So beyond Good and Evil there is only as much good as you can do for yourself... Doing good is easy. Doing evil takes more effort more creative work and then one must know how to stand back from the rewards."

Charlie: "You (all of us) are the God who rules... where evil and good starts and ends in balance and harmony beyond all the words and thought patterns."

Charlie and Ted have transcended morality, and are free of the crushing adherence to moral codes. They are, then, amoral. They feel no twinges of conscience, no pangs of guilt. Charlie feels no conscience and no guilt. Charlie and Ted are happy with their deeds.

Charlie: "I am content with myself"; "I like being with myself."

Charlie: "I haven't got any guilt about anything because I have never been able to say any wrong."

Charlie: " ...there is no wrong. I don't do wrong."

Ted: "The guilt or innocence — all those things that are really meaningless... its not a matter of caring. It doesn't have any meaning for me."

Ted: "Well, a lot of people are encumbered with a kind of mechanism that is called guilt. To a degree, I have certainly experienced it, but much less so now... I mean I don't feel guilty for anything!"

Ted: "Guilt? It's this mechanism we use to control people. It's an illusion. Its a kind of social control mechanism — and its very unhealthy!"

Ted: " ...the guilt doesn't solve anything, really. It hurts you. You don't need to feel badly. You don't need to regret."

Ted: "I have a stronger self-image than I ever had before... Its a revelation. It's marvelous."

They have transcended reason. They don't have to make sense. Words are a barrier, so why bother with them? Sheheit dislikes words. So why then trust words coming from this New Human? Sheheit can adopt any position, then drop it for another contradictory position at will. Sheheit believes in nothing.

> Charlie: "You reach a stage of nothing. You reach a stage of no thought."
> Charlie: "A free mind creating thought may seem in raw form to be mad. I'm not of your school-thought. Your world's thoughts are just as mad to me as I may seem to you."
> Charlie: "...the MIND is endless and set in total perfection, and PERFECTION is beyond human brains."

The Enlightened Ones have transcended emotion. So when Sheheit seems to feel something, the feeling may or may not be genuine. Feelings like beliefs come and go. Sheheit is a chameleon. Sheheit loves pretending, loves playing the Cosmic Game. Fear, hate, love, and warmth have nothing to do with a Bundy kill, with the rush and power of a human hunting campaign. The void expands from within to possess the other without.

> Ted: "On most occasions (during the hunt) there was a high degree of anticipation, of excitement, of arousal... it was... a possession."
> Charlie: "You don't know how to survive. You're weak. You have emotions, you play little games with your mind. You chase your tail."
> Ted: "Oh I felt good! I felt good. I felt the drive, the power. I had what it took... my karma was so right." (describing his escape from jail for murders already committed).

Charlie's Brothers live in the Cosmic Now. Each moment changes, so Sheheit holds no allegiance to any promises made. The promise lives and dies with the moment.

> Charlie: "...all that is real to me is right now."
> Charlie: "I have never lived in time."
> Charlie: "I don't believe in anything past now. I speak to you from now."
> Charlie: "In my mind I live forever."
> Charlie: "Time is man-made and an illusion and controls must be put on it or it will spin the minds into destruction."
> Ted: "We're always straining reality... prison forces me... to live in the here and now."
> Ted: "I don't think I need to feel guilty anymore, because I try to do what's right, right now!"
> Ted: "I've learned to live absolutely and completely and totally in the here and now. Buddhism and Taoism and spiritual-physical traditions of

the East are much in tune with the way I have become."

The Brothers have transcended humanity. They think they have become God, that they are God, that they are in charge of their own reality, that they create their own reality. They think they are everywhere, in everything. Charlie is the elder and wiser brother here:

Charlie: "My reality is my reality, and I stand within myself on my reality."
Charlie: "But I'm only what lives inside of you, each and every one of you."
Charlie: "Total awareness, closing the circle, bringing the soul to now. Ceasing to be, to become a world within yourself. Locked in your own totalness."
Charlie: "One must realize a perfect universe within oneself."
Charlie: "I am my own court and judge, my own world, my own God."

As the elder brother, Charlie seems to have a plan:

Charlie: "I am Abraxas, the son of God, the son of Darkness... I'm God's messenger from and in the truth... I am the 666... my 666 Beast is running free outside,... the same God I speak of is all gods in ONE GOD. One world. One court. One government. One order. One mind."
Charlie: "The words I send you... play in your illusion and bring down the Christian thought placing new value on life being death and death being life."
Charlie: (sings):
  If we're gonna do something in this world
  We've gotta do it right
  Underneath all that ever was
  Reasons and rhymes wound up tight
  Astral flight, my spiraling staircase dreams
  Lucifer, my brother...

And so Charlie sings to Lucifer. In the Luciferan spiraling staircase of hierarchical devouring, Charlie is at the bottom, but he is at least looking up the staircase in the right direction, and he knows his true brother, Lucifer.

We invent descriptions for these brothers. We call them insane, or character-disordered, or sociopaths, or psychopaths, or whatever. This helps us cope with the unpleasant truth that they swim in a coherently articulated spirituality, whether we understand and like it or not. For Luciferans, this spirituality is puerile. Nevertheless, it heralds their own, and is closer to Luciferism than any other known spirituality. Cleckley may have known about this spirituality, but was probably constrained by the limits of psychology and scientific tradition. Cleckley's psychopaths seem to have transcended themselves beyond psychology and science into the void, into that-which-is-not-human, into prototypes of the New Luciferan Humans.

How many psychopathic human prototypes are out there? When asked the question: "What do you say to those people that say Charles Manson is a psychopath?" Manson responds: "So? There's a lot of us nowadays."

Who ever said the psychopathically voided ones wouldn't find a cosmically spiritual laugh in the pain and dismemberment of others? Who said that spirituality and transcendence could only be loving? The New Human need not be loving at all. Sheheit can be unattached, unbonded, depersonalized, self-centered and cold. He adheres to no moral code, and his promises are worthless. The emerging New Human, transformed and re-wired, might decide to be nice. Or Sheheit might be a horror beyond comprehension. Our future Masters may be ecstatic saints or cruel psychopaths. There are no guarantees. There are no promises.

Despite the pleasantly reassuring words of New Agers, transcendence guarantees nothing. Spirituality is not necessarily synonymous with love. To say that only higher order beings can climb the spiritual ladder ignores the nature of the climb. Charlie is behind Buddha, and closing fast. I think I hear his Brothers cheering. Their chorus is rising.

For Luciferans, Sheheit is birthing itself now because the late twentieth century is an inviting time. Sheheit is manifesting itself in the birth of psychopaths everywhere. And every one of these lower order predators represent the potential flowering of advanced Luciferan consciousness.

NATURAL BORN KILLERS

Whether lots of little Charlie prototypes are being born or not, his psychospirituality is certainly spreading into a marvelously receptive audience: Charlie's spirit has apparently possessed the entertainment industry. The anti-hero has become hero. Hannibal Lechter, the serial killer from the movie *Silence of the Lambs* has all the life, enthusiasm, energy and dynamism of a true hero. So do Mickey and Mallory, the killer couple from Oliver Stones' powerful movie *Natural Born Killers*.

Listen to Mickey's invocation of his own spirituality as he and Mallory drive down "Highway 666":— "Baby, by the power vested in me as God of my world, I pronounce us husband and wife."

And listen to Mickey's answers to questions posed by Wayne, a Geraldo-like television host questioning Mickey after his capture, a capture which catapults Mickey and Mallory to superstardom:

Q: Mickey Knox, when did you first start thinking about killing?
A: Birth. I was thrown into a flaming pit of scum, forgotten by God. I came from violence. It was in my blood. My dad had it, his dad had it. It was all just my fate. My fate.
Q: How can you kill an innocent man?
A: Innocent, who's innocent? It's just murder, man, all God's creatures do it, some form or another. I mean, you look in the forest, you got species killing other species, our species killing all species including the forest. We just call it industry, not murder. A lot of people walking around out there already dead, just need to be put out of their misery. That's where I come in, fate's messenger. See, if the corn or wheat falleth to the ground it abideth alone, but if it die, it bringeth forth much fruit. The wolf don't know why he's a wolf, the deer don't know why he's a deer, God just made it that way.
Q: Maybe you're right Mickey, I don't think so, but maybe you're right. Corporate predators, environmental predators, nuclear predators, life is a hunt. So tell me Mickey, any regrets?
A: I don't spend much time with regret. That's a wasted emotion. Well, I wish that Indian hadn't got killed... He saw it.
Q: Saw what?
A: The demon, he saw the demon.
Q: The demon? What demon?
A: Everybody got the demon in here (points to himself), the demon lives in here, it feeds on your hate, cuts, kills, rapes, it uses your weakness, your fears, only the vicious survive. We all come from no good piece of shit from the time we could breathe. After a while you kind of become bad... Same dream I've had since I was kid, I guess, I just a runnin', runnin' with the animals in the darkness... Death, death just kind of becomes what you are, after a while you begin to like it. Know about realization, Wayne? I mean all this (points around)... just illusion. Moment of realization is worth a thousand prayers.
Q: You're crazy, man.
A: Wayne, I don't think I'm any crazier than you are. I'm extreme, dark and light, you know that (shows Yin-Yang symbol). That's your shadow on the wall. Can't get rid of your shadow can you Wayne? You know the only thing that kills a demon? Love.
Q: Was it worth it?
A: You mean was an instant of my purity worth a lifetime of your lies,

Wayne?

Q: Please explain to me, where's the purity that you couldn't live without in the fifty-two people who are no longer on this planet because they met you and Mallory? What's so fucking pure about that? How do you do it?

A: You'll never understand, Wayne. You and me, we're not even the same species. I used to be you, then I evolved. From where you're standing you're a man. From where I'm standin', you're a ape. You're not even a ape. You're a media person. Murder? It's pure. You're the one made it impure. You're buyin and sellin' the fear. You say "why?" I say "why bother?"

Q. Are you done? Great. Now let's cut the BS and get real! Why this purity that you feel about killing? Why, for Christ's sake, why? Don't lie to me!

A: I guess Wayne you just got to hold that old shot gun in your hand then everything becomes clear, like it did for me the first time. That's when I realized my one true callin' in life.

Q: What's that Mickey?

A: Shit man, I'm a natural born killer.

So there it is. Mickey is his own killer-God. Life is a hunt. Only the hunters are honest and pure. Only the killers are natural, and they are evolving beyond other humans. Only they have a lock on the truth. And only they will thrive and prosper. In the words of brother Charlie: "Murder! There's no murder in a holy war, man... The whole thing's a holy war." To say it another way: if we are all gods, and all gods are holy, then murder does not exist. It is all just a holy war, a war of gods against gods.

What happens to Mickey and Mallory? They become famous, they break from jail, they escape, they have children, and they live happily ever after, unbothered by their crimes and certain of the rightness of their truth.

Stone's movie offended many audiences because of its apparent celebration of violence, murder, and psychopathology. But Stone only reflects what seems obvious. He knows that we love, adore, and honor our psychopaths. Our enraptured fascination bonds us to them. They have become the fulfillment of Clockwork Orange.

According to Charlie, "there's a lot of us nowadays."

LUCIFERANS AND PSYCHOPATHS

Psychopaths may be evolving their own spirituality, a way of living which is everywhere "in the air." Luciferism can then be understood as the ultimate evolution of psychopathic faith. Luciferism seems to accept and extol the basic psychopathic personality traits, and to support psychopathic predatory urges with the compelling force of religious conviction and the hope of ultimate transcendent power. One could argue that Luciferism might attract psychopaths, and then mold, direct, and expand the placental consciousness of the basic psychopath beyond psychopathology itself and toward Luciferism.

But a chasm exists between psychopaths and Luciferans. Their similarities pale compared to their differences. Hare's Psychopathology Checklist shows just how significant these differences are. Psychopaths, according to Hare, are (or show):

1. *Glib and superficial.* Luciferans are not, unless they feel it is to their advantage to appear this way.

2. *Egocentric and grandiose.* Luciferan egocentricity is that of the higher self, not lower selfishness. Luciferans are indeed grandiose, but believe they have the practical means to achieve their goals; psychopaths seldom if ever follow through with their grand plans.

3. *Lack of remorse or guilt.* Luciferans once had remorse and guilt, but consciously decided to kill them. Psychopaths seldom remember ever experiencing these emotions, and probably never have.

4. *Lack of empathy.* Psychopaths do not know anything about empathy; Luciferans know it but do not want it.

5. *Deceitful and manipulative.* Describes both, although Luciferans proclaim a higher purpose to their deceit.

6. *Shallow emotions.* Psychopaths do not truly feel much of anything. Luciferans feel deep passions, impulses and driving needs, although not the "nice" variety. Luciferans appreciate subtle nobility and applaud real power.

7. *Impulsive.* Luciferans are never impulsive. They plan, think, anticipate, and delay gratification (especially during the hunt). Impulses have to be rigidly contained, controlled, and redirected.

8. *Poor behavior controls.* Luciferans try to control everything, especially their own behavior. Self control is vital at all times.

9. *Need for excitement.* Luciferans never seek excitement for its own sake. Excitement junkies leak and lose precious power. Satisfying the lust for excitement is stupid and wasteful.

10. *Lack of responsibility.* Luciferans are deeply responsible to their own quest for power acquisition and godhood. Psychopaths lack all responsibility, except for the satisfaction of base needs and desires.

11. *Early behavior problems.* Probably true of most psychopaths. May or may not be true of Luciferans.

12. *Adult antisocial behavior.* True for psychopaths. Definitely not true for

Luciferans, who would never appear antisocial, and who would fear the loss of hierarchical power should they appear too antisocial.

The only links between psychopaths and Luciferans are lack of conscience, compassion, and empathy. But in all other ways they differ. To Luciferans, psychopaths are sub-human; Luciferans believe themselves to be trans-human or post-human. Theirs is a conscious choice for evolutionary advantage, not an imposed or inherited pathological condition.

Yet the links are there: I have described psychopaths as Luciferan Neanderthals. But some Luciferans would disagree. They find absolutely no connection between themselves and despicable psychopaths. They would argue that Luciferans are to psychopaths as Christians are to televangelists. There is a loose connection, perhaps worth exploring. But just as Christians cannot be equated with televangelists, so too Luciferans cannot be equated with psychopaths. They are connected, like distant cousins, and that is all. Psychopaths are the fungus of Luciferism, like televangelists are to Christianity.

Other Luciferans would argue that even if this is true, such lower order psychopaths could nevertheless be harnessed by Luciferans for certain purposes. Such purposes might include "dirty jobs", such as the abduction of specific targets, or the commission of certain crimes.

For the most part, Luciferans despise psychopaths. Luciferans see themselves as higher-order beings. As such, they have "tried" morality, virtue, compassion, faith, and all the other trappings of "goodness", and simply found them phony, incomplete, and ineffective. They have transcended beyond such concerns, and do not wish to return to them. Psychopaths, on the other hand, have never experienced normal life, and are only defective humans, nothing more. Who knows if they would actually reject normal human life if they had the chance to experience it? Who knows if they would follow the higher Luciferan call, or simply fall prey to human emotions like love?

These questions aside, what is certain is that psychopaths have not consciously rejected compassion and conscience, because they have never known them. Psychopaths are only the products of genetic or social forces they cannot possibly understand or comprehend. They are victims themselves, and hence beneath the contempt of most Luciferans.

Psychopaths do not even rate as good food for devouring, because they lack nourishment. Luciferans cannot live off them. Hence the great disrespect that Luciferans have for psychopaths. They are not even worth the effort of predation. At least other victims stand for something — for decency, love, compassion, morality. Their stand gives them a certain kind of nobility (and hence edible energy), albeit the nobility that the predator assigns to his prey. But psychopaths have never possessed this nobility and never will. As a result, they are to be despised and destroyed, not cultivated. They are an experimental prototype only, and not worth supporting or even devouring.

This debate will probably remain unresolved. Some Luciferans will try to cultivate and use psychopaths, others will simply erase them whenever possible.

All Luciferans will agree that psychopaths are a different order, a lower order, not to be confused with the real force of the Luciferan evolutionary impulse. Psychopaths may perhaps constitute a new prototype, but they most likely represent a dead-end evolutionary attempt at the New Human, an entrapment to be avoided, an impediment to be annihilated and replaced by true Luciferans who grasp the full transcendence and freedom of Luciferan psycho-spirituality.

Luciferans know that psychopathology is beneath them, but that its attractions — the love of killing and violence as pleasurable ends in themselves — can become potential entrapments, handicaps as disabling as any other. In the same way, they know that two other potential prisons stand between them and the total freedom of godhood: organizations and satanism.

CHAPTER NINE

LUCIFERAN ORGANIZATIONS

Men are forever creating organizations for their own convenience and forever finding themselves the victims of their home-made monsters.

— Aldous Huxley, Themes and Variations

... organizations often consume and exploit their employees, taking and using what they need while throwing the rest away...

— Gareth Morgan, Images of Organization

Totalitarianism occupies its victims, making them incapable of rebellion... totalitarianism has no end; either it grows or it dies.

— Earl Shorris, Scenes From Corporate Life

... thanks to its peculiar ideology and the role assigned to it in this apparatus of coercion, totalitarianism has discovered a means of dominating and terrorizing human beings from within.

— Hannah Arendt, The Origins of Totalitarianism

You must love Big Brother. It is not enough to obey him: you must love him.

— George Orwell, 1984

Luciferans are radical individualists. They despise dependence on anything or anyone, and wish only to expand Selfhood. They seek total freedom from all limiting conditions, including the condition of being part of any social group. They despise the sickness of human relationships, and never submit their individuality to serve any kind of human organization: like psychopathology, organizations are just traps to be avoided.

For Luciferans, human groups and organizations have only one use:—sustenance. Luciferans see human organizations in predatory terms, as sources of potential power acquisition. Despite their potential threat to the Luciferan's freedom, organizations can yield concentrated food energy faster and more powerfully than a series of individual victims. Some Luciferans even believe that only the collective energies of human organizations offer sufficient nutrition for higher-order Luciferan activities. An organization, in other words, can feed a Luciferan. Instead of feeding on one individual victim at a time, the Luciferan can absorb the collective energies of individuals within organizations.

Such predation is complex and difficult, requiring special predatory skills. In order to harvest an organization's energy, the Luciferan has to first control and then re-engineer it. All organizational efforts must be contained, controlled, and directed up the organizational hierarchy to the Luciferan, who can then devour and possess the physical, financial, emotional, cognitive, and spiritual energies of the organization's members. The organization serves only one function which is to enhance the Luciferan's power acquisition by attracting and processing energy, and then funneling it upward for the Luciferan to devour.

If the Luciferan is skilled enough to conquer and control an organization, she has two ways to take advantage of its energies. She can leave the organization's structure basically as she found it, and then proceed to slowly, secretly, and incrementally drain its vitality without the overt knowledge of anyone in or outside of the organization. This kind of drainage has its limitations for obvious reasons: fear of discovery, limited time and opportunity to devour, and other related problems prevent full predatory access. The organization's energy is not flowing directly into her, so she has to settle for what she can get.

A second alternative is to make the energy flow directly to her by transforming the organization into a totalitarian pyramid which she controls. Such organizational transformations are difficult, but the results can be astonishing. If the organization's culture can be re-engineered to overtly serve, honor, and feed its Luciferan leader, then the leader can swell exponentially with the power acquisition.

Taking over and then re-engineering an existing organization can be extremely difficult even for skilled Luciferan predators. The Luciferan can meet resistance from the organization's existing leadership, from the ethics embedded in the organization's culture (especially if the organization is religious, charitable, or politically idealistic), and from other forces flowing from the organization's past.

To avoid this problem, some Luciferans instead create their own organizations designed for personal power acquisition. Everything about the organization— culture, purpose, design, vision, mission — serves to add power and energy to its Luciferan founder.

Such organizations are totalitarian in the Orwellian sense. Power is held solely by the organization's Luciferan leader, who uses it to ruthlessly exploit, possess, and devour all available organizational energies. Totalitarian organizations allow easy predation for the Luciferan, because members, as a condition of belonging, must surrender themselves unconditionally to their organization and its leader. Their entire purpose becomes to enhance their leader's power and emulate the leader's example. The organization's culture thus becomes predatory, competitive, aggressive and hungry for power. In other words, it becomes an extension of its Luciferan founder and an expression of her personality.

Creating a devoted organization might absorb the predatory energy of a Luciferan's entire physical life span, but the results can be worth the effort and predatory patience required.

A note before beginning our exploration. Luciferan organizations, like Luciferism itself, are on the cultural horizon, and are not in full conscious existence. As I make no claims to truth about Luciferans or Luciferism, I also make no claims about Luciferan organizations: what follows is speculative. I will be using the *as if* perspective — writing about Luciferan organizations in the present tense as if they already existed. I ask that readers continue to appreciate, understand, and accept the power and value of this approach.

As with Luciferism itself, however, some of you may recognize Luciferan traits in real organizations you know intimately, and some of you may even recognize the Luciferan style animating the actual leader of a familiar organization. As Luciferans would say, welcome to reality, and welcome to the brave new world of Luciferan organizations.

PREDATORY LUCIFERAN ORGANIZATIONS

An organization created by a Luciferan for personal power acquisition is always built on predatory Luciferan principles. Such organizations can therefore be recognized by their totalistic culture of devouring, possession, violence, and disguise. They are relentless in their hunger for power, expansion, and ultimate influence. Their cultures adopt the predatory nature of Luciferism, although without necessarily promoting Luciferan psycho-spirituality consciously or openly. These organizations can be corporate, political, national, familial, educational, religious, charitable, feminist, or therapeutic in nature. By action, however, they are predatory. No matter what their outward mission, vision, or apparent purpose, their actual intentions are always self-centered. They exist to serve the ultimate purpose of all predators: the acquisition of power and energy for personal survival. By necessity they strive to be exclusive, successful, powerful and influential in their quest to absorb energy for their respective Luciferan leaders.

Such organizations have an identifiably totalistic design similar to Orwellian political totalitarianism, and comparable to cults. It seems that just as all predators assume certain design features to enhance their predation (faster speed, sharper eyes, powerful claws), so Luciferan organizations tend to adopt features and traits that enhance the predatory advantage of the Luciferan founder.

I would like to examine these design features now, beginning with the organization's overall structure (which I compare metaphorically to a "psycho-spiritual cone"), and then finishing with a profile of its various traits.

THE PSYCHO-SPIRITUAL 'CONE'

A predatory totalistic Luciferan organization can be visualized as a cone with its tip above and base below.

At the tip of the cone is the leader. Proceeding downward in concentric circles are the immediate inner circle of elevated followers closest to the leader, followed by ever lower elements of the hierarchy, down to the newest recruits. Promotion up the hierarchical order depends on a number of factors, the most important being the degree of obedience to the leader.

All members can be pictured as forming a circle at their level of authority.

They look "inside and up" toward the cone's center and apex to worship the leader. Their awareness, consciousness and life's energies are directed outside themselves to the leader at the top. All other influences, thoughts, and ideas from outside the cone are relevant only to the extent that they can be used to strengthen the leader. Members believe that personal survival, protection, meaning and purpose can only be found by serving the leader and expanding the cone's influence in the world.

The cone's boundaries are a membrane: information goes out into the world from the leader's wisdom, but little feedback — especially negative — is allowed to penetrate the cone from the outside. The leader's word is absolute, and the flow of truth is one-way. Members promote this truth to the outside world, where it may be experienced by outsiders as propaganda, zealotry, and aggressive proselytizing, or as advertising, enthusiasm, and *truth-sharing*.

Information from the outside world is heavily restricted and limited. Contacts with 'tainted' outsiders are discouraged, and all criticism is placed through filters built and monitored by the leader and the group's inner higher circle. These filters effectively dismiss outside criticism by defining it as evil persecution or as the manifestation of an enemy conspiracy.

The cone's structure envelopes all who enter it. Once inside, the new recruit is taught to see the outside world as absurd or evil, and comes to believe that truth, life, hope and power can only be found within the cone's protection. The recruit's sole purpose is to serve the leader and to expand the leader's influence by expanding the cone itself.

The cone expands by increasing dedicated membership, financial resources, material acquisitions, and social influence. As it grows it becomes ever more energized to serve the leader. The cone can be thought of as "spinning": the more it grows, the bigger it gets, the faster it spins. As it gathers and spins with crackling energy, centrifugal force acts to draw members inward and upward, to convince them that such movement is the only path to freedom. As it spins, the cone gains momentum with every new believer drawn in. Some Luciferan cones grow, spin fervently, and then die, having failed to maintain momentum and growth, and having succumbed to the centripetal forces pulling it apart. Others stabilize and enter into a kind of truce with the outside world. Still others grow to the point that they actually take control of the wider culture within which they were created. One only need think of Nazism or the Bolshevik to understand how a small group of dedicated followers can usurp power. Outsiders who challenge the organization's growth will be harmed. Since all truth and power exist only within the cone, then any means can justify the end, which is defined as the cone's triumphal growth, empowerment, and prosperity.

The following profile outlines the raw traits of such predatory organizations.

The ideal Luciferan organization is a predatory machine designed by its charismatic Luciferan founder to serve its creator's purposes. Here is how such organizations can be recognized.

Predatory organizations have a charismatic leader or founder. He or she is magnetic, electrifying, and articulate. She creates a utopian vision of peace, joy, and harmony powerful enough to draw the enthusiastic energy of dedicated followers. She radiates brilliance and sometimes even genius.

She tends toward messianic proclamations. If the organization is religious, then she is God or the Absolute, or at the very least, God's Closest Prophet. To obey her is to obey God; to disobey is to betray God. She is a divine source, and as such commands total obedience, respect, and submission from followers.

If the organization is corporate, then the leader is the bringer of great profit, power, and lifelong employment, the author of security and safety for all employees. If political, the leader is of course the prophet of inevitable historical change, the savior of the masses from powerlessness and poverty.

Upon closer inspection, however, the leader of a predatory organization has a darker side. He or she is authoritarian. She is a power and control junkie, obviously taking great pleasure from her power. She commands total obedience, complete submission. Any sign of individuality within her close inner circle of followers is discouraged or even ruthlessly crushed. Criticism from followers cannot be tolerated. Punishment to offenders is swift and often severe. Such leaders expect every whim to be fulfilled immediately by followers, because total obedience is an outward manifestation of her total control.

A predatory leader is usually self-appointed, accountable to no tradition or outside body. She is a law unto herself; what she says and does is always interpreted by followers as correct and perfect; what is against her and her teachings is immoral, evil, negative, or simply a form of lower order vibration. She defines reality for her followers. She drains her followers of money and property, which they lovingly surrender to her, thanking her for removing the "burden of bad karma" implied by material wealth, and impressed that she has the spiritual strength to carry this suffering on their behalf.

Or he could use his followers sexually because they only want to reciprocate their deep gratitude to him for "activating their sexual chakras and beginning the Kundalini journey toward enlightenment." He might ask his followers to kill his enemies as an act of kindness, thus releasing these targets from the bondage of their corrupted physical bodies and allowing them to evolve into his truth on the astral level. He might ask his followers to kill themselves communally as an act of ultimate loyalty and personal sacrifice to the cause, thus strengthening its future and guaranteeing their own personal salvation. Normal standards of compassion, conscience, morality and law do not apply to him because he has transcended such lower-order concerns.

The Luciferan leader is self-serving. While followers live in poverty, he lives in opulence. Decadent material wealth can be justified as 'gifts' from the divine source, as the gratitude of followers, as a necessary 'teaching device' to show lower order beings that when they are spiritually advanced enough then they too will be able to live in opulence without being corrupted by it. If material wealth is 'bad karma' or 'spiritual pollution', then the leader offers to take on the bad karma to save his followers. Hypocrisy, rationalizations, and lies are thus spiritualized to serve the leader's needs.

The leader is intolerant and often dogmatic. The truth is as he speaks it at the moment. If the truth changes, if a prophecy is not fulfilled, then he has simply decreed that this in turn should be the new truth. Critics, whether inside his organization and out, are all enemies by definition. His truth is absolute and timeless, even if it changes. It cannot be questioned. He or she is manipulative and capable of deceit, lies, and chameleon-like transformations. For the news camera he is sincere and pious; hidden from view he can be monstrous.

Some of these leaders may descend into psychopathology and develop a delusional paranoia and even criminal behaviors, often indulging in their illnesses at the expense of their followers. These indulgences may involve 'teaching devices' such as physical assault, sexual abuse of adults and children, extortion, corruption, and murder. Higher-order predatory leaders would of course shun any such psychopathic indulgences unless higher level *powaqqatsi* advantages could be obtained from them.

For those in thrall to their leader, absolutely nothing is wrong. Nothing can be wrong, for their leader is perfect. Those followers who see the negative side tend to dismiss it or simply reinterpret it as some kind of special spiritual teaching.

When a leader of this nature has absolute control over an organization, and if his pathological sickness deepens, then the organization will sicken along with him. It will dutifully reflect every aspect of his personality, and will seek to socialize new members into submission. Ultimately, new members will want to replicate the 'perfect master' in every way possible. If the leader is a higher-order Luciferan, then the organization will drift toward the Luciferan impulse as an imprint to be emulated.

If the leader is effective with this imprinting, then he or she will carve her pattern deeply into the organization even after death. Thus the organization will revere and promote individuals whose personality best fits that of the Luciferan founder. The leader can then virtually live on through future generations of followers: Luciferans believe their organizations will continue to feed them in the next life and thus provide a predatory advantage over other competitors. In this way the organization itself will become as predatory as its founder. This predation will be anchored deeply within the organization's myths, rituals, ideology initiation or socialization practices.

SECRECY, DECEPTION, CAMOUFLAGE

Secrecy is essential to the predatory organization. Without it, the organization's true impulse would be seen openly, and potential victims might rebel. Disguise is an absolute weapon against enemies and potential victims who would reveal the truth. Without camouflage, such organizations would be seen as they are — ruthlessly predatory — and would then be in open conflict with their victims. Competitors could use this truth to damage or destroy the organization's credibility. Predatory organizations desire absolute power and certainty, and so do not want to allow uncontrollable impulses to enter into the devouring game. They need secrecy and lies.

Such organizations *have* to appear other than what they are. If predatory, they must seem giving. If violent, they must appear peaceful. If devouring, serving. If possessing, giving. If protean, honest. They must maintain the appearance while practicing the deception.

This deception must extend not only to outsiders — the public, victims, competitors and enemies — but also to followers lower in the organization, who must initially believe that they are serving a noble cause when in fact they are simply serving the Luciferan leader's power acquisition. Their submission to the leader must be based on their perception of him as an exalted being of great compassion and wisdom. They must not suspect — at least at first — that their service is causing them to become as predatory as their leader. Rather, they must believe their predatory actions are justified by the nobility of their leader and his cause. Such actions can include deceiving potential recruits, lying to the press and the public, engaging in deceptive money-making schemes, and harming perceived enemies. Lies and deceptions crafted by the Luciferan leader must guide the actions of lower-order members. Only an inner circle of initiates advanced in the organization's hierarchy must know the full truth, and even they have must be manipulated by the ultimate manipulator in the organization. If this leader fails, then one within this inner circle will rise to take the power and promote the plan.

Protean camouflage is always necessary. The organization will not show its true face until forced to do so by intense examination. Some Luciferan organizations may even temporarily eliminate or sacrifice certain key predatory processes in order to gain a camouflage advantage. This may cause a loss of power by interfering with predation, and may even delay the leader's plans, but the advantage of an outwardly ethical appearance usually outweighs such losses. The organization can then operate without interference behind a pleasing facade.

ISOLATION AND ELITISM

All of these layers of lies and secrecy effectively isolate the leader from lower followers. Despite the leader's importance as an object of worship for members, only an inner circle of devoted initiates have real contact with him, and even this contact is limited. The leader needs isolation and secrecy to hide his true nature. Such isolation adds to his mystique and enhances his status with his followers while simultaneously preventing them from fully comprehending his true motives.

The organization itself also has to be isolated from the outside world. Financial matters must be hidden, and the inner workings of the organization must remain secret. Isolation may be geographical or psychological: the organization can be physically separated from the outside world by occupying and guarding a remote location, such as a commune, or it can be psychologically isolated by cultivating a culture of elitism and solidarity within members, who will then refuse to disclose anything about the organization's inner nature with outsiders. The group can thus exist in society and yet be as emotionally disconnected as a group living in the jungles of Guyana.

Because the leader's hold over his organization is threatened by competing information sources, he must ensure that his followers remain isolated from intimate contact with outsiders. The leader will therefore attack outside sources relentlessly. These sources may include the media, science, other philosophies and organizations, and even the concerned families of his followers who question his methods. In short, anyone or anything competing with or criticizing *the* great mission.

Such outsiders are always described in derogatory terms, and critics are attacked with vicious verbal or even physical assaults. Only the Luciferan leader's doctrine is the True Doctrine, sanctified by an Ultimate Source (God, Truth, Light, Financial Profit, Growth, Health, Historical Political Change, etc.). Truth is black and white. Followers either accept all of his doctrine or none at all. Isolation from other contaminated sources protects the organization's purity and strength.

In brief, the leader encourages isolation because it increases group solidarity, decreases competing sources of information from the outside, and enhances control over members.

In their proud isolation from the contaminated outside world, the members

244

of predatory organizations always consider themselves superior. They are the specially saved, the superior elite. All other beings are inferior, and are always described in derogatory terms: they are "meat", "wogs", "systemites", and so on.

Elitism shuts down communication with the outside world, thus increasing isolation and secrecy. Why listen to input from inferior outsiders? Their thoughts are polluted, degraded and degenerate, not worthy of consideration. Such outsiders will never understand the Program, will never "get" the message, and will live in ignorance forever. They may be pitied, but never welcomed, except as potential members or as victims.

Such elitism is vastly different from healthy pride. I can be proud of my football team, proud of my country, or proud of my profession. But this does not touch the same emotional chord as elitism. Healthy pride encourages contact with other organizations, and is comfortable with openness and freedom. Elitism snubs others, closes contact, and limits thought.

Elitism attracts members because they can then feel superior to outsiders. Secure in their superiority, they feel safe and strong. Luciferan leaders know that elitism can easily translate into hateful aggression, especially when outsiders cease to be objects of simple ridicule and pity, and instead become an enemy threat.

Such elitism operates within the organization as well: a member's value depends on his place in the cone's hierarchy. Thus lower members wish desperately to climb higher, not only to gain respect, but to get closer to the leader. The organization is designed to reward and encourage this urge. It is to become a prime directive for every member. If strong enough, the urge-to-climb will then dominate all other concerns for the member, including morality. To climb up the ladder, the member will do anything required. Such members have obvious value for the Luciferan leader.

To create this kind of devoted follower, the Luciferan simply has to exploit the natural human instinct to feel superior, then all else follows. Luciferism itself can be considered as a kind of religious elevation of superiority and elitism. Luciferans intimately understand this instinct, so they know how to use it as bait to attract and manipulate members. The member's life energies will then flow in and up the organizational hierarchy to the feed the Luciferan at the apex.

OUTSIDERS AS ENEMIES

Camouflage, secrecy, isolation and elitism all work together to enhance group solidarity and power, which in turn helps feed the Luciferan leader. This solidarity is further deepened when the group unites against an enemy.

Luciferan leaders use an enemy to help unite and focus their organization. The enemy is everywhere, without and within. The enemy is powerful, cruel, cold, vicious, manipulative, and power-hungry. He is the cosmological enemy, a kind of archetype of evil. The enemy cannot be reasoned with, only shunned, destroyed and consumed.

The enemy is hated passionately. In Luciferan organizations, hatred of the enemy swells: immense energy is directed strategically to attack or defend against this enemy. In such organizations, outsiders are left with the impression that, despite the leader's utopian and loving ideology, the organization itself is more concerned with hatred and devouring than with love.

The enemy is assigned a number of characteristics, some of which have been catalogued by Sam Keen in his powerful book *Faces of the Enemy*. The enemy is the stranger, the aggressor, faceless. He is also the enemy of God or of the group's conception of the Absolute. He is a barbarian, greedy to possess all that the group has fought so long and nobly to create. He lies and deceives and cheats. He is a criminal, probably a torturer, rapist, or thief as well. He is comparable to the lowest forms of life on the planet, and is like a beast, a reptile, an insect or germ. He is the bringer of death, the destroyer. He is a disease. He is, in other words, reprehensible and disgusting, less than human, not like members of the group.

Thus demeaned and diminished, the enemy can then be condemned, segregated, assaulted or even slaughtered. The Nazis used all of these images to depict the Jew, and other political and religious groups continue to use them today. Evil enemy images are the stuff of propaganda, so wherever war is about to break out, enemy imagery runs at fever pitch.

Predatory organizations use enemy imagery not only to justify attacks on outsiders, especially critics, but to enhance separation, elitism, and secrecy. Members will simply refuse to associate with outsiders for fear of contamination, and so will voluntarily separate themselves. They will see themselves as a special elite, saved, enlightened, transcendent, above and away from the masses beneath them. And they will never share the group's privacy and secrecy with the hated enemy. Thus the group then binds itself together into a unified whole, where all hatred, anger, and fear can be projected onto the enemy "out there."

The group's particular religious philosophy helps define these enemies. If the group is New Age, then the outsider might represent the "lower-order vibrational energies", if Christian, then the "Satanic", if Muslim, then the "infidel", and so on. Anyone can become defined as an enemy — whether critics, family, friends, the general public — all who do not embrace the leader's inspired truth. There is no middle ground because all humanity is either with the organization or against it.

Luciferans also encourage and cultivate such imagery in their followers because all internal disputes and personal angers can be safely redirected toward the enemy. The leader can then escape any potential hostility from his own membership, even when he clearly deserves it. Using enemy imagery, the Luciferan leader can use his own members as weapons to control or intimidate anyone who might expose him. Internal anger is deflected to the enemy, and the enemy is effectively intimidated by followers who come to believe that they are doing something noble for their cause.

CONSPIRACIES

Whenever enemy imagery, elitism, isolation and secrecy take hold of an organization, conspiracy theories usually follow. Thus the evil enemy is everywhere, working against the just cause, united in a worldwide conspiracy of overwhelming proportions, waiting and planning and plotting to take over. The enemy has tentacles reaching everywhere. Only the organization and its leader can save the world from this nefarious enemy. Perhaps conspiracy theories grow so easily within predatory organizations because they themselves seek absolute expansion of their power. As a result, they are hyper-alert for potential enemies or competitors, and easily project expansionist and conspiratorial intentions onto their enemies in order to deflect attention from their own predatory devouring, possession, and violence. Conspiracy theories, therefore, function to disguise the organization's predatory intent from both outsiders and naive insiders.

Additionally, conspiracies enhance group solidarity. When conspiracy theories are running at a fever pitch then the evil enemy is everywhere. The organization's members become engaged in a heroic struggle against this invincible and omnipresent enemy who must be crushed at all costs. The organization therefore swells with the energy, drive, and zealous enthusiasm of its members, and its emotional tone becomes frenetic. Enormous crises are imminent. The 'world' is about to invade them. Satan is staging an attack. Backsliders, sinners, revisionists or communists are ruining the organization. Unless all members give 100% right now, doom is imminent. Members therefore donate obsessive levels of work and effort, giving years of free time devoted to "the cause", and happily sacrificing everything to enhance the organization's growth. They attack the leader's enemies and competitors and, if successful, neutralize them. The organization's power and influence therefore expands, permitting the Luciferan leader to get stronger by feeding on this energy.

Graumann and Moscovici articulate the basic elements of conspiracy theories in their book *Changing Conceptions of Conspiracy*. Basically, such theories always refer to a secret group with clandestine agents who are masked to look just like you and me, but who have sinister dark intentions of destruction. The group is all-powerful, almost omniscient, omnipresent, and omnipotent with endless financial resources and power.

The enemy conspiracy has high solidarity: it is a highly organized, efficient machine which completely controls obedient legions of automatons. They have a subversive plan or plot designed to attack the integrity, purity, and cohesiveness of "my" social body. Their plan is massive, and has been launched against us and all that is good and just. They are infiltrating us everywhere. They appear like us but are disloyal, treacherous betrayers who only wish us harm. They are really alien outsiders, and wish to abduct us into their evil ways. They are behind every calamity, and are responsible for every problem. If they did not exist, then we-the-good would prosper. They bring contamination, and are like a disease. They are the evil enemy incarnate. And unless we wake up, an absolute crisis is imminent. We have to hunt them out ruthlessly and expose them for what they are. They must be removed from power and brought to justice.

Examples of this are legion: anti-Semitism, the infamous "Protocols", Nazi ideology; the Inquisition and witch trials, and the Stalinist gulag. Massive logical fallacies are used to identify the evil enemy: guilt by association, guilt by appearance, guilt by accusation. If you associate with known enemies then you are one of them, if you look like the enemy then you are, and if you are accused then you must be guilty. Evidence is sifted through the sieve of the conspiracy theory, so that even innocent behavior is seen as sinister. The conspirators must be publicly exposed in show trials, where evidence is actually fragile and confusing, where "lurid details" feed public fascination, where the accused are often coerced into confessing, and where the emotionally loaded language of stock phrases and jargon prevails over the reasoned examination of truth.

Conspiracy theories are ultimately unverifiable because most physical evidence is shaky or non-existent, with a heavy reliance on the memories or confessions of alleged perpetrators. There is usually an imaginative literary quality to the conspiracy theory, which is created in written documents over time in a fictionalized manner. One author contributes a few ideas, another references these ideas and then embellishes them, and so on. The result is what Moscovici calls a "figurative or imaginary core of social representation", somewhat like a morality play.

When conspiracy theories are in full force, they serve to enhance group solidarity and mobilize group energies. Authority can be deepened to deal with the emergency. Enemies can be attacked more easily, with less regard for conscience or compassion. Members' frustrations, hatreds and fears can thus be vented on the enemy scapegoat who is after all absolutely evil. These enemies are reduced to one mass without individuality; the complexity of the individual enemy becomes the single simple fact that he is the evil agent of an evil system. All problems are reduced in this way, so members have a simple causal explanation for all problems: "it's the Jew", "it's the Wog", "it's the Corporations", "it's the Satanist." Each member can thus feel profoundly important, part of a historical movement, a knight on an eternal quest. Members and leaders can avoid all feelings of guilt or remorse for their actions. After all, such feelings are only the tools of the conspiracy. Members feel all-powerful, certain, free of the burdens of self-examination, self-doubt, and complex thought.

Conspiracy theories are strangely logical and coherent, possessing an internal consistency more profound than reality itself. They are precise, detailed, and passionate. They allow for no doubt or alternative explanation. All possibilities are covered, all events interpreted, all eventualities predicted. As bizarre as this might seem to outsiders, conspiracies feel like absolute truth to insiders. Logic is not expelled but simply shackled to serve the conspiracy. Conspiracy theorists weave complex networks of logical inference, induction, and deduction without ever examining or challenging their core beliefs: accept that Jews are evil, and all else follows logically, including the gas chambers. Luciferans understand and use conspiracy theories as weapons against their enemies, and will create and use them in organizations they control.

TRUE BELIEVERS

The ideal member of a Luciferan organization is the "true believer", a person so dedicated to the leader that all other concerns are secondary.

The longshoreman philosopher Eric Hoffer describes the true believer as a certain sub-type of human being who becomes passionately dedicated to a cause. This dedication is an uncompromising and complete devotion to the "one eternal truth" and holy cause. Hoffer describes such people as appearing poised, self-assured, and autonomous in their monolithic certainty. They see themselves standing above those who do not know the truth and who belong to the lower ranks of the uninitiated.

Hoffer goes on to say that the true believer's real self is altogether different. The true believer is consumed: by self-hatred and self-contempt, by the hatred of everything presently interfering with his future utopian ideal, and by a profound sense of dislocation from everything around him. According to Hoffer the true believer is incomplete, insincere, frustrated, estranged, worthless, inadequate, and filled with guilt and purposelessness. The grand "cause" is a kind of antidote against disconnection. The cause fills the believer with purpose, meaning, direction, and esteem. Without it, the believer is nothing. Without the believer, the cause is nothing. The cause and the believer thus enter into a kind of mutually supportive symbiotic relationship benefiting both but frequently harming other individuals or society as a whole.

A totalitarian leader who can galvanize such disconnected loners, losers, and "misfits" into a cohesive whole can achieve ferocious power.

Hoffer's archetypically inadequate "outsiders" may be useful to the Luciferan predator in a similar way, however, but they also bring problems. Their excesses can be hard to control, their impulsiveness can bring trouble, and their commitment to the Luciferan's cause can easily shift to another.

Luciferans therefore try to recruit more connected and successful members of society. Such individuals have followed society's blueprint for happiness, have risen successfully to influential positions of power, but have found only despair, unhappiness, depression, and restless emptiness. Their acquisition of career, wealth, reputation, and position have not filled the void. They lack something, and seek it desperately. They are starving for meaning and purpose despite their success, and often feel dislocated, forgotten, isolated and miserable, even though others see them as paragons of success and happiness.

The astute Luciferan can gradually convince them to serve his cause, and can then use their social connections and their wealth to his advantage. Powerful group dynamics and psychological assault can transform susceptible lawyers, doctors, teachers, social workers, entrepreneurs, and other professionals to become as dedicated to the cause as other true believers, and lead them to jettison conscience and compassion to ensure the survival and growth of their new cause.

The Luciferan leader can exploit these individuals because their despair is so acute and painful. They surrender themselves to him in exchange for relief from anomie and despair. Like any other salesman, the Luciferan senses the victim's personal pain and uses it as an advantage.

Society's "outsiders" and "insiders" can both therefore respond with equal joy and enthusiasm to the Luciferan's call to become true believers in his cause. The Luciferan understands the universal human desire to escape suffering, and simply asks his followers to surrender personal autonomy for the relief he offers, the relief of truly believing and belonging to a noble cause.

True believers can be found in political movements, corporate adventures, business pyramid sales schemes, therapeutic movements, religious cults, environmental societies — in any type of organization that will promote and reward them. Luciferans are attracted to such organizations because true believers are easy to manipulate and control. They do not ask questions, they serve the cause relentlessly, and they eagerly jettison conscience and compassion for the greater good of their cause and so will engage in predation, violence, or any other act commanded by the leader. They can be used as weapons against enemies or competitors while believing they are serving a nobler, higher cause.

True believers easily become armies of psycho-spiritual salesmen. They have "the truth" and want you to have it as well. Argument is irrelevant to them. They have the truth and your arguments are meaningless. They sell the Cause everywhere, at every opportunity. Intimate personal relationships are displaced by the cause, so that even close friends and partners sense only the "program" and not the person carrying it, as if the person dispensing the message had been displaced or even destroyed by it.

The organization creates incentives for their best recruiters. These are seldom financial — recruiters may proselytize for twenty hours per day, seven days a week, and then feel guilty for four hours of sleep. Incentives are usually less substantial: praise from the leader, elevated group status, promotion, and a sense of personal fulfillment.

By "sharing the vision" and constantly recruiting, they bring in more resources for the organization. More members to be exploited, more money, power, and influence, more energy and drive. Because they are blind to the motives of those controlling their beloved cause, they can be coldly used to bring great harm to enemies or competitors. They become weapons to be used at the discretion of their Luciferan masters.

Of course not all organizations whose members practice heavy proselytizing are Luciferan, but such organizations offer themselves as beacons for Luciferan predators, who often ruthlessly and easily obtain positions of leadership, control and power. A well-tuned army of uncritical recruiters is a prize to be taken and possessed by an astute Luciferan predator.

OBEDIENCE

Obedience is valued and rewarded in Luciferan organizations. Obedience is essential. Lower-order members must be prepared to follow the leading elite's directives over all other personal concerns of compassion or conscience. Without this depth of obedience, organizational power acquisition is limited and easily lost to internal conflict and stalemate. Obedience is essential.

For the Luciferan leader, disobedience is cancerous for his organization. It must be ruthlessly destroyed, especially if it grows from compassion or conscience. One way to counter disobedience is to appeal to loyalty. Members can be told: "You may not like manipulating this old man to donate his estate to us, but your obedient dedication will help the group to grow, thrive, and survive. This is a higher good than your petty concerns about the old man. If you love me, you will do as I ask."

Another is to appeal to a higher cause, which takes precedence over all lower moralistic concerns. The cause is noble and perfect, so any action promoting the cause must be moral and ethical. If the noble cause is the promotion of racial purity, then killing lower races is a rational and moral act of goodness and kindness. Thus morality and truth become redefined or reframed for the member/victim, who can then interpret her obvious act of brutality and cruelty as an unpleasant but necessary step toward a higher good. Once a Luciferan controls a higher cause loved by millions, then the cause can be twisted to serve power-ends never understood or even suspected by its followers.

If loyalty and higher cause don't work, then Luciferans can appeal to personal ambition: "You may not like what I am asking you to do, but do it and I will appreciate it. We both know this means great prosperity, success, and power for you." The message here is simple: obey and you will prosper. Disobey and you won't.

A Luciferan leader can also appeal to authority. The experimental psychologist Stanley Milgram showed how normal individuals easily give up their internal moral compass when directed by an authority figure.

In his book *Obedience to Authority* he described a series of experiments in which a scientist asked experimental subjects to participate in a study of learning. Subjects were told that the scientist wanted to study the effects of punishment on another subject's ability to learn a series of tasks. The subject was thus asked to become a "teacher", and the other subject the "learner". Both scientist and learner were part of the experimental team, however, so only the teacher was the real experimental subject.

A scientist in a white smock instructed each teacher to shock the learner for every mistake. A dial of ascending voltage from 15 to 450 volts was placed in front of the teacher, labeled "Slight Shock, Moderate Shock, Strong Shock, Very Strong Shock, Intense Shock, Extreme Intensity Shock, Danger: Severe Shock, and XXX". Shock intensity was to be incrementally increased after each mistake.

The learner, meanwhile, was trained to react in a different way for each level of shock administered by the teacher, starting with an initial "ouch" and leading ultimately to a convincing scream of pain and then the silence of apparent unconsciousness. The teacher was visually separated from the learner, but could hear every reaction.

Initial predictions by a group of psychiatrists was that most subjects would not go beyond the 150 volt, or "Strong Shock" level. In fact, only 8 out of forty subjects stayed in this level. Two went as far as "Intense Shock", five to Extreme Intensity Shock", and a whopping 25 to "XXX" shock.

All the teachers apparently believed that the victim's pain was real, and most wanted to stop immediately. Only the coaching of the white-frocked scientist kept them going. Their moral compasses swung to the magnetic authority figure and so they followed his directions. Milgram says of his experiment: "Nothing is more dangerous to human survival than malevolent authority" and "The abrogation of personal responsibility is the major psychological consequence of yielding to authority." Those who surrender to authority "have given themselves to the authority; they see themselves as instruments for the execution of his wishes; once so defined, they are unable to break free."

Luciferans understand Milgram's results perfectly. His authority in the experiments was the presence of a scientist in a lab coat; theirs the profound presence of charisma and apparent godhood. Luciferans know that most of us will submit to the right authority figures, and so try to position themselves to take advantage of this weakness. They know we are often as obedient to an authority as animals to a herd leader. This weakness can be exploited.

Milgram calls this weakness the *agentic state*: "The agentic state is.. the state a person is in when he sees himself as an agent for carrying out another person's wishes. He... no longer views himself as responsible for his own actions." Milgram adds: "Moved into the agentic state, the person becomes something different than his former self, with new properties not easily traced to his usual personality".

Milgram believes that "ideological justification is vital in obtaining willing obedience, for it permits the person to see his behavior as serving a desirable end." In his experiment, this desirable end was serving the cause of science. Luciferans know how to expand this ideological service far beyond the call of science to include whatever ultimate good the victim aspires to serve: God, Allah, The Great Brotherhood, personal enlightenment, *samadhi*, cosmic consciousness, political revolution. Ideology is key here. Says Milgram: "control the manner in which a man sees his world, and you have gone a long way toward controlling his behavior."

Milgram concludes: "It is this ideological abrogation to the authority that constitutes the principal cognitive basis of obedience. If, after all, the world is as the authority defines it, a certain set of actions follows logically. The relation between authority and subject therefore cannot be viewed as one in which a coercive figure forces action from an unyielding subordinate. Because the subject accepts authority's definition of the situation, action follows accordingly."

Luciferans exploit this ideological surrender to authority ruthlessly. But if followers still do not submit, then Luciferans will use any kind of coercive technique to break down the member's resistance and gain absolute control of his beliefs and actions. These range from sophisticated psychological assault itself to simple threats, intimidation, and fear tactics. The message here is easy to understand: "criticize me, and I will badly hurt you or those close to you."

All of these techniques — appeals to loyalty, higher cause, personal ambition, authority and threat — have the same objective: "obey, obey, obey".

Conformity

Conformity is as essential to Luciferan organizations as obedience. If obedience to authority fails to influence a member's conduct, then conformity to group norms and expectations can take over. The psychologist Solomon Asch used a fascinating experiment to demonstrate the power of conformity to the group. Basically, Asch used a group of confederates to influence the behavior of a target subject, who was prompted to believe that the entire group was also new to the experiment. Each subject was asked to look at drawn lines, some of which were shorter and longer than others: the experiment was allegedly about visual perception.

At the end of the process, confederates were prompted to lie about which of two lines was longer, and the experimental subject — the last of the group to respond — was finally asked his opinion.

Asch expected that all subjects would reject group opinion to follow the evidence of their own eyes, but such was not to be the case. A full third of test subjects dismissed the evidence of their own eyes to follow the dictates of the group.

This was only a simple perceptual task, something quite clear and obvious to the senses. It also occurred with a group of people that the subject had just met. Asch did not explore how this might manifest with respected and known "confederates", or with less clear questions such as "is my nation right and just?", or "is my faith real and true?" Where ambiguity reigns, then a fair assumption is that reference to group norms takes over. As such, conformity-to-the-group becomes a powerful force modifying individual perception and core-beliefs.

The Luciferan leader knows this truth. Conform to what everyone around you is doing, or else be considered unfit. Merge into the herd, because in it you will find identity, belonging, believing, and certainty. You will find the essence of yourself only when you give yourself up to the group. The group norm is wisdom, and this wisdom will guide you to peace, security, and happiness. Sameness is blessed, and blessed is sameness. Give up the burden of difference and individuality, let the group-mind penetrate you and relieve you of the pain of maintaining a different opinion. Fall into the joy of belonging, and let all your personal cares float away. You are the group, and the group is you. Your life is empty and meaningless apart from the group, and the group will wither without you. You are needed by the group, and you need the group.

Conform, and all blessed things will come to you. Disobey, and you will feel the pain of separation. Such conformity is a powerful weapon for the Luciferan, and is used with devastating effect to control members and align them with the organization's purpose.

DREAD AND FEAR

Luciferan leaders also use dread and fear as control mechanisms. Members are conditioned to think that if they disobey, leave or betray the organization then they will be cast out into an insufferable existence. Identity, belonging, believing, security, truth, happiness, and purpose will all be lost.

This can be as threatening for an aging mid-level manager in the corporation he has served all his life, as for the member of an intense religious cult. The manager faces the dread of unemployment and disconnection from the source of his identity and prestige. The cult member faces the dread of excommunication and disconnection perhaps from God himself. The result is the same: intense fear and profound dread.

Submit to a power greater than yourself, a power which you cannot possibly understand, or experience the fear and dread of isolation, rejection, poverty, and even death.

Submit, or be cut off. This is an essential weapon for the Luciferan leader. If you cannot submit, then leave the tribe and face the outer darkness alone and unprotected. A simple choice. Give your soul to the organization, or be cast out to suffer loss, deprivation, or even death. Few people can resist such power, especially after having committed their primal life's energies to serve an organization, its leader, and its cause.

PSYCHOLOGICAL ASSAULT AND MIND CONTROL

Psychological assault is another weapon of choice for Luciferan leaders. It is safe to use because it is not illegal, and yet it yields deep control over members when properly used.

Psychological assault allows the Luciferan leader to penetrate deeply into each member's core self and take up residence. Psychological assault was defined earlier: its main intention is to gain control of a person by controlling what she believes to be true. That is, by boring deep into Rockeach's layers of belief (he is the psychologist who described beliefs from external/superficial to internal/essential like the layers of an onion), the organization's leadership inserts itself into the target member's core beliefs. This is probably best accomplished when the target is young in years.

The target's inner core is cracked open and filled with the predator's "truth", then sealed over again. The target then becomes filled with love for the organization, seeks to serve it passionately and totally, and defends it against all enemies by even dying for it if necessary. Such targets may never realize why they love the organization so deeply. Their devotion becomes primal.

If members eventually question these beliefs — whether nationalistic, religious, or familial — then they experience a kind of primal fear, despair, and depression akin to the fear of death. Their questions leave them isolated, fearful, alone, defenseless. And so they stop questioning, because to question is to risk dissolution.

This is the power of "mind control" in its absolute sense. The mind cannot pursue questions of personal doubt without threatening the kind of profound loss suggested by absolute extermination. Luciferan leaders want to install this depth of control by using psychological assault. Take control of the member's core beliefs through psychological assault and the leader takes control of the person.

RIGID HIERARCHY OF CONTROL

Luciferan organizations usually have a strong, rigid hierarchy of control. This chain of command may not exist officially as an organizational chart, but will be clearly understood by followers. The leader is at the top of the chain, and dictates directions downward throughout his organizational "cone". His span of control is usually tight for he trusts few people except an inner elect who have submitted totally to him. His directions must be followed as if they came directly from God.

In its more extreme form, this rigid hierarchy of control becomes so authoritarian that followers can surrender control over even simple matters of everyday life. Physical appearance, friendships, time management, behavior: all of these and more become controlled. Followers literally hand over personal autonomy, and are punished for any expression of personal opinion. The Luciferan leader, through her organization, penetrates and possesses every aspect of her follower's existence.

Questions, doubts, and concerns cannot be expressed. Their presence indicates either betrayal, 'bad vibrational energies' or 'Satanic' influence. Followers usually have to appear constantly happy, enthusiastic, and 'saved'.

They are expected to share this happiness with outsiders through constant proselytizing and recruitment: not to attempt to recruit others indicates lack of belief and belonging.

Totalistic control can deepen to include even the private thoughts of followers. Privacy is evil because it is selfish: it suggests that the member is holding something from the organization and is therefore not completely devoted. Constant confessions of internal sin and non-compliance are the only way to convince the leader that utter submission has been achieved. The hierarchy of control must penetrate beyond the realm of behavior and appearance and into the very core of the follower's identity.

This degree of control has obvious advantages for the Luciferan organization: members will obey commands that clearly violate morality and conscience, and will even commit atrocities in the name of the "movement" that they would never contemplate as individuals.

LAW BREAKING

Since Luciferan leaders want their organizations to expand at all costs, then social laws and norms that impede this growth are only obstacles to be overcome. Laws based on social conscience or compassion simply do not matter. If a goal can be reached by breaking a law, and the chances of being caught are slim, then the organization will proceed. Expediency, efficiency, and success are the only guiding forces.

In accordance with the Luciferan leader's belief in his own godhood, his organization sets its own laws. Laws directing the conduct of lesser humans and less successful organizations do not apply: "Do what thou wilt shall be the whole of the law". If a law interferes with the organization's expansion, it must be ignored, challenged, or changed by lawyers or politicians bought for the purpose. Law is flexible, designed to serve the needs of the strong and dominant. Moral and legal relativity mean that the law can be adjusted to suit the predator's needs.

Organizational image is of course essential. The appearance of propriety and good citizenship must be maintained always. If ultimately successful, such organizations can obtain the absolute political power to define laws for others. Luciferan organizations seek power and expansion above all else, and are only satisfied when bottom-line growth, power and influence transcend all other concerns.

PREDATION

Luciferan organizations are, in sum, as predatory as their founders. Constant growth, expansion, and devouring, destruction of the enemy, warfare, and relentless competition:— all of these define Luciferan organizational culture. Luciferan organizations pursue predation with great fervor to overcome all potential enemies or competitors, to rise to the top, to corner the market of power and influence, and to expand, consume, control, and dominate. Apart from the obvious advantages of power, money and influence that the control of a predatory organization can bring, such control also unleashes an "army" of true believers who will then act as agents to recruit new members, that is, to bring them into the organization so they can be possessed by it.

If the Luciferan controls the organization's culture, he will also control all its new recruits. He can then take personal control of vastly more individuals than would be the case if he had to possess them singly, one at a time. He can in fact live deeply within the core beliefs of those who follow him, and can devour their energies at will.

Some Luciferans believe that upon their personal death, they can live on through the organization and its members' devotion. Some even believe they can use this devotional energy to assist their rebirth on the physical plane. Others want to use the organization's accumulated energy to "finance" their rise up the hierarchy of competing Luciferan hugods. Their capital is locked in the depth of worship, devotion, and service offered by their followers: the more followers gathered and the deeper their devotion, the stronger the Luciferan becomes.

Controlling the Organizational Beast

Luciferans believe that when a predatory organizational cone "spins" hard enough, it can create a centrifugal force strong enough to disorient and overcome even its founder and leader. Organizational extramemes are therefore as potentially lethal to their creators and controllers as to outside enemies: like any weapon, they must be understood and mastered.

Mastery is difficult, time-consuming, and demanding. It requires specific skills along with the accumulation of sufficient personal power. The organization becomes a beast on a leash, and the Luciferan leader has to know how to cage it. If he does not, the beast will devour him.

Thus, even though Luciferan leaders enhance their power potential by cultivating and controlling an organization, they realize that they simultaneously place themselves in danger. Two threats are possible: first, a competitor can take control of the organization and turn it against its Luciferan founder and, second, the organization itself can assert control over its creator like a powerful extrameme rebelliously out of control.

A takeover by another Luciferan from inside or outside the organization is a constant threat, especially if the organization is effective in delivering pure energy to the leader at the top. If other Luciferans are strongly attracted to the organization, they will want to remove its leader and assume control so the organization's energy will be theirs to devour. Their attack may be frontal, as when one entrepreneur openly assaults a corporation in a deliberate attempt to take it over, as in the movie *Wall Street*. Or the attack may be more subtle, from within, where the Luciferan competitor replaces the current leader by pretending obedience until he is able to convince key members of the organization to follow his mutiny.

Luciferans believe any organization can outgrow its controllers or creators. A Luciferan leader understands that the best way to control his organization is to implant his personality so deeply into its members they will never be able to even contemplate independent life. However, such control is seldom absolute, especially if some of his followers are Luciferan themselves.

Luciferan leaders are therefore chronically alert to the possibility of attack from without or within. This hyper-alertness may seem paranoid or delusional to others, but is an absolute necessity for the Luciferan leader, who knows that competing Luciferan hugods will try to rip his prize from him just as the stronger cougar will steal food stalked and killed by the smaller bobcat. This is why the Luciferan wants to possess his organization so utterly and completely, and why he subjects even his inner circle of dedicated followers to constant loyalty tests. If another Luciferan competitor takes over his organization, the Luciferan knows that he will probably be destroyed in the process. He will become the ultimate enemy in the eyes of his followers, who will turn on him and even celebrate his destruction. At the very least, he knows he will lose a lifetime of energy expended to build his organization.

Luciferans therefore struggle constantly against other predators. But they also remain alert to a second threat, the organization itself. Their fear is based on the belief that organizations are alive, that like intramemes and extramemes they have an existence separate from the individuals within them. If properly controlled, the organizational entity can act as a kind of extension of the Luciferan's power and influence. It can harm enemies or competitors, gather power, and become a living weapon. Like a hawk tethered to its owner's arm, however, the organization can become lethal if it is not effectively controlled. The Luciferan leader has constructed his organization to be ruthlessly predatory, like a kind of vicious animal on a leash. But the collar can never be removed. If it is, then the Luciferan's own organization can become just another enemy or competitor to be fought.

The idea that an organization might be alive is probably as difficult for most of us to accept as the possibility that intramemes and extramemes are also alive. Even more difficult is the notion that organizations, intramemes, and extramemes might act in a selfish manner to promote their own interests. We assume that this ability to promote one's own needs must be limited to an individual with a brain sufficiently large enough to allow for thinking, planning, and related cognitive processes. How can an organization plan against its founder when it is not a consciously aware entity?

The answer is not difficult: billions of living organisms operate to maximize their own survival, and few if any of them have complex neural systems. Bacteria struggle against antibiotics and other bacteria while insects develop strategies to capture prey, avoid predators, and kill competitors. Evolutionary biology adopts the axiom of struggle and competition as a guiding principle for all life forms, including human beings. Reductionists and materialists refuse to allow any application of foresight, planning, cognition, or other "anthropomorphisms" to these creatures, and yet these same scientists insist that each one struggles for existence by developing responses that look suspiciously like the outcomes of rational planning, plotting, and scheming. In this context, I personally have no difficulty accepting the idea that organizations will struggle for survival as frantically as a single-celled organism.

Luciferans go further. Because they accept spiritual (i.e. non-physical) realities as existing in their own right — some endowed with cognition and some not, but all struggling to survive in the theater of spiritual warfare — they have no difficulty going further than this and accepting that organizational entities are individuals, endowed with more or less cognitive awareness, intelligence, maturity, and power.

A brief detour into the idea of living organizations having a specific "character" or "personality" might therefore be useful at this point, because although organizations are a huge part of our lives, few of us, unlike Luciferans, have likely ever considered just what kind of beast they might be.

ORGANIZATIONAL CHARACTER: VITALISM VERSUS REDUCTIONISM

We all seem to accept that individuals can become pathological: sadists, serial killers, and psychopaths exist. In the same way, many social workers and psychologists are now realizing that family systems can become abusive, that a pathological culture can infest a family system so deeply that all members are infected. The pathology cannot be isolated as the personal individual possession of each family member, but exists instead within the familial system shared between them.

This idea can be expanded to include organizations larger than the family system, such as churches, therapeutic movements, corporations, political movements, and new religious movements. Any one of them can create an abusive culture. Families are not unique in this regard.

An interesting possibility then emerges. Individuals involved in an abusive organizational culture may become pathological due to their involvement alone, not because of any inherent individual personality problem they may possess. Thus an otherwise healthy individual who joins a pathological organization may become pathological by belonging.

In other words, the pathology can be located in the organization itself, not just the individuals within it. A person may join the organization, act pathologically, then leave the organization and, by doing so, leave behind the pathology. The organization itself is the diseased organism, not each individual member. Strangely enough, virtually nothing has been written about such abusive organizations, despite the impact that organizations generally have on our lives.

Think about the organizations affecting everything we do: we are born within huge medical organizations called hospitals; we are educated within the bowels of immense educational institutions; our food is delivered to us through a chain of complex organizations from farms to the local supermarket; most of us find work within organizations; our political lives are governed by political parties which in turn utilize enormous bureaucracies; and even our deaths are governed by an array of organizations from legal firms to undertakers. We depend on them for everything, including basic survival.

Imagine civilization without organizations. Nothing could be achieved. Without effective political organization, political rhetoric is mere rant. Without organized government, chaos and anarchy are inevitable. Without a religious organization the prophet's words desiccate and scatter on the dry winds of history. Organizations are the conduit through which dreams, visions and plans are made real.

We live, breathe, move and die within the loving embrace of organizations designed to make our lives better. And sometimes they do make us better; sometimes they create terror, fear, and unbelievable horror instead.

Despite their omnipresence in our lives, we know fearfully little about human organizations. Perhaps we know so little about them because most of the thinking about organizational theory seems to rest with professors of management and administration in universities, who really only serve the business community. These professors graduate MBA candidates who are trained to think in terms of the bottom-line profit for the corporations ultimately hiring them. The rest of us learn little and know even less about how power, influence and control are utilized in organizations — business, political, religious, educational or otherwise. Knowing little, we cannot evaluate them. That which is beyond evaluation is beyond judgment. And that which is beyond judgment is beyond accountability.

So just what is an organization? As with all other fields of thought, opinion is divided. Mechanistic/reductionist perspectives hold that organizations are no more than their component parts — humans — and that humans are no more than their chemical and physical components directed by known scientific laws. Organizations thus do not have independent life or consciousness, and any implications drawn from this possibility are illusory and fallacious. Holistic/ vitalistic perspectives, however, hold that organizations are always more than their component parts, that just as humans are greater than the sum of their parts — organs, tissues, matter — so too organizations are in some way autonomous. In the words of Ludwig von Bertalanffy, the founder of General Systems Theory: "the contest between the mechanistic and vitalistic conceptions is like a game of chess played over nearly two thousand years. It is essentially the same arguments that always come back, though in manifold disguises, modifications, and forms. In the last resort, they are an expression of two opposing tendencies in the human mind."

In the field of biology, theorists like Lovelock with his Gaia hypothesis represent the vitalistic side of this dialectic, while Edward O. Wilson in *On Human Nature*, and Richard Dawkins in *The Blind Watchmaker* advocate absolute reductionism to the social/biological and genetic levels respectively.

The same debate is raging in the field of neuropsychology. Some researchers are stating unequivocally that "mind" is simply the effect of neurochemical processes of the brain, and that "soul" and other concepts simply do not exist. Francis Crick in his work *The Astonishing Hypothesis* says: "You, your joys and your sorrows, your memories and your ambitions, your sense of personal identity and free will, are in fact no more than the behavior of a vast assembly of nerve cells and their associated molecules." The debate has also animated the history of psychology, as represented by behavioral versus gestalt approaches. To my knowledge, the debate has not yet reached as heavily into organizational theory, possibly because the field has been dominated so completely by reductionism and by the practical expediency of MBA production.

As should be clear by now, I would like to take a vitalistic perspective to describe organizations. Vitalism brings us closer to understanding the Luciferan belief that organizations are alive. Without it, the Luciferan leader's fear of his own organization is impossible to comprehend.

Vitalism is defined by Webster's as either the doctrine that the functions of a living organism are due to a vital principle distinct from physiochemical forces, or the doctrine that the processes of life are not explicable by the laws of physics and chemistry alone and that life is in some part self-determining. To include human organizations with living organisms requires a leap of faith without sufficient proof. However, just as biologists are beginning to toy with this idea by applying it to bee hives, aspen groves, and earth itself, I would like to see where it takes us when applied to organizations.

A way to begin is to think of organizations as a special form of extrameme. As with Dawkin's memes, organizational extramemes only exist within human culture; they survive by implanting themselves in the minds of members, and then drawing loyalty, enthusiasm, and commitment from them. These energies can be considered "food" for the organizational extrameme, because without this food it will wither and die. If the organizational entity is successful, it will survive its founder by moving across generations to inhabit the minds of new recruits.

An organization, therefore, can be considered as a special type of extrameme. It is not physically alive, but rather exists as a controlling entity in the minds of the human beings it inhabits. The organizational extrameme can only exert control through the human minds it inhabits, or possesses. The meme is not physical: actions committed by the organization are always committed by individuals within it, not by any kind of direct action from an organizational "ghost." The non-physical extrameme possesses individuals, and directs them to behave according to approved patterns.

Such extramemes may begin life as a successful meme cluster (i.e., a group of ideas) which attracts human interest. If this interest is deep and wide enough in the human community, then humans may get together to share their reactions to the meme. If these reactions in turn are powerful enough, then those humans attracted to the meme may gather together to form an organization. The organization may then grow on the enthusiasm and commitment of its members. If successful, the meme may then become an organizational extrameme, a powerful entity capable of inhabiting, directing, and controlling the lives of its members.

For our purposes, organizations will be conceived as extramemes which are vitally more than the sum of their parts. Beyond this, we can pretend that they may even be a form of sentient life, as per previous discussions regarding memes. This means that they each have their own character or personality existing separately from their human component parts. They can therefore be described as *individuals* along with other individual entities on all levels complex life. Julian Huxley says: "The existence of a species or race, a procession of similar individuals descended from a previous one, as well as of what we usually call individuals, the separate beings that at any one moment represent the species, leads of necessity to the separation of two distinct kinds of individuality; one belonging to the race and one to the persons that constitute the race".

The same argument can be applied to any entity comprised of parts, whether it be an individual, a colony of ants, a species, or an organization. Arthur Koestler called all such entities "holons": composed of parts, and yet transcending these parts with a "wholeness" not explicable by the parts alone. Living organizations can therefore be thought of as individual organisms which take on certain traits, including Luciferism:— an assumption that animates and vitalizes everything that follows.

The Vitalism of the Luciferan Organization

If such organizations exist, then we can assume they probably act relatively freely among us. They could predate, possess, and cause violence with only minimal need for disguise. They could create a predatory culture or "personality" that we won't perceive because we only see the actions of individuals within the organization but not those of the organizational entity itself. We would thus become easy prey. This is why Luciferans seek to use such organizations to enhance their power and influence.

We are simply taught not to think of organizations as living entities and are therefore not trained to notice the signs and symptoms of predatory organizations. We still think of predation as something perpetrated by individuals. The criminal, the psychopath, the cruel and the sadistic — these are figures we recognize. But a predatory organization? Few of us could actually sit down and draw up a list of features defining such organization. We might think of the "Mafia", or of a particularly frustrating encounter with bureaucracy, or of a kind of amorphous "them or they." But beyond that, could we really clarify the nature of any predatory (never mind Luciferan) organization? Probably not.

Luciferans, however, have no trouble identifying predatory organizations, because they deliberately seek or create them. Not all predatory organizations are Luciferan, just as not all human predators are Luciferan: but if organizations are alive, then like all living things they have to engage in the predatory arts to one degree or another, or die. Organizations are therefore at war with one another. They fight for human members, for physical space and buildings, and for control of planetary resources. Organizations compete like all other life forms, and only the strong survive.

Organizations as Living Predators

All successful organizations need to grow. The only way they can do this is to inhabit the minds of human beings. Their task, therefore, is to inhabit as many human minds as possible by attracting more members than other organizations. A huge membership is good for the organizational extrameme, but large numbers alone are not enough. For example, millions of people might belong to, say, a book or record club through the mail. But their commitment is superficial: the organization has no deep hold on the loyalties of members. Such organizations can therefore perish in an instant. Long term survival depends not just on large size, but on depth of commitment as well.

Depth of commitment does not flow just from the money, prestige, and security offered by the organization in exchange for human energy. Organizations built on this exchange can become enormous, but members attracted for these reasons alone will never hold the organization together. Any number of crisis will cause members to desert the organizational extrameme: a higher bid from another organization, a temporary failure of the organization's profit and productivity — in short, any interference with the exchange of money, prestige, and security.

Truly powerful organizations seek deeper bonds from members, so that loyalty and commitment remain solid even in the face of overwhelming adversity. This depth of commitment can only flow from the complete physical, emotional, cognitive, and spiritual devotion of its members. The deepest expression of this kind of loyalty and commitment shows itself in those members willing to sacrifice or even die for the organizational entity's survival. This is the real strength of a nation state, political movement, religion, or Luciferan organization — that its members will remain loyal even during difficult times, and that they will even die to ensure the organization's survival.

The deeper the organization's hold on members, the longer it can survive and prosper. The most effective organizations therefore offer far more than the trinkets of money or prestige. They offer self-actualization or spiritual fulfillment in exchange for their members' deep commitment and energy. From the Luciferan perspective, these survival efficient organizations penetrate members so deeply that they actually possess them, as was discussed earlier. The longer a person is possessed by the organization, the more difficult it is to leave. Social connections, personal contacts, security and even identity itself intertwine deeply within the organization's existence, thus ensuring its survival.

A number of methods have been designed to elicit such intense commitment from members. For example, children born into the group can be socialized at an early age. Early instruction of the young is a powerful method of control for organizations seeking long term survival over centuries. Nation-states are effective in this regard: witness the powerful installation of patriotism in children living in the United States, for example, and compare that to Canada. One of them remains strong, the other is threatened with break-up. Young members of any organization must feel deep love for it, or else its time is limited. This love is food for the organization.

The organization can also strengthen itself through the manipulative proselytizing of committed members capable of bringing in large numbers of recruits, as with cults. Once into the organization, these new recruits can be psychologically assaulted, resulting in the replacement of their core beliefs and identity structures by the organizational extrameme. This control can then be solidified through powerful techniques of social influence such as those used by cults. Initiation rituals, loyalty tests, and other techniques can also ensure ongoing loyalty and commitment. Luciferans would argue that all attempts to induce loyalty, no matter how inspired by apparently "higher" motives, are essentially predatory. As with all living things, organizations seek to perpetuate themselves. Luciferans would argue that even apparently charitable organizations have to ensure the loyalty of their members by possessing them. Predation is absolute, even for organizations apparently built on higher motives.

Thus, an organization created for truly charitable purposes and protected by its founders' system of checks and balances (usually in the form of a constitution or something similar) would appear safe from predatory impulses, especially if, over the years, the organization's culture evolved a rich tradition of compassion, honesty, pride and fair service. Such a tradition could initially defeat the invasion of other more predatory energies, much as a pine tree will pitch out a boring beetle. But should the organization hit hard times, or should it eventually wish to expand its power and influence, then predatory strategies may suddenly seem more inviting.

In other terms, Luciferans assert that all living things seek to perpetuate themselves through predation, and so do organizations. As with individuals, those that consciously adopt successful predatory principles will survive and prosper. Those that do not will simply perish.

Organizations can enhance power or drain it from a Luciferan. An organization can open up predatory advantage or become a trap as potentially destructive and debilitating as psychopathology or Satanism.

CHAPTER TEN

SATANISM &
RITUAL ABUSE

"Until hard evidence is obtained and corroborated, the American people should not be frightened into believing that babies are being bred and eaten, that 50,000 missing children are being murdered in human sacrifices, or that satanists are taking over America's day care centers... An unjustified crusade against those perceived as satanists could result in wasted resources, unwarranted damage to reputations, and disruption of civil liberties."

— Kenneth Lanning, the head of the FBI's special unit in charge of investigating claims about satanic-cult crimes

There has been intense public and professional fascination with Satanism and ritual abuse in recent years. For most of us, "Lucifer" means "Satan" or "Devil", and so "Luciferism" should then be synonymous with Satanism. But Luciferan psycho-spirituality is only loosely connected with Satanism. Although "Lucifer" and "Satan" are often used interchangeably, Luciferism and Satanism are distinct and separate.

Contemporary Satanism seems to be the mixed child of different seeds, including myth, hysteria, the proclamations of self-proclaimed Satanists such as Anton Lavey, biblical definitions, religious prophecy, various syncretic New Age influences, official police reports, testimonies from children and adults who seem to have been ritually abused by a Satanic cult, beliefs and conjectures by therapeutic professionals, and the media. There seems to be little coherence between these sources, and so the monstrous child lurches from lurid exposure in the *National Inquirer* to serious discussion in the *New York Times*, and from law enforcement's *File 15* to academic journals. Experts on Satanism have cycled their views through endless media appearances and professional seminars, and the child grows more monstrous with each telling. Coherence, reason, and balance are not part of the monster's anatomy, so there is no way to tell which body part is expressing the truth.

For example, LaVey's version of Satanism is radically different from his rival Michael Aquino's (see Selected Bibliography), and both of these bear little resemblance to the fantastic cultic horrors described in tabloid accounts of murdered babies and sacrificial killings.

Early media coverage of lurid tales of ritual abuse — and subsequent therapeutic and police interest in the matter — roused passions that have been intense and often confusing. Opposing camps of ardent believers and equally passionate skeptics have drawn battle lines which have ultimately led to today's skirmishes about the validity of recalled memories by adults ("False Memory Syndrome"), the believability of testimony by very young children, and the lack of professional objectivity by psychiatrists, social workers, mental health professionals and child-rights advocates who have believed disclosures from alleged victims of Satanic ritual abuse.

Balance in this emotional storm has been rare: how are we supposed to respect both the real pain and terror of those who have shared their disclosures of ritual abuse, and yet also respect the rights of those who were unfairly caught in the wide net of alleged perpetrators? The professional communities have been even harder to understand. Each side has lined up platoons of PhD's, MD's, and other titled warriors, and each has had its obvious extremists, true believers, and zealots.

I was intimately connected with the "Satanism scare", as some have called it, and was for a time consulted as a Canadian "expert" on the subject. I worked with families of victims reporting ritual abuse, and with the victims themselves. I took part in police investigations, gave seminars on the subject, and generally did what I could to inject as much balance and reason as possible into the debate. But the issue took on a momentum all its own, sometimes helpful, sometimes not.

The following material is designed to explore the similarities and differences between Satanism and Luciferism, and not to offer any "final word" about Satanism or ritual abuse. Given the way the whole issue has progressed, from an initial massive overexposure with thousands of instant "experts" to the more recent embarrassed silence of previously enthusiastic professional advocates, (the number of books and articles about ritual abuse and Satanism have about dried up in the past four years). I am afraid that readers are going to have to come to their own judgments about the reality of Satanism or ritual abuse. For the sake of efficiency, an annotated bibliography will provide the references used in this chapter, and may help readers wanting to pursue the "Satanism scare" in more detail.

WHAT IS SATANISM?

Satanism is a religion. Like other religions, it is protected by legislation. Satanism is recognized by the American military: personnel can be married, blessed, and buried by Satanic priests if requested. As a religion, it is at least as old as Christianity and perhaps predates it under other names. Like other religions, many sects and varieties of Satanism have appeared. Recent additions include the Church of Satan, the Temple of Set, and the Process Church. Common elements of this religion seem to include: worship of the flesh — lust and primal emotions are good; celebration of ego — narcissism and selfishness are good; celebration of material wealth; celebration of power and control — power over others is good; rejection of love and compassion for enemies, but not for friends; rejection of Christian moral codes and their replacement by

270

ethical hedonism and pan-Satanism (Satan governs all creation, not God); celebration of a force or personality known as Satan; incorporation of various anti-Christian symbols (i.e., inverted crosses, "666"); and fascination with the dark or evil side of human nature.

Satanic believers seem to fall into a few broad categories: a) self-appointed, isolated, unsophisticated individuals, teenagers or small groups, b) psychopathic or psychotic career criminals who claim to serve Satan, c) religious Satanists who openly celebrate their faith (Church of Satan, Temple of Set, etc.), d) alleged Satanic cults believed to be secret, sophisticated, perhaps international and linked in a conspiracy.

The first three are all real. Actual teenagers have proclaimed themselves Satanists. I worked with many of them in Toronto in the late eighties and early nineties (see my article "Teen Satanism" in Langone's *Recovery From Cults*). Psychopathic killers such as David Berkowitz (Son of Sam) and Richard Ramirez (The Night Stalker) have claimed that their allegiance to Satan motivated their killings. Actual Satanic churches do exist.

Secret Satanic cults, however, have not been proven to exist. Such cults are held to be responsible for ritually abusing children and adult victims, and are alleged to be highly secretive, multi-generational, multi-national, and historically rooted in European history. They allegedly form an underground religion that flowers at night, in the dark, hidden.

They are described as being highly influential, with members primarily drawn from the upper classes of society (hence their ability to form a conspiracy to prevent real investigations). No compelling physical evidence has been shown to support their existence other than the testimonials of ritual abuse victims.

Satanism is often associated in the public mind with spirit possession, the black mass, human sacrifice, cannibalism, and other criminal activities. These associations usually stem from media accounts, fictional stories or movies, and other similar sources. But clearly, not all self-proclaimed Satanists are criminals.

Satanism is also frequently associated with Witchcraft, Santeria, the occult, or cults generally. Witchcraft, or Wicca, is a pagan religion unconnected to Satanism. It is not anti-Christian like Satanism, but rather non-Christian, like paganism. Modern Wiccans tend to be well educated, law abiding, and socially concerned. Santeria is a mixture of African tribal beliefs and Catholicism. It was linked to a well-publicized case of ritual crime in Matamoros, Mexico, but is not itself Satanic or criminal.

The Occult simply means hidden or secret, and includes hundreds of non-Christian traditions, few of which are even remotely criminal. Wicca, Santeria, Occultism, Paganism, and other related traditions have been defined as Satanic by some Christian sources. Such definitions are theological in nature, and valid only within a Christian framework.

A cult can form around any ideology (political, religious, therapeutic, commercial). Practitioners of Satanism may or may not be part of a cult. I personally have never found evidence supporting the existence of an actual Satanic cult. Teenage dabblers, psychopathic Satanists, and Satanic Churches — yes, but Satanic cults, no. This does not mean they don't exist, but that their existence is hard to prove and therefore questionable at this time.

What Is Ritual Abuse?

Many different definitions exist, all reflecting various perspectives. My own definition of ritual abuse satisfies the criteria that I think are important, and so I will use it here. Ritual abuse can be defined as: systematic abuse committed by a religious or cultic organization in a stylized ceremonial manner consistent with the group's belief system and approved by the group's leadership.

The key elements of this definition include a high level of organizational sophistication and the notion that leadership, organizational style, and ideology drive the abuse. In other words, the abuse is not driven by individual psychopathology but by group dynamics based on a well organized ideology. In this sense ritual abuse can be considered a form of organized crime.

Ritual abuse can be Satanic, but can also be based on other ideologies. By the definition above, ritualized abuse has occurred in other cultic settings (i.e., Nazism) and is likely to occur again in the future.

In the current literature, ritual abuse and Satanism are synonymous. This is unfortunate for a number of reasons. First, it ignores the reality that not all Satanic groups are violent. Second, it ignores the equally strong reality that ritual violence is also committed by non-Satanic groups. Despite this, ritual abuse will probably remain cemented to the idea of Satanism. Current thinkers in the area seem unwilling to cut Satanism free from ritual abuse, just as some anti-cult activists seem unwilling to disconnect new religious movements from destructive cultism.

What Is Satanic Ritual Abuse?

Satanic cults are allegedly sophisticated, international, professional, secretive, and highly organized. They have apparently existed for at least the past four generations according to victims. Again, none have been proven in a court of law to exist.

Recent evidence from children claiming to be victims of Satanic ritual abuse has been widely publicized. The children are usually between the ages of 2 and 7, and are frequently found to have suffered severe physical and sexual abuse. In addition to this abuse, they often disclose that they were forced to eat and drink noxious substances such as blood, urine, feces, animal and human remains, and drug mixtures, that they participated in bizarre sexual practices such as bestiality, group sex, and sadism, that they observed, suffered, and were forced to perpetrate physical assaults, torture, sacrificial murder, and other sadistic acts, and that they were subjected to isolation and confinement in coffins, graveyards and similar settings.

All of the above seem to have occurred in settings which were ceremonial (altars, candles, robes, special symbols), theatrical (perpetrators and victims apparently wear masks and costumes to assume the identities of animals, monsters, superheroes, and more familiar figures such as doctors, judges, policemen, and so on), and organized (many perpetrators, many victims). Perpetrators seem to include family members linked through multi-generational abuse. There seems to be a clear hierarchy of perpetrators: leaders and followers emerge, and usually one figure dominates as the overall leader. Often the entire process is reported as being recorded, usually by video cameras.

Similar evidence has emerged from adult victims who recall ritual abuse from childhood and details are almost exactly the same. Adult victims seem to be overwhelmingly female. Memory recall seems to emerge spontaneously, in therapy, or in treatment (usually for Post Traumatic Stress Disorder, Multiple Personality Disorder, or other dissociative disorders). Victims' reports emerge from different geographical areas and time periods, yet contain similar content.

Apart from disclosures by child and adult victims, little if any supporting physical evidence seems to be available, despite the sometimes powerful support of legitimate authorities in law enforcement, mental health, and social services. Criminal prosecutions of Satanic ritual abuse have generally not been successful because physical evidence supporting the existence of a sophisticated network of Satanic cultists has simply not been found. Child custody hearings of Satanic ritual abuse have had mixed success, but have received massive media coverage. Seemingly legitimate victims and their professional supporters often appear to be handicapped by a sometimes bizarre collection of 'ex-breeders', 'ex-Satanic high priests' and so on, who have come forward to claim expertise and, apparently, to hunt for attention. Lacking credibility or evidence, they seem to harm rather than help advance our understanding of ritual abuse.

Since so little is known about Satanism, cultism, occultism, and so on, apparently dubious information from questionable sources has at times been accepted and promoted uncritically by professionals.

ARGUMENTS AGAINST THE EXISTENCE OF SATANIC RITUAL ABUSE

Various individuals and groups have reacted to allegations of the existence of Satanic ritual abuse with skepticism and doubt. Several compelling arguments have been advanced.

First, there is no evidence except the testimony of victims, despite several massive police investigations. No single cult has been uncovered, and the testimony of child or adult is seldom if ever supported by physical evidence. Given the massive numbers of murders reported by thousands of victims, at least a few bodies should show up somewhere. Sooner or later one cult conspirator should lead police to real evidence, but none have.

Second, the whole scenario seems illogical. How could such a massive conspiracy exist undetected? Cults cannot remain totally secret. What about defectors for example? To exist, it would have to be the "greatest criminal conspiracy of all time", as the FBI's Kenneth Lanning has stated repeatedly. No group could cover evidence this perfectly for this long. Furthermore, as popularly portrayed, the 'Satanic cult conspiracy' is inconsistent with known attributes of cults generally: specifically, most cults love to announce themselves to the world as saviors and educators.

Thirdly, critics hold that the testimonies of adult "survivors" of Satanic ritual abuse victims are not credible. Survivors are "obviously" driven by self-interest because they gain attention, money, and other remuneration from their testimonials. Many such survivors seem mentally ill, leading skeptics to believe that no real Satanic abuse has occurred. Such survivors might be suffering from post-traumatic stress disorder, multiple personality disorder resulting from early childhood trauma, or from false memory syndrome. They might have been hurt, but are now fabricating and exaggerating their abuse under the influence of outside professionals exploiting their suggestibility.

Some critics also believe that the testimony of children is suspect and should be corroborated before being believed. These critics assert that children are even more vulnerable to suggestion than mentally ill adults, and cannot always be believed, despite the passionate rhetoric of child advocates. Such advocates are often professionals who promote or believe in ritual abuse. For skeptics, they are all suspect, and can be found among police, mental health professionals, media, educators, consultants, and so on. Many are well meaning but are: a) unprofessional; b) naive and easily manipulated by the newest 'fad'; c) encouraging victims to expand their testimony to ever more lurid and extreme levels. Many are motivated by self-interest or a hidden agenda which might include money, professional advancement, attention from public and media, or promotion of personal religious beliefs, especially Christianity.

Along this line of thinking, skeptics believe several special interest groups are also promoting this issue for their own ends. Such groups include various fundamentalist Christian leaders, anti-cult organizations, and media, especially of the tabloid variety.

Fourthly, skeptics state that conspiracy theories generally should be suspect. Such theories tend to grow in confusing times, and usually target and blame scapegoats. In this case, the scapegoat is the illusory "Satanic cult" which, like the "saucer aliens", are usually claimed to exist without real evidence: "I know someone who knows someone who saw them...." Such unsupported conspiracies usually cause terrible social harm when believed (i.e. the Salem witch trials). Ritual abuse stories are simply new forms of older "atrocity tales" which indict a specific group and hold them responsible for horrific evils, usually to justify violence against them. Skeptics state emphatically that such tales have a long and dubious history, and should not be believed.

Ritual abuse tales are also similar to urban legends, which are stories that gather enough credibility as they are told and retold that they become almost believable. Any real facts are lost as such rumors evolve into contagions which are then believed uncritically. Tabloid media help disseminate the legends to an audience of millions. Skeptics, finally, claim that Satan is not real, therefore Satanism is not real. Ritual abuse represents a return to superstition similar to witch trials and the Inquisition, with equal potential for destructive harm to innocent victims — in this case those who are accused of ritual abuse. Ritual abuse atrocities are simply not possible because people cannot be this barbaric. Civilization has advanced too far, and human nature is not that perverted or twisted.

ARGUMENTS SUPPORTING THE EXISTENCE OF SATANIC RITUAL ABUSE

Other individuals and groups believe fully in the existence of Satanic ritual abuse. They tend to make the following arguments.

Physical evidence exists, but it has not been found because Satanic cults are very sophisticated and hide evidence well. Members of these cults occupy high positions of power in society and prevent real investigations. Dead bodies and other physical evidence are disposed of carefully, leaving no evidence. Victims are not listed as missing because:

a) 'drifters' and other unknowns are carefully chosen
b) women breed children especially for sacrifice and do not register them at birth
c) victims are 'bought' from poor countries.

Believers often point out that police and other investigators do not know what to look for, and have bungled most real cases because their supervisors mock them, they are not trained, and they lack sufficient resources.

Satanic cults exist but are secret and sophisticated, having had centuries of practice in the arts of concealment. They have operated easily because no one has been looking for them until now. No one believed such activity was possible, so previous disclosures from victims were ignored (just as disclosures of child abuse twenty years ago were ignored). Other cults were able to hide their actions for years (i.e., Jonestown) because outsiders could simply not believe such abuse was possible, or that members could enter into a conspiracy of silence to protect their abusive leaders.

Believers note that effective investigation techniques by police to penetrate abusive cultic settings have not been developed. Cult crime can be considered a form of organized crime and therefore requires specialized training no different than needed for biker gangs or mafia-like criminal organizations. Satanic cults have not been uncovered or properly handled because investigating law enforcement organizations have no background, training, or experience to find them or deal effectively with them. Waco, Aum Shinrikio, The Solar Temple, and Heaven's Gate are obvious recent examples.

Furthermore, victims should be believed because the detail of their disclosures is just too specific and internally consistent over time to be fabricated. Disclosures from victims separated geographically and in time share consistent content. They point to a similar set of experiences which could only be produced by a well organized conspiracy.

Respected professionals are taking these disclosures very seriously. Children and other victims should be believed. We shouldn't blame the victim, nor should we repeat similar patterns of denial when the first disclosures of child abuse came forward decades ago. Young children simply could not fabricate such disclosures of brutal sexuality, torture, and violence unless they were directly exposed.

Believers feel that skeptics should be exposed to the real victims, most of whom are sane, intelligent, and motivated only by their desire to find the truth. Most victims of ritual abuse disclose their stories with obvious emotional pain and catharsis. The information emerges in a way that suggests they were subjected to "brainwashing" or "thought reform" techniques. Such techniques leave a certain "emotional fingerprint" on victims, a pattern very different than that left by simple repression, dissociation, or post-traumatic stress disorder. Such techniques require sophistication, time, massive energy, and organization. So when the children mention that their abuse occurred over time in a group, and thought reform techniques appear to have been employed, then there must be truth to their statements. How could a young child fabricate the complex emotional fingerprint of such sophisticated techniques?

Supporters go on to argue that we ought to trust the professional judgment of the hundreds of legitimate psychiatrists, psychologists, social workers and other professionals who have come to believe their clients' ritual abuse disclosures. Certainly some of these professionals may be self-serving, unprofessional, or naive, but not the majority. There are just too many qualified and credible professionals describing this problem. It is easy to find one or two professionals who over diagnose the problem, who see ritual abuse as the source of all their clients' problems, and who are themselves obviously unstable, but this is true for all professions and all professionals. To point to these unstable individuals and then to generalize their instability to all other professionals is simply logically fallacious. Every serious issue attracts dubious extremists and self-serving agents: the issue cannot be dismissed by blaming extremists. Most professionals have more to lose than to gain by supporting their clients' disclosures about ritual abuse, especially in light of the recent backlash against them. Supporters argue that such professionals are only messengers, and they shouldn't be blamed for the message.

Regarding "urban legends", conspiracy theories, belief in Satan and other similar "superstitions", believers respond that these criticisms may be true of extreme reactions to ritual abuse by the tabloid media, but not of the large numbers of reasonable professionals and victims whose stories will simply not disappear no matter how uncomfortable they make everyone (especially law enforcement) feel. One does not have to believe in Satan to believe that others do, or that others might act on their beliefs.

OTHER POSSIBLE EXPLANATIONS OF SATANIC RITUAL ABUSE

There are some other interesting interpretations of Satanic ritual abuse apart from the idea of an international cult conspiracy or an equally grand conspiracy of malicious self-serving therapists. These arguments all assume that victims are reporting what they really saw and believed to be true in their own experience, but that the ritual abuse did not necessarily happen physically in the precise way described by victims.

Please note that these interpretations are not presented here as fact, but rather as summaries of various points of view which are either already present in the literature or likely to show up shortly. Let's view some psychological and parapsychological perspectives on this problem: the first, psychological, holds that Satanic abuse is not physically real, but that victims' experiences are real. That is, there is no physical evidence and victims are telling the truth. The explanation is that powerful psychological dynamics are at work. The experiences may then be a new form of mental illness not yet defined. Or they may be the invasion of a new form of subconscious 'archetype' of another as yet unknown psychological mechanism.

They may be ultimately interpreted as a new form of dissociative disorder. Many adult survivors seem to also suffer from some degree of dissociation or multiple personality disorder. Many therapists have stated their belief that such dissociation is the end result of early massive abuse — that it is a device used by children to cope with great horror. Thus the child literally breaks into pieces and "stores" the horror within a personality not normally available to the everyday self. These memories eventually explode from such containment, usually as a result of therapy. Because they have been hidden in the subconscious for so long, they may well have evolved from, say, "normal" sexual abuse to a full-fledged archetype of ultimate evil. The subconscious mixes archetypal images of ultimate horror to an already festering memory in ways articulated by Carl Jung and others.

The field of anomalous psychology — the study of strange or otherwise odd experiences often interpreted as psychic or spiritual — has historically tried to explain such experiences as the outcome of basic neurological, perceptual or psychological variables. Ritual abuse memories will likely find a home in this branch of psychology with other anomalies such as near-death, past-life, alien-abduction, out-of-body and channeling experiences.

Other psychological interpretations will likely flow from the massive and mounting literature on early childhood abuse: ritual abuse memories may be the child's way of making sense out of the chaos of sexual or physical violence.

The point here is that endless varieties and variations of psychological interpretations are likely to take shape in the next few years, especially from those clinicians whose early belief in the objective reality of Satanic cults perpetrating ritual abuse has been shattered by the lack of corroborating physical evidence.

PARAPSYCHOLOGICAL EXPLANATIONS

Parapsychological explanations offer a second possibility: ritual abuse occurs in an as yet unknown realm of experience. Such explanations usually are based on the occult notion that we have more than one body, that we exist as layers of energy from the physical to the "astral", "spiritual" and so on. Consciousness is not linked to the physical brain alone, but can detach from it and move on different levels of reality such as those experienced during shamanic journeys. These levels are held to be just as real as the physical, requiring special organs of perception not available to most of us linked only to physical reality. In this conception, ritual abuse occurs while the victim is in his "second body." The abuse is therefore experienced as real, but did not occur in physical reality. Victims confuse the two different types of experience — hence Law Enforcement's inability to find sufficient physical evidence.

The psychologist Kenneth Ring has explored this kind of explanation by examining near-death experiences and UFO encounters in his book The Omega

Project. Ring is a professor of psychology at the University of Connecticut at Storrs, and he defines these experiences as expanding our capacity for "imaginal perception" in an "imaginal body" (i.e. astral body in occult jargon) which bring us into contact with a "higher transcendental order." We are being spurred to "psychological evolution and higher states of consciousness" by these real, yet non-physical, experiences. Something he calls "mind at large", a "benign transpersonal aspect of mind that is conscious, purposive, intelligent — and capable of interacting with matter" is guiding us into this alternate realm of experience which is "objectively self-existent." To my knowledge no one has yet applied this kind of argument to ritual abuse experiences, but their close similarity with important details of UFO abduction experiences suggests this may only a matter of time.

John Mack comes close to the same territory in his book *Abduction: Human Encounters with Aliens*. Mack is a professor of psychiatry at the Harvard Medical School, and claims that UFO abduction stories "have the characteristics of real events" because they are highly detailed, there is correspondence of detail over time and between physically isolated individuals, and there is intense emotional and physical impact and trauma in victims." This is exactly the same pattern found in ritual abuse victims. Mack feels that abduction experiences pose intense philosophical and spiritual challenges which may lead to an evolution of human consciousness guided by some sort of alien intelligence.

It is probably safe to say that parapsychological explanations of Satanic ritual abuse — as they gain momentum over the years — will lead in the same general direction.

Spiritual explanations offer a third option: some Christians, for example, believe that the organizing factor in ritual abuse is the presence of a spiritual entity known as Satan. His presence has been described and predicted in the Bible. The manifestation of massive numbers of cases of ritual abuse indicates the advent of the end times as suggested by the *Book of Revelation* in the New Testament, signaling the end of the world as we know it. Those who believe in this interpretation seem to also view the symptoms of MPD and other similar psychological manifestations as evidence of possession by evil spirits loyal to Satan. This explanation is supported by some groups and individuals within Christianity, but certainly not all.

These Christian believers tend to argue that Satanic cults cannot be found because they are protected by supernatural forces controlled by Satan.

Other Christians familiar with the ascetic tradition of the early desert fathers might argue that ritual abuse stories represent spiritual attacks similar to those described by St. Athanasius in *The Life of Antony*. Most of the desert fathers tell of being assaulted by demons in various forms, beings capable of assuming physical form but leaving no physical evidence.

Still other Christians familiar with the contemplative monastic traditions might argue that ritual abuse experiences represent a kind of "dark night of the soul" sent to test and strengthen the innocent.

Other non-Christian spiritual sources might argue from their own traditions in a similar way, and place ritual abuse in the context of their own spiritual beliefs. The point here is that they will all share the same basic belief in the spiritual nature of the abuse, meaning that it cannot be understood by psychological or parapsychological explanations.

GROUP DISGUISES

A fourth possibility is that ritual abuse is real but that it has been committed by various unrelated groups for the pursuit of widely different motives. For example, it could have evolved naturally within a dysfunctional family where deviant sexual and sadistic urges have taken an unusually bizarre and twisted turn, perhaps fed by images from horror movies, paperback "Satan" novels, and "true crime" books. The motive here is uncomplicated, and can be understood as the simple satisfaction of twisted sexual power drives.

Another possibility is that ritual abuse could represent the natural evolution of bizarre sexual practices by groups meeting to explore the dangerous edge of sexuality and violence, such as some extreme S&M organizations. Such groups might wish to enter the raw gutters of sexual practice and expand the range of their cruelty and sadism, especially in the realm of psychological assault. They would, in effect, be adding "spice" to new areas of deviance and decadence.

To follow this possibility to its logical end-point, perhaps there are only so many ways that sexual perversion and deviance can progress: activities such as eating and drinking noxious substances (urine, feces, insects, menstrual blood etc.), copulating in forbidden/taboo ways (with children, animals, in group settings), mixing terror and sex, invoking sadistic cruelty — may represent the inevitable extension of perverted personal appetites pursued to their ultimate destination.

Ritual abuse disclosures systematically list these extreme deviancies almost as if the alleged perpetrators were deliberately setting out to be as obscene, unnatural, cruel, and bizarre as possible. Perhaps the truth is that there are only so many ways to do this, and different unrelated groups across the country simply stumble upon them in much the same way that, say, successful serial killers find remarkably similar ways to kill successfully without detection.

Criminal organizations, particularly those selling sex and pornography could also produce elaborate theatrical mockups of the Satanic mass. Such a practice would serve three obvious purposes: intimidation of innocent child victims, enhancement of sexual stimulation for those so inclined, and the protection of the identity of perpetrators by wearing masks, robes and other disguises. The constant mention of cameras, video cameras, disguises, masks, and related materials by children, along with multiple murders (without bodies or other physical evidence) could indicate support for this explanation. Even if children disclose abuse, their stories would seem so extreme as to cause doubt about their credibility, therefore protecting the entire criminal enterprise.

A final possibility is that memories of ritual abuse stem from CIA experiments in brainwashing. The arguments seem to go something like this. The CIA wanted to test the brainwashing hypothesis by taking, exploiting, and programming an apparently unrelated group of young children from middle-class families because of the "communist scare" of brainwashing in the fifties. They wanted to see if brainwashing was effective. They wanted to see if they could instill experiences in the memories of small children that would later emerge as testimonials about Satanism. In other words, they wanted to see if they could alter the young child's perception of experience, reality, and truth.

THE INEVITABILITY OF RITUAL ABUSE

Whatever else it may be, and however we might try to understand or explain it, ritual abuse — or something like it —seems to have a certain compelling necessity and inevitability. By this I mean that, given the debauchery and illness present within human moral history, it would seem surprising not to find pockets of ritual abuse throughout society. The temptations for those so inclined are immense: the permission to indulge in erotically charged sexual variations and perversions, power over helpless victims, sexually charged secretive group psychodrama, loss of self into the group and release of primal emotions — to name just a few.

Furthermore, ritual abuse can be considered a logical extension of certain historical, cultural, and psychological trends that have always been present in human history. In this light, ritual abuse is not only likely, but probably inevitable, unless we assume that these powerful historical forces have simply vanished with the progress of "enlightened civilization."

For example, consider the long history of human sacrifice. An argument could be made that sacrifice is simply too deeply embedded in human history and too all-pervasive historically in most cultures to have completely disappeared. Subterranean remnants of various types might well exist in our time. Sacrifice may seem barbaric to us, but it has its own compelling spiritual logic. I offer something precious to my god — a human life — and the god then thanks me by keeping my group whole and well. Or, I absorb the sacrificial offering's vital power and energy by killing him in a ceremonial manner designed to prevent the flight of his spiritual energy after death. Once certain assumptions are accepted — "my God wants me to sacrifice in his honor", or "I can strengthen myself by absorbing my victim's suffering and ultimate death" — then the actual physical act becomes a coherent extension of these core beliefs. Interested readers might want to consult books like Girard's *Violence and the Sacred* for more about the logic of human sacrifice.

There is the equally compelling history of human cannibalism, which may not be as remote from our culture as we think. It could be returning or simply emerging from secrecy, as Tierney suggests in his book *The Highest Altar: The Story of Human Sacrifice.*

A strong history of sacrifice and "spiritual cannibalism" exists within central Christian dogma and ritual itself: Christ offers himself as a sacrifice for us, and the Eucharist celebrates the eating and drinking of Christ's flesh and blood. Those wishing to invert Christianity might logically eat and drink something opposite to Jesus, such as the blood and flesh of human and animal victims, feces, and other similar substances.

Add to this the history of magical thinking, which attracts and fascinates people today. Satanism can be considered the darker expression of occult magic (i.e. absorbing another's life force by killing, serving a God through ritual sacrifice, or gaining special powers by offering sacrifices).

Consider as well that some people might worship the "dark side" of human nature. Why assume that all religions worship only the positive side of human experience? Why should "spiritual" necessarily imply loving, kind, and good? And considering our collective fascination with violence, brutality, and all that is "darkly evil", it only seems logical to expect that some groups might well worship this dark side.

In media culture there is a growing attribution of heroism to traditionally evil characters such as serial killers (i.e., "Freddy Kreuger" in the *Nightmare on Elm Street* movie series), vampires (especially Anne Rice's characters), Charles Manson and the like. In the movie *Natural Born Killers* we are actually invited to sympathize, empathize, and root for the psychopathic killers. We are fascinated by the sociopathic mode with its desensitization, pleasure in power and violence, and lack of conscience, compassion, or moral code. If the sociopathic mode is so fascinating to us, then why wouldn't some individuals or groups take this fascination to the heights of religious worship?

And speaking of groups, the history of the cultic mindset itself speaks to the likelihood that groups of "normal people" acting on abnormal beliefs (i.e., Jonestown) can participate in the most horrific crimes imaginable and still justify their actions by defining them as a spiritual necessity based on loyalty to the group's leader, who as the Ultimate Power's representative knows what is best for us and for his victims.

Finally we might consider various Darwinian explanations. As disgusting and sick as this might seem to comfortably modern folk, the point could be made that groups practicing ritual abuse, especially cannibalism, might be better adapted to live in a possibly chaotic and overpopulated future world devoid of civilization and basic food resources.

One food resource would be abundant: human flesh. Groups that have an organized psychological, cultural, social, and spiritual foundation to permit cannibalism without guilt or remorse would have an obvious advantage.

In a similar way, individuals living in the sociopathic mode would be better adapted to survive in a world of moral relativity where traditional identity structures (family, community, religion) have deteriorated, where unpredictable change occurs at an accelerated rate, and where daily threats to existence (war, environmental collapse) require a kind of detached non-feeling and disconnection.

If these arguments have any merit at all, then the emergence of ritual abuse disclosures should be no surprise. If one particular case or even a large percentage of cases have no physical foundation in fact, that cannot then automatically mean that all cases are to be dismissed, or that the possibility of ritual abuse itself can be disregarded. Given human nature and human history, it seems inevitable that groups will gather for the sole purpose of expanding their deviant, violent, and abusive potential. Add to this a coherent spiritual belief system such as Satanism and a cultic mind-set, then the possibilities for perpetrators are open and endless.

LUCIFERISM AND SATANISM

To sum up: Satanism should not be naively embraced as an immanent worldwide conspiracy, but nor should it be dismissed as complete foolishness. There has been an overblown "Satanism scare", but there has also been an equally inflated "Satanism denial." Hopefully the information above sheds some balance and sanity on the situation.

The point of this discussion about Satanism and ritual abuse? Simply this: the significance of Luciferism does not depend on the truth or falsehood of a worldwide network of Satanic cults practicing ritual abuse. If ritual abuse testimonials are ultimately proven wrong, this will have little bearing on the new Luciferan prototype, which I believe exists and grows despite fanciful urban legends surrounding it.

The Satanism scare can perhaps be compared to the vampire legend. It merely explores our deepest fears and terrors. If vampires represent our own fear of being devoured by a stronger predator, then Satanism represents our fear of being completely annihilated, body, mind, soul, and spirit, by an organized group of even stronger predators, a group rising from us the way we seem to have risen from apes.

Satanism and Luciferism share some elements: for example the killing of compassion and conscience, the infatuation with power, the hatred of rules. But they differ so completely in other important ways that they can only be understood as very distant cousins.

Luciferism is a sophisticated yet coherent religious philosophy. Satanism in its modern form has its own rigorous coherence, but is lost in a bizarre mixture of pathetic theatrical exhibitions of the type displayed by Anton Lavey and his entourage of Hollywood imitators. Luciferism shuns the odd, the bizarre, the weird. It is not interested in media attraction while Satanism embraces all of these.

Luciferism shuns psychopaths; Satanism seems to attract them. Satanism speaks to a hedonistic expansion of base animal instincts and the satisfaction of pleasure, no matter how twisted. Luciferism seeks to transcend all this and rise to a higher and more sophisticated level of power acquisition within the hierarchy of devouring. For them, Satanists are lower order predators. Luciferans would never waste precious energy on the personal satisfaction of instinctual energies, whether sexual, aggressive, violent, or egocentric. They would view such activities with disdain for leaking precious energy instead of devouring and storing it for future advancement up the hierarchy. All of these differences revolve around one core idea: Satanism seeks to expand ego, whereas Luciferism seeks to expand Self.

If Satanism is the expansion of ego through predation, then Luciferism is the expansion of Higher Self through predation. In Luciferan terms, ego is beneath Self. Self is thus the Higher Self of new age, transpersonalism, occultism, and gnosticism, as described earlier.

For Luciferans, ego expansion is ultimately illusory and pathetic because it is a dead end, whereas expansion of the Higher Self is limitless and infinite in power-potentiality. Expanding the ego is like expanding the stomach: it sags and then passes obnoxious waste, ultimately disabling the body feeding it if overfed. Such predation is indulgence, and indulgence is weakness, so when Lavey trumpets indulgence as freedom, he displays his ignorance and weakness. Luciferans are drawn to asceticism more than indulgence, and have no respect for those unable to control and limit their passions and personal tastes. Furthermore, the ego dies when the body dies, but the Higher Self does not, so investing any energy in the satisfaction of lower-level ego pleasures is wasteful and ultimately ludicrous. For Luciferans, Satanists are therefore beneath contempt, even lower than middle-class victims. Their energy is hardly worth devouring. Some Satanists may see Lucifer's light and answer a higher calling, but few seem to do so because they become trapped in their own limited ego-cages. Satanism thus attracts ego-centered lower-order individuals such as psychopaths, neophytes, and thrill seekers.

Luciferism on the other hand attracts Self-centered higher-order predators who wish to expand into ultimate potential, not contract into the prison of egoicity.

If Luciferism is the evolving ideology of a new type of human-hugod predator, then perhaps we all sense their presence and are struggling to name them and know them. Satanic cults might then be urban myths generated to explain this instinctive fear, somewhat like an archetype from the unconscious.

If this is true, the myth will continue to maintain a powerful hold on our imagination and attention. We won't be able to dismiss it because unconsciously we will be trying to understand it. Maybe this same unconscious hold led me to try to penetrate beyond, beneath, and behind Satanic mythology. As mentioned in the Introduction, I believe Satanism is one possible doorway into the "beyond and behind" I have called Luciferism, along with psychopathology, cultism, and predatory competition.

But other doorways exist. Other connections can be found. Luciferism, like all other belief systems, is part of a wider ecology of ideas. It has not been inserted abruptly into the world of ideas, but has grown and matured from within. It is related to what we already know and believe. I would like to explore some of these relations now, and show that Luciferism is just as connected to our Western intellectual ecosystem as it is grounded in our daily experiences of devouring, possession, violence, disguise, and predation.

CHAPTER ELEVEN

RELATIVES: LUCIFERAN
IDEOLOGY IN THE
WESTERN WORLD

From whence did Dante take the material of his hell but from our actual world? And yet he made a very proper hell out of it. But when, on the other hand, he came to describe Heaven and its delights, he had an insurmountable difficulty before him, for our world affords no materials at all for this...
— Arthur Schopenhauer

Until now I have referred to Luciferism in two ways: as an evolving spiritual ideology, and as a way of being that exists in its own right with or without conscious adherence to Luciferan ideology. As an ideology it is nascent, but as a way of being — as predatory power acquisition — it has clearly existed for as long as human history has been recorded. We have always had power-predators and probably always will. Having said this, I do not mean to imply that every hustling power-player is a Luciferan. As already mentioned, Luciferism involves the deliberate and conscious destruction of conscience and compassion for power advantage, along with a specific supernatural belief in the human transformative potential to become god. Actual Luciferism is only now emerging on the world scene; the Luciferan style, however, is all around us, especially in the world of ideas.

I would like to begin with Arthur Schopenhauer, quoted above, who many would suggest was nothing but a gloomy, bitter, pessimistic old philosopher with deep personal problems derived from a poisonous relationship with his mother. Others would argue that his vision is simply realistic, that our world is a vicious pit of despair, inequality, and cruelty for all but a select minority of the privileged, wealthy, and powerful. Luciferans would agree with his vision, and would suggest that others agree as well, including Machiavelli, Darwin, Freud, Hobbes, Nietzsche and other influential thinkers.

Life on planet earth is a war of all against all, an unending competitive battle more like traditional visions of hell than of heaven. Luciferans just accept this reality, and proceed to adapt themselves to it with strength, pragmatism, courage, and will.

Take this idea of adaptation a little further! If Luciferism is the extension of Darwinian evolutionary principles into the religious and spiritual realms, and if Luciferans represent a new form of successfully adaptive human life, then by evolutionary principles, they must somehow "fit" better into our current intellectual, social, and physical environments.

This "fit" is not hard to show. Luciferan psycho-spirituality is not remote to our late twentieth century world. It is not disconnected. It does not flourish as an esoteric conspiracy. It does not thrive in dark obscurity removed from everyday existence. On the contrary, I would like to assert that it is openly nourished by the ground of Western thought and spirituality.

I say this not because I am "anti-Western" or because I nurture hostility toward science, individualism, competition or any of the Western intellectual traditions about to be explored. I love my life as a "Westerner", and appreciate the freedom and honesty it provides. I treasure individuality and privacy and I am not afraid of competition. All of the traditions about to be discussed were not created or promoted by Luciferans for Luciferan purposes. On the contrary, their founders and promoters had entirely different intentions. Luciferism chooses certain of these traditions and emphasizes specific core ideas to enhance their own interpretation, an interpretation which I believe is rational, compelling, and likely to draw many adherents in the next few decades. These core ideas have saturated our culture for centuries. They include survival through predation on the hierarchy of devouring, and the exaltation of Self to God.

Luciferan spirituality simply links these ideas, adds the destruction of conscience and compassion, applies this synthesis to all levels of existence from physical to spiritual, and then creates a new vision of human potential which speaks directly to our desires and aspirations for ultimate power, control, and success.

Very few Westerners would accept Luciferan principles openly, and would be deeply offended to be called Luciferans. Although we might grudgingly accept our own direct familiarity with the predatory impulses of devouring, possession, violence, and disguise as everyday realities, we would be far less willing to admit familiarity with the spiritual ideology of Luciferism. Becoming God? Climbing to the apex of the psycho-spiritual hierarchy? These core Luciferan ideas appear to be radically foreign, unnatural, and deeply disconnected from our own treasured belief systems and reigning cultural truths.

Christians, for example, understand themselves as the people of God, not of Lucifer. God told them to multiply and prosper. God is with them, and they have risen to worldwide power because of His approval of their actions, not because they have followed Luciferan principles. God is their God, not Lucifer.

Humanists, to take another example, are their own people, accountable only to humanity itself and not to God, Lucifer, or any other falsely imagined deities. Atheists and agnostics would likewise bristle if their ideas were linked in any way to Luciferism, and would probably either ignore such an accusation or fight it with indignant outrage.

As with devouring, possession, violence, and disguise, however, I would like to introduce hugodhood and the psycho-spiritual hierarchy as the familiar old friends they really are, as relatives of some of our most treasured systems of belief and truth.

These two core Luciferan ideas — becoming God and climbing the hierarchy — are connected to some of the most influential social movements, conditions, and thinkers of our time from which none of us are immune. Just as devouring, possession, violence, disguise and predation illuminate our daily actions, so does becoming god and mounting the hierarchy illuminate our minds through some of the most powerful thought-systems animating the Western world. Luciferism simply adds a particular twist to them by applying the methodology of predation: climb the psycho-spiritual hierarchy of devouring to become God by expertly applying the predatory arts.

To repeat: if Luciferism is the use of predatory techniques for scaling the hierarchy to achieve godhood, then it is connected to us through our love of all three key ideas, personal godhood, success on the hierarchy, and competitive predation. Regarding competitive predation, enough has been said. Regarding hierarchy and godhood, however, I would like to show how these ideas resonate with some of the belief systems that drive our lives.

The point here? Simply this. The ideology of Luciferism is not alien. It is close. It is related to us. We are bound to it as relatives by blood. This chapter will therefore explore the adaptable fitness of predatory Luciferan psycho-spirituality to the thought-life of Westerners about to enter the new Millennium.

Human Gods

For those of us raised in the post-God world, a world of reductionism and naturalistic materialism stripped clean of magic, mystery, and spirituality, becoming god is absurd and impossible. We waited for Godot, and he didn't show up. God is not dead, because he never existed in the first place. Death is for living entities, not fanciful imaginary gods. There is no God. Therefore, becoming God is meaningless. The idea is absurd and daft.

For those of us raised beneath the righteousness of the jealous God who said, "*I am the Lord your God, you shall have no other gods before me,*" the idea of becoming God is blasphemous. Beyond that, it is impossible. We are the creatures, not the Creator. We are limited beings created by the limitless God. We cannot become God. Such insolent absurdity is the sinful source of Lucifer's fall.

For those of us raised in the loving embrace of liberal humanism, we politely respect the right of others to pursue godhood, but would rather pursue personal growth, empowering relationships, physical fitness, job satisfaction, or a new car instead.

But still, there is something about the idea that compels interest. It seems somehow familiar, a bit fascinating, maybe even slightly intoxicating. Those who pursue the idea of personal godhood can surprise themselves by finding a widespread network of movements and traditions as close to us as classical Greek philosophy, Human Potentialism, Transpersonalism, New Age, Gnosticism, Occultism, Science, and even Christianity: all of these flow from deep wells in our culture, and all of them contain within their boundaries the idea that we are God or that we can become God in some way.

There are variations on this idea. For example, I might believe that I can become God in the same way that a drop of water becomes the ocean: I merge into a larger whole, and my identity is lost to the higher whole. Or I might look within and find that my core essence is God, that a spark of divinity resides in my being. I realize that I am part of God, but that others are also part of God as well. Or I might take the advice of certain sages and conclude that I can imitate or become like God by following a diligent path of spiritual discipline or by adhering to codified rules of behavior. I could become convinced that I can merge with God in ecstatic union as described by mystics. I might even conclude that I am a God already, and simply need to recover that fact.

Regardless of how variant the concepts, the same basic idea is foundational. My identity is one with God's. Luciferism simply goes further, by suggesting that I can usurp God. This ultimate step seems to be the sole property of Luciferism: just as Lucifer attempted to replace God, so Luciferans follow the same quest. But others have also decided they can replace god by denying his existence and inserting something else: the blind mechanical chance of evolutionary science or the pursuit of personal pleasure are two obvious examples. The single most compelling difference between the Luciferan idea of hugodhood and the traditions to be discussed below seems to be the Luciferan's refusal to accept that godhood rests in the amplification of *goodness* or *virtue*. Luciferism anchors its quest in the pure will of *powaqqatsi* devoid of any traditional sense of morality or goodness. For the Luciferan, the devouring hierarchy extends to God. There can be no blending, melding, or union with such an entity, only its annihilation.

Despite this difference, however, Luciferism is not radically disconnected from these other traditions. They are all related to this one central idea: becoming God. It might amaze you (as it has me) to discover just how deeply this idea has embedded itself in our culture.

PHILOSOPHERS

The idea of humans becoming gods, or God, or godlike, has traversed its way in and out of philosophical traditions since Plato. I would like to take a brief look at some of the philosophers who have "hosted the hugod meme." To do so, I have relied heavily on Sahakian's *History of Philosophy* and *Ideas of the Great Philosophers*, Will Durant's *The Story of Philosophy*, and other similar books which summarize philosophy for non-specialists.

I have explored the actual writings of many philosophers, especially Nietzsche, but I am new at it, and do not want to appear more knowledgeable about philosophy than I actually am. As with most of my generation, philosophy came to imply something stale and irrelevant, like Latin. The triumph of empiricism and naturalistic materialism has been absolute in the Universities: I do not remember taking even one philosophy course. Yet I now believe that philosophy is crucial, that science rests on it (in the form of naturalistic materialism — see Phillip Johnson's books *Darwin on Trial* and *Reason in the Balance*), and that the western mind cannot be understood without it. I think I need another lifetime to absorb the power and beauty of Western philosophical thought; I only wish I had started earlier in this life. Any errors of interpretation are therefore strictly mine, and I remain happily open to any criticisms from interested professionals.

PLATO, BERGSON & ALEXANDER

As one of the most influential representatives of classical Greek philosophy, Plato's thought is seminal. He contrasted the temporary, contingent, impermanent, and imperfect nature of this life with the perfection of the next life after death. Every individual seeks perfection, and according to Sahakian, "gradually achieves a godlike state liberated from the limitations of space and time, of corporeal existence, and of sensory (phenomenal) experiences."

Such self-realization is the goal of all our striving, and once achieved, transports us into a god-like state. We yearn to achieve this god-like condition, which is the ultimate good. Says Sahakian about Plato's position: "the successful effort to become like God rewards man with the highest state of blessedness — perfect happiness. Resemblance to God, then, is the ethical end of man."

Plato is obviously not Luciferan, but he articulates the deep human yearning to become more, to become god or god-like. This idea weaves and bobs its way through western culture despite being pitted against a heavyweight Christian opposition: no matter how hard Christian fighters whacked at the hugod meme, it always seemed to bounce into the ring ready for another round. Nietzsche promoted it, along with the evolutionary philosophers Bergson and Alexander. Even Sartre put on the gloves and took a round.

Bergson was a philosophizing biologist whose work early in this century found its focus in his concept of *elan vital*, a vital force animating and directing world evolution. For Bergson, the idea that random chance, accidental mutation, and natural selection could alone account for the evolution of complex life was absurd. The world is not mechanically or materially driven, and reductionism alone is inadequate to explain life. Only the *elan vital* explains life — his famous philosophy of creative evolution is based on the *elan vital's* relentless drive, which leads ultimately through human beings to godhood.

According to Sahakian, "Bergson referred to the world as a 'machine for the making of gods' for nothing is beyond the capacity of the *elan vital* to accomplish." When empowered by the *elan vital*, religion can only take one real form, which Sahakian suggests is "based on the identification of the human will with that of the divine, uniting the two in mystical union"... "The mystic teaches us how to become gods, for the "essential function of the universe... is [that of] a machine for the making of gods."

Samuel Alexander also wrote in the first half of this century. He developed the philosophy of emergent evolution, which suggests that new life emerges in ever more complex forms with properties greater than the sum of its antecedent parts or components. He describes five levels of emergent evolution, culminating in mind. He claimed that a sixth is on the way, though: *deity*.

Deity is not God, but rather "the next stage of emergence in the process of evolution." As such it represents a higher force than humans, a kind of Super Being. Alexander apparently did not describe this new stage, claiming that we are only responsible for encouraging its appearance. He felt that we should be cooperating with God to bring in Deity — to in fact encourage our own evolution to Deity.

Nietzsche

Some Luciferans would argue that Nietzsche is a conducive philosophical host for key Luciferan arguments, and that his ideas are about as Luciferan as one can have without an actual conversion to the faith. I am sure that the supporters of Nietzsche in the philosophical academy would disagree.

Regardless, Nietzsche's idea of the superman comes close to what Luciferans mean by the hugod, even though Nietzsche did not fully elaborate the exact nature of his exalted prototype. He did make clear, however, that the superman would evolve from lower humans, and that it would transcend our sick moralities to find strength, power, and authority by pursuing the will-to-power.

His perspective is evolutionary. A new human is coming to replace the old. This new human will evolve from us as we advanced from apes. Here is how he puts it (all quotes in this section are from *Thus Spake Zarathustra*; all italics are Nietzsche's):

Man is a rope, fastened between animal and Superman — a rope over an abyss.... *I teach you the Superman.* Man is something that should be overcome. What have you done to overcome him?

All creatures hitherto have created something beyond themselves: and do you want to be the ebb of this great tide, and return to the animals rather than overcome man? What is the ape to men? A laughing-stock or a painful embarrassment. And just so shall man be to the Superman: a laughing-stock or a painful embarrassment.

Nietzsche asks us, through his prophet Zarathustra, to sacrifice ourselves for the superman: I love those... who sacrifice themselves down to the earth, that the earth may one day belong to the Superman.

I love him who lives for knowledge and who wants knowledge that one day the Superman may live. And thus he wills his own downfall. I love him who works and invents that he may build a house for the Superman and prepare earth, animals, and plants for him: for thus he wills his own downfall.

The Superman is coming to replace humans. He also comes to replace God; God is dead, and so the Superman can be born: And this is the great noontide: it is when man stands at the middle of his course between animal and Superman and celebrates his journey to the evening as his highest hope: for it is the journey to a new morning.

The man, going under, will bless himself; for he will be going over to the Superman; and the sun of his knowledge will stand at noontide.

"All gods are dead: now we want the Superman to live" — let this be our last will one day at the great noontide!...

Once you said 'God' when you gazed upon distant seas; but now I have taught you to say 'Superman'.

God is a supposition; but I want your supposing to reach no further than your creating will.

Could you *create* a God? — So be silent about all gods! But you could surely create the Superman.

Perhaps not you yourselves, my brothers! But you could transform yourselves into forefathers and ancestors of the Superman: and let this be your finest creating!

But to reveal my heart entirely to you, friends: *if* there were gods, how could I endure not to be a god! *Therefore* there are no gods... .

The beauty of the Superman came to me as a shadow. Ah my brothers! What are the gods to me now.! ...

Very well! Come on, you Higher Men! Only now does the mountain of mankind's future labor. God has died: now we desire — that the Superman shall live.

For Nietzsche's Zarathustra, "The Superman *shall be* the meaning of the earth. I want to teach men the meaning of their existence: which is the Superman, the lightning from the dark cloud man."

There are differences between the Superman and the Hugod: the Superman is physical, not supernatural; the Superman is not god, but a replacement for all the dead gods. Nietzsche asks us to sacrifice ourselves for the coming Superman, a decidedly un-Luciferan thing to do.

Despite these differences with Luciferism, Nietzsche's vision of will-to-power, of the celebration of power over weakness, of his disgust with the morality of "goodness" and of his evolutionary Superman place him in resonance with Luciferan thought. God is dead, and the Superman replaces god.

SARTRE

Sartre's position is that God has abandoned us by throwing us into the world. We face the fear of nothingness, and so have a driving "desire to be." This desire leads us, says Sartre, to want the state of "Being-in-itself-for-itself," which is the same as being God.

Thus, according to Sahakian, Sartre holds that "the fundamental project of man is determined by his desire to be God."

Sartre himself puts it this way: "To be man means to reach toward being God. Or if you prefer, man fundamentally is the desire to be God...."

EDWARD O. WILSON

Readers familiar with E. O. Wilson know with absolute certainty that he would never promote the acquisition of human godhood. He is the reductionist's reductionist, the materialist's materialist, and the mechanist's mechanist. He has been so thoroughly possessed by the naturalistic scientific spirit that even the idea of godhood, never mind God, would be a ridiculous fallacy not even worth consideration.

To go even further, and to include Wilson with other philosophers, would rile not only his loyal readers, but certainly the man himself. For Wilson and other materialistic scientists, the philosopher is an absurd weaver of fables, a clown and fool without value. From the time that science, in the works of Bacon, Galileo and the other giants of the seventeenth century, first turned its broad back on philosophy, it has thankfully never looked back, and good riddance to philosophy and all armchair rationalists.

Yet I must agree with Alfred North Whitehead, who argued in his book *Science and the Modern World* that Science has never abandoned philosophy, but has simply rejected an open and honest philosophical pursuit of its core axioms: "We are so used to ignoring the implications of orthodox scientific doctrine, that it is difficult to make evident the criticism upon it which is thereby implied," and "we forget how strained and paradoxical is the view of nature which modern science imposes on our thoughts" and "one main position in these lectures is a protest against the idea that the abstractions of science are irreformable and unalterable." Reductionism and materialism are philosophies only, not absolute truths, a point echoed eloquently and forcefully by Phillip Johnson as well. As philosophies, they have implications far beyond the scientist's "fact-finding" intentions, one of which is that God must be replaced (killed?) by science.

For example, consider Wilson's words (from his book *On Human Nature*), an obvious philosophical treatise claiming to be objectively scientific:

> *"Recall how God lashed Job with concepts meant to overwhelm the human mind: Who is this whose ignorant words cloud my design in darkness?*
> *Brace yourself and stand up like a man;*
> *I will ask questions, and you shall answer...*
> *Have you descended to the springs of the sea or walked in the unfathomable deep?*
> *Have the gates of death been revealed to you?*
> *Have you ever seen the door-keepers of the place of darkness?*
> *Have you comprehended the vast expanse of the world?*
> *Come, tell me all this, if you know.*

Wilson's response to "Yehovah's" challenge is an astonishing philosophical statement, said with an apparently unblushing and unapologetic hubris:

> *"And yes, we do know and we have told. Yehovah's challenges have been met, and scientists have pressed on to uncover and to solve even greater puzzles."*

Wilson goes on to boast about science's achievements, which have apparently surpassed anything the Old Testament writers could have conceived even in their wildest revelations. The war between "irresistible scientific materialism and immovable religious faith", as Wilson defines it, has been won. Science is the victor. God has been dethroned, cast down, and destroyed.

In other words, God has been outdone and replaced. Surely this resonates with the Luciferan impulse to kill and replace God just as deeply as Nietzsche's vision. Wilson would never admit that humans were becoming gods, but nevertheless boasts that we have surpassed and replaced God.

Some would call this blasphemy; others would call it hubris. Many would call it an obvious statement of fact: Wilson is not the only scientist displaying the brightly colored feathers of self-certainty and supreme confidence. According to him, we already possess truths beyond even Yehovah's imagination, we are close to knowing everything essential about the universe, including life on earth, and we only need to fill in the details without reference to God, gods, or religion. Whether he likes the idea or not, Wilson the Scientist has thus usurped God's throne and become godlike by replacing god.

TEILHARD DE CHARDIN

Teilhard was both a scientist and a Catholic priest. His vision of cosmic evolution working through human beings and bringing us to the ultimate "omega point" was an attempt to reconcile Christianity with evolutionary science. My point here is not whether he succeeded, but that he saw human beings as part of an evolutionary process that has direction, purpose, and meaning leading us onward and upward to greater heights of god-like consciousness.

According to Teilhard, there is "something greater than ourselves moving forward within us and in our midst." He believes that "man discovers that he is nothing else than evolution become conscious of itself," and that we are moving higher and higher to ever more transcendent states of being.

He praises "the outcome of the world, the gates of the future, the entry into the super-human" which awaits us all. Is he suggesting that we will become gods by replacing god? No, because a Catholic priest is not likely to promote human godhood. But the germ of the idea of human transcendence is there in his work: the super human at the omega point of evolution.

Leaving the philosophers behind now (actually an impossibility, because they are the ghosts in the western scientific "mind machine", refusing exorcism by the high priests of science), I would like to explore some modern movements which also promote the idea of human godhood.

These movements include Human Potentialism, Transpersonalism, Gnosticism, the Perennial Philosophy, New Age and, surprisingly, even Christianity itself. After this exploration, I will briefly highlight the hugod idea within three specifically Western notions: the creative genius, rugged individualism, and evolutionary thought.

THIRD FORCE PSYCHOLOGY AND HUMAN POTENTIALISM

Human potentialism has probably had at least as much impact as Christianity or Science on Western daily thought and life in the latter half of the twentieth century. It is rooted in philosophy, especially existentialism, but emerged for public consumption primarily under the influence of academic psychology. It quickly spread to business and management literature, to educational thought and practice, to local bookshelves as pop psychology and self-help, and even to the mystico-religious marketplace of personal transformation and spiritual development. Its impact is probably immeasurable, like trying to estimate all the ways that television, cars, or technology have changed our lives.

Psychological potentialism began as a reaction against the reductionism and apparent dehumanization served up by the behavioral psychology of Skinner and others, who declared their interest in scientifically understanding and controlling human behavior. Skinner asserted that we are all empty black boxes filled at birth by social conditioning. Learn to manipulate the conditioning process, and you control the type of person created (this was the theme of his stiff novel, *Walden Two*).

Such bleak determinism seemed to rage against the dignity and freedom of the human spirit. It was matched in its relentless reductionism and determinism by Freud's psychoanalysis, which asserted that we are ruled by toxic passions buried deeply beneath consciousness, and that our conscious minds are governed by unconscious forces beyond our control or comprehension. Genetics, neuropsychology, and related areas added to the bleak picture by stating that humans were only the sum total of the biological, genetic, and physiological functions driving them. Humans, in short, were defined as little more than organic machines driven by conditioning, unconscious forces, and biochemical processes.

Humanists righteously opposed this deterministic reductionism, and stood like so many bold knights defending their noble cause against a relentlessly evil enemy. Their movement — variously called Human Potentialism, Radical Humanism, or Third Force Psychology (Behaviorism was 'first force', and Psychoanalysis the second) — spread like soothing cream to those who felt burned and scarred by Skinner's relentless determinism and Freud's sexual reductionism. Their books became immensely popular with the general public, taking their authors far beyond the boundaries of academic psychology and into the domesticity of the household name: Maslow, Frankl and Fromm are just a few. They all asserted the same opposition to first and second force psychology: far from being limited products of forces beyond their control, they claimed, human beings are free, limitless in potential, and vibrant with unknown possibilities.

Their legacy lives on. It has blossomed into what many would now call an *almost* religious movement. Its fundamental principles, based on the limitless possibilities of human potential, have flowered (or the opposite, depending on your point of view) into the clearly stated belief that humans have no limits at all, meaning that ultimately we can become "as god." This in turn has evolved into what some call Fourth Force, or Transpersonal psychology, to be discussed shortly.

Maslow is a good starting point for understanding this evolution from psychology to spirituality. His invention of the "peak experience" concept and his ideas on religion stand at the gateway between Third and Fourth Force psychology, between humanism and transpersonalism.

In the chapter on transcendence in his book *The Farther Reaches of Human Behavior*, Maslow states that "one can be an end, a god, a perfection, an essence, a Being (rather than a becoming), sacred, divine." Man can be a God, says Maslow.

Elsewhere he states that during some of his own peak experiences, "I can then even feel some subjective equivalent of what has been attributed to the gods only, i.e. omniscience, omnipotence, ubiquity (i.e. in a certain sense one can become in such moments a god, a sage, a saint, a mystic)." He goes on to relentlessly attack traditional religion, particularly Judeo-Christianity, by associating it with all that is dry, dead, limited, imprisoned, atomized, submissive, and repressive.

Maslow *prophesied* a new race of men, the "self-actualizers". Like Bucke in his powerful book *Cosmic Consciousness*, he anticipates their emergence on the world scene.

This new man will actualize all of his potential, including his potential to be a God. He will achieve this through the transcendent state, through direct personal experience of pure spirituality and pure energy. According to Maslow, such actualizers are "becoming a single party of mankind, the earnest ones, the seeking, questioning, probing ones... the explorers of the depths and of the heights, the 'saving remnant.'" He refers here to the evolution of a new human prototype, of human beings who become like God. He feels they are an elect group of humans who will transcend all limitations, and who will then obtain God-like status, a sort of humanistic superman. I don't think I need to overstate how closely this resonates with the Luciferan position.

Maslow is not the only early spokesman for the Human Potential Movement. Traces of the hugod idea can be found in the works of Erich Fromm as well. Fromm developed very powerful concepts of human dignity and freedom, also in reaction to the overwhelmingly depressing determinism and reductionism of psychoanalysis and behaviorism. Man (they said "Man" back then) is self-determining, has a core power of will, of responsibility, and of spiritual power, and is driven by the need to find meaning and purpose. The enemy of the free man is that which reduces, atomizes, and mechanizes him, that which undermines his limitless human potential.

Erich Fromm goes much further than this, though. Ultimate human potential is godhood. He tells us that *You Shall Be As Gods* (the actual title of his 1966 book). This kind of "radical humanism," according to Fromm "considers the goal of man to be that of complete independence." This means independence from all that hinders humanity's higher human potential, including rational thought, belief (vs. 'direct experience', which is desirable), submission or obedience to authority, and so on. The lesson of the *Old Testament*, according to Fromm, is that we are to be as gods. Through what he terms the *X-experience*, which he defines as that kind of transcendent religious experience found in mysticism and in the core reality of religions everywhere, we can follow our human potential to its logical conclusion, to godhood. "The idea that man has been created in the image of God leads not only to the concept of man's equality with God, or even freedom from God, it also leads to a central humanist conviction that every man carries within himself all of humanity."

In another book, *Psychoanalysis and Religion*, he speaks favorably of what he terms humanistic religion, saying for example, that "in humanistic religion conscience is not the internalized voice of authority but man's own voice, the guardian... Sin is not primarily sin against God but sin against ourselves." Toward the end of the book he states that "the underlying theme of the preceding chapters is the conviction that the problem of religion is not the problem of God but the problem of man; religious formulations and religious symbols are attempts to give expression to certain kinds of human experience."

In other words, by attempting to penetrate human spiritual reality apart from the "encumbrance" of traditional religious thought, Fromm has adopted a different form of religious thought. The idea of direct experience of divinity, of man's potential to be God, of the power of human will to produce a state of total unconditional freedom, of the transcendence of lower self or ego, and so on — all of these are in his work, and all of them animate his conception of human and divine reality.

Fromm's Radical Human Potentialism thus promotes humanity to a kind of godhood. It makes claims of ultimate truth. It attacks Judeo-Christianity relentlessly, and can therefore be considered part of the tradition of apologetic attack rather than the tradition of psychology.

This idea can also be found in the works of Carl Jung. Some Jungians might argue with this, but to me the evidence seems clear. Jung is probably not a "humanist," but his influence on psychology has been immense, probably equal to humanistic psychology itself. His psychology is based on the notion of individuation, of how the individual can expand potential, and of how this expansion is itself the essence of human purpose. In a review of Richard Noll's new book *The Jung Cult: Origins of a Charismatic Movement*, Leonard George (himself an influential 'potentialist') states in the journal *Gnosis* (No. 35, Spring 1995) that individuation for Jung meant becoming god: "In this book Richard Noll presents a startling reason for (Jung's) appeal: the Jungian world view has an intrinsically religious structure and intention because Jung's original aim was *to found a religion* (Noll's italics)... Jung's mission statement is thoroughly religious and nonscientific in content. It discusses the need for those who would follow the way of individuation to undergo an experience of self-deification — of becoming gods *themselves* (my italics) — then to descend psychically to the underworld to engage in a 'struggle with the Dead'... Noll links this amazing speech with another even more astonishing text: Jung's description of his own experience of becoming a god..."

The idea of human godhood in the works of Maslow, Fromm, and Jung is clear enough, but when third force psychology transforms itself into "fourth force" or Transpersonal psychology, human godhood becomes an even more central preoccupation.

FOURTH FORCE PSYCHOLOGY OF TRANSPERSONALISM

Roberto Assagioli was an Italian pioneer of psychoanalysis as early as 1910, but grew to feel that psychoanalysis ignored real human spirituality. He asserted that human spirituality could only be reached after the individual fully realized and explored his subconscious mind, and then ultimately through an investigation of what he called the "higher" or "spiritual" self. Assagioli was influenced by a variety of spiritual teachings, including Hindu yoga, Theosophy, Buddhism, and Christian mysticism. He developed a system called Psychosynthesis from these sources, and became deeply involved in New Age centers in California such as Esalen (his books are part of a series sponsored by Esalen).

His psycho-spirituality distinguishes between the "I" and the "Self". The Self stands behind the daily manifestation of "I" in the world. Assagioli urges what he calls "disidentification from I", which means discovering that the Self is not desire, thought, activity, or role. As one disidentifies with the impermanent "I", one finds one's consciousness expanding to embrace the higher mysteries discussed in ancient religions, and one begins to directly experience divinity. This higher Self, also called the Transpersonal Self, is "at One" with a higher energy known to us as God. When in this exalted state, the Transpersonal Will is activated to identify with the Universal Will. At this stage, the Self realizes that it is God. Assagioli expresses it this way:

> This consummation is vividly expressed in the Sanskrit saying *Sat-Chit-Ananda*: "The blissful awareness of Reality". And finally in the triumphant affirmation: *Aham evam parm Brahman*: "I indeed am the Supreme Brahman."

The basic beliefs of Fourth Force psycho-spirituality are all here: the primacy of the experience of spiritual realities, the hierarchical structure of levels of consciousness leading to the Higher Self which is at one with the universal God-force, and the necessity of transcending the lower self to become like God. Assagioli had an enormous impact on the development of transpersonal psychology, and I understand that his Psychosynthesis has formed a devoted gathering of followers who believe they have in fact actualized their higher realities.

Ken Wilbur is one of the most highly acknowledged gurus of Transpersonal Psychology. Although not academically aligned with a University, his works (A Sociable God, The Atman Project, Transformations of Consciousness and others) seem to have set the structure and much of the terminology of TP. His books are impressive monuments of intellectual and literary power: his reach of understanding and his global vision of the relationships between the world's spiritual traditions defy comparison.

Like Assagioli, Wilbur distinguishes between the "egoic" self and the Higher Self. Growth is a constant redrawing of boundaries — "I" is more than body, than mother, than ego, than desires, than thought, than roles in life. As one's boundaries expand, various possibilities open up, possibilities held by religions to be sacred possessions of their particular system but which are, according to Wilbur, normal aspects of human existence.

These possibilities can develop when we encounter the Higher Self, an encounter which purportedly leads us to the concrete experience of serenity, wisdom, and ecstasy, to the awakening of various extrasensory faculties, and to visions of God, revelations of light, and cosmic bliss. These are all conceived in terms of a highly structured and intricate hierarchy of development, too complex to detail here. But once the individual discovers the Higher Self, he discovers that he is "at cause" with the Universal Will and so passes beyond personhood into a kind of godhood, as this has been known and described in various mystical systems in history. Because the Self transcends personality, it lives forever, and can reincarnate throughout time.

Stanislov Grof, author of Beyond the Brain and The Adventure of Self Discovery, has emerged with Wilbur as one of the reigning gurus of TP. His credentials are more solid than Wilbur's — he was Chief of Psychiatric Research at the Maryland Psychiatric Center and Assistant Professor of Psychiatry at Johns Hopkins University School of Medicine.

Like Wilbur, he investigates the transpersonal realm of higher human potential. All the key elements of Transpersonalism are in his work; the belief in a Higher Self which must be reached through various psycho-spiritual techniques, the existence of personal experiences such as "cosmic consciousness" which transcend space and time, the fascination with mystical teachings from all times and cultures, the idea that the Self is at one with the Ultimate Cause, and so forth.

Grof, more than Wilbur and Assagioli, integrates TP with traditional psychotherapy. He explores the methodology by which "spiritual emergencies" can be handled by the trained therapist, and insists that much of what has been classified traditionally as mental illness is in fact an excursion by the individual into realms of higher consciousness. His material is complex, and his system of classifications impressive. His ability to synthesize extraordinary realms of experience, from psychic phenomena to *satori* is remarkable.

He says, "there exists ample evidence that the transcendental impulse is the most vital and powerful force in human beings." Like Maslow, he seems to think that the world will somehow be saved by those who undertake this heroic inner journey, and that through this process, new social structures will evolve to better reflect true human spiritual reality. (He does not seem to accept the possibility that some of those on the inner journey with him will be Luciferans, however).

Transpersonal Psychology itself has been defined in the following way. The emerging "Fourth Force" is specifically concerned with the study, understanding and responsible implementation of such states as being, becoming, self-actualization, expression, and actualization of meta-needs (individual and "species-wide"), ultimate values, self-transcendence, unitive consciousness, peak experiences, ecstasy, mystical experience, awe, wonder, ultimate meaning, transformation of the self, spirit, species-wide transformation, oneness, cosmic awareness, maximal sensory responsiveness, cosmic play, individual and species-wide synergy, optimal or maximal relevant interpersonal encounter, realization, and expression of transpersonal and transcendent potentialities, and related concepts, experiences, and activities.

This was written by Maslow in the then emerging *Journal of Transpersonal Psychology*, which is home to the writings of most notable Transpersonalists. One central point upon which most seem to find agreement — the ultimate expression of transpersonal and transcendent potentialities allowing advanced humans to share the experience of what others have previously called godhood.

Transpersonal psycho-spirituality has probably had less public exposure than Human Potentialism, but its influence may yet be felt in the next century. It seems to conduct itself with a kind of quiet dignity "behind the scenes", much like Gnosticism or like Aldous Huxley's *Perennial Philosophy*, both of which I will examine next.

GNOSTICISM: THEOMORPHIC CHRISTIAN HUGODS

Between Plato and the evolutionary philosophers of the twentieth century, the idea of human godhood seemed beaten by Christianity. Apparently it was only hiding — in the secret world of Gnosticism.

Gnosticism has returned; some would say it never left. With the publication of Elaine Pagel's book *The Gnostic Gospels*, Gnosticism's immense influence on Western life, thought, and spirituality has come to light. Her book is based primarily on ancient scrolls called the Nag Hammadi texts, uncovered in Egypt in 1945. These scrolls revealed the existence of a type of early Christianity very much at odds with the traditional versions we know today.

As commonly understood, Gnosticism is considered a Christian "deviation", although it is more likely a translation of an earlier pre-Christian spiritual tradition into Christian terminology. It is eclectic, apparently having roots in many traditions and cultures. According to Jaroslav Pelikan, a respected scholar and authority on early Christianity, many gnostic systems occurred in early Christian times, and gnosticism itself can be found in at least three other milieus: the Syrian, the Iranian, and the Jewish.

Much of our knowledge of early Christian Gnosticism before the Nag Hammadi texts came from the historical records of its victorious enemies within mainstream Christianity. Gnosticism was considered a heresy, possibly the greatest of all heresies. The early Church defined itself primarily by its opposition to Gnosticism: much of the canon, creeds, beliefs, and rituals of mainstream Christianity evolved during its battle with Gnostic heretics.

Despite its almost complete obliteration, however, Gnosticism has survived; I would suggest that it will always survive in one way or another. It is a complete way-of-knowing opposed to institutionalized religion with its creeds, rituals, and dogmas, pointing instead to the experience of something deeper, more personal, more direct. It also advances many of the key ideas articulated by Human Potentialism and Transpersonalism, articulating the hierarchical layering of consciousness and the possibility of actualizing human potential to become God or godlike.

Gnosis is the Greek term for knowledge. In Gnosticism it becomes the esoteric knowledge of spiritual truth held by an elite group of wise adepts who believe that salvation rests in gnosis, not faith. This gnosis can be understood as the direct apprehension of spiritual truth through intense personal experience transcending matter, feeling, thought, thought-systems, and other worldly-bound illusions.

Matter itself is evil, and was created by a lower-order "God" or "demiurge". The God of the *Old Testament* is considered a demiurge. For Gnostics, Christ represents a force in direct opposition to the old Jewish God Yahweh, who cast us from our spiritual home (symbolized as Eden) into this material world of viciousness, cruelty, and insanity. Yahweh's motivation was jealousy: he was afraid that we would uncover our true nature and inheritance of divinity, and thus become his competitors. Salvation is thus the act of breaking free from Yahweh's prison of matter, from the illusion of worldly space and time. But salvation is only the sole possession of a special elect few who penetrate the hidden secrets of existence, and who use this gnosis to climb up and out of the lower realms of existence as represented by created matter. The higher realms are home to us, not earth. We are spirits of light — sparks from God — descended into the prison of matter and held captive here by evil sub-gods of various degrees of power. Thus there is a hierarchy stretching from base matter to sublime spirit, from the world of lust, greed, and "ego" to the higher worlds of pure spirit. The adept climbs this hierarchy because this is the only way to achieve salvation. No higher power is going to reach down and haul us out; only our own efforts can release us from the prison of matter.

In Christian versions of gnosticism, Christ came to show us the way out of this earthly prison. Thus Christ was a kind of friendly guide showing us the way to redemption, which meant struggling free of matter and rising up through the hierarchical "aeons" or manifestations of the true God who is "uncontainable, invisible, eternal, and ungenerated in quiet and in deep solitude for infinite aeons." (God was often conceived in terms of depth rather than height, although the same sense of hierarchy still applies). These emanations extend outward from God to eventually end in our own world of fallen matter.

Gnosticism was saturated with magic formulæ, arcane rituals and so on, all of which were designed to free the divine spark within from its material prison.

Valentinus and Marcion, considered to be the "fathers" of Christian Gnosticism, were attacked rigorously and suppressed. But their ideas resurfaced in fourth century Manicheism, which was also considered a serious threat by the church. Church opposition lead ultimately to the formation of many common Christian beliefs, especially that God is the creator of matter and hence that matter is not evil.

Christian Gnosticism could be bizarre, but it could also be sublime. Listen to the words of one early gnostic teacher quoted by Pelikan:

"Abandon the search for God and creation and other matters of a similar sort. Look for him by taking yourself as the starting point. Learn who it is within you who makes everything his own and says, 'my God, my mind, my thought, my soul, my body'. Learn the sources of sorrow, joy, love, hate. Learn how it happens that one watches without willing, rests without willing, becomes angry without willing, loves without willing. If you carefully investigate these matters, you will find him in yourself."

Or listen to these words from the Gnostic *Gospel of Thomas*:

Jesus said to them: "When you make the two into one, when you make the inner like the outer and the outer like the inner, and the upper like the lower, when you make male and female into a single one, so that the male will not be male and the female will not be female, when you make eyes replacing an eye, a hand replacing a hand, a foot replacing a foot, and an image replacing an image, then you will enter the kingdom."

Gnosticism continues to fascinate and attract generation after generation of North Americans. In his book *The American Religion*, the literary critic Harold Bloom goes much farther. He claims that North Americans have their own unique kind of spirituality, which at its core is gnostic. He calls it the American Religion, and suggests that true "made in America" Christian sects such as Mormonism, Christian Science, the Southern Baptists, Seventh-day Adventism, and Pentecostalism are fundamentally Gnostic, not Christian.

One example is the archetypical American religion, Mormonism. In his famous "King Follett Discourse" given shortly before his death, the prophet and founder of Mormonism Joseph Smith articulated the "man-is-god theme" (this passage is quoted from an article by Lance Owen in *Gnosis*, No. 35, Spring 1995): "There are but very few beings in the world who understand rightly the character of God," he said. "If men do not comprehend the character of God, they do not comprehend their own character." Within human-kind there is an immortal spark of intelligence, taught the Prophet, a seed of divine intellect or light that is "as immortal as, and coequal with, God Himself." God is not, however, to be understood as one and singular. Turning to an oddly kabbalistic exegesis of the first three works of the Hebrew text of Genesis, Smith pronounced that there are a multitude of Gods which have emanated from the first God, existing one above the other without end. He whom humankind calls God was Himself once a man; and man, by advancing in intelligence, knowledge, and consciousness, may be exalted with God, *may become as God.* (authors italics)

Bloom supports the same Gnostic interpretation of Smith's spirituality. If Bloom is right about the American Religion then we have to accept the widespread presence of basic Gnostic ideas in the Western world, even the western Christian world. This would also then include the presence of two primary Gnostic concepts: psycho-spiritual hierarchy and becoming God.

There is a word for "becoming God" — theomorphism — which means "rising to become God." Bloom suggests that the heart of the American Gnosis is represented by theomorphism, by the "exalted man self-elevated into Heaven," who "lessens the difference between God and man" to actually become God through an "eternal progression to godhood." God is within, and can only be encountered personally, alone, away from the crowd. God's within-ness is God, and is one with the divine spark animating human nature. We are all, at root, God — or potentially God.

Gnosticism can be found in other influential religious and intellectual movements. I suggest that Human Potentialism (at least that stream of it described above) and Transpersonalism are essentially Gnostic. Beyond these two powerful movements, one need only examine the widespread appeal and influence of the Gnostic analyst Carl Jung; Stephen Hoeller dedicated an entire book to Jung's gnosticism in *The Gnostic Jung and the Seven Sermons to the Dead*.

So, becoming God is one of the basic beliefs driving Bloom's American Gnostic religion. My point here is not to debate the merits or historical details of Gnosticism, but simply to point out that this influential movement contains an idea basic to Luciferism: theomorphism.

This idea also appears in another powerful synthesis of ideas promoted by Aldous Huxley, which he calls the Perennial Philosophy. Huxley claims that this philosophy drives not only American religion, but all religions worldwide.

THE PERENNIAL PHILOSOPHY

Huxley defined the Perennial Philosophy in his book of the same name. It contains ideas basic to Luciferism, ideas which at first may appear foreign, bizarre, heretical, or just plain dizzy, but which have deep roots in Western spirituality. The significance of Huxley's Perennial Philosophy for Luciferism is that he postulates the universality of these ideas across time and culture, a central idea of which is that humans can become like gods.

The Perennial Philosophy states something like this: matter, the material world, does not exist as an independent, objective reality. It is an extension of our consciousness. To change reality, therefore, we must change consciousness. Change consciousness, and then enlightenment becomes possible.

Enlightenment, transcendence, and salvation depend on this change, this transformation of consciousness. According to the Perennial Philosophy (or "PP"), we are trapped in a prison of matter. Like Gnostics, Huxley asserts that we are divine sparks seeking release. Enlightenment occurs only by transcending matter. This concept of salvation is also expressed by Pagels and other interpreters of the Nag Hammadi scrolls, and is thoroughly Gnostic. The Gnostic intellectual William Irwin Thompson, author of *The Time Falling Bodies Take to Light*, and *Darkness and Scattered Light*, articulates the same basic idea. We have to escape the trap of illusion, the trap of *Maya* spun by three-dimensional reality. Much of Western Occultism, including Theosophy, holds this same belief. Human beings are spiritual in nature, not material;

spirit determines matter and not the reverse; we can only know ourselves by transcending the prison of matter and finding our true Self, or Source.

There is only one way to do this. The seeker must transform and open himself to higher states of consciousness through the use of specific consciousness-altering techniques and disciplines. That is, he must find his own salvation, because no God is going to gracefully or freely offer assistance.

Huxley asserts that these techniques are probably ancient, and likely known to every culture. They include meditation, trance induction, and psychoactive drugs. Altered states can also be reached with ecstatic dance, yoga, rhythmic group ecstasies, sensory bombardment or sensory deprivation, food deprivation, isolation, deep primal emotions such as profound fear, terror, guilt, euphoria, and sexual orgasm. Breath control, deep relaxation, visualization, repetitive vocalizations such as mantras and concentration exercises can produce powerful states as well. Finally, various systems of rites, rituals, and ceremony can combine all of these elements to produce powerful transformations.

Once the altered state is achieved, the seeker then enters another realm of experiential reality. Having transcended his lower material self (otherwise described as ego, consensus consciousness, etc.) and surrendered to the higher spiritual realities, he is given divine power. This is the trance walk of the shaman, the magical flight of the initiate, psychic gifts such as clairvoyance, clairaudience, and so on. These gifts can be accompanied by the kinds of profound physical, mental, and emotional experiences described by Bucke in his book *Cosmic Consciousness*. The seeker might experience himself falling into the "oneness" of the universal force, he might be filled with overwhelming surges of electricity, of euphoria and ecstasy, he might be washed clean by a deep and pervasive sense of calm and peace, or he might sense a bright white light causing him to burst into tears of joy and surrender.

When all of this occurs, however, the "journey" has just begun. The seeker must now keep going higher, through yet more rarefied levels of vibration, through a hierarchy of levels of consciousness. The ultimate end is the Higher Self, Atman, True Self.

This Higher Self is the reality behind personality, the truth behind all the manifestations of one's own particular time and place. The Higher Self is at one with God and is in fact the same thing as God.

The god of the Perennial Philosophy is something like the "Force" in the movie *Star Wars*. This is not the personalized biblical God, but is non-personal, neither good nor evil, completely immanent in creation (everything is God, from the smallest rock to the newborn infant is alive and animated by God), and the Ground of Reality itself.

So the seeker discovers that he is God, or Divine Reality, or Ultimate Ground. Huxley says that the Perennial Philosophy "finds in the soul something similar to, or even identical with, divine Reality," and "The divine Ground of all existence is a spiritual Absolute, ineffable in terms of discursive thought, but (in certain circumstances) susceptible of being directly experienced and realized by the human being."

Being one with God, being god, the seeker knows he will live forever. Hence the movement's promotion of reincarnation:— the temporal self is nothing more than a particular manifestation of the Self in a given time or place. Being God, the seeker also knows that she is in charge of her own reality, that there are no accidents or coincidences, that she wills her own life in every detail. All sicknesses, disasters and setbacks are her own creation. She is totally and completely responsible. Mistakes made during this incarnation will be corrected and balanced in the next, until she truly learns that she is a cause because she is God.

Attaining God-union, however, is not the muscular expansion of Higher Self as in Luciferism, but the annihilation of self all together. Huxley: "For the more there is of self, the less there is of God." Luciferans might deny lower egoic selfhood so that the Higher Self can expand to replace God, but selfhood remains primal. Followers of the Perennial Philosophy, however, seek to merge with God. The methodology of ultimate spiritual attainment may differ between the PP and Luciferism, but both seek godhood.

Having discovered oneness with God, the seeker is now truly free, truly enlightened. She is the sole arbitrator of her own reality and morality. She has transcended mere belief and faith to directly experience the God-force. She has transcended the limitations of words, logic, reason, thought and concepts to rise to a higher understanding. She is in fact a super-being, no longer driven by the ego, by the world, by desires. She has detached herself from the lower human condition. She has annihilated her lower self, and transcended time and space, living instead in the eternal Now. She has evolved into a Higher Being.

The elements of PP — its focus on technique to attain altered states, the centrality of Will, its emphasis on transcendence of all that belongs to the lower self or ego (personality, reason, logic, words, feelings, desires, and so on), its search for direct experience of the Divine within, the Higher Self, its insistence on the reality if the hierarchical structure of consciousness — are all present in Luciferism as well. If Huxley is right in his assertion that "rudiments of the Perennial Philosophy may be found among the traditional lore of primitive peoples in every region of the world, and in its fully developed forms it has a place in every one of the higher religions," then we have to accept that these elements of Luciferism also resonate worldwide.

If Gnostics and "PP'ers" are a bit remote and esoteric, going about their business with quiet dignity, New Agers seem to have no such love of reclusive spirituality. Even Human Potentialists and Transpersonalists, themselves no strangers to pop culture and self-promotion, pale against the flushed declarations of personal Godhood made by some New Agers. The phrase "I am God" has even come to symbolize the New Age movement itself.

General New Age beliefs were outlined previously, and so will not be repeated here. Instead I would like to quote from a few representative and well-known New Agers regarding their position on theomorphism. I am not suggesting that all New Agers would agree with these statements, nor am I interested in defending or attacking the idea of personal godhood itself. As before, my intention at this point is only to show that the idea is widespread.

I could quote from literally hundreds of New Age sources, but will turn to only two, Shirley MacLaine and J. Z. Knight's channeled entity Ramtha. In fairness to more responsible New Age thinkers, these two choices might be unfair: both have been held up for public ridicule by the media, and both are so self-promoting that only televangelists seem as equally dedicated to the accumulation of "green energy" (or as the rest of us call it, money). Nevertheless, both sources articulate a theomorphism echoed one way or another in virtually every New Age text that I have ever read.

Here is what Shirley MacLaine has to say about the New Age possibility of godhood in her book *Going Within*:

> "I, for example, do a silent mantra with each of my hatha yoga poses. I hold each yoga position for twenty seconds and internally chant, *I am God in light*." "Since the Higher Self, the soul, is our personalized reflection of the Divine spark ... Therefore, self-realization is God-realization"
> "We are each within God. God is within Us. There is no separation between God and Us."
> "This understanding brings us to the most controversial concept of the New Age philosophy: the belief that God lies within, and therefore we are each part of God. Since there is no separateness, we are each Godlike, and God is in each of us."

Ramtha is the "entity" trance channeled through J. Z. Knight. He presents himself as a powerfully spiritualized warrior from a previous stage of human history who wishes to help us. In Knight's book *Ramtha*, he says:

> "Now. Yeshua ben Joseph, who you call Jesus of Nazareth, is a great god,

just as you are a great god. But he is not the only son of God; he is a son of God. He was a man who became God, just as you will become God. You are here, master, to become God." (my note: "master" is a term Ramtha uses for all of his human followers):
"You are already God."
"Then I knew that man truly was, in his essence, God."
"You are God."
"Now, I have told you in every conceivable way — and over and over and over again — of the grandest truth you will ever know: you are God."

Quotations like these can be pulled from books lining the shelves in any New Age bookstore. If New Age thought is as widely accepted as it seems to be, then the idea of human godhood is also widely known. The point here is simple: Luciferans are not alone in their pursuit of Godhood.

CHRISTIANITY

Traditional Christianity abhors the notion of personal Godhood. There has been one "god-man", Jesus Christ, and there will never be another. God is God, and humans are humans. One is the creator, the other the created. One is omnipotent, omniscient, omnipresent, perfect and limitless; the other is a creature limited by time and space. One directs, the other receives. The relationship between God and man can be intimate, but in no way implies a unity, merging, or identification. God speaks to humans through Jesus Christ, and humans — separate from God — are commanded to listen.

Despite this radical separation between God and humans, the Bible itself provides fascinating hints about other possibilities, about the potential of humans to become God. For example, consider this passage from the *Gospel of John*, chapter 10, 31-36 (my emphasis in italics):

Then the Jews took up stones again to stone him.
Jesus answered them, "Many good works I have shown you from My Father. For which of those works do you stone me?"
The Jews answered Him, saying, "For a good work we do not stone You, but for blasphemy, and because You, being a Man, make yourself God."
Jesus answered them, "Is it not written in your law, 'I said, you are Gods'? If He called them gods, to whom the work of God came (and the scripture cannot be broken), do you say of Him whom the Father sanctified and sent into the world, 'You are blaspheming,' because I said, 'I am the Son of God'?"

Jesus here refers to Psalm 82, which has God saying: "They know not, neither do they understand; they go about in darkness; all the foundations of the earth are shaken. I said: You are gods, all of you sons of the most High. Yet like men you shall die, and fall like any prince."

Traditional Christianity interprets these passages to mean that only Jesus is the son of God. But the passages seem to suggest otherwise. At the very least, they bring forth the idea that humans can become God, or gods, and that some of the "Jews" who stoned him were offended and obviously frightened by the idea.

These are not the only biblical passages referring to human godhood. When Adam and Eve were tempted to eat the fruit of the tree of knowledge of good and evil, (despite God's warning that they would die if they did) the serpent encourages them with: "You certainly will not die! No, God knows well that the moment you eat of it your eyes will be opened and you will be like gods who know what is good and what is bad."

God's reaction to their transgression is fascinating: "Then the Lord God said: 'See! The man has become like one of us, knowing what is good and what is bad! Therefore, he must not be allowed to put out his hand to take fruit from the tree of life also, and thus eat of it and live forever.'" Adam and Eve are thrown out of Eden, and prevented from reentering, as if their potential godhood somehow threatened God's own power. God's response here seems suspiciously hierarchical and predatory, as if the threat of human godhood was real and therefore needing prevention by any means possible, no matter how drastic.

I leave the theological implications of this to others. But it seems clear to me that the entire Biblical narration of human history begins with, and is therefore built upon, the threat that humans might become equal to God. This idea, this possibility, is therefore inseparable from Western Christian history. Even Christ himself is defined as God-man, fully human and fully God. He is also called the "second Adam": did he finish eating the fruit Adam was unable to reach after his expulsion? And how are we, as God's children made in His image and likeness (we are like God?), to understand our own potential? Listen to Christ's strange words:

> "Most assuredly, I say to you, he who believes in Me, the works that I do he will do also; and greater works than these he will do." (John 14:12).

Whatever all this means, and however we might want to interpret it, the idea of human godhood (or God's humanhood) — either as blasphemy or as hinted human potential — is a central, vital, and essential dynamic of Judeo-Christian thought. Luciferans would agree, and would add their agreement to the Gnostic belief that God, or Yahweh, is just a lower order archon trying to squash the threat of competitive human godhood. God is therefore an enemy to be overcome: if you see Yahweh on the road, kill him.

THE CREATIVE GENIUS

If some western religious, spiritual, and psychological movements have toyed with the idea of human godhood, then so too have some artists. There are connections between God and the artist, because both create. Some artists feel compelled to understand their creative impulse in ultimate terms, and to describe their creativity as a kind of godhood in itself. The literary critic George Steiner puts it this way in his book *Real Presences*:

> The poet, the master craftsman as 'another god' is a Renaissance commonplace. It runs like a bright thread, at once hubristic and pious, through Cellini's memoirs and informs, uncannily, his great carving of Christ on the Cross now in the Escorial. This motif of alternative divinity may well be the decisive clue towards the mania of invention and design in Leonardo, towards the unmistakable paradigm of the likeness of God the Father in Leonardo's self-portraiture. In his preface to an exhibition catalogue of Gauguin (1895), Strindberg is acerbic: Gauguin is "the Titan who envies the creator and in his spare time makes his own little Creation." A Creation, one would add, obsessively Edenic, almost vehemently intent on a cancellation of the Fall. Striking is the force and persistence of the *topos* of the artist as god, of God the rival, in an age reputedly secular. "God is in reality nothing but another artist," (*otro artista*) declared Picasso whose own appetite for invention, for self-recreation was, indeed, that of a demiurge. Having completed his paintings in the Chapel of the Rosary at Venice, Matisse ruled: "I did it for myself." "But you told me you were doing it for God," objected Sister Jacques-Marie. Matisse: "Yes, but I am God."

Steiner feels that such statements are "legion", and argues that these artists are God's rivals who are "wrestling for primacy" through an "imperious act of *second* creation" in order to achieve the mastery of total freedom. The artist thus asserts his own absolute singularity against a "rival master" by bringing into being a kind of "counter-creation."

To become God; to find ultimate personal freedom by displacing God; to fight and wrestle with a jealous God unwilling to surrender sovereignty: such is the Luciferan pulse, and such, says Steiner, is also the vital pulse of artistic genius.

Is artistic genius Luciferan and therefore "evil"? No: once again, my intention here is only to illuminate our culture's profound familiarity with the idea of personal godhood.

To use a computer analogy, human godhood has been copied into the "operating system" of the human cultural "biocomputer" through psychology, religion, spirituality, and artistic creativity.

Luciferans accept the basic fact of this struggle for personal godhood, and invoke it as a vital primal impulse and key component of their belief system.

RUGGED INDIVIDUALISM

Along with the creative genius, the western world has birthed, nourished, treasured and exalted the idea of the individual. Rugged individualism is the opposite extreme of self-loss by, say, absorption into a god, another person, or a group. Losing identity to a group is horrifying for the individualist, who wants little to do with groups, organizations, governments or any other kind collective entity. Perhaps our North American ancestors instilled this fear in us: most of them fled the stifling tyranny of various organized entities in Europe, from governments to religions. Or perhaps the rugged frontier instilled individual initiative and rewarded the individualist's love of self-reliance.

Whatever the source, we North Americans treasure the individual. We celebrate the heroic warrior who tackles and defeats the might of the powerfully repressive organization. We love the achievements of individual genius, and adore the individual who rises from rags to riches with nothing other than his own courage, tenacity, and wits. Horror for us is not expulsion from the tribe, but absorption by the tribal entity, as Orwell articulated in 1984.

For us, the self-reliant and self-sufficient individual is primal. But this is also true for Luciferism, which elevates rugged individualism to godhood. For the Luciferan, Self is all, Self is center, and Self is god.

This possible evolution of rugged individualism from frontier ethic to Luciferism is, I submit, clear to see. Its seeds are present in Emerson's philosophy, and have fertilized Human Potentialism and Transpersonalism as well. For example, listen to Emerson, the North American prophet of self-reliance. His sense of the sacred is grounded only in the individual: "Nothing is at last sacred but the integrity of your own mind." "We are all divine because we all possess selfhood," and "self-existence is the attribute of the Supreme Cause." God is in all of us, "we learn that God IS, and that he is in me" and that we do not ever need to bow low before God as beggars because "as soon as the man is at one with God, he will not beg." God loves the self-reliant man: "welcome evermore to gods and men is the self-helping man." The man who truly trusts himself is almost godlike: "and truly it demands something godlike in him who has cast off the common motives of humanity, and has ventured to trust himself for a taskmaster." Few of us realize our divinity, because "we but half express ourselves, and are ashamed of that divine idea which each of us represents." Those who are ashamed are also limited, and "men cease to interest us when we find their limitations. The only sin is limitation."

As with all prophets of rugged individualism, Emerson dislikes and distrusts society: "Society everywhere is in conspiracy against the manhood of every one of its members." Religious traditions are equally repressive: "What have I to do with the sacredness of traditions, if I live wholly from within?" Even good and evil themselves are just categories that the true individual must subvert to his own Self or Center: "Good and bad are but names very readily transferable to that or this; the only right is what is after my constitution, the wrong what is against it."

Emersonian individualism is the North American cultural ethic, an ethic which resonates with Luciferism in its elevation of the Self, its celebration of Self as center, and its distrust of any and all limitations, from society to arbitrary ethical categories of good and evil. Luciferism is perhaps the *dark side* of this ultimate individualism. The Luciferan's vision is the desire of the individual for the ultimate self-reliance of godhood itself.

Of course, Emerson and Luciferans are also universes apart, as is the case with all of the traditions mentioned here: none of them — except maybe Nietzsche's — link human advancement with the destruction of conscience and compassion, and none of them suggests that competition, struggle, and evolutionary Darwinism extend into the spiritual realms as well. As far as I know, only Luciferism sees compassion and conscience as impediments to human actualization.

EVOLUTION, TRANSFORMATION, NEW PARADIGMS

If the power of individual genius and the centrality of Selfhood express the essence of Western culture, then the idea of constant change is even more essential. Everything changes for the Western man. Nothing stays the same, ever. The Greek philosopher Heraclitus was right: all is in constant change and flux. He said, and we concur, that "all things flow, nothing abides." The river I saw yesterday is not the same river today. Even the body I possess today is not the same one I had yesterday, because its cells have changed. My form remains constant, but its parts do not; even my body's form itself changes from birth to death.

All things change and transform constantly, relentlessly, from cellular levels of organization to world nation states. Only change is constant, and even it is fickle and unpredictable.

This infatuation with change breaks through into our intellectual culture constantly. We hear about "context shifts", "paradigm shifts", "transformations", and "revolutions." Everything, including our thinking, apparently evolves. Darwin's metaphor of natural evolution fills our culture like expanding smoke, drifting into everything from the marketplace of consumer goods to the spiritual marketplace, saturating everything with the burning odor of competition and selection.

Everything evolves; all things change. Luciferans accept this truth and just "flow with it" because they believe that evolution has an historical inevitability and momentum flowing upwards to the state of Luciferan godhood itself, a state which ultimately transcends space and time and therefore even evolution itself. No matter how it is expressed or by which authority, Luciferans can demonstrate that evolution is "on their side."

For example, Julian Huxley, the influential promoter of Darwinism, believed that biological progress is defined by the successful competitor's "greater control over the environment," and "greater independence from the environment." Yet these are also central preoccupations of the Luciferan path: controlling others, controlling the environment, controlling their own inner worlds of conscience and compassion, and achieving ever greater godlike independence from the material, natural, and human environments.

Huxley feels that successful organisms will gradually raise the "upper levels" of this kind of cumulative and progressive control. Luciferans believe that they represent the dream of achieving the absolute upper limit of godhood.

We can leave behind classical evolutionary philosophy and take an example instead from the developing science of complexity. Stuart Kauffman and his colleagues at the Santa Fe Institute have been trying to discover the laws of self-organization apparently displayed by all complex systems from simple cells to nation states and planets. They claim that complex systems tend to display ever increasing powers of self-organization apparently designed to defy the various forces seeking to dissolve them, from simple entropy to other organized competitors. Kauffman's book At Home in the Universe and Lewin's Complexity: Life At The Edge of Chaos both promote this notion of increasing self-organization as an inherent property of complex living systems, and as the primary "unit" upon which Darwinian selection acts.

Thus the properties of self-organization apparently strengthen survival. If the organism cannot maintain its own integrity, coherence, and order against the massive forces of universal chaos and change, then extinction soon follows. And it is precisely these properties of self-organization that Luciferan's claim to master: their quest for the ultimate power of godhood is the essence of pure self-organization standing eternally against the aligned forces of chaos, disorder, disintegration, dissolution, and relentless change. Luciferans embrace the principles of self-organization, but reject the apparently inevitable end of every self-organizing entity: death and extinction.

The Luciferan quest for godhood extends even into the nature of change itself. Postulate progressive change, and Luciferans insist that they represent the ultimate cumulation of that change. Promote a coming "paradigm shift" from human to trans-human, and Luciferans are there already. Suggest the evolution of a New Human, and Luciferans offer themselves as its epitome. Luciferans consider themselves the masters and rulers of change, not only because of their mastery of Protean shape-shifting, but because of their inheritance of the primal, restless, and relentless drive of progressive evolution:— a process which, they believe, expresses itself fully and completely in their drive toward godhood.

THE DEVOURING HIERARCHY

If the idea of human godhood thrives within Western intellectual and spiritual history, then so does the notion of hierarchy. Hierarchy saturates Western traditions. For example, consider how Christianity layers existence from God to Satan, angels to devils, bishops to monks, saved to unsaved, and heaven to hell. Consider also Gnosticism, which ranks an elite group of spiritually evolved souls above lower-order humans, which arranges spiritual being in an ascending and descending order of levels on the tree of life, and which places all spiritual levels above matter. New Age thought has its own hierarchies as well, such as higher vs. lower Self, and higher vs. lower vibrations, as does Transpersonalism with its higher vs. lower levels of consciousness.

We are saturated in hierarchy. But before going any further, I would like to define the term — or at least clarify how I will use it. I agree with Arthur Koestler, who said in *Janus: A Summing Up*, "Unfortunately, the term 'hierarchy' itself is rather unattractive and often provokes a strong emotional resistance. It is loaded with military and ecclesiastic associations, or evokes the 'pecking hierarchy' of the barnyard, and thus conveys the impression of a rigid, authoritarian structure...". Koestler went on to describe a very different type of hierarchy of biological life characterized by autonomy and flexibility at each level. By hierarchy, therefore, I am not implying the kinds of value judgments that concerned Koestler and which have become the focus of so much feminist and Marxist rage. As defined and used here, hierarchy is not evil or good in itself, but just exists. Huston Smith, the great interpreter and scholar of world religions, said in an issue of *Gnosis* (No. 37, Fall 1995): "The notion that hierarchies as such are oppressive is simplistic, misguided, and flatly untrue."

So what exactly is hierarchy? If we leave aside value judgments and unpleasant associations, what is left?

In its simplest form, hierarchy just means an order of levels from top to bottom. The levels may involve increasing authority, as in a corporation, increasing complexity, as in recent biological thought, or increasing intelligence, as in IQ testing. Hierarchy is prepositional: "higher" and "lower" levels are always involved, and so hierarchy can be visualized vertically from top to bottom. The term is obviously saturated with value judgments and noxious historical associations, and may never truly be free of them despite Koestler's protests. But again, my point here is not to judge the concept of hierarchy in Western thought, but only to point out its ubiquitous presence.

To comprehend the full influence of hierarchical thinking on the Western mind, we need only look at three "down to earth" cultural forces that have undeniably shaped us: science, capitalism, and socio-economic realities.

SCIENCE

Our compulsion to order all things from top to bottom, higher to lower, stronger to weaker, better to worse, complex to simple, is primal. We do it in our sciences, in our social organization, in our personal preferences. Hierarchical thinking is not just primal, but of an even deeper essence. We frame reality in hierarchical terms, perhaps unconsciously, perhaps (as Luciferans would argue) because this is how reality operates, perhaps because there is simply no other alternative.

Whatever the reason, hierarchy dominates. Despite attempts to cast a pejorative spin on hierarchy by some feminists (hierarchy equals male, equals evil), socialists (hierarchy equals rich ruling elite, equals evil), anarchists (hierarchy equals fascistic control of individual freedom, equals evil) and others, the principles and brute reality of hierarchical organization persist. Hierarchy overpowers even those violently determined to destroy it. The Marxist revolution was at root an attack against a higher level of social hierarchy by a lower level, but its fruit was a communist state every bit as hierarchically structured as the society it sought to replace.

Mother Nature herself seems to embrace and love hierarchy. The Romantic ideal of the innocently pristine and sublime natural world free of ugly hierarchy is an illusion. All of nature resonates hierarchy in its basic structure. Atoms form molecules, which form elements, which form tissues, which form complex organic bodies. These bodies then form social organisms within which hierarchy rules: the pecking order welds together not just chicken culture, but virtually every animal society we have been able to study, including ourselves. And each society then enters into competition with others, so that a hierarchy of societies evolves both within species and between them. This manifests for us as the hierarchy of nations, each competing to establish itself as the most dominant, powerful, and influential. Hierarchy and competition and predation: these seem so ubiquitous in all life forms as to be self-evident.

Mother Nature has apparently given birth to this vicious hierarchy of predation. The human eats the fish which eats the smaller fish, which eats even smaller fish, which eats other life forms. We call this the "food chain", but it is really just another hierarchy. The hierarchical food chain apparently produces higher and more effective predators through the cruel process of evolution, where the strongest and fittest lord it over the weaker and unfit. So says the science of biology: from Darwin to the sociobiologist Edmund O. Wilson, the message is the same. The hierarchy of dominance exists, and the big fish eats the little fish. It is as simple as that. Despite recent research on cooperation by game theorists such as Robert Axelrod, who wrote *The Evolution of Cooperation*, and who is fascinated by altruism, reciprocity, and kinship, no one has seriously challenged or diffused the scientific impulse to see nature's creatures as bound to one another through hierarchy, competition, and devouring.

The actual layer or unit of hierarchical focus seems almost irrelevant. All living things seem to be systems, and each system is made up of parts organized into a hierarchy. Arthur Koestler called this the Janus principle, the notion that all things are simultaneously independent wholes and dependent parts of an ascending and descending hierarchy of complexity. Like the two-faced God Janus, all things share an organized coherence as independent entities, while simultaneously belonging to a higher whole of some kind. All things are *holons* as Koestler coined them, partly whole, partly dependent on other wholes. And they are all organized hierarchically, from cell parts to whole cell, from cell clusters to tissues, from tissues to bodies. Without hierarchical order there could be no organization, and without organization there could be no life.

Hierarchical thinking extends into every science. In biology, it has been encoded in the idea of the increasing complexity of organisms through evolution. In the taxonomic system developed by Linnaeus it is demonstrated by the methodology of dividing all living entities according to ever more inclusive categories beginning with the "lowest" level, the species, and rising up through genus, family, order, class, phylum and kingdom.

Hierarchical principles (as well as morphological and developmental similarities) organize this system of classification; species are also categorized by various systems according to increasing complexity, evolutionary adaptation, and displays of higher order functioning. Other sciences, such as chemistry, use similar principles to classify the increasing complexity of non-organic and organic substances.

In psychology, hierarchical thinking frames our definitions of how the brain organizes sense perceptions through various layers of hierarchical neural processing; for example, a visual sense perception begins with the rods and cones in the retina and proceeds through ever more complex layers of brain tissue to "terminate" in the tertiary areas of the visual cortex. Hierarchical thinking also defines how psychologists describe motivational theory as epitomized by Maslow's hierarchy of needs. The same is true of developmental theory, from Kohlberg's hierarchically conceptualized description of moral development to Piaget's hierarchically defined articulation of the child's cognitive development. We conceptualize human development as climbing a hierarchy from kindergarten to grade twelve, from first year University to Ph.D., from the bottom rungs of employment to the top.

Again, the point here is not to argue whether this is good or bad, but simply that it is. Even our conceptions of the afterlife are hierarchical: Heaven is up there. Apparently we have to behave and think in a certain way to get into Heaven, and once admitted, we fit into a hierarchy with Jesus and God at the top and various layers and levels of angels in between.

We place ourselves into hierarchies relentlessly, unconsciously, and automatically by constantly comparing ourselves with others who might be better looking, smarter, more qualified, wealthier, happier, or whatever. We do it in our personal lives, in our sciences, and especially in the way we organize ourselves as a society.

CAPITALISM AND THE SOCIO-ECONOMIC HIERARCHY

Capitalism and Darwinism fit. Capitalism can be understood as the application of Darwinian competitive principles to economics. The strongest survive. The weak perish. Services and products evolve and improve through the competitive process, just as life-forms improve through evolution. One organization preys on another. And within the whole enterprise, the hierarchy of the successful is imperative. This view of economic reality has roots in the "dog eat dog" philosophy of Thomas Hobbes, and then formally with the British economists Adam Smith through Thomas Malthus and David Ricardo to the present day.

Hobbes in particular seemed to resonate with Luciferan sentiment. He stated that all people are at war with one another: "The condition of man ... is a condition of war of everyone against everyone." His book *Leviathan* is a gloomy testament to "the life of man, solitary, poor, nasty, brutish, and short." Hobbes believed that "force, and fraud, are in war the two cardinal virtues." Only enlightened self-interest has allowed the creation of the *social contract* of rules, laws, and social order; that is, each person gives up freedom in order to gain relative safety and justice. If possible, however, each person will try to break these rules for personal advantage, so only "Leviathan" can ensure that the laws are followed. Leviathan might be a king, a god, a democratic assembly, or any other entity vested with authority. Leviathan needs to enforce the laws and punish those who transgress. But Leviathan is above all laws, and does not have to follow them. Luciferan ideology parallels Hobbes; the goal of every serious Luciferan is to control "Leviathan" and therefore society, to use the legal system against opponents but to live above it himself, to climb the hierarchy of worldly power to its apex and beyond.

The business world embraces hierarchy. To organize and expand a business means to incorporate a hierarchy. There have to be bosses, and there have to be workers — those with power, those without. Despite recent attempts by many corporations to decentralize decision-making power and "flatten" their organizational charts, such decentralization can only go so far. Beyond that is chaos, like allowing the heart to decide when it wants to beat, or the foot deciding to step wherever it wants. Organization automatically implies hierarchy. The executive suite remains the apex of the hierarchy: even our architecture reflects this obvious fact.

The capitalist system is based on the accumulation of wealth and power. It is maintained by individual self-interest. Each individual in effect competes with all others to rise in the hierarchy of power, wealth, and influence.

Socio-economic status refers to one's place on the social hierarchy, and has to do with wealth, power and influence. A select few are on top; some are in the middle, and a lot are on the lower rungs. No one argues with this basic reality; no one disagrees with the assertion that, say, the "middle class" exists. Disagreements center only on which class should control social power. Socio-economic status is all about hierarchy, and every sane individual knows his place in this pecking order exactly. Most social revolutions seem to involve little more than violent protests by those on the lower levels wanting to rise up the hierarchy.

Again, I make no judgments here about capitalism or socio-economic status. I personally feel very comfortable living within the bounty of North American democratic capitalism. I do not claim that hierarchy itself exists exclusively in the Western world. India has its caste system, and African tribal groups have their own hierarchies of power. If anything, the Western world is just more honest about the whole thing. The point is simply that hierarchy is everywhere. Luciferans simply extend this concept all the way to God, and then offer the possibility that any one of us can climb all the way to the top, to become the "Executive of all executives".

Are capitalism and the socio-economic hierarchy Luciferan and therefore evil? In themselves, no: competition, predation, and the power hierarchy tend to elevate and celebrate the same personal qualities promoted in Luciferism, but that doesn't mean they are identical, any more than an agnostic's love and compassion for others means he is a Christian.

Many find hierarchical capitalism offensive; personally, I would rather be a member of a western democracy built on capitalism than any other society built on more "sublime" ideologies. I appreciate honesty, and I prefer reality over fantasy. But if the heart of Luciferism is that it has no heart, that it seeks power, control, and domination, that it sees compassion, empathy and love as impediments, that it devours and expands by absorbing the life of other beings, then Luciferism, not Christianity, resonates more deeply with the forces driving the modern socio-economic world.

Luciferans would say that capitalism works because Luciferan principles produce results: more power, growth, and dominance. Corporate executives purchasing and absorbing copies of such classics as Sun Tzu's *The Art of War* or Machiavelli's *The Prince*, or who enjoy more recent books such as Wess Roberts' *Leadership Secrets of Attila the Hun*, which celebrate predatory power acquisition as a joyful, real, noble and necessary pursuit, are certainly buying their share of Luciferan-like philosophy. As Michael Douglas' character, a predatory speculator and financier in the movie *Wall Street* says: "Greed is good. Greed is great." Such capitalists assert that they are just recognizing reality, that the world is as it is — a devouring hierarchy which rewards both personal and collective ruthlessness and selfishness. Luciferans would agree, and would heartily endorse such sentiments.

OTHER RELATIVES

Various other thinkers, writers, artists, and entertainers have articulated pieces of Luciferan psycho-spirituality. They cannot be considered Luciferan as defined here, nor can their work be classified as Luciferan. But aspects of their work resonate with the Luciferan impulse, and since the purpose of the chapter is to show that core elements of Luciferan ideology are not removed or remote from our history, culture, and perhaps even our destiny, I would like to look at some of these other "relatives" now.

NIETZSCHE AGAIN

No philosopher better articulates brute Luciferan ideology about power than Nietzsche. He writes beyond the *Superman* here, as described earlier, to penetrate deeply into the essence of Luciferan reality. His writings on competition, war, compassion, conscience, and power acquisition are astonishing, and could be included in any canon of Luciferan writings. I am not claiming that he is Luciferan or evil, simply that his writings are yet one more example of the osmotic proliferation of basic Luciferan ideology in our culture. Nietzsche speaks his mind clearly and directly, and so I will present his thoughts without commentary (all quotes are from Nietzsche's *Twilight of the Idols* and *The AntiChrist*):

> On Obtaining Power:— "What is good? — All that heightens the feeling of power, the will to power, power itself in man. What is bad? — All that proceeds from weakness. What is happiness? — The feeling that power increases — that a resistance is overcome."
> "Not contentment, but more power; not peace at all, but war."
> "I consider life itself instinct for growth, for continuance, for accumulation of forces, for power: where the will to power is lacking there is decline."
> On Competition and War:—"War has always been the grand sagacity of every spirit which has grown too inward and too profound; its curative power lies even in the wounds one receives."
> "And war is a training in freedom."
> "Freedom means that the manly instincts that delight in war and victory have gained mastery over the other instincts — for example, the instinct for 'happiness'."
> "The free man is a warrior."
> "What does not kill me makes me stronger."
>
> On conscience, compassion, and remorse:— "Remorse of conscience is indecent."
> "Every error, of whatever kind, is a consequence of the degeneration of instinct, disintegration of will: one has thereby virtually defined the bad. Everything good is instinct — and consequently easy, necessary, free."
> "Strong ages, noble cultures, see in pity, in 'love of one's neighbor,' in a lack of self and self-reliance, something contemptible."
> "One must be superior to mankind in force, in loftiness of soul — in contempt...." "What is more harmful that any vice? — Active sympathy for the ill-constituted and weak — Christianity."
> On Christianity:— "... and out of fear the reverse type [i.e. reverse of the "superman"] has been willed, bred, achieved: the domestic animal, the herd animal, the sick animal man — the Christian."
> "Christianity has taken the side of everything weak, base, ill-constituted; it has made an ideal out of opposition to the preservative instincts of strong life."

"Christianity is called the religion of pity — Pity stands in antithesis to the tonic emotions which enhance the energy of the feeling of life: it has a depressive effect. One loses force when one pities."

"The anti-natural castration of a God into a God of the merely good would be totally undesirable here. One has as much need of the evil God as of the good God."

SCHOPENHAUER

Will Durant called Arthur Schopenhauer's greatest work, *The World as Will and Idea*, "that great anthology of woe." Schopenhauer's philosophy was pessimistic, based on his observations that most human beings endure short lives of suffering, confusion, pain, and despair. He believed that the world was evil, and that it was driven by a force he called "Will."

Schopenhauer's *Will* is not the same as human will, but rather a restless, brutally indifferent and relentless force which intrudes into human life in the form of instincts, such as the desire to reproduce and to survive. This Will fills us with endless desires which we cannot hope to fulfill; hence we are left in a state of chronic unhappiness.

Schopenhauer's Will is close to *Powaqqatsi*. Here is how he describes it:—
"... the will must live on itself, for there exists nothing besides it, and it is a hungry will"... "Thus the will to live everywhere preys upon itself, and in different forms is its own nourishment, till finally the human race, because it subdues all the others, regards nature as a manufactory for its own use. Yet even the human race... reveals in itself with most terrible distinctness this conflict, this variance of the will with itself; and we find *homo homini lupus* (Man is a wolf to man)." In other words, all life competes with all other life, and predation — not love — is the dynamic driving all life forms.

The Will is absolutely indifferent to me, the individual. No loving God watches over me, nothing "out there" protects my interests. I am protected only to the extent that I can protect myself: Schopenhauer used to sleep with pistols beside his bed. Sexuality is a pernicious aspect of the Will which works on behalf of the species, but which is indifferent to the individual: "The sexual impulse is to be regarded as the inner life of the tree upon which the life of the individual grows, like a leaf that is nourished by the tree and assists in nourishing the tree; this is why that impulse is so strong, and springs from the depths of our nature... all this points to the fact that the life of the individual is at bottom only borrowed from that of the species... Death is for the species what sleep is for the individual...."

Life is therefore essentially evil as far as each individual is concerned, and is governed by a relentless Will which serves only its own interests. Luciferans agree with Schopenhauer's basic conception that life is driven by a cold, impersonal, and relentless Will which is absolutely indifferent to our suffering, and which only uses us as temporary vehicles for the propagation of the species. With a few minor additions and deletions, this is also the philosophical view of evolution presented by Richard Dawkins: "will" or "life" is everywhere at war with itself, and everywhere seeking its advancement. "Will" equals "nature", which in current terminology equals the force of evolution described by Dawkins and others as blind, cold, and absolutely indifferent to us.

Happiness, said Schopenhauer, only comes to those who are able to transcend the prison of Will and who are strong enough to reject its power and its impulses, including sex. Those able to accomplish this kind of transcendence can find peace: "Then all at once the peace which we were always seeking, but which always fled from us on the former path of the desires, comes to us of its own accord, and it is well with us. It is the painless state which Epicurus prized as the highest good and as the state of the gods; for we are for the moment set free from the miserable striving of the will."

Luciferans would disagree with Schopenhauer's method of escaping the prison of the will and finding peace, however, which was to transcend the Will through asceticism, compassion, and a deep appreciation of genius, art, and philosophy. Schopenhauer saw in Christ the actions of one who refused to participate in life dictated by the Will: as one who loved his enemies, who refused to fight, who refused to reproduce, and who even refused to save his own life. Luciferans argue the opposite, that transcendence can only occur by defeating the "Will" at its own game, by flowing with the Will and using its predatory essence to ascend the psycho-spiritual hierarchy to godhood and therefore achieve a state beyond the grasp of even the Will itself.

But Schopenhauer's basic vision of nature as a relentlessly nasty and evil force paradoxically parallels both the Christian vision of the "world" as an evil dominion dominated by Satan, and the modern scientific view of nature as the result of blind chance mutations absolutely indifferent to morality. Even his ideas about the power of sex predate Freud's, who could easily have been one of Schopenhauer's many disciples. The gloomy philosopher's ideas deeply influenced Nietzsche, and seem to have found a welcoming home in modern science.

In other words, his vision resonates with Luciferism, and can be considered yet one more close relative on the Luciferan "family tree".

THE FAUST LEGEND

Let us shift now from philosophy to art; specifically, to the Faust Legend. Marlowe's Doctor Faustus and Goethe's Faust warn about the apparent dangers of Luciferan power acquisition. Goethe's Faust is a doctor of great learning who believes he has mastered all human knowledge, yet who hungers for more power, higher potential, and deeper satisfaction. So he embraces the black arts, and soon signs a blood-bargain with the demon Mephistopheles who promises him untold knowledge, power, and god-like influence for a price: his eternal soul.

Says Goethe's Mephistopheles to Faust:

> "For you there is no boundary or measure," to which Faust replies: "I want to taste within my deepest self. I want to seize the highest and the lowest." "What am I," he adds, "if I can never hope to hold the crown of my humanity which is the aim of all my senses?"

What can be wrong with such a noble desire? In itself, perhaps nothing. But Mephistopheles makes clear his real intentions to one of Faust's students also seeking great knowledge and truth, and who tells Mephistopheles that he wants to "drink more deeply from your wisdom." Mephistopheles responds by writing the following passage: "You will be like God, knowing Good and Evil," and adds "Follow the ancient words and also my cousin the snake. That godlike spark in you will have you quaking soon enough."

Becoming God? Faust asks "Am I a god? The light pervades me so!" Faust wants more than human life. He laments that "the ecstasies that launched us on this life, congeal in the muddled business of living." He is disgusted by his human limitations. "I, the godhead's image, who thought myself close to the mirror of eternal truth" find instead that: "I am not like the gods — I feel it deeply now. I am the worm that burrows in the dust and, seeking sustenance in the dust, is crushed and buried by a casual heel."

Faust asks "Shall I obey my inward yearning?" He wants more of everything, especially power. Power is all. "It is written, 'In the beginning was the Word!'" ...yet adds that "The text should be 'in the beginning was the Power!'". Mephistopheles has been called, and he responds by offering Faust everything he wants.

But after obtaining everything he thought he wanted, Faust finds himself empty and lost, alone and damned, and so he desperately tries a last-ditch communion with the *Exalted Spirit*:

> "That nothing perfect falls to Man I know so deeply now. With all my bliss which brought me close and closer to the gods, you gave me the companion (Mephistopheles) which I now can no longer do without, though cold and insolent, he humbles me before myself, and with a single word he perverts your gifts to nothing. Untiringly he fans within my soul

a seething fire for that radiant image. So I plunge from lust to consummation, and in its throes I crave for lust."

The more Faust seeks godlike perfection, the more he curses that he has become welded "to this odious creature (Mephistopheles) that feeds on suffering and feasts on destruction." A chorus of invisible spirits sings in despair about his lust for godhood: "Woe! Woe! You have destroyed the lovely world with a heavy blow. It falls, it is shattered! Smashed by a demigod's fist."

Christopher Marlowe's Doctor Faustus is an earlier journey into the same territory.

Faustus says: "A sound magician is a demi-god! Here tire my brains to get (beget) a deity!" Faustus wants it all. He wants power, and knowledge. He says to himself: "The god thou serv'st is thine own appetite." Faustus wants power, all power. He wants to rule the world.

By "desperate thoughts against Jove's deity" he finally surrenders his soul ("had I as many souls as there be stars, I'd give them all for Mephostophilis") so that Mephostophilis will be forced "to give me whatsoever I shall ask, to tell me whatsoever I demand" and believes that "by him I'll be great emperor of the world."

Mephostophilis naturally has other plans, but encourages Faustus' power-lust, saying "And then be thou as great as Lucifer!" Mephostophilis is joined by an evil angel, who adds:

"Go forward, Faustus, in the famous art (magic)
Wherein all nature's treasure is contained.
Be thou on earth as Jove is in the sky,
Lord and commander of these elements!"

Faustus falls for the temptation, and so is damned. He is warned by a heavenly chorus, and told that he is tempting the edges of human possibility and power, but to no avail. He hasn't listened, and so is condemned. A heavenly chorus sings (somewhat gloatingly perhaps):

Till swoll'n with cunning, of a self-conceit,
His waxen wings did mount above his reach (like Icarus)
And melting, heavens conspired his overthrow! ...
Cut is the branch that might have grown full straight
And burned is Apollo's laurel bough
That sometime grew within this learned man.
Faustus is gone: regard his hellish fall,
Whose fiendful fortune may exhort the wise

Only to wonder at unlawful things
Whose deepness doth entice such forward wits
To practice more than heavenly power permits.

Luciferans laugh at such a fate:— if Faustus allowed himself to be imprisoned in an endless hell of pain and suffering at the hands of the archon "Jove", then this only proves his weakness, nothing more.

The Faust legend contains the key Luciferan idea of becoming god by climbing the power hierarchy. Both authors offer dire warnings about the horrible fate awaiting those who tempt the laws and limits of the heavenly Father. Luciferans might use this kind of threat to undermine competitors, but for them, Faust is noble, daring, human, vital, and alive. He is only staking claim on what is his, but God is jealous — Faust was just not strong or smart enough to avoid God's wrath.

The dangers of tempting God's wrath by pushing the limits of knowledge has been encoded in hundreds of schlock science fiction movies and novels, and can also be found in classics such as Frankenstein. The ingredients are stock: a mad scientist (i.e., Faust) goes into forbidden territory — bringing back the dead, obtaining superhuman powers, living forever, and so on. Like Icarus, he flies too close to the sun, and suffers the penalty. Or like Pandora's box, a new and lethal knowledge is opened and set loose on earth by his impudence, a knowledge that threatens to expel us from existence just as we were expelled from Eden. We always push too far, we humans, and we always pay the price for betraying God's limits and laws. We pay, say Luciferans, because God is afraid of us.

Marathon & Doom

Lets go now from the sublime worlds of philosophy and literature to the frenetic future world of video gaming. These worlds are not so far apart, at least from a Luciferan perspective.

Take the games *Doom* and *Marathon* as examples. Punch up the icon, and the screen opens. In both games, you view the screen as if it were your visor, as if the camera lens and your eyes viewed the same scenes. You are armed, and you have enemies. In *Marathon*, your job is to clear out evil aliens. You work your way through corridors, dark rooms, and hidden chambers. Aliens seek to kill you at every step. You gather weapons, ammunition, energy and special powers if possible. You kill them, or they kill you. If you kill enough of them — if you are a good predator — then you move to the next level of the hierarchy. Your enemies become more evil and powerful as you move up the hierarchy, and your predatory skills have to swell exponentially or else you will be annihilated. You use whatever weapons you can; you expect no mercy and are given none in return.

This ideology rages throughout the world of gaming, and can be found in even more concentrated form in various role playing games such as *Dungeons and Dragons*. It is a world of danger, deceit, and power acquisition. The entire point of such games — especially D&D and its spin-offs — is to acquire power exponentially, to obtain enough energy to overcome all obstacles and enemies.

Various parent watchgroups rigorously condemn such games, and seek to limit their availability. Luciferans would argue that such campaigns are useless because these games faithfully articulate the real game of life here on planet Earth:— rising up the hierarchy with predatory skill. The young know this truth instinctively, and are thrilled to have the opportunity to demonstrate their mastery of the predatory arts of killing, possessing, devouring, and tricking their enemies, even if only in play and imagination. These games are eternal, natural, and normal, say Luciferans, and accomplish what all play in the animal kingdom is designed to do: preparing the young ones for the real world. Limiting such play only limits children's predatory instincts and thus their human potential.

LUCIFER'S PRINCIPLE

Apparently I am not alone in my analysis of the widespread presence of Luciferan principles in our Western worldview. In the nine years it has taken to complete this work, I have never encountered another writer working on similar ideas, at least until now. In the summer of 1995, I found a copy of Howard Bloom's *The Lucifer Principle: A Scientific Expedition into the Forces of History*. I was enthralled. I was also surprised.

Bloom is not a scientist, but rather an entrepreneur who has run a PR firm for popular personalities like Prince, the Jacksons, Bette Midler, the Talking Heads, and others. He has written for *Rolling Stone* and *Omni*, for the *Village Voice, Cosmopolitan*, and the *New York Post*, and who is cited as having assisted with cancer research. He is not exactly an exalted figure in the scientific world, but his ideas are fascinating.

Despite its title, Bloom's book is not about Lucifer or Luciferan psycho-spirituality.

It is instead his vision of nature as a relentlessly vicious and competitive struggle, a vision which makes explicit what is implicit in our scientific worldview since the seventeenth century. The Lucifer principle, he says, "is a complex of natural rules, each working together to weave a fabric that sometimes frightens and appalls us." These rules, he says, are essentially evil: "nature does not abhor evil, she embraces it." In a statement invoking

Schopenhauer's spirit, he claims that Mother Nature is callously indifferent to life, creating endless streams of living pawns "who suffer and die to live out her schemes."

To overcome the Lucifer principle we need "to dismantle the curse that Mother Nature has built into us" because "evil is woven into our most basic biological fabric." He states that "we need to stare directly into Nature's bloody face and realize that she has saddled us with evil for a reason. And we must understand that reason to outwit her."

Bloom notes that "Lucifer, in fact, is Mother Nature's alter ego... For Lucifer is almost everything men like Milton imagined him to be. He is ambitious, an organizer, a force reaching out vigorously to master even the stars of heaven ... he is part of the creative force itself." In Bloom's mind Lucifer is of course only a metaphor; no such being actually exists. But Lucifer stands for a force that lurks coiled within our basic biological, historical, and cultural existence, a force which relentlessly rewards the most intelligently aggressive and vicious individuals, ideas (memes), or societies (which he calls superorganisms).

His book is a fascinating journey through apparently unrelated fields of study — everything from cultural history to ethnology. His basic idea is that all life and all manifestations of life, including human thought and culture, are based on *powaqqatsi* (he does not use this term, but it nevertheless summarizes the theme of his book).

Luciferans would agree with his analysis of 'the way things work in the real world', but would ridicule his suggestion that humans can somehow transcend "Mother Nature, the bloody bitch" by trying to "invent a way in which memes and their superorganismic carriers — nations and subcultures — can compete without carnage." There is no hope that "we may someday free ourselves of savagery" by creating "a world where violence ceases to be." We can never hope to "escape our fate as highly precocious offspring, as fitting inheritors of nature's highest gift and foulest curse, as the ultimate children of the Lucifer Principle."

Such escape, claim Luciferans, can only be found by following the Luciferan path. The only other alternative is death and extinction. Our only hope for survival is to embrace reality and merge with its vicious rhythms and cruel impulses because all else is illusion: Luciferans would point out that Bloom himself offers over three hundred pages to describe the "evil" state of things on planet Earth, but devotes a scant two pages at the end of his book to empty appeals for peace, perhaps because Schopenhauer was right in asserting that "our world afford no materials at all for this ... ."

There is no peace. There will never be peace, because peace and life are incompatible: peace can't be imagined because it is not possible. It is unnatural, as Luciferans would claim that Bloom himself has shown. Nature is Luciferan, and so is the entire universe.

Lyall Watson, author of *Supernature*, has written a more recent book *Dark Nature*, which like Bloom's *Lucifer Principle*, defines nature as the source of evil: Watson believes that we need to "see evil as a force of nature, as a biological reality," as something having "separate survival value and its own strange agenda."

Watson states, "I believe it will help to know that evil is commonplace and widespread, perhaps not even confined to our species." He adds, "Evil exists and seems to me to have sufficient substance to give it credence as a force in nature and as a factor in our lives. It is part of the ecology and needs to be seen as such."

Luciferans agree with him: Darwinian evolutionary selection is a relentlessly vicious and non-moral force which has encoded its selfish ruthlessness into the human animal.

Says Watson: "... as a biologist, I know that nature is basically relentless and unfeeling, with little in it to match the sympathy of a child who stops and takes the time to turn a beetle over on its feet. It's a jungle out there, a war very often of all against all ..." Watson then quotes the writer Annie Dillard, adding his own comments as well: "'The universe that suckled us,' rails Dillard, 'is a monster that does not care if we live or die.' And that too is true. Nature has little, in a moral sense, to commend it."

Strong words. And there are more like it. "Nature is morally bankrupt and stands condemned." Watson quotes other biologists and thinkers such as Edward Wilson, who he quotes as saying "I would concede that moral indifference might aptly characterize the physical universe. But for the biological world, a stronger term is needed." That term, adds Watson, is *evil*. He quotes the words of yet another thinker, George Williams, the "godfather of evolutionary biology": "Mother Nature is a wicked old witch," and "Natural selection really is as bad as it seems and that, as Huxley maintained, it should be neither run from nor emulated, but rather combated."

And so combat is what Watson goes on to recommend. Like Bloom, he asserts that the natural evil existing within us and passed to us genetically by our "selfish genes" has to be fought, *hard*. Our "dark nature" — the Other, the Enemy, the Beast — is within us, and we have to control it.

Our weapons are the ethical forces of conscience and compassion which, unlike our dark nature, are *unnatural*: we are caught by a "conflict between an old set of impulses which are, by design, very strong; and a new set of values which are, inevitably, unnatural." Watson argues that our genetic programming has encoded its dark nature within us, and that "What matters now is that the best we can do with our genetic programming, once it has done its job of getting us to the starting line, is to use it as a model of how not to run the race, or the species." The "enemy" is thus within us, and is us. We have to fight our "immoral, mindless genetic government," this "old genetic enemy" our Jungian shadow, which is "inevitably selfish, angry, jealous, lustful, greedy, suicidal and murderous; as well as infantile, emotional, vital, neurotic and creative in an unfocused sort of way." Our shadow, claims Watson, is also "dangerous, disorderly, fugitive, distasteful, sensual, stupid, and lacking in spirituality."

His strategy for fighting it? "We need to learn to love our differences." We need to "rise above nature." We need to create "an expanding web of trust, obligation, and affection." We need to find "balance" and "equilibrium", combining "just enough" goodness and badness to find the natural ecological balance. We need to "confirm the dark shadow" because "health lies in integrating good and evil" (he accepts and promotes the Jungian position on this). Because we are the children of a natural evolutionary process which is "completely amoral, devoid of empathy and long-term concern," we must fight for conscience and compassion, for something new, and different, and unnatural: "It is up to us to provide these moral qualities, to give life on Earth a *conscience*" (my emphasis). He concludes his book with: "The choice is ours. It is the capacity to choose that makes us special, giving us the ability to select a course for nature, instead of just submitting to the course of natural selection."

I do not want to argue either for or against Watson's position, but just point out that his vision of nature is purely Luciferan: nature is as Darwin described it, viciously competitive, amoral, indifferent. About this position there is no argument, either from Watson or from the other expert biologists he quotes. It is apparently accepted as fact, beyond discussion. Like Bloom, Watson feels that Mother Nature, our parent, is a "bloody bitch," and that we have to confront her with our moral arsenal or else submit to her pathological promotion of endless violence and brutality.

Luciferans would agree with Watson's analysis of the problem, but, of course, not with his solution. They would point out that, like Bloom and Milton and all the other fools who describe evil in loving detail but who become mute when trying to describe its opposite, Watson can only mouth hopeless platitudes that amount to little more than "be nice", "don't be nasty", "be moderate" and so on.

For Luciferans, this nonsense is exactly what Watson calls it, unnatural. Only Luciferism is natural and therefore real. Luciferans know that the Darwinian rules governing the natural world extend to all levels of reality, including the human and spiritual domains, and that encouraging compassion and conscience is fruitless. Watson promotes this nonsense because he is too cowardly to face reality as it is — as science has proven it to be. Watson's "solution" is impossible, impractical, and unreal. It won't happen because it can't happen.

Facing reality and truth is hard; only strong Luciferan warriors can stare into the abyss and survive. Only the Luciferan warrior faces the truth of the serpent beast within, not by combating it, but by embracing it, inviting it into human nature, and therefore making it smarter. The serpent — Watson's "enemy other" — is knocking on the door wanting in. The Luciferan simply opens the door and invites in the "intelligent serpent" to assume its rightful place in human nature so that humans can incorporate its truth and so evolve upward and outward to godhood itself.

Evil

The terms "Lucifer" and "evil" are welded in our culture; most of us, if asked to find a truly Luciferan "relative" in western culture, would turn to the concept of evil. As such, evil needs to be included here. But I include it reluctantly, for several reasons.

First, by calling Luciferism evil, we put it "out and away." It becomes something *not-me*, something foreign, ugly, and slimy. My purpose here has been to show the opposite, that it is "in-here-now" and is currently evolving in a natural way from our western heritage.

Second, I am not a philosopher or theologian, and the topic of evil leads in so many difficult and complex directions that I would be lost before taking the first step forward (as seems to have happened to many others over the centuries, including "experts" on the subject).

Thirdly, evil implies judgmental condemnation, and I have struggled to avoid taking a stand on the platform of the moral hierarchy, preferring instead to view Luciferism as it is, from the inside.

Having said this, I have to reluctantly concede that Luciferism and evil are related. I accept their correlation — but only by redefining evil. That is, evil and Luciferism can be considered related only if evil, as commonly understood, is given a new meaning.

Before examining this new meaning, however, I will first take a very brief look at some of the more common definitions of evil: their inability to capture the full essence of Luciferism will be obvious. I would like to spare us the joyless task of sorting through every historical definition of evil; Evil has had many faces, many interpretations. Here are a few to consider.

Evil has been understood as the smelly refuse of moral degradation (such as bizarre sexual activities); as anything hurting me or my kind; as political cruelty (Nazis, etc.); as criminal activity (especially serial killing); as sadism and cruelty, and so on. This is the territory of what philosophers call "moral evil" — evil that humans do. Most books outside the religious stream seem to describe evil in moral terms, as some horrifying act committed by apparently ruthless perpetrators. A "who's who" rogues gallery of morally evil perpetrators can be found in most of these books: Lt. Calley and the MyLai incident in Vietnam, Nazi atrocities, and serial killers are a few of the more common examples. Examples of books viewing evil in this way include *Facing Evil* (an outgrowth of Bill Moyers' PBS special), *Evil* (also based on a television production, from England), *The Roots of Evil* by Ervin Staub (an examination of genocide and group violence), and Peck's *People of the Lie*.

Evil has also been understood as disaster and destruction. The train wreck, the typhoon, illness, death: they all destroy. In its positive aspect, destruction "cleans up" history, making way for the new. In its darker aspect, it signifies destruction for its own sake: nihilism, anarchy, and destruction of order. Philosophically, destructive disasters and related events are called *natural evil*. In corporate insurance terminology they are called, strangely, *acts of God*.

Evil has been described a third way, as a necessary oppositional counter to good: no good exists without evil, and vice versa. Thus the Yin and the Yang are two equal forces that cannot exist without each other any more than *up* can be separated from *down* or *dark* from *light*. All living beings need evil in order to survive. In the end evil enhances our growth because it tests and strengthens us. This is the territory of what philosophy calls *metaphysical evil*. Mircea Eliade brilliantly explores this understanding of evil in his little book *The Two and The One*.

Metaphysical evil has also been conceptualized as a kind of force or entity deliberately limiting our growth, keeping us in sleepy ignorance, dominating us and directing our lives. This force, which is neither human nor natural, allegedly opposes true human growth and keeps us enslaved to greed, selfishness, and ruthless competition with one another so that we will remain blind to its power and unable to fight its impulse. Various belief systems describe this force or entity with different names: Satan, The Dark Lord, and so on.

Deviation from God's will (as defined by one religious group or another) is yet another example of Metaphysical evil: evil is defined as the willful disobedience of God's laws. Different Gods have different laws, so evil would also then vary in different cultural settings at different times. Needless to say, "God's Will" is often inextricably bound to prevailing cultural norms as defined by the current ruling elite: it may be evil to commit suicide in one culture, but applauded in another.

The relativity of moral standards across cultures and generations has led many recent thinkers to abandon any hope of finding one absolute standard of metaphysical evil. Recent attempts to deconstruct evil with the hammers of moral relativity and philosophical humanism have not solved the problem; on the contrary, we have been left more disoriented and confused than ever.

Carl Jung epitomizes the non-traditional psychological exploration of evil as the "shadow" within all of us, existing in the depths of the unconscious as repressed personal material or as repressed archetypes. The therapeutic community has marched into this traditionally religious territory with a few recent offerings, most notably Scott Peck's *People of the Lie*. But for one reason or another, most of us remain uncertain about therapeutic definitions of evil: Peck's perspective is Christian, but what criteria do other therapists use to categorize evil? Humanistic values? Therapeutic values? If so, why would one of them be any better than another? Why would we be inclined to passionately serve any one of them? Such "man-made" spiritualities usually fall flat against the religious imagination, like the idea of making love with someone who is at best uninteresting and at worst disgusting.

Add to this confusion the recent offerings by Bloom and Watson (*The Lucifer Principle* and *Dark Nature*), in which "Mother Nature," not Satan, seems responsible for evil, and the problem of evil remains the intellectual labyrinth it always has been.

Augustine's definition of evil as the absence of good — as a kind of void or darkness — and Hannah Arendt's well known phrase "the banality of evil" which she applied to faceless Nazi bureaucrats like Eichmann, simply spin the problem in different directions, and seem to satisfy no one.

Our ideas about evil fail to capture its essence. Yet we remain fascinated with evil. It seems real, close, vital, and powerful. We devour paperbacks by Clive Barker, Stephen King, and Dean Koontz to taste evil primally, directly. We rent horror and science fiction videos for the visual feast they provide. We want to know about evil because even though our logic and reason cannot wrap around it, our emotions and instincts easily accept its concrete reality because we experience it directly.

THE EXPERIENCE OF EVIL

Putting the experience of evil into words is difficult. An idea or image of evil is one thing, directly experiencing it another. In George Steiner's sense, the experience of evil is primal and hard to translate.

How do we translate the direct encounter of evil? It always seems so immediately concrete, specific and personal: my child is killed by a low-life murderer who enjoys killing; my friend's mother sobs quietly every morning when she stares at the scars from the concentration camp and mourns her husband.

To put it another way, how do we put the experience of good into words? Like evil, we sense that it is real, a force, something in its own right. But the imagination fails, and the words never surface.

We are trying to describe the evil thing in itself, as Kant would say, when maybe this is just not possible, as Kant would also say. Some things exist, but defy reason and sense, and mock both rationalistic and empirical explanations.

Kant is probably right about our limitations. Not only evil and good elude us, but just about everything else important to us as well, from love right through to hate. All we can do is refer to examples: we think of My Lai, or the Holocaust, or Ted Bundy or some other instance when evil seems present.

What do we experience? Perhaps revulsion, fear, horror, or stunned silence. How do we react? Maybe with outrage, anger, or demands for justice. But the experience itself?

It affects us in real ways, but we just cannot seem to capture it. I believe I have had my own direct experiences with evil. For me, evil feels old, extremely old. It carries a cold malevolence. It watches, and is interested in human life. It seems to enter into situations and individuals and transform them: I have felt evil in something as innocent as an offhand remark from someone I do not even know, and in something as vile as someone taking obvious pleasure in deliberate cruelty to an animal. My body reacts. Things feel slow, thick, and turgid, as if I was wrapped in something tightening. I know I am in the presence of evil, perhaps signaled distantly to me by an ancient sensory network almost atrophied.

I feel this kind of evil most powerfully when I am near certain types of human beings, but never when I encounter natural disasters or metaphysical thoughts about evil.

As mentioned in the introduction, I have tried to penetrate into the nature of this presence, and have found it to have something to do with being deceived, of being assaulted, of being devoured, of being possessed. It is the experience of being an object in the eyes of your devourer, of being nothing but food for her power lust, of having no other worth or purpose in her eyes. It is the experience of being reduced to your component parts, like the slowly turning wooden cases decorated with body parts in Clive Barker's movie series, *Hellbound*.

From this experience, I have developed the following definition of evil. It may confuse things further, or it may clarify and cleanse the problem of evil for you as much as it has for me.

Evil is defined here as the deliberate, conscious, and rational choice to kill compassion, conscience, empathy, and love in order to obtain ultimate power.

A personal transformation necessarily follows this choice, because a new human is born. This new being is utterly different from the old, and is driven by a radical alteration of deep internal core beliefs, motives, and intentions.

As defined here, evil is a choice, an action of deliberate inner transformation, what Kant calls radical evil. Behaviors which flow from this choice may bring benefit or harm to others (as is probably true for all human beings no matter how noble, compassionate, or loving), so evil is not found in consequences: evil resides in the source and not the outcome, the cause and not the effect.

Augustine described evil as the void of good, as a negative or non-existent result of the absence of love, which for him equaled the absence of God. But as defined here, evil is the choice to willingly enter into the domain of no-love, a region not characterized by an absence or a void, but rather by the swelling euphoria of powaqqatsi. Evil is not a lack of, but a choice of and movement toward, a different way of being.

As such, evil is distinctly human. As far as I understand the animal kingdom, even predators do not make a conscious choice to kill compassion and conscience: they simply make the instinctive choice to survive. Evil is possible for us because we are cognitively capable of imagining the possibility of extending our natural powers of violence, possession, and devouring to unknown limits — all the way to godhood. The lynx is not evil when it rips apart a snowshoe hare even though violence, possession, and devouring are all present.

Evil therefore cannot be seen in actions disconnected from intentions. The Luciferan's support for a worthy charity is radically other than the same support offered by a person of good intentions and honest compassion. The charity may use both donations for good or ill — the charity might be a scam, it might honestly provide food for the poor, it might purchase arms for an apparently noble counter-revolutionary force, it might keep an innocent impoverished child alive who grows up to become a vicious criminal or dictator — any number of permutations can flow from two very different motivations. But the evil exists at the source, not the outcome. Evil is within, not without.

Human evil seems to inevitably violate the natural balance of things, even though it seems, like Luciferism, to be grounded in natural principles. If this balance is understood as the equal giving and taking of energy for survival (in the sense that plants provide food and oxygen to mammals, while mammals spread seeds, carbon dioxide, and nutrients for plants), then the choice for evil is the intention to tip the balance:— to take, but not give back. Evil can be understood as *powaqqatsi* without the willingness to eventually give oneself up to be devoured as well, to offer back something to those who have given their lives up for the sake of your life. Evil always takes in, endlessly expanding its possessive power. It never gives back, never gives out, and never gives in.

True evil rips open the natural order of things. It is always conscious, deliberate, knowing, and cold. As Watson indicates, it is life out of balance, or as the Hopi call it, *Koyaanisqatsi*. Historically, when any one life form or civilization has claimed to have achieved ultimate power, the natural world has responded with disease, new predators, and a host of other enemies to limit and even destroy the usurper. Truly malignant evil human beings, however, seek to eliminate any such impediments, limitations, or enemies. They seek to transcend the limits of the natural world. They seek a total freedom of will not available to any other natural life form.

This definition of evil fits with Luciferism. Defined this way, and provided that other definitions of evil don't intrude, then evil and Luciferism are compatible relatives. Used as defined here, evil applies to Luciferans. Used in some of the other cultural, historical, and religious ways described above, it does not, at least not directly.

Luciferans themselves would accept their association with evil, provided again that its meaning is restricted to the definition above. But they would have much more to say about the experience of the inner transformation that evil implies. For Luciferans, evil is not Augustine's empty void, but something more vital, real, and alive, something that energetically annihilates the sickly emotions of love and pity, remorse and guilt. Evil is understood as that force or power entering true Luciferans who make the necessary sacrifices. It is life itself, Schopenhauer's Will, the force that animates all known existence. They see it as the actual essence of life, empowerment, and evolutionary will. Unlike its weak opposite abstraction good, evil is easy to understand and embrace because it is real, solid, and alive.

Do Luciferans rip open the order of things? Are they truly "life out of balance" because they take but never give? They certainly attempt the ultimate imbalance: one life absorbing and controlling all others by becoming God. And yet Luciferans themselves would claim that they are only following the natural order of things, pursuing power up the hierarchy to its God-apex. They would claim that their pursuit is natural, balanced, ordered and logical — and therefore ecologically sound. They would also add that the destruction of conscience and compassion are natural aspects of normal human growth, like losing baby teeth or growing pubic hair. For Luciferans, evil does not exist as an empty concept or void, but as the vitally living dynamic of power acquisition. For them, the order of things is ripped open by love and its sick derivatives, not by *powaqqatsi*. For them, evil is desirable, while good is repulsive.

So why do some humans choose the Luciferan bargain and adopt evil? I personally don't believe that the choice has anything to do with "nature or nurture" controversies. Such a choice cannot be encoded in the genetics of a child, nor can it be imposed in a child's mind because of upbringing. Evil is not the child with brain abnormalities or the infant born into a home of abusers and therefore patterned to repeat the abuse in adulthood. Some children may be born with "bad genes" or "bad parents", but I believe that each and every one of them has a choice to either amplify the "bad" or combat it.

A child raised in a brutal home may become part of a cycle of abuse, and as an adult may perpetrate the same brutality. This is not evil. This is simply ignorance. The same child, however, who through some means is permitted to understand his cycle and who then proceeds to consciously enjoy it anyway, steps toward evil.

By definition, those who make the choice for evil are always aware of their choice. Their decision is purposeful, and calls for the deliberate destruction of all capacities designed to restrict their predatory abilities. This means, again by definition, that they must have experienced compassion and conscience in order to fully, consciously, and deliberately destroy them. Luciferans celebrate this destruction, and invite others to kill everything restrictive within them to fulfill the bargain for power.

THE LUCIFERAN BARGAIN

I work with children whose violent behavior seems to demand analysis: "go ahead," they seem to say, "figure me out. Make my day. I dare ya." My temptation is to believe that through "analysis", or "psychology", I will be able to understand them and therefore "fix" them.

So legions of people-mechanics like me try to figure them out. One says, "they had bad parents." Another says, "they have bad genes," or "they have bad brain wiring." Yet another says, "bad society made them this way." I long ago tired of this, and yet I still keep at it, like the rat who keeps pressing the bar in his cage even though the food pellets no longer roll out magically like they used to. I think: "if only I can understand the cause, I can change the result." I think: "if I keep at it long enough, the truth will set the child free." And so the analysis game continues, like Sisyphus pushing his rock up the hill.

I face the same temptation with the human dynamics surrounding the Luciferan bargain. I want to believe that I can "figure it out" — that is, reduce it to its component parts, and therefore weaken its impact. But I personally do not believe in this kind of reductionistic analysis any more, so I will try to avoid the analytic temptation and offer instead a few brief observations (perhaps laced with just the slightest tinges of analysis).

Evil begins with an invitation. The invitation is sent out when conscience and compassion are betrayed. Their destruction creates a vacuum. Evil then fills it. This is the meaning of the Luciferan bargain — the destruction of conscience and compassion in exchange for power. Power then becomes possible — evil inevitable.

When life becomes overwhelming, the Luciferan bargain becomes more and more attractive. Early childhood abuse, deprivation, pain, suffering, loss, sorrow, failure, loneliness, emptiness, fear, confusion, guilt, remorse: all of these human experiences demand a choice. The choice is simple: do I take the suffering and the pain, or do I shut it off? If I take it, then I become responsible for changing it, for learning from it, for making sure that I don't pass it on to people around me or to my children. I suffer, but I don't inflict others with my suffering. I don't dig for sympathy, I don't display my pain for gain, I don't whine or swim in self-pity. I choose not to be twisted by my suffering. Instead, my pain becomes a friend, something to guide my compassion and conscience: I know what suffering is and what it does, and so my empathy swells to a strength that would never permit me to inflict pain, abuse, and suffering on other beings.

If on the other hand I refuse to take the pain, then I will deny or repress it. This usually means becoming numb. The pain is compartmentalized and repressed. It simmers below consciousness, threatening to erupt, and it drains energy and cripples the full spectrum of emotional life. Drugs, alcohol, addictions, and other escapes mask this withdrawal. Such repression and denial are commonly encountered by therapists and healers, and are probably the most common causes of emotional illness and despair.

Luciferans also refuse to take the pain, but they make a different bargain. They do not deny their pain. Instead they choose to inflict pain and suffering on others before it can be inflicted on them. To do this they commit an act of emotional surgery. They cut away that which normally prevents such cruelty: conscience and compassion. They sacrifice their moral and emotional lives for the temptation of obtaining power over the horror of suffering, pain, and weakness.

They do this because the experience of suffering horrifies them. Suffering means failure, powerlessness, and loss of freedom. Suffering is like being devoured as prey. Suffering is for losers, not victors. The powerful inflict suffering on the weaker, and those ahead in the hierarchy cause the lower to suffer. Power is the ability to inflict pain and suffering on other beings through devouring, possession, and manipulation. We either inflict pain or we have it inflicted on us. For a Luciferan there is no other choice.

Suffering itself is a signal of loss, humiliation, and weakness. If not prevented, then suffering drains power and energy. The only way to regain this loss is to steal energy from other beings. And the only way to do this is to inflict pain: as the victim suffers, the Luciferan draws strength and energy from the suffering. Energy is thus devoured and possessed, and the cruelty required to cause the suffering deepens the Luciferan bargain by cutting and sacrificing yet more compassion and conscience.

Once the bargain is accepted — once a person agrees to kill conscience and compassion to have power over suffering — then a cycle begins. Suffering is reduced, but it demands a price to keep silent. This price is simple: inflict suffering on others. The more others suffer, the less suffering and pain the perpetrator will feel. A kind of euphoria or ecstasy replaces personal suffering and pain: the more pain is inflicted on others, the more the perpetrator feels power, strength, life, and joy. Like any other such bargain, however, more and more is required as time goes on. For the alcoholic, more alcohol; for the drug addict, more heroin; for the Luciferan;— more violence, possession, and devouring. The cycle may begin with the desire to kill personal suffering and pain, but always ends with an escalating need to inflict it on others. Ultimately, true Luciferans seek to transcend even this escalating need for more power, killing, devouring, and possessing by gathering just enough energy to launch them into godhood. In this way they hope to transcend everything, including their response to suffering.

Luciferans embrace this bargain as a spiritual quest. If Buddhists try to rise above suffering by stoically transcending it, and Christians by loving it, then Luciferans attempt to eliminate suffering by killing it and replacing it with euphoric sensations of power and *powaqqatsi*.

The bargain invites what I am calling evil, because evil thrives in the void created by the destruction of conscience and compassion. Evil is therefore intensely personal, because only individuals can make the choice to invite it.

THE FINAL CHOICE: PURE EVIL

I do not know how to communicate the nature of pure evil in any cosmic, religious, or transcendent context. The more we extract, analyze, and abstract it from actual human choice, the thinner and more remote it becomes. Great religious and philosophical cosmologies have placed it solidly in one infinitely expansive scheme or another with grandly sweeping concepts and mighty words. I cannot vouch for any of them, and prefer instead to take a thoroughly pragmatic philosophical position. My experience is that the further we move from the individual's choice, the more remote evil becomes. Individuals seem to be carriers of evil: individuals might then be considered as the interface between the ultimately mysterious force of evil and human existence.

This suggests that evil transcends humans, that it exists as some kind of force which enters those who have made the ultimate sacrifice and bargain. If it exists independently of human beings — that is, if it enters individuals who make the Luciferan bargain, and is something other than this bargain, as is suggested in myth and religion — it exists beyond my comprehension. I have only experienced it intuitively: in this I agree totally with J. B. Russell, who also believes that pure evil can only be directly experienced and directly intuited because it transcends other methods of capture.

I do know, however, that once conscience and compassion are totally eradicated, then the Luciferan bargain is complete. This is perhaps what our ancestor's called *loss of soul*, a condition that seems as real as evil itself.

The *soul-lost* state is poorly understood. Individuals choosing it are not always easy to discern, because their bargain may have resulted in success, prestige, wealth and immense influence. The decision to serve evil is thus also a spiritual choice, having little to do with psychological pathology, bad upbringing, or an "oppressive society." Sophisticated Luciferans are infinitely more dangerous than those pursuing simple human depravity.

They have become transformed, and have left human nature behind. Evil brings something new to its followers, something spiritual. It transforms by inviting its own kind of rebirth.

THE TENACITY OF ENTRENCHED EVIL

Once invited, evil is hard to eradicate. First, it has momentum. Like any other habit, the more we choose it, the more likely we are to choose it again — Carl Goldberg (in his book, *Speaking with the Devil: Exploring Senseless Acts of Evil*) articulates his vision of how individuals gradually forge an evil personality through the momentum created by a series of small concrete choices over time. The momentum carries itself, and builds energy over time: the more we seek to kill conscience and compassion today, the more likely we are to make the same choice tomorrow. This seems as true for alcohol and drugs as for evil.

Second, the more we choose evil — that is, the more we allow conscience and compassion to wither — the weaker these voices become. Conscience and compassion have to be invited, used and exercised in order to grow, otherwise they atrophy. The very force needed to reverse the Luciferan bargain is therefore weakened.

Because the original choice for evil might have meant flight from pain and suffering, a third reason that evil is hard to fight becomes clear: in order to erase the evil and re-energize compassion and conscience, we have to face the original pain. This becomes harder and harder the longer we delay. The repressed pain is literally demonized; what was hard to face initially becomes monstrous ten or twenty years later.

Therapists from Freud onward have known this, and their healing methods have been designed to lance the malignant poison of repressed pain. Those who have chosen the Luciferan path but want to reverse their steps therefore have to fight the momentum and growing strength of evil within them, while at the same time realizing that success only means opening themselves to the original horror they refused to handle. Added to this is the realization that the forces needed to overcome it all — compassion, conscience, and warmth — are weak. The individual is easy prey for despair, depression, fear, and hatred, and therefore to a reinvocation of the Luciferan bargain.

As if this wasn't enough, a fourth problem seems to emerge: the evil comes to life within. I say "seems to emerge" because I am not entirely certain, and am only describing my own personal experience with evil individuals. Something other than a void seems to enter such people, something I have felt and intuited but not seen or touched. The Luciferan bargain seems to be a kind of birth: as conscience and compassion die, something else replaces them. This something else seems to be alive: the Luciferan choice seems to create a non-physical life form which struggles for survival like all other life forms. This probably feels absurd to some readers. But if true, then not only does the Luciferan individual have to face her weakened state and original pain, but she also has to cope with the momentum of a malignant life form fighting for its own survival within. This life form, or energy, or whatever it is, appears to operate with intelligence and deliberation, to actively prevent its destruction, and to insist on pursuing the quest for absolute godhood.

Such a life form would seem to counter my contention that the choice for evil is free, deliberate, conscious, and rational. That is, it seems to shift responsibility from the chooser to the new life form itself. But remember that the choice for evil — the Luciferan bargain — is a transformative event. The human becomes trans-human, or unhuman, inhuman, superhuman, or subhuman, depending on one's point of view. A new life force or form enters, and an old one leaves. In this sense the decision may be irrevocable, like the choice to amputate a limb or the act of killing another human being. Something is lost that can never return. But the initial choice is always conscious; we are all free to choose or not choose the Luciferan bargain.

Finally, the tenacity of evil is compounded by a simple fact of human life: we begin to love that which we choose and with which we become familiar. We become attached to it, secure in it. Even if we find the strength to overcome

344

its momentum and its survival strategies, even if we can rediscover the compassion and conscience we sought to kill, and even if we can face the original horrors we ran from, we still have to encounter our love of, and attachment to, the life we have created.

This is similar to the strange phenomenon of multiple personality: patients actually come to love and cherish some of their created personalities, even those which bring pain, confusion, and destruction to the patient's life. Whatever else the metaphysical purpose and origin of the Luciferan's "evil child" might be, it is, after all, a child. The Luciferan invited it and gave it a home. More than that, the Luciferan agreed to sacrifice his own emotional and moral existence to enable the transformation — the birth of a new life — to occur. The Luciferan simply does not want his old life back, no matter what regrets might later surface.

For all these reasons — and probably more than I am able to conceive — the Luciferan bargain is seldom, if ever, reversed. Once the contract is signed and the deal complete, evil entrenches itself tenaciously within its host.

RECOGNIZING EVIL INDIVIDUALS

Those who accept evil know themselves. They recognize themselves, but are also recognized by those who have consciously refused to embrace evil. Human history has been defined by those who accept evil. It has also been defined by those who have not.

We sense evil only obliquely, darkly, from an angle. Its essence is as mysterious as love, life and existence itself. Yet we can come to know it in the same way we come to know any spiritual reality: we can know it through those who serve it, those it inhabits. These are easy words. But Luciferans are not going to proclaim themselves openly. Like all predators, they thrive on camouflage, hunting skill, and protean disguise. They will never willingly reveal themselves. Despite this, I have come to accept certain ideas about the nature of people embracing evil, those I call Luciferans. Some of these beliefs are obvious and self-evident, others are not.

To summarize the nature of Luciferans: first, their emotions are dead, although they can mimic real feeling at will. Second, they do not follow standard moral codes, although they pretend to. Third, they never feel guilt or remorse about anything they have done, although they may mimic these emotions for effect. Fourth, they are predatory parasites: they draw energy from other human beings without reciprocity, without giving anything in return. They prey on other humans for survival just as we prey on lower forms of animal and plant life. Fifth, they believe that they represent the birth of a new trans-human order, the outcome of an evolutionary leap. They understand

and consciously accept this transformation. Luciferism is not just a new ideological belief system; it reflects the real and substantial evolution of a new life form, which is now, or soon to be, in active competition with existing human forms.

By the definition above, this new life form is "evil"; Luciferans would argue that their resonance with other relatives of our Western traditions guarantees its emergence and survival in the next century. Luciferans would submit that their way of being completes the evolution of Western culture in the new millennium.

LUCIFERISM 2000; LUCIFERAN SURVIVAL

Luciferans assert that they are appearing as a new survival prototype to cope with society and civilization in the twenty-first century — in other words, that the Luciferan mode has Darwinian survival-value for the new millennium.

If Western intellectual and practical culture already echoes basic Luciferan impulses and resonates with core aspects of Luciferan thought as described above, then I can only assume that this identification will become more public and open and that it will emerge from the darkness in the same way that Freud opened the doors on sexuality or Darwin on our animal origins. If this occurs, then Luciferism (or something similar with a different name) will become a religion in the next century because it will be best adapted to the world we have created.

This socially constructed world of ours, at least as I have come to understand it, welcomes and rewards the Luciferan style. In Darwinian terms, it favorably selects Luciferans, because in addition to all the points of correspondence between our intellectual culture and Luciferism mentioned so far, the western world also treasures and embraces the following elements, all of which suit Luciferan needs: rapid change, broken connections, numbing, moral relativity, narcissism, existential freedom, appearance over substance, and rabid competition.

These "Luciferan social trends" all resonate with basic Luciferan beliefs and behavior, thus encouraging Luciferan "fitness." They also allow Luciferans the freedom of easy predation. These are fat times for Luciferans, and if these trends continue to deepen their hold on Western thought and action, then Luciferans will prosper and swell with success.

RAPID CHANGE AND BROKEN CONNECTIONS

It is a truism of our times that everything changes, all the time. New inventions, new material goods, new friends, new husbands or wives, new managerial theories, new governments: we are the people of the change. All is in flux, nothing is ever certain, little is predictable. The word "new" is an advertising icon, possessing a positive spin of its own, implying an automatic improvement on everything before it.

But constant change is scary, and so we reach for the unchangeable, for that believed to be true and permanent for all time. We feel powerless and victimized by the massive forces of change as the new millennium approaches. We try to grab onto something permanent, but it usually twists from grasp and transforms into something not expected and not wanted. And so we feel lost.

Luciferism offers answers. Focus on self, gather power, become strong, mold reality until it holds still, grab it and hang on until it knows that a God is present. Make it become still, make it revolve around me, not the reverse. And while reality is thus being shaped, the Luciferan can move, flow and writhe in sync with Protean flexibility and malleability. The Luciferan believes that she can become the center of the universe, and so can make the constant turmoil of rapid change come to an end. By becoming the eye of the hurricane, the Luciferan aspires to control the reality-swirl first by riding its predatory external winds, and then by taking command of its center, the source of all life.

Connections are breaking everywhere. Families are fracturing. Old allegiances are dying. Fault lines are opening along racial, cultural, linguistic, and sexual lines. Connections with ancient and revered cultural beliefs, traditions, and institutions are eroding. Broken connections are so clearly evident in modern life that, like constant change, we now take them as normal and inevitable.

And that is exactly the point: broken connections are inevitable — even normal and natural — in our minds. But how many broken connections can we be expected to endure?

We know from research on early childhood that children who suffer a string of broken bonds, first with their parents and then with a series of foster parents, eventually give up. They become numb. And why not? Why invest the intense emotional energy of trust and commitment to yet one more relationship doomed to fail? This is likely true as well for adults who swing from one relationship to another. After a while, why bother? Why surrender to trust and love when the only result is pain and disappointment?

Why not just get cold on the whole thing? Why not take control over the pain, and refuse to commit to the self-destructive legacy of love and trust? Why not just shut down? Kill love, and compassion, and all the painful emotions associated with them? In other words, why not take the Luciferan option? It is easier, safer, and more reliable. It works, because it eases the pain of helplessness and promises control. It also accepts the inevitability of the loneliness and abandonment that are the legacy of broken connections: it says that you are alone and will always be alone because such is the destiny of all gods and those who aspire to godhood. Luciferism turns the tragedy of broken connections — helplessness, loneliness, and futility — into an intoxicating offer of power, noble destiny, and absolute redemption from suffering.

The Luciferan answer to broken connections? Do not make them in the first place. Kill the part of you that needs connecting to others, and then take predatory advantage of others' weakness, which is their inability to transcend their need to connect. Become so strong that broken connections will never again have the power to weaken or harm you. And then learn to move rapidly from one connection to another, coming in and out of relationships with other people, organizations, or belief systems without the impediments of regret, remorse, or conscience, always the winner in every energy exchange, always stronger but never ever truly connected. Like Proteus, flow from one scene to the next, and never endow the scenes with anything other than their potential for power acquisition.

Broken connections then become irrelevant, meaningless, and spiritually transcended through the Luciferan choice.

Numbing

Rapid change and broken connections create stress, and if the stress becomes too great then something snaps. Something gives way, and the person's normal emotional processes change. A kind of numbness sets in to distance the sufferer from further suffering. Lifton calls this psychic numbing. Psychiatry has many names for it, including post-traumatic stress disorder, and every one of us knows something about this state. Just remember the time when everything seemed too much, too overwhelming, too extreme, perhaps during a family crisis of some kind, or some other cumulation of extreme stress.

The state can be considered the emotional equivalent of the medical shock that follows serious physical injury: the emotional being has been injured, and gathers all its resources and energies into a concentrated inner core as a defensive measure, just as the body gathers its resources around key internal organs during severe blood loss.

During this state we become listless, disorganized, unable to think or feel. Little problems become immense, and immense problems are ignored. Pavlov called this the paradoxical phase of inhibition in his stress experiments with dogs: when the animal finally determines that its situation is unwinnable, it simply folds up and retreats. It shuts down. And so do we.

Too much bad news, too many rapid changes and broken connections beyond our control, and we want to give up. We want to shut down. We want the uncontrollable pain to go away. In other words, we are already moving toward the Luciferan bargain.

Luciferans naturally despise the weakness implied by numbing, the shutting down of resistance and the giving up of control. True Luciferans believe that no force on earth could ever cause them to numb their warrior spirit. Perhaps they are correct, perhaps not. But numbing itself could very well be a prelude or push toward the Luciferan bargain: if we feel this kind of de-energized hopelessness and fatigue for long enough, some of us are bound to fight for recovery. And once recovered, some would search for any form of protection or strength to prevent a recurrence. Some would deeply desire to shut down all receptivity to emotional trauma, loss, regret, and guilt. Some would therefore joyfully embrace the Luciferan bargain.

MORAL RELATIVITY

Rapid change, broken connections, and numbing would perhaps be less devastating if we had some kind of inner resource to depend upon. This resource would tell us what do, how to react, how to understand and transcend the shock. It would inform us about right and wrong responses, and help us interpret the pain.

But no such standard remains. For most of us, ours is the age of uncertainty, of moral relativity. No absolutes remain, and so we feel lost.

Perhaps these absolutes were only shams all along, pleasant fallacies and fantasies invented by us out of ignorance and weakness, nothing but an "opiate for the masses" as Marx called them. But their truth value is not the point here; their functional value was what counted. For they provided a moral point of reference, and a compass to guide us toward that point where truth and beauty were believed to dwell.

Our loss of this moral center has been no less earth-shaking than our discovery that the earth is not the center of the universe. We simply do no know how to respond. We are lost.

We are told that one lifestyle is equal to all others, that truth is relative to culture, race, gender and any number of other factors. We are told that truth is relative to the perceiver, that no truly objective truths exist, that no absolute guide to moral behavior can ever exist. The only objective truths we allow are those claimed by science, which accepts only naturalistic, materialistic, reductionistic, and deterministic philosophical positions. We are locked into two possibilities: accept the nothingness of relativity, or the nothingness of a material universe created by chance and accident without purpose or direction.

And so we fall back on whatever we can find. Many of us retreat to a kind of extreme Emersonian position where we set our own standards according to the sacred divinity which is our own personal nature. Says Emerson: "Nothing is at last sacred but the integrity of your own mind ... No law can be sacred to me but that of my nature. Good and bad are but names very readily transferable to that or this; the only right is what is after my constitution, the wrong what is against it." In other words, morality is what I determine it to be by measuring it against my nature, my sacred self.

And thus some of us incline toward personal godhood, which is the ultimate destiny of Luciferism. Luciferans simply promote radically different means of getting there, ways which suit the *animus* of our times and the spirit of the West.

NARCISSISM

Following Christopher Lasch's book *The Culture of Narcissism*, individualism took on a pejorative spin in the minds of many Westerners: the grand nobility of Emerson's self-reliance and rugged individualism devolved into the shallow self-indulgence of superficial narcissism. Lasch describes the degraded banality of the modern self, emotionally shallow, plastic, and without depth, "perpetually unsatisfied, restless, anxious and bored." The narcissist has not penetrated the depths of self but instead "it is their very psychic selves that have gone numb." The narcissist is "unappeasably hungry for emotional experiences with which to fill an inner void," and yet often display a "protective shallowness in emotional relations." Lasch feels that this narcissistic style "appears realistically to represent the best way of coping with the tensions and anxieties of modern life."

If Lasch is even partially correct, that "new social forms require new forms of personality," then I would suggest that our social world requires traits associated not only with narcissism, but also with the Luciferan personality style. Narcissism is, according to Lasch, a "flight from feeling." Luciferism offers the same escape.

But Luciferism also differs. Instead of running from the "void within," the Luciferan says to the narcissist: put your Self in the center of the void, and make the void over into your own image.

Luciferism offers a practical solution to the narcissist; one she can understand because it starts from familiar territory, from the terrifying experience of self loss and emotional numbing to a self-ness which is still nevertheless self-centered: the narcissist can be invited to conclude the journey of selfish-ness and take it to its logical conclusion, which is Luciferan godhood. Luciferism has the potential to take the civilized narcissist far beyond her inconsequential and pathetic self-centeredness into a true Self-Centeredness. Thus Luciferism appeals to the narcissism of our era as much as to its psychopathology: the narcissist will be as intrigued by Luciferism as the psychopath.

EXISTENTIAL FREEDOM: FACING THE VOID

Moral relativity and scientific materialism have, along with atheism, destroyed the beliefs that used to nourish us. Only physical matter is real, and only chance and randomness shape us. There is no meaning to our existence. There has been no universal designer, and we are not loved. The universe could care less about us. We have no purpose; we come into life from dark nothingness, and return to nothingness after death.

We are surrounded by the void: look up, and it is there, look down and it is there, look in or look out, and it is there, it is everywhere. We are orphans in an indifferent universe. The molecular biologist and Nobel Prize winner Jacques Monod put it this way: "The ancient covenant is in pieces; man knows at last that he is alone in the universe's unfeeling immensity, out of which he emerged only by chance."

The scientists who have given us this wonderful gift of "truth" do not seem to care about its impact. As deliverers of "objective reality" they seem as coldly indifferent to us as the universe they describe. So just how are we supposed to digest their truth? How are we supposed to respond to the relentless coldness of the positivistic universe?

Existentialism is one way. Ours can be called the age of existential despair, perhaps the first era to truly explore life without God or any other comforting spiritual force. Sartre describes existentialism as "nothing else than an attempt to draw all the consequences of a coherent atheistic position." God is dead, says Nietzsche, and yet we go on living. Our lives exist against the reality of the dark void, the nothingness from which we came and to which we will return. Nothing guides us, rules us, or owns us. We are absolutely free: we first exist, and then we define ourselves afterwards. We are not defined in advance: "existence precedes essence" is the slogan used by existentialists to summarize the unconditional and absolute freedom of human nature. Being free, we are also totally responsible for ourselves. We choose what we are to be, and by our choices we define ourselves for good or bad. This awful responsibility is dreadful, but we are condemned to live it. Despair is inevitable because the void is as absolute as our absolutely isolating freedom. There are no gods, there is only me and the void I face.

Luciferans agree emphatically with the idea of existential freedom: I am primal, I am absolute, and only I can create my own meaning within the boundlessness of my own freedom. For Luciferans, this means that we are all absolutely free to extend our freedom to godhood.

Luciferans disagree with existentialist morality, which is nothing more than the extrapolation of Christian-like weakness, and which can only handicap the true warrior-hero who has the guts to face the void. The dark void exists, but so what? It can be transcended, but only by those strong enough to emulate our coldly efficient universe and become even colder, harder, tougher, and more *real*. Only power is real, and only power acquisition is real. The answer to existential despair? Get tough and fight back. Don't whimper in supplication to some higher order predator you think is a God; don't hide in addictions or repressions; don't stir in despair like some kind of negativity junkie. Get tough. Get real. Fight, and fight hard against the void until it gives in to your will.

For Luciferans, existentialism is a step in the right direction, because for existentialists, everything is possible and nothing is restricted. As Dostoevsky has one of his characters in *The Brothers Karamazov* state: "But you see, if there were no God, everything would be possible!" But because there is no god there are no rules or limits except those we accept in weakness. If we are, as the Existentialists assert, absolutely limitless and free to transcend every limit placed before us, then the only possible endpoint of our limitless transcendence is the state of godhood. And the only way to get there is to follow the good advice of that nascent Luciferan Nietzsche: get tough, kill the pity, live like a man and a warrior, and invoke the Superman. For Luciferans, existentialism fits. It does not cause despair, but joy; Luciferans are beautifully equipped to live in the existentialist universe.

PROTEAN APPEARANCE OVER SUBSTANCE

Western culture is infatuated with appearances. Appearance is everything, substance little. Physical beauty, wealth, intelligence, success, and status are all on display. I am a commodity for sale, and my selling value depends on my appearance. Politicians obey this truth or they perish. We know who they are by what they display; and I know who you are only by what you show me, by how you appear.

A whole tradition in psychology, behaviorism, is built around this fundamental idea: I can never know you except by your behavior, by how you appear to me. Your appearance is everything. And since appearances are so fluid — aging, clothing, makeup, hobbies, work, experience, and training can all change how you appear to me — then you are always going to be fluid to me. You are always changing, always in flux, never permanent. All is protean, all is surface. Appearance matters more than substance, because your substance can only be communicated to me by your appearance.

If appearance is everything, if you are how you appear, then it follows that Luciferans have a wonderful advantage in our world. They are the shape shifters, the masters of predatory disguise, and because they cultivate the art of disguise, their range of possible appearances is vast, and therefore their ability to fit into any number of environments — from a religious revival to a corporate boardroom — is legion. This protean flexibility and adaptability is a survival advantage: Luciferans embrace protean flexibility because of the predatory advantages it provides, just as they embrace rapid change, broken connections, numbing, moral relativity, narcissism, and existential freedom.

Rabid Competition and the Cult of Success

This aspect of our culture has been so well analyzed and accepted that it has become a truism. We are the people who compete for success. Success is the elixir in the grail cup, the sole goal and purpose of life. Success ideology cranks out pop-psychology's perennial best-sellers: from the positive thinking movement generated by men like Norman Vincent Peale to the more ambitious and lucrative offerings of promoters like Anthony Robbins, the cult of success finds a willing reception in the millions of success-seekers who devour these books, tapes and seminars. We believe that only stiff competition fuels progress, change, and growth on all levels — remove competition, and you remove the innovation, initiative, and entrepreneurial spirit driving all levels of cultural growth. Just look at the failed communistic experiments worldwide for verification.

The message is always a variation of one simple theme: to succeed you have to win, and to win you need a competitive advantage over others. Success, therefore, is an extension of the same brutal game played by evolution and by life itself. No one else can do it for you; you have to fight and overcome, or else fail. To be a winner or to be a loser — that is the question.

Luciferism embraces and elevates success ideology to spiritual dimensions. There are winners and losers in the spiritual game too, and only those with an edge, with special methods and techniques, will survive. The spiritual hierarchy is as unforgiving of losers as the political, social, and economic hierarchies. The ultimate success story is not the richest man heading the largest corporation, but the most powerful being crowning all creation as its god and master. The stakes are higher, but the game is the same. So just as Luciferism appeals to narcissists and psychopaths, it also appeals to those whose lives revolve around the altar of success. The Luciferan would say to our most successful and powerful icons: "you have only just begun to realize your full human potential — carry on, keep going, there is more power available to you than your paltry mind can even conceive," or, as a character in Clive Barker's novel *Everville* says: "you can put every fear you harbor in this world aside, for power awaits you there, that I promise you. Power that would seem to you unlimited, for your skull does not contain ambition enough to exhaust it."

No Limits

In his extraordinary book *The True and Only Heaven: Progress and Its Critics*, Christopher Lasch identifies a powerful ideology that has animated North American culture: the idea of progress, the sense that we have no limits, that if limits exist they are as yet unknown. Progressive ideology applies to all spheres of Western life, from the development of ever-better consumer products and industrial technology to human self development. Progress is endless, cumulative, and human-driven: we improve through our own efforts, not through the intercession of any supernatural agencies. There are no limits to human progress except those we impose on ourselves. Science is the outstanding model of cumulative progress: the circle of knowledge keeps expanding, and each new fact is added to the historical bank account of previously discovered facts.

My point here is not to argue Lasch's assessment of the centrality of progressive ideology in our culture, because I think it is self-evident. I simply want to stress that, like the cult of success, progressive ideology saturates our culture, and that Luciferan ideology articulates and translates this ideology into a coherent plan of action for individuals who want to progress to the ultimate heights of competitive success — godhood. If progress is truly limitless, if human beings have no limits, if all limits are just obstacles to be overcome, and if progressive ideology extends beyond just consumer goods, technology, and science to include spiritual development as well, then Luciferism has to be understood as a logically coherent belief system grounded deeply within progressive ideology itself.

The Luciferan Pond

Luciferism, in summary, should emerge publicly and swell with adherents because it fits into the Western mind as a coherent, consistent philosophy of life. Another way to explore this *fitness* is to think of an imaginary "Darwinian pond." All kinds of life grow there, from tiny micro-organisms to fish and frogs. The pond's temperature remains at a steady state around, say 68 degrees. This temperature favors the frogs and fish and micro-organisms living there. On the edges of the pond, another life form struggles to exist: it lives at 68 degrees, but with difficulty. The pond is not welcoming; the creature survives, but has few offspring.

But then the temperature changes. It gets colder, first reaching sixty, and then fifty five, and then fifty. The creature thrives in this cold, but the frogs and fish don't. They begin dying off, and the new creature asserts its primacy. If the pond is our culture, if the moral temperature of our civilization is dropping and if conscience and compassion are withering while *powaqqatsi* thrives, then the new Luciferan creature may be just now entering a welcoming cultural climate. Luciferans would agree: the "pond" is cooling in their favor.

It might seem at first that the Luciferan style would bring about such disorder that it would ultimately destroy even those who adopt it. In a world of endlessly competing hugods, how could anything get done? Without cooperation, dog eats dog and chaos results. But isn't this the essence of capitalism? If the so-called "invisible hand" of capitalism somehow unites individual self-interest and greed into a thriving and dynamically communal social enterprise, then cannot the same "hand" unite the actions of a society of Luciferans dedicated to personal power acquisition above everything else?

Luciferans would argue it can, that in fact it already is, because society is already overwhelmingly Luciferan in action if not overtly by belief. Luciferans claim they are part of the next inevitable wave of evolution, that they are the next evolutionary leap about to appear on planet earth.

Luciferans acknowledge, however, that evolution has a wider perspective than individual survival, or even the survival of a given species. Evolution is blind and indifferent. It might favor Luciferans right now, but then change suddenly in the near future. The triumph of the Luciferan style might not lead to a unification by the invisible hand but instead bring about complete destruction of current society, a society which has bloated beyond the confines of earth itself to absorb. In this alternative scenario, Luciferans might then be nothing more than agents of evolution or of Gaia to tear down society from within, filled with immense strength, burning desire, and fanatical intensity designed only to destroy, like the barbarian hordes of history.

No matter. True Luciferans will adapt. If the world of culture and civilization as we know it is disintegrating, then Luciferans are primed to survive: they will thrive on anything, including human flesh if need be. They have evolved the ideological foundations necessary for absolute ruthlessness, violence, devouring, and possession, and will do whatever is necessary to survive. Even if the world of culture moves in the opposite Orwellian direction toward absolutely centralized power, Luciferans will survive there as well, and will rise to top positions of influence.

Luciferans believe that only one of these two options can happen: human society is *cooling down*, and the lower temperature will force us to centralize and submit to tyrannical order, or will cause us to decompose into chaos and barbarism. Either way, Luciferans feel confident of their survival skills, and are ready to take advantage of either possibility. This new world is their niche.

As their niche grows, so grow their numbers. The inner city, the war-zones of suburbia, the soul-killing environment of upper and lower class despair — here is where they can be found. They swell on despair, pain, hatred, and loss. They do not judge these things from any point of view other than power acquisition. They suck on these energies, and grow healthy on them.

In a way, Luciferans may actually be helping to transform civilization into a theater of battle compatible with Luciferan needs and desires. If they grow in numbers and influence, they might actually help decrease the pond's temperature, because the more trees and rocks of morality and conscience they strip away, the cooler the pond becomes.

Luciferan hugods wish to prosper and multiply, they wish to tear this world apart until it bleeds every drop of energy and sustenance. If their success should lead to planetary disintegration, they are not concerned. They will absorb what they can take, and then leave the mess behind, like loggers in a primeval forest or strip miners on a mountainside.

To summarize this book: I believe I have sensed or intuited or encountered a real presence standing behind Satanism, destructive cultism, and other related phenomena. I have tried to define the basic features of this unknown presence by calling it Luciferism; my guess is that these features will resonate intimately with what most readers see, know, feel, and understand about the way of things on planet Earth.

Just as Christianity somehow called out to followers two thousand years ago, so too Luciferism may well call out to people now. It may simply codify and state in obvious terms what many of us already believe, and as such may take on organizational and even institutional form in the next millennium.

Is its success inevitable? Are there alternatives? I would like to finish with an exploration of at least some alternatives available to those who want to face reality but who do not want to pursue the Luciferan bargain.

CHAPTER TWELVE
ALTERNATIVES

The desire for absolute singularity cannot be ruled out. But neither can the dread of solitude.

— George Steiner

I suspect that few readers will argue with some basic aspects of the Luciferan analysis of nature and reality: that our world is constructed as a hierarchy of devouring, that predatory skill determines success on the hierarchy, and that life is a struggle for survival from the first breath to the last. Most readers will have recognized and understood that these predatory principles dominate life as we know it, and that this perspective has solid support from evolutionary science.

Some of the more extreme features of Luciferism — hugodhood, the vital animism of intramemes and extramemes, the belief in trans-physical or supernatural forces and personalities, and the extension of predation into the spirit world — might seem fanciful or bizarre, but nevertheless remain grounded in the same principles of predatory competition, natural selection, and evolutionary philosophy.

Argue as you will, life without devouring is impossible. All living things eat and possess. All commit violence. All seek personal advantage, whether for self or family, tribe or country. Life apparently thrives when it openly embraces these forces, but dies out when it ignores them: their reality seems beyond question, and their impact on us beyond doubt. The prevailing philosophies of natural materialism and scientific reductionism have it that we are apparently animals, nothing more, and that nature is red in tooth and claw: our fingers aren't dripping blood at this instant only because we pay others to get their hands red and dirty — soldiers, police, farmers, ranchers, and butchers.

But, you might say, altruism and cooperation also exist. People can be kind, selfless, and even self-sacrificing. Nature provides as many examples of cooperation as competition — perhaps more, if the new sciences of complexity and self-organization are true — beginning with the cooperation of component parts of cells and leading all the way up the hierarchy to include collectives such as human societies and perhaps even *Gaia* herself. But the Darwinian reductionists can explain this apparently altruistic force embedded in nature as nothing more than a superior survival weapon for one collective or another: cooperation and altruism, in other words, are just advanced weapons in the chronic struggle for survival, and natural selection simply works on the collective rather than its component parts. The cells in one human body unite and struggle for survival against the cells united in a different human body; the members of one animal species unite and cooperate to overcome the members of another; one tribal group unites to defeat a neighboring tribe; one racial group unites through language and common genetic history to rise up and defeat another; one nation unites to destroy another in war.

The ethos of our age has shown us that we are imprisoned in powaqqatsi; our choices seem limited to either joining the war for life, or dying. Many of us experience helpless resignation and even despair in light of this harshly predatory vision of existence, a resignation made even more overwhelming because of the scientific, philosophical, and common-sense evidence supporting it. Add the relentless morbidity of reductionism, materialism, and various related determinisms, and life seems little more than an accidental occurrence in a vast void of "unfeeling immensity", as Monod describes it.

Our fate seems to be nothing more than serving our "selfish genes", competing against other beings for survival, and then ceasing to exist at death. Apparently we exist in a "powaqqatsi prison" designed solely to feed the brutal cycle of birth, life, and death on planet earth.

THE *POWAQQATSI* PRISON

Luciferans argue that we are all part of this cycle of brutality; we are all prisoners of *powaqqatsi*. Our prison is inescapable because it is not a building of brick, mortar and concrete, but is constructed of our living organic flesh and blood. We cannot escape because to escape is to die. Our flesh demands food, and food acquisition is powaqqatsi. Our flesh needs warmth, so we have to acquire clothing and shelter, an acquisition which demands yet more *powaqqatsi*. We seem to need sex, love, and social position, all of which can demand even more *powaqqatsi*. Our prison sentence begins at conception and does not end until death.

We are programmed by a set of rules built into our flesh, rules that demand compliance and tolerate no disobedience. Those who disobey simply disappear from the face of the earth. We are compelled, driven, and forced to participate in devouring, possession, violence and disguise no matter how we might feel personally. We therefore all face a dilemma, which I will be calling the predator's dilemma. I would submit that the predator's dilemma is, or soon will be the central philosophical issue of our times. To eat or not to eat, to possess or not possess, to kill or not to kill, to deceive or not deceive: these are the questions that may well drive twenty-first century philosophy.

The stark predatory reality of life on the hierarchy of devouring thrusts a dilemma upon us. No matter how distant we are from the actual carnage needed to keep us alive and safe — and we in the West are removed by layers of institutional insulation — we are still caught in the dilemma: do we participate and thrive, or do we refuse to participate and wither?

We are like Anne Rice's vampires. In her book *Interview With the Vampire*, for example, Rice recasts the vampire Louis as a creature of morality, as one who initially does not want to kill the humans he needs for food. He is not the amoral evil killer of past vampire portrayals, but is instead a creature of sympathy. We are attracted to him; we sympathize with his plight.

This is probably because his plight is a dilemma we all face. Kill, or die. Follow the impulses built into our organic machinery, or face extinction. Louis' organic machinery differs only slightly from ours, because now he needs human blood instead of animal flesh; the only difference is that he is supposed to kill humans, while we are supposed to kill animals and plants. His machinery commands him to follow a set of predatory rules he cannot resist. He is confined to the hierarchy, just as we are.

At first he refuses to kill. He cannot destroy his conscience and compassion for humans, and so he lives on lower creatures, debasing himself with the blood of rats and other despicable creatures. Rice's book details the vampire's struggle with this dilemma. We are fascinated by it because it is our own as well.

The vampire Lestat has no such dilemma, however. Lestat "created" Louis, and tries to teach him the morality of the higher-order predator. Says Lestat: "evil is a point of view. We are immortal. And what we have before us are the rich feasts that conscience cannot appreciate and mortal men cannot know without regret. God kills, and so shall we; indiscriminately He takes the riches and the poorest, and so shall we; for no creatures under God are as we are, none so like Him as ourselves, dark angels not confined to the stinking limits of hell but wandering His earth and all its kingdoms."

Louis discovers Lestat's teachings to be real: "I knew peace only when I killed, only for that minute" ... "we must kill to live"... we must never hesitate to bring death, because it is how we live" ... "I know what he is saying is true, that when I kill there is no longing; and I can't bear this truth, I can't bear it."

But bear it he must, and so must we: like the vampire, we are compelled to indulge in acts we detest. We struggle to rise up the socio-economic hierarchy, we kill other life forms, we compromise ourselves daily. And yet what are the alternatives? Poverty? Illness? Powerlessness? Death?

How are we supposed to reconcile our love of the gift of life with the commitment to predatory principles that this implies? If I love this earth despite the predatory principles ruling it — if I love this world and want to be in it — then I have to kill, devour, and possess. How can I truly enjoy the forest or the pond when I know the cruelty needed to sustain them? Do I have the right to possess, devour and destroy other life forms in order to advance my own life? Are there any real alternatives?

It seems to me, therefore, that the central ethical question of our time is this: how should we respond to *powaqqatsi*, predation, and the devouring hierarchy, to the Darwinian spectacle of life on planet earth?

Luciferans have their answer: simply accept *powaqqatsi* reality, adapt to it, extend it into all possible spiritual realms, and then gather enough personal energy through predation to transcend the whole mess by becoming god. Other options might be available, however, and I would like to explore some of them now.

ALTERNATIVE POSSIBILITIES

A menu of responses to the *powaqqatsi* prison and the predator's dilemma seem possible. Most, if not all, have been attempted historically by one philosophical school or another, or by one religion or another. They can be summarized as follows.

First, we can try to ignore, avoid, deny, or transcend the dilemma.

Alternatively, the dilemma can be accepted as real, but fought or resisted. Or, it can be accepted, and a compromise sought. Or we can accept the dilemma but refuse to play and simply quit the game by giving up and dying. Or the dilemma can be fully accepted and we can consciously offer ourselves up for devouring.

Another set of possibilities involves embracing the predatory principles of competition and success, and ceasing to care about any ethical concerns. When taken to its extreme, this embrace can lead to the Luciferan faith itself.

One surprising alternative is also available: Christianity. Christ's message seems designed specifically as a response to the dynamics of predation, *powaqqatsi*, and the devouring hierarchy.

I will now briefly explore each of these possibilities.

THROUGH IGNORANCE

One way to handle the dilemma is to pretend it does not exist. Problem? What problem? Devouring, predation, hierarchy and all the rest: just ignore them. I do not have to worry about killing other life forms to survive, because someone else does it for me. Farmers raise the meat, butchers slaughter and package it, and I just buy it. I am not involved. The dilemma is not mine, because I personally do not possess or devour anything or anyone. I am not violent. I am not predatory.

And so, let others do the my killing; I get my meat nicely wrapped. My conscience is clean. I do not want to know where my leather wallet comes from. I do not want to hear about how gasoline gets from that third world country to my gas tank. I am innocent. It is not my fault. The world might be nasty, dirty, unclean — but not my little piece of it. My world is sanitized. I am not guilty of anything, because what is there to feel guilty about? The answer to the dilemma? Don't think about it. Create a sanitized middle-class sanctuary behind the walls of a closed community. Lock the doors, and keep it out. My conscience is as clean as my toilet — sanitized and free of the germs of complicity.

By Avoidance

If the problem cannot be ignored, then it can be avoided in countless imaginative ways. For those who sense the truth of the predatory hierarchy, who cannot lock it out or wipe it away with disinfectant, and who become cynical, world-weary and disillusioned as a result, the possibilities of avoidance are multitude. If escape from the dilemma's soul-numbing spiritual gridlock is desired, then such escapes can be easily found.

Drugs are marvelous. From alcohol to the hallucinogens and mood enhancers, drugs offer temporary relief from the hierarchy's relentlessly depressing pressure.

Sex and relationships can also offer alternatives. To become infatuated with someone, and then to move from that person to another before the deadly daily realities of life on the hierarchy can intervene — the need for food, shelter, job, money, and child support — means playing a kind of frantic game of musical relationships that, for a time at least, can make the predatory hierarchy seem remote.

Immersing oneself in work and career is effective as well. Climbing the hierarchy of success and focusing entirely on the job at hand can provide merciful relief from despair, hopelessness, and fear about the real world of hierarchy, predation, and competition. Work is "what I do" without guilt. Hence the corporate executive can make decisions that destroy the already depleting resources of the planet without feeling responsible. It is just my job, it is what I do, and I do it well. I do not need to worry about the consequences, about how I might be hurting or even killing others, because it is just not my problem. Period.

Another possibility is the wonderful avoidance tool called television. Turn on the box, and get numb. Add a few beers, overeat to silence the fear, and the problem is solved. Popular entertainment culture is a haven for those wanting to avoid reality, and even seems deliberately designed for that purpose. The relentless reminders of our devastated world on the daily news — crime, violence, death, mutilation, disasters — really do not mean much, because I am safe and warm on my couch. I am a voyeur to others' despair and pain, but I am remote from it. It doesn't touch me. I am only a disinterested observer.

Religious and spiritual consumerism can bring the same results. One need only shop in the psycho-spiritual marketplace, buy a sweetly convincing belief system which dogmatically avoids predatory reality, and the results can be as soothingly effective as any narcotic, especially if the new belief system tells me that the predatory hierarchy is just illusion, a problem of perspective, a reality I have created which I can simply uncreate with daily meditation. It is not real, and it need not concern me.

In a similar vein, I can invent wonderfully idyllic utopian fantasies of a world that might be (if only everyone embraces The Truth) or a world that was (the noble savage living in harmony with nature; the golden age when my culture was truly young, vibrant, and powerful), and pretend that somewhere, sometime, the predatory hierarchy was/is/will be overcome.

For reasons already discussed earlier, Luciferans despise those who ignore reality or avoid it by embracing one type of fallacious addiction or another. But they are easy prey, and Luciferans devour their energy constantly. For Luciferans, such "ignorers" and "avoiders" aren't even worthy to be called sheep; they have no real strength at all, and are simply begging to be killed.

In Denial

Instead of ignoring or avoiding the predatory dilemma, another alternative is to deny it by concluding that the predatory analysis is simply wrong. Life is not constructed this way, and does not follow these rules. Altruism, sympathy, and helping are woven into creation just as deeply as competition and predation. Cooperation evolves naturally in systems, as Robert Axelrod (in his book *The Evolution of Cooperation*) and others have attempted to show. Life cannot exist without cooperation between and within species. Competition is real, but is only part of the picture, and a small part at that. The full flowering of competition could only lead to chaos, with every created entity competing fiercely against all others. The Darwinian interpretation is only partial, despite its domination of today's intellectual climate.

Darwin's interpretation of predatory competition on the hierarchy of devouring only appeals to the deterministic naturalism and materialistic ethos of our age, which, as mentioned, states that there is no purpose, that soul does not exist, that matter is everything, that the lower determines the higher, and that the past determines the present. According to this ethos, there is no teleological or vitalistic source directing creation; only chance, coincidence, and the void actually exist. But other interpretations are possible.

For example, a rich tradition of philosophical alternatives suggest that reality is more than just the grim competition of force against force. From Plato's Idealism through the German Idealists Kant and Hegel, philosophers have presented other explanations and theories of life, including the possibility that soul is real, that mind and soul determine, organize, and create physical reality, that life as a whole is evolving to some future perfection, that non-physical vitalistic forces shape material reality, and that matter is also shaped teleologically by causes other than those existing in the past. Life is more than just relentless competition; it is suffused with meaning, beauty, and purpose beyond the daily struggle for survival. This tradition of thought has been dismissed as nonsense by the triumphant forces of modern scientific reductionism and materialism, but nevertheless may once again capture human imagination in the future.

Even some recent scientists contest this relentlessly grim vision of predation on the hierarchy. For example, David Foster's book *The Philosophical Scientists* presents an exploration of the ideas of a group of scientists led by Sir Arthur Eddington called "The Cambridge Club" who examined scientific evidence supporting the belief that "the stuff of the world is mind-stuff" and that life could not possibly have evolved from simple chance events. Connie Barlow offers other alternative interpretations of the evolution of life from authors such as James Lovelock, Lewis Thomas, Julian Huxley and Arthur Koestler in her fabulous book, *From Gaia to Selfish Genes*. My point here is not to present or defend these alternative theories, but simply to note their existence. Not everyone believes that the predatory reality of the Luciferan hierarchy is the only possible description of life on earth.

Luciferans would deny the reality of all such armchair speculations and sweetly mystical nonsense. Life is as it is, and no amount of empty philosophical daydreaming can change this basic fact. To deny the devouring hierarchy is to be like the man pretending that the truck bearing down on him is not really there, and who is free to enjoy his illusion for approximately two seconds, at which time both he and his illusion will be crushed.

To Transcend

Beyond these philosophical and scientific alternatives, other religious traditions have interpreted the hierarchy differently. Zen advocates a position above the dueling opposites of good and evil, higher and lower, predator and prey, yin and yang. This state beyond competition, pain, tension, and war is available for all those wishing to transcend war on the hierarchy.

The Buddha offered a similar transformation beyond competition, stress, and pain through inner transformation. His Four Noble Truths of dukkha, karma, detachment and the Eightfold Path supposedly lead to Nirvana, which is a state of removal from competition and strife, a state in which complete detachment, enlightenment and peace have been attained. Nirvana literally means "blown out", and so the Buddha's solution was to blow himself out of the hierarchy of devouring, pain, competition, and desire. Dukkha, traditionally understood as the imperfection, incompleteness, alienation and suffering caused by attachment to the "fire of life", can perhaps also be understood as the outcome of powaqqatsi and the predator's dilemma. If so, then Luciferans would point out that the sweetly compassionate Buddha still had to eat, and that his followers have all embraced powaqqatsi in order to spread his message.

In Jainism, an ancient Indian tradition, the problem of devouring is addressed through an absolute respect for all life forms, in which the doctrine of non-violence is absolute. All life is held to be sacred, and no being has the right to deny life to another. Hence the Jains are exclusively vegetarian. They wear cloth across the mouth to avoid inadvertently killing insects. They promote radical asceticism, and hold the belief that true existence is a spiritual transcendence beyond the hierarchy of devouring and predation. Hosts of other spiritual traditions have promoted the same basic theme.

In Western spirituality, for example, the monastic and ascetic traditions defied the demands of the hierarchy directly. Athanasius's *Life of Antony* is an example. Antony retreated to the desert, took minimal energy from other beings by eating little or nothing, remained aloof from the social power hierarchy, and put all his faith and trust in God. Some later Christian saints claimed that they took no energy at all from earth, but only directly from God. They seemed to believe that energy, life, and vitality could be obtained in other ways than just through powaqqatsi. The entire ascetic tradition itself, where the monk renounces all claims to worldly power, competition, and violence, is a way of life based on principles other than predatory Darwinism. St. Francis is an obvious example here, but hundreds of other saints have expressed the same basic message throughout Christian history.

Of course, Luciferans would argue that anyone who denies the reality of power acquisition is idiotic, and hence easy prey for Luciferan predators. They would argue that no matter what the Buddhists, Jains, ascetics and others might believe and no matter how they might act, they are permitted to exist only because others do their dirty work: even St. Francis begging in the streets for food depends on the network of merchants, farmers, politicians and others whose adherence to the principles of hierarchical devouring and possession ensure that the food will be available.

Transcendent solutions can probably best be summarized by the ancient aphorism that we should "be in the world but not of it." Unlike ignoring, avoiding, or denying the predator's dilemma, transcendental solutions acknowledge the world of hierarchy, predation, cruelty, and violence but attempt to go beyond it, to invoke the presence of some form of transcendent experience, state, or reality into this world of woe and pain. By doing so, the individual expects to transform both himself and the world in which he lives, moves, and has his being.

Luciferans would suggest that no such transformation occurs, that the individual simply fades into the backdrop of illusion and impotent powerlessness that is the fate of all but those truly heroic Luciferan warriors who accept the dilemma and answer it by embracing predation.

RESIST!

Most of us living at the end of the Twentieth Century cannot easily deny, ignore, avoid or pretend to transcend the predatory hierarchy. One look at the newspaper's business pages, a brief perusal of the atrocities committed by one nation against another, or a short glance at any recent biology textbook will reinforce the awesome truth that only the fittest survive in the war of all against all.

For those who refuse to ignore, avoid, deny or transcend this reality, a number of options are available. The first is to fight against the devouring hierarchy by refusing to accept any part of it. It must be opposed on all levels, relentlessly and energetically. Whatever compulsions and limitations the predatory hierarchy imposes on human beings must be rooted out, exposed, and fought.

Communism, in its original form, was a declaration of war against capitalism and the various social philosophies supporting its existence, which in turn, I believe, was a declaration against the formidable domination of the predatory hierarchy in every aspect of human life. Communists wanted a utopian state in which absolute justice ruled, in which everyone worked selflessly for the good of all others, in which wealth was evenly distributed between the powerful and the weak, in which all forms of personal possession (of property, capital, etc.) would be eliminated, and in which crime, poverty, and all the other vicissitudes of modern living would be annihilated. Communists refused to acknowledge the awesome power of personal power acquisition, possession, and devouring, while capitalist democracies embraced it: Luciferans would have us all note which of them survived and prevailed.

The predatory hierarchy can also be fought through radical asceticism, voluntary poverty, and other similar forms of "tuning in, turning on, and dropping out." The sixties generation was one more example of the historical urge to fight the incessant pull of the hierarchy's demands: to accumulate wealth and power, to get stronger, to dominate others.

Sixties' idealism was a direct assault on the values of the capitalist state. Hence the hatred of corporations, the distrust of all authorities culpable and guilty of compromise with the establishment "beast", and the search for alternative ways of survival, including communes and new forms of sexual relationship. But Luciferans laugh about such puerile experiments, and would note how few of them have survived. That the radical sixties revolutionary would become a Wall Street speculator was as inevitable as death itself, and Luciferans sarcastically point out that the ex-revolutionary's neat two car garage hides no rusty Volkswagen vans.

Luciferans would state that radical asceticism, poverty, and denial of predatory impulses might be possible for the occasional saint, but absolutely impossible and remote for all other human beings. Appetites, desires, and other predatory impulses are just too powerful.

The Stoics of ancient Greece found another way to fight. They accepted the nasty realities of this world — to do less was to betray reason and hence to lose virtue, because virtue (a Socratic ideal treasured by the Stoics) depended on honestly matching one's intellectual understanding with reality. In other words, Stoics refused to deal in fantasy. But to accept reality was to live in pain, stress, and despair, creating our dilemma.

Stoics did not want to live in distress; they desired peace of mind without sacrificing their acceptance of reality. Such peace of mind was a state therefore sought by all Stoics, a kind of tranquillity, serenity, and undisturbed stability. Predatory impulses, disgusting passions, the drive for power acquisition and all the well known "evils" of their day and ours could destroy peace of mind and mental tranquillity, so the task facing every human being was to deny such passions. Only an iron will prepared to overcome all these impulses and endure any resulting deprivation or pain could achieve and maintain mind peace. Passions from within or terror and pain from without haunt all of us: Stoics claimed that the only answer is to accept such painful realities but to fight them with personal strength, endurance and will power.

Another way of fighting the relentless power of the predatory impulse is to devote one's life selflessly to others in need, without hope of reciprocation, reward, or recognition. Volunteer in a food bank, work with the underprivileged, help out in poor countries: the possibilities are endless. Even my own work with COMA was driven by this kind of impulse. I worked for free most of the time. I refused to compromise with various interest groups in order to obtain money from them: funds from Christian groups disappeared because I stated that Christian cults were possible and that cultism itself was not the sole property of new non-Christian religious movements. Corporate donations dried up when I went on record in *Canadian Business* that cultism could be found in some corporations, and that various businesses were importing cultic trainers in order to achieve a business advantage. I felt very noble; but in the end COMA was crushed, I became drained emotionally and financially, and the noble enterprise ended. Luciferans would have predicted this outcome: no one can challenge the predatory order of things on planet earth and survive. Even the apparently selfless armies of volunteers have a selfish end in sight: adoration from the community, a rush of "do-gooder" emotion, and so on. Moreover, behind these volunteers stands a spouse, organization or other entity providing the money for the noble gesture, and this money always comes ultimately from predatory principles themselves.

Political systems, asceticism, philosophy, volunteerism: these and hundreds of other options have been created to fight the relentless determinism of the predatory hierarchy. Luciferans respond with great humor to the obvious irony implied by all such resistance. As resistance, it is in effect a declaration of war against the predatory hierarchy, but war is the very stuff of the hierarchy itself. To fight the fact that we have to fight and struggle against one another, is still to fight. To vigorously oppose the hierarchy is to become the hierarchy, by definition. Noble motivations in the name of a higher cause are irrelevant. To struggle against the predatory hierarchy is to embrace the very principles and behaviors being fought. Hence the Russian communists became even worse than those they hated, fought, and defeated.

Luciferans explain this by noting that to fight a thing, you have to focus on it, hard and constant like a cat stalking a bird. You have to learn about its weaknesses, amplify hatred against it in yourself and others, focus on it intensively and passionately, draw upon the martial energies of stalking and killing. Those who do this relentlessly and vigorously will therefore become the very thing they hate. William Blake expresses his caution this way: "they became what they beheld."

William Irwin Thompson cites Greek sources who called this odd phenomenon *enantiodromia*: becoming that which you resist. Hence the odd modern phenomenon of radical feminists demonstrating patriarchal hatred of their enemies and embracing the worst forms of demagoguery and coercion to get what they want. Fight away, chuckles the Luciferan. Hate the predatory hierarchy and resort to any action, moral or immoral, to destroy it. All such actions only confirm the hierarchy's power. The Emperor in the movie series *Star Wars* embodies this ironic Luciferan chuckle: go ahead, he says to the

369

noble hero Luke Skywalker, hate me and try to kill me — do this and you will become like me, a walker of the dark side.

Compromise is the alternative probably chosen by most of us: accept the reality of the dilemma of predatory competition on the devouring hierarchy, but compromise with it. Accept that existence is structured this way but reduce its impact by accommodation. Make your deal!

I can do this by accepting my place in the power order. I am never going to be a political power broker, great thinker, or influential artist. I am just another citizen, and I can live with that. Live and let live. Don't mess with me, and I won't mess with you. I rely on the social systems in place (government, law, education, medicine, etc.) to protect and preserve me, and I will surrender a certain amount of freedom and wealth to them. I will get my share — not too much and not too little. I am not so naive as to give my money to the needy or to devote my time freely to others, but then again I won't unfairly gouge anyone either. I will simply try to live as honestly and ethically as I can, knowing that I have to commit some devouring, possessing, and killing in order to do so. Others can kill my food for me, and my nation can take advantage of other nations far away so that I will always have cheap consumer goods. I will look after myself and those closest to me, because I am alone in this world except for my family and friends. I will preserve as much conscience as I can, providing the cost is not too great. Other compromising options are also possible. I can get back to the land like Thoreau, and find my own little Walden paradise. My personal devouring, possessing, and killing will therefore be reduced, and I will live as honestly as possible. I will kill my own chickens, gather my own eggs, tend my own garden. My killing will then at least be honest and straightforward, devoid of illusion and plastic-wrapped distance. My impact on planet earth will be as soft and kind as possible. I won't fight the devouring hierarchy, because I cannot. I will simply work as realistically and ethically with it as I can. The demands of the hierarchy thus become like death and taxes, something to be accepted but not embraced. The devouring hierarchy is after all only natural, and natural is good. I may not like it, but I can learn to live with it

Politically, I can fight for causes which seem to reduce the impact of the devouring hierarchy. Green eco-politics, animal rights, recycling, vegetarianism: the list is endless.

I can embrace the "neo-native" option, the idea that native Americans honored that which they had to kill. They would kill the Caribou and offer thanks to the animal's spirit. Other life forms have to give up themselves in order for me to exist, and so I will honor this sacrifice, and be prepared to sacrifice myself. I accept that existence is structured this way, that something has to become less in order for me to exist. This is just the way of things. I will kill because I have to, but will do so with ultimate respect and honor for that which gives its life force up to me.

There are undoubtedly endless varieties of compromise. I mean nothing pejorative by this word, but instead suggest that mitigating, ameliorating, accommodating, or reducing the hierarchy's impact is an option which includes acceptance of its existence combined with an honest attempt to accommodate and reduce participation in its demands. I suspect that this has been the choice of *Everyman* throughout time, those not wishing to embrace the hierarchy but also not wishing to simply fold up and die.

PURE REFUSAL

Folding up and dying — this is yet another possible reaction to the devouring hierarchy. The option is simple: accept the absolute victory of predatory principles controlling existence on planet earth, but refuse to participate. Life here is absolutely corrupt, absolutely evil, absolutely vicious and cruel. There is no hope of change, because this world is based solely on the predatory hierarchy. To remain in it is to essentially become it, no matter what kind of compromises are made. Ignoring it, avoiding it, denying it, fighting it or compromising with it: these choices are all the same, all despicable, all part of the dark ugliness and evil of life on the hierarchy.

The only answer is to refuse all possession, all devouring, all killing, and all disguise. In other words, the only answer is to leave existence and die. Death is the only possibility, the only state in which no devouring (of food or the energy of other beings), no possessing (of property, clothing, money), no killing (of other animals, insects, plants) and no disguise (without which we would be naked, exposed and utterly defenseless) is possible. Without predation on the devouring hierarchy, life is impossible and death is the only alternative. This death might be honorably self-imposed by suicide. Or it might be imposed by any agent serving the devouring hierarchy: disease, starvation, other human predators, all of which are ready to take the life of any being refusing to participate in predation. But the end result is the same: refuse to engage in the hierarchy, and therefore refuse to engage in life itself.

SACRIFICE YOURSELF

This option was most clearly articulated by Jesus Christ. His message went far beyond the usual positions taken by most world religions and moral systems, all of which prohibit or discourage excessive possession, violence, devouring and disguise as articulated in moral codes such as the Ten Commandments and the Great Commandment to "do unto others as we would have others do unto us." Christ said that all of these moralities are good, but that they are not enough: even the Pharisees and the unbelievers are moral in their own ways.

Christ said that his followers have to go further, and offer themselves up for sacrifice to those forces seeking to possess, kill, eat, or trick them. They should not deny, ignore, avoid, transcend, fight, compromise or refuse these forces, but simply give in to them and let them have their way. Thus, if someone asks for your shirt, then give it to him; if someone slaps your face, let him strike you again. Give away your possessions, and move consciously into the servitude of God. Depend on nothing but God. Make peace with those who hate you by loving your enemies and all who spitefully use and abuse you. Do not return their attack. Worldly power acquisition is useless. Satan offers Christ power over all earthly kingdoms for all time, a temptation which he turns down.

Instead Christ offers himself up as a sacrifice to be tormented, humiliated, tortured, and unjustly killed. Christ says that when we give ourselves up as sacrificial offerings, when we let others eat our bodies and drink our blood just as he offered himself to us, then a strange thing happens: we get stronger. The first become last, and the last first. The body may be destroyed, but the spirit grows strong. Death is followed by rebirth, especially for those who die a martyr's death. Emptiness is followed by fullness, poverty by heavenly riches, and sorrow by joy.

When like Christ we give ourselves up to the "Prince of this world" then we enter the kingdom of Heaven, which is not a physical but rather a state that exists between us, within us, among us, and in God. It grows like a small mustard seed into something huge; it is infinitely valuable, and it causes us to "rise up" like new bread. The more we strip from ourselves, the closer heaven gets. When we become as children again, then we enter it, or it enters us. We call it down to earth every time we pray "Our Father who art in heaven, Thy kingdom come ...", and we expand its power every time we refuse to engage in the devouring hierarchy's demand for *powaqqatsi*. The kingdom of Heaven is completely unnatural in the biologically Darwinian sense: the lion lays down with the lamb, and all competition, violence, possession, devouring and disguise cease because every inhabitant draws all he needs straight from God. Needless to say, Heaven escapes our imagination: sexless winged creatures playing harps and gamboling through the clouds seems to be about the best we can do.

True Christianity is a mysterious testament against the *powaqqatsi* prison, and its answer to the predator's dilemma is clear: depend on God and let go of the foolish and fruitless pursuit of predatory power acquisition.

If we refuse to deny, ignore, avoid or transcend predation, if fighting it seems useless and even stupid, if compromise seems weak and ignoble, if death is to be avoided at all costs, and if personal sacrifice is horrifying, then another option is to accept the reality of the hierarchy and embrace its principles, impulses, dictates and laws.

Once this choice is made, then the world opens like a happy oyster, and anything becomes possible. Any desire can be sated, any impulse can be indulged, any wish fulfilled. To live according to the predatory hierarchy is to love devouring, possession, violence and disguise in all their multi-colored splendor.

"Success ideology" celebrates this option. Think positive thoughts, set goals, take action, and succeed! Positive Thinkers and success merchants like Napoleon Hill, Maxwell Maltz, Norman Vincent Peale, Anthony Robbins and their imitators and successors have preached the doctrine of success to receptive audiences for generations. In this religion, success is heaven, failure is hell. Success is simple: formulate a plan, accumulate as much money and power as possible, follow the dictates of the hierarchy and possess wealth, status, social position and power. These are the only realities; all else is illusion and foolishness.

Others follow the dictates of the hierarchy even further. For them, conscience and compassion are all right in themselves, as long as they do not interfere with success. When a clash seems inevitable (cheat on your business partner or don't get the money you need and deserve; sleep with the boss or forget promotion; destroy that competitor with a smear campaign or watch your profits fall) then concerns about conscience and compassion are always secondary. The world is a tough place where only the strong survive. Things need to be done, unpleasant things, but that is just the way of life. Struggle, battle, and conflict are the only realities; there is an eternal war between competitors for scarce resources. Get powerful and get rich or roll over and take defeat. Get with the program or join the ranks of the weak, the stupid, and the defeated.

Life is hard, no one else is fair, and no one will give you a break unless you take it by force or by stealth. The game of success has simple rules, just like the jungle. One rule is to seem to be kind, ethical, and fair minded while engaging in the acquisition of power. To join the ranks of the wealthy and influential, one has to learn the rules of social interaction and civilized conduct. But this is all disguise, and anyone with real power knows it. Tough realism and smart, harsh action regardless of consequences to others (especially competitors) is the only way to survive and prosper. All else is foolish, false illusion.

"Greed is good, greed is great" was preached to an audience of investors. Entrepreneurial possession, devouring, violence and disguise are the engines of progress and without them stagnation, entropy, and death result. Western culture has triumphed because it has accepted lovingly, understood keenly, and embraced these impulses. We will fall to the bottom of the hierarchy of nations if we ever forget, deny, or fight this basic truth. Individuals who forget will also fall to the bottom of the socio-economic hierarchy. There is no higher justice or morality in such failure. There is only stupidity, weakness, and waste.

PURSUE ABSOLUTE LUCIFERAN SINGULARITY

Some of those embracing predatory success may want to pursue yet one further option, one other way to handle the dilemma of the predatory hierarchy. For them the full flowering of Luciferan religion is attractive because simple success, no matter how awesome, is not enough. Such individuals want more than just success, power, and wealth: they want to climb even higher up the psycho-spiritual hierarchy. Luciferan spirituality shows the way, a path to power acquisition, predatory expertise, spiritual survival and even the godhood discussed in this book. But one consequence of the Luciferan way needs to be considered: Steiner's state of absolute singularity.

If Luciferism is the spiritual elevation of selfhood to godhood, then as the Luciferan climbs the hierarchy, fewer and fewer competitors would be encountered. Each one would be dangerously powerful, but the psycho-spiritual hierarchy allows no power sharing. There is one king, one chief executive, one absolute leader. The higher the position on the hierarchy, the fewer competitors are left. As the self inflates, other selves must give way. There can thus be only one endpoint for one God: the unity of absolute singularity.

The attainment of such unity has occupied religious thinkers throughout time. It has been centered on surrendering selfhood to a higher sense of oneness and perfection. Luciferans invert the equation: do not surrender the singularity of selfhood to a wider and deeper unity of oneness, but instead force the greater unity to surrender itself to the singularity of a fully empowered selfhood. This submission of the universal "allness" to the "oneness" of the Luciferan soul is the essential Luciferan quest. In other words, do not cave into God, make God cave in to you. Absolute singularity, absolute power, absolute freedom — such is the Luciferan way. To pursue *powaqqatsi* is to deepen solitude, until enough power is gathered to eliminate everything other than Self from consciousness.

Such absolute singularity is deeply attractive, but also implies something else: absolute solitude. Absolute singularity means absolute isolation from other beings. It is the life of the lonely predator, but a predator with immense power and influence, a god to all beings lower on the hierarchy. When self inflates to god, then the universe becomes self, and nothing else matters. All else is secondary, peripheral, inconsequential. To be absolutely all-powerful and above all other beings is to be absolutely alone. Such aloneness is awesome, unthinkable, and impenetrable to us, not something that many of us are likely to desire.

As always, Luciferans have a response to what the rest of us think we might or might not desire. Of course, most human beings shrink before such awesome responsibility, which is why they will always be nothing more than victims. Their need for affiliation and communion is their weakness. Selfhood is too hard for them, and so they fail to fulfill their potential. Selfhood means the absolute singularity of deep solitude, and is a gift to be endured only by the hard and the strong.

But Luciferans would point out that no matter how frightening the specter of singularity and absolute solitude might seem to us, we all share it. After all, aren't we just miniature kingdoms of isolation anyway? We have friends, lovers, children, family, and associates. We are all ultimately alone, aren't we, like floating specks of light in a dark and endless sea? We communicate, we love and hate, we interact, but ultimately we are alone in our own skulls, removed from everything except ourselves. We can leave the social stage any time to find ourselves absolutely alone and isolated behind the set. We enter, we play a part, and then we leave, alone. We are born alone, we live our most intense moments alone, we die alone, and no amount of wishful thinking changes this basic fact. Communion is an illusion for the weak and the soft, a lie built on the false dreams of love, compassion, conscience, and empathy.

Luciferans accept this alone-ness as the inevitable outcome of the competition of all against all. They accept that such isolation is the way of things, and that it must be heroically embraced, celebrated, and deepened. To find absolute peace and power in the solitude of one's own Self is for the Luciferan a magnificent goal, available only to the strong, the fit, the realistic, and the predatory.

There is a mystery here, a mystery hiding in the infinite darkness of absolute personal solitude. And here is where I am forced to stop, because I cannot penetrate further.

I remain ambivalent: part of me mistrusts the mystery like a coyote contemplating a skillfully constructed scent-baited trap; another part is tempted like one of Kubrick's apes to reach up and grasp a gloriously powerful future of unlimited power and evolutionary potential.

I cannot penetrate this mystery, but only assert once again my conviction that the Luciferan Age is dawning and rising among us, within us, and between us, and that Luciferism describes a reality we know intimately as our own. Alternatives exist, but few seem to fit the spirit of our age quite as well as Luciferism and these alternatives are *exceptional* and perhaps always have been. The Luciferan message about our new age is that human evolutionary progress excludes ethics and morals, that spiritual growth bypasses love, that higher powers of consciousness invoke only higher powers of predation, and that the New Human will be a predator to behold with great fear and trembling.

BIBLIOGRAPHY

These are some of the books and articles I've used; direct quotations or references to their content can be found in the editions listed below.

I have more or less used basic APA (American Psychological Association) style with each listing below, but have not used other standard APA methods in the manuscript itself. Because I tried to avoid an "academic" feel to this book, I did not specify the page number of quotes in the text itself or in footnotes. If some of the books, movies or television programs mentioned in the manuscript are widely known, then they haven't been listed here (i.e., Anne Rice's or Frank Herbert's novels).

Arendt, Hannah. 1951. The Origins of Totalitarianism. 1986 edition, London: Andre Deutsch.

Athanasius. 1980. (trans. Robert C. Gregg). The Life of Antony and the Letter to Marcellinus. New York: Paulist Press. (original: circa 350 AD).

Axelrod, Robert. 1984. The Evolution of Cooperation. New York: Basic Books.

Babuta, S. and Bragard, J. 1985. Evil. London: Weidenfeld and Nicolson, in association with Channel Four Television Company Limited.

Barker, Clive. 1994. Everville. Harper Paperbacks.

Barlow, Connie. (Ed.) 1991. From Gaia to Selfish Genes: Selected Writings in the Life Sciences. The MIT Press.

Barlow, Connie. (Ed.) 1994. Evolution Extended: Biological Debates on the Meaning of Life. The MIT Press.

Becker, Ernest. 1973. The Denial of Death. New York: The Free Press.

Becker, Ernest. 1975. Escape From Evil. New York: The Free Press.

Bertalanffy, Ludwig von. Quoted in Barlow, C. (Ed) 1991. From Gaia to Selfish Genes. MIT Press.

Blake, William. 1958. In William Blake. (J. Bronowski, Ed). Penguin. (Original Poems from Songs of Innocence and Songs of Experience pub between 1789 and 1794).

Bloom, Harold. 1992. The American Religion: The Emergence of the Post Christian Nation. New York: Touchstone.

Bloom, Howard. 1995. The Lucifer Principle: A Scientific Expedition into the Forces of History. New York: The Atlantic Monthly Press.

Bromley, D. & Shupe, Anson. 1989. Public Reaction Against New Religious Movements in Cults and New Religious Movements. Edited by Galanter, M. Washington: American

Psychiatric Association.

Bucke, R.M. 1973. Cosmic Consciousness: A Study In the Evolution Of The Human Mind. Secaucus, N.J: The Citadel Press. (first pub. in 1901).

Burgess, Anthony. 1972. A Clockwork Orange. London: Penguin. (Originally published in 1962)

Capaldi, N. 1979. The Art of Deception. Buffalo, N.Y.: Prometheus Books. (Originally published in 1971).

Caputo, Philip. 1977. A Rumor of War. New York: Ballentine Books.

Cialdini, R. 1984. Influence: The New Psychology Of Modern Persuasion. New York: William Morrow And Co.

Cialdini, Robert B. 1984. Influence: The New Psychology of Modern Persuasion. New York: Quill.

Cleckley, Hervey. 1988. The Mask of Sanity. (fifth edition). Emily S. Cleckley. (originally published in 1941).

Cohen, Leonard. 1993. Stranger Music: Selected Poems and Songs. Toronto: McClelland and Stewart.

Conway, F. & Siegelman, J. 1978. Snapping: America's Epidemic Of Sudden Personality Change. New York: J.B. Lippincott Co.

Conway, F. and Siegelman, J. 1978. Snapping. Dell.

Crabtree, A. 1985. Multiple Man: Explorations in Possession and Multiple Personality. Toronto: Collins.

Crapanzano, V. and Garrison, V. 1977. Case Studies In Spirit Possession. New York: John Wiley & Sons.

Crick, Francis. 1994. The Astonishing Hypothesis. Touchstone.

Cronkite, Kathy. 1994. On the Edge of Darkness: Conversations About Conquering Depression. New York: Doubleday.

Crowley, A. 1987. The Book Of The Law. York Beach, ME: Samuel Weiser. (Originally published in 1938).

Csikszentmihalyi, Mihaly. 1990. Flow: The Psychology of Optimal Experience. New York: Harper and Row.

Dawkins, Richard. 1976. The Selfish Gene. New York: Oxford University Press.

Dawkins, Richard. 1986. The Blind Watchmaker. New York: W.W. Norton & Co.

Dennett, Daniel. 1995. Darwin's Dangerous Idea: Evolution and the Meanings of Life. New York: Touchstone.

Doctorow, E. L. 1994. The Waterworks. Signet.

Dostoevsky, Fyodor. 1981. The Brothers Karamazov. New York: Bantam. (originally published in 1880).

Durant, Will. 1961. The Story of Philosophy. New York: Touchstone. (originally published in 1926).

Emerson, Ralph Waldo. 1995. Self Reliance and Other Essays. New York: Barnes and Noble. (Originally published in the latter half of the eighteenth century, in various different publications).

Fiore, Edith. 1987. The Unquiet Dead: A Psychologist Treats Spirit Possession. New York: Ballentine Books.

Foster, David. 1985. The Philosophical Scientists. New York: Barnes & Noble.

Frank, J. 1961. Persuasion and Healing. 1973. New York: Schocken Books.

Fromm, Erich. 1950. Psychoanalysis and Religion. Yale University Press. Fromm, Erich. 1966. You Shall Be As Gods. New York: Fawcett Premier.

Girard, Rene. 1977. Violence and the Sacred (Patrick Gregory, Trans.). Johns Hopkins University Press. (Original work published in 1972).

Goethe, Johann Wolfgang von. 1962. (Trans. by Peter Salm). Faust, First Part. New York: Bantam. (originally published in 1808).

Goldberg, Carl. 1996. Speaking With The Devil: Exploring Senseless Acts of Evil. Viking Penguin.

Goodman, F. 1981. The Exorcism of Anneliese Michel. New York: Doubleday.

Goodman, F. 1988. How About Demons? : Possession and Exorcism in the Modern World. Indiana University Press.

Goodrick-Clark, N.1985. The Occult Roots of Nazism. The Aquarian Press.

Hare, Robert D. 1993. Without Conscience: The Disturbing World of the Psychopaths Among Us. New York: Pocket Books.

Harrington, Alan. 1972. Psychopaths. New York: Touchstone.

Hesse, Hermann. 1951. Siddhartha (Hilda Rosner, Trans.). New York: New Directions Publishing Corporation. (Original work published in 1922).

Hobbes, Thomas. Leviathan. Originally printed in 1650.

Hochschild, A.R. 1983. The Managed Heart: Commercialization of Human Feeling. University of California Press.

Hoffer, E. 1951. The True Believer. New York: Harper and Row.

Huxley, A. 1985. The Perennial Philosophy. London: Triad Grafton Books. (first published in 1946).

Huxley, A. 1987. The Doors of Perception and Heaven and Hell. London: Collins. (first published in 1954).

Huxley, Aldous. 1989. Brave New World. London: A Triad Grafton Book. (Originally published in 1932).

Huxley, Julian. Quoted in Barlow, C. 1991. From Gaia to Selfish Genes. MIT Press. Johnson, Phillip. 1991. Darwin on Trial. Downers Grove, Illinois: InterVarsity Press. Johnson, Phillip, 1995, Reason in the Balance. InterVarsity Press.

Johnson, R. H. & Blair, J. A. 1983. Logical Self-Defense. McGraw-Hill Ryerson. (Originally published in 1977).

Katz, Jack. 1988. Seductions of Crime: Moral and Sensual Attractions of Doing Evil. New York, Basic Books.

Kauffman, Stuart. 1995. At Home in the Universe: The Search for the Laws of Self-Organization and Complexity. New York: Oxford University Press.

Keen, Sam. 1986. Faces of the Enemy: Reflections of the Hostile Imagination. Harper and Row.

Klimo, J. 1987. Channeling. Los Angeles: Jeremy P. Tarcher, Inc.

Koestler, Arthur. 1978. Janus: A Summing Up. New York: Random House.

Lasch, Christopher. 1979. The Culture of Narcissism: American Life in An Age of Diminishing Expectations. New York: W. W. Norton & Co.

Lasch, Christopher. 1991. The True and Only Heaven: Progress and Its Critics. New York: W. W. Norton and Company.

Laski, Marchanita. 1961. Ecstasy in Secular and Religious Experiences. Los Angeles: Jeremy P. Tarcher.

LaVey, Anton. 1989. The Satanic Witch. Los Angeles: Feral House (Originally published in 1970).

Le Bon, Gustave. 1969. The Crowd. New York: Viking Press. (originally published in 1895).

Lewin, Roger. 1992. Complexity: Life at the Edge of Chaos. New York: MacMillan Publishing Co.

Lewis, C. S. 1941. The Screwtape Letters. New York: New American Library (1988). Lewis, C. S. 1965. Screwtape Proposes a Toast. London: HarperCollins.

Lewis, I. M. 1989. Ecstatic Religion. (2nd Ed.). New York: Routledge. (Originally published in 1971).

Leyton, Elliot. 1986. Hunting Humans: The Rise of the Modern Multiple Murderer. Toronto: McClelland and Stewart.

Lifton, R. 1961. Thought Reform And The Psychology Of Totalism. 1969 edition, New York: W. W. Norton & Co. (see chapter 22)

Lifton, R. 1976. The Life of the Self: Toward a New Psychology. New York: Touchstone.

Lifton, R. 1987. The Future of Immortality and Other Essays for a Nuclear Age. New York: Basic Books, Inc. (see chapter 15)

Lifton, R. 1991. Cult Formation. Cultic Studies Journal, 8, (1), 1.

Lifton, R. 1993. The Protean Self: Human Resilience in an Age of Fragmentation. New York: Basic Books.

Lilly, John C. 1973. The Center of the Cyclone: An Autobiography of Inner Space. Bantam. (Originally published in 1972).

Loftus, E. & Ketcham, K. 1994. The Myth of Repressed Memory: False Memories and Allegations of Sexual Abuse. New York: St. Martin's Press.

Mack, John. 1994. Abduction: Human Encounters with Aliens. New York: Charles Scribner's Sons.

Magid, K. & McKelvey, C. 1987. High Risk: Children Without a Conscience. Bantam.

Malcolm, Andrew I. 1972. The Pursuit of Intoxication. Toronto: PaperJacks.

Malcolm, Andrew I. 1973. The Case Against the Drugged Mind. Toronto: Clarke, Irwin and Co.

Malcolm, Andrew I. 1973. The Tyranny of the Group. Toronto: Clarke, Irwin & Co.

Marlowe, Christopher. 1969. Doctor Faustus. (Sylvian Barnet, Ed.). Signet. (Original work published in 1604).

Martin, Malachi. 1976. Hostage To The Devil: The Possession and Exorcism of Five Living Americans. New York: Thomas Y. Crowell.

Maslow, A. 1984. Religions, Values, and Peak-Experiences. New York: Penguin. (Original work published in 1964).

Maslow, A. 1985. The Farther Reaches of Human Nature. New York: Penguin. (Original work published in 1971).

McDougall, W. 1920. The Group Mind. Cambridge University Press.

Michaud, G. & Aynesworth, H. 1989. Ted Bundy: Conversations With a Killer. New York: Signet.

Milgram, Stanley. 1974. Obedience to Authority. New York: Harper & Row.

Milton, John. 1994. Paradise Lost, in The Works of John Milton . Wordsworth Editions, Ltd. (Original work published in 1667).

Monod, Jacques. Quoted in Evolution Extended by Connie Barlow.

Monroe, Robert A. 1971. Journeys Out of the Body. New York: Anchor Press.

Morgan, Gareth. 1986. Images Of Organization. Sage Publications.

Nelson, C. Ellis. 1973. Conscience: Theological and Psychological Perspectives. Newman Press.

Nietzsche, Friedrich. 1968. Twilight of the Idols and The Anti-Christ (R. J. Hollingdale, Trans.). Penguin Books. (Original work published in 1889).

Nietzsche, Friedrich. 1969. Thus Spoke Zarathustra. (R. J. Hollingdale, Trans.). Penguin Books. (Original work published in 1883).

Ofshe, R. & Watters, E. 1994. Making Monsters: False Memories, Psychotherapy, and Sexual Hysteria. New York: Charles Scribner's Sons.

Orwell, George. 1989. Nineteen Eighty-Four. Penguin. (First published in 1949).

Oshry, Barry, and Oshry, Karen. 1980. Middle-Group Dynamics: Ramifications for the OD Unit. In Trends and Issues in OD, (Burke and Goodstein, Eds.), San Diego: University Associates, Inc.

Osterreich, T.K. 1921. Possession: Demoniacal and Other Among Primitive Races, In Antiquity, The Middle Ages, and Modern Times. 1966 edition, New Jersey: University Books.

Pagels, E. 1981. The Gnostic Gospels. New York: Vintage. (first pub. 1979)

Pagels, Elaine. 1995. The Origin of Satan. New York: Random House.

Peck, M. Scott. 1983. People of the Lie: The Hope for Healing Human Evil. New York: Simon and Shuster.

Pelikan, Jaroslav. 1971. The Christian Tradition: A History of the Development of Doctrine, Volume One. The University of Chicago Press.

Person, E. S. 1986. Manipulativeness in Entrepreneurs and Psychopaths. In Reid, Dorr, Walker, & Bonner (Eds.), Unmasking the Psychopath: Antisocial Personality and Related Syndromes (pp. 256-273). New York: W. W. Norton & Co.

Reed, Graham. 1972. The Psychology of Anomalous Experience. London: Hutchinson & Co. LTD.

Reid, William. (Ed.) 1978. The Psychopath: A Comprehensive Study of Antisocial Disorders and Behaviors. New York: Brunner/Mazel.

Ring, Kenneth. 1992. The Omega Project: Near-Death Experiences, UFO Encounters, and Mind at Large. New York: William Morrow.

Rokeach, Milton. 1960. The Open and Closed Mind: Investigations Into The Nature Of Belief Systems and Personality Systems. New York: Basic Books.

Rokeach, Milton. 1972. Beliefs, Attitudes, and Values: A Theory of Organization and Change. Jossey-Bass.

Russell, Jeffrey Burton. 1988. The Prince of Darkness: Radical Evil and the Power of Good in History. Ithaca, New York: Cornell University Press.

Sahakian, William. 1966. Ideas of the Great Philosophers. New York: Barnes & Noble.

Sahakian, William. 1968. History of Philosophy. New York: Barnes & Noble.

Sargant, W. 1957. Battle For The Mind: A Physiology of Conversion and Brain-Washing. London: Heinemann.

Sargant, W. 1974. The Mind Possessed: A Physiology of Possession, Mysticism and Faith Healing. 1974: J.B. Lippincott Co.

Sartre, Jean-Paul (no date listed). Existentialism and Human Emotions. Secaucus, N.J.: Castle.

Schein, E. 1961. Coercive Persuasion. New York: W.W. Norton.

Schopenhauer, Arthur. The World as Will and Idea.

Schreck, Nikolas. (Ed). 1988. The Manson File. New York: Amok Press.

Shengold, Leonard. 1989. Soul Murder: The Effects of Childhood Abuse and Deprivation. New York: Fawcett Columbine.

Shorris, Earl. 1981. Scenes From Corporate Life: The Politics of Middle Management. 1984 edition, New York: Penguin.

Shupe, A. Bromley, D. 1980. The New Vigilantes: Deprogrammers, Anti-Cultists, and the

New Religions. Beverly Hills, CA: Sage.

Shupe, A. Bromley, D. 1984. The Anti-Cult Movement in America: A Bibliography and Historical Survey. New York: Garland Publishers.

Singer, M. and Ofshe, R. 1986 Attacks on Peripheral versus Central Elements of Self and the Impact of Thought Reforming Techniques. In Cultic Studies Journal, Vol. 3, No. 1.

Singer, M. T. 1979. Coming Out Of The Cults. In Psychology Today, p72, Jan.

Singer, M. T. 1990. Thought Reform Programs and the Production of Psychiatric Casualties. In Psychiatric Annals, p188, Vol. 20, #4, April. .

Singer, M. with Lalich, J. 1995. Cults In Our Midst: The Hidden Menace In Our Everyday lives. San Francisco: Jossey-Bass.

Sklar, D. 1977. The Nazis and the Occult. New York: Dorset Press.

Smith, Michelle and Pazder, Lawrence. 1980. Michelle Remembers. New York: Congdon & Lattes.

Snow, C. P. 1959. The Two Cultures and the Scientific Revolution. Cambridge University Press.

Staub, Ervin. 1989. The Roots of Evil: The Origins of Genocide and Other Group Violence. Cambridge University Press.

Steiner, George. 1989. Real Presences. The University of Chicago Press.

Thompson, William Irwin. 1989. Imaginary Landscape: Making Worlds of Myth and Science. New York: St. Martin's.

Thouless, Robert H. 1974. Straight and Crooked Thinking. London: Pan. (Originally published in 1930).

Tierney, Patrick. 1989. The Highest Altar: The Story of Human Sacrifice. Viking.

Watson, Lyall. 1995. Dark Nature: A Natural History of Evil. New York: HarperCollins.

Weber, Max. 1958. The Protestant Ethic and the Spirit of Capitalism. New York: Charles Scribner's Sons.

Weinberg, Steven Lee. (Ed). 1986. Ramtha. Eastbound, WA: Sovereignty, Inc.

Wilbur, Ken. 1985. The Atman Project: A Transpersonal View of Human Development. Wheaton, Ill: The Theosophical Publishing House. (Originally published in 1980). Wilson, Colin. 1987. A Criminal History of Mankind. London: Grafton. (Originally published in 1984)

Wilson, Edward O. 1978. On Human Nature. Harvard University Press.

Woodruff, P. and Wilmer, H. 1988. Facing Evil: Light at the Core of Darkness. LaSalle, Ill: Open Court.

Yeakley, Flavil R. (Ed.) 1988. The Discipling Dilemma. Nashville: Gospel Advocate Co.